Y0-BYX-028

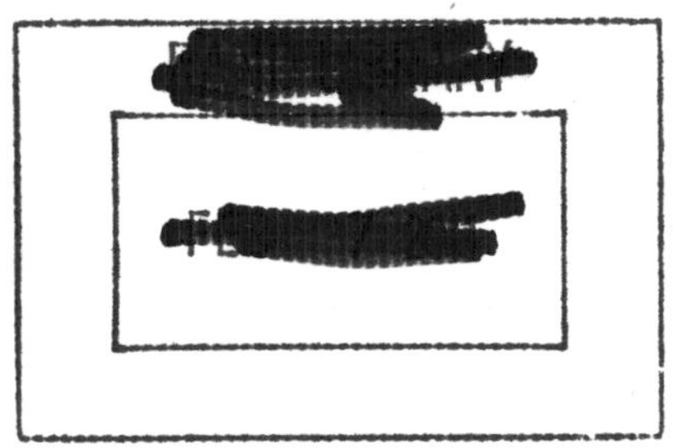

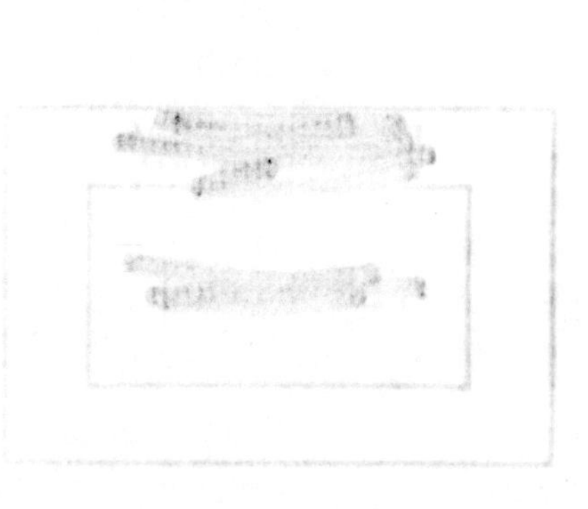

The Consequences of Counterterrorism

THE CONSEQUENCES OF COUNTERTERRORISM

MARTHA CRENSHAW

EDITOR

RUSSELL SAGE FOUNDATION • NEW YORK

The Russell Sage Foundation

The Russell Sage Foundation, one of the oldest of America's general purpose foundations, was established in 1907 by Mrs. Margaret Olivia Sage for "the improvement of social and living conditions in the United States." The Foundation seeks to fulfill this mandate by fostering the development and dissemination of knowledge about the country's political, social, and economic problems. While the Foundation endeavors to assure the accuracy and objectivity of each book it publishes, the conclusions and interpretations in Russell Sage Foundation publications are those of the authors and not of the Foundation, its Trustees, or its staff. Publication by Russell Sage, therefore, does not imply Foundation endorsement.

Library of Congress Cataloging-in-Publication Data

The consequences of counterterrorism / Martha Crenshaw, editor.
p. cm.
Includes bibliographical references and index.
ISBN 978-0-87154-073-7 (alk. paper)
1. Terrorism. 2. Terrorism—Prevention. 3. Emigration and immigration—Government policy. I. Crenshaw, Martha.
HV6431.C6526 2010
363.325'16—dc22

2009035321

The paper used in this publication meets the minimum requirements of American National Standard for Information Sciences—Permanence of Paper for Printed Library Materials. ANSI Z39.48-1992.

Text design by Suzanne Nichols.

RUSSELL SAGE FOUNDATION
112 East 64th Street, New York, New York 10065
10 9 8 7 6 5 4 3 2 1

Contents

Contributors

Martha Crenshaw is senior fellow at the Center for International Security and Cooperation (CISAC) and at the Freeman Spogli Institute for International Studies (FSI), both at Stanford University, and professor of political science by courtesy at Stanford University, as well as professor emerita of government at Wesleyan University.

Rogelio Alonso is associate professor of politics and security studies in the Department of Public Law and Political Sciences at the University Rey Juan Carlos, Madrid.

Giovanni Capoccia is professor of comparative politics in the Department of Politics and International Relations (DPIR) at Oxford University.

Chantal de Jonge Oudraat is associate vice president of the Jennings Randolph Fellowship Program at the United States Institute of Peace (USIP) and adjunct associate professor at the Edmund A. Walsh School of Foreign Service at Georgetown University.

John E. Finn is professor of government at Wesleyan University.

Dirk Haubrich was formerly research officer in the Department of Politics and International Relations (DPIR) and Nuffield College, Oxford University, and has since taken on managerial and advisory roles for the U. K. government.

Gallya Lahav is associate professor of political science at the State University of New York at Stony Brook.

David Leheny is the Henry Wendt III '55 Professor of East Asian Studies at Princeton University.

Jean-Luc Marret is senior research fellow at the Fondation pour la Recherche Stratégique (FRS) and senior fellow in residence at the Center for Transatlantic Relations (CTR), at the Paul H. Nitze School of Advanced International Studies (SAIS) at Johns Hopkins University.

Ami Pedahzur is an associate professor in the Departments of Government and Middle Eastern Studies at the University of Texas at Austin.

Arie Perliger is Lady Davis Fellow in the Department of Political Science at Hebrew University and the 2008–2009 Schusterman Visiting Israeli Professor at the State University of New York, Stony Brook.

Jeremy Shapiro is director of research for the Center on the United States and Europe and fellow in foreign policy studies at the Brookings Institution.

Acknowledgments

The idea for this project came from the Russell Sage Foundation, where Jitka Maleckova, then a program officer, helped immensely to guide it through the early stages. Suzanne Nichols expertly shepherded the volume through to publication, with the help of April Rondeau and copy editor Cynthia Buck. Two anonymous outside reviewers provided thoughtful comments. I especially want to thank my colleagues who contributed to the volume for their efforts and their patience during what must have seemed to be endless revisions. At CISAC, Kate Chadwick ably assisted me in the details of editing and production.

CHAPTER 1

INTRODUCTION

MARTHA CRENSHAW

In examining the political consequences of government countermeasures designed to combat terrorism and the policy outcomes that change democratic institutions, processes, and values, this volume addresses two important but often-neglected questions: What are the political consequences of counterterrorism measures taken by liberal democracies and the international institutions that link them? And how severe are the negative effects of counterterrorism on civil liberties, the rule of law, and patterns of democratic governance?

We focus here on advanced liberal democracies other than the United States in order to provide historical and comparative perspective.[1] The effects of the American global war on terrorism have been studied extensively, but the discussion is not always situated in a broader international context.[2] This volume does not deal specifically with the United States, but several of the chapters consider the American case within a comparative framework. Many of the discussions are also concerned with the divisions between the United States and Europe in dealing with contemporary terrorism. Also, since the shock of the 9/11 attacks, legal scholars have addressed the effects of counterterrorism much more energetically and thoroughly than have political scientists. This volume is the beginning of an effort to fill the gap in our understanding of the political as well as the legal impact of democratic responses to terrorism.[3]

Counterterrorism policy is controversial, and it is almost certain to become more so if governments continue to strengthen their response to terrorism. Democratic governments do not initiate counterterrorism policy with the express intent of undermining democracy, but they may be too ready to accept the idea of an inevitable trade-off between security and liberty; to think that because terrorists might exploit democracy, attractive "loopholes" must be closed; or to deny the real costs of counterterrorism. Fears of failing to prevent a disastrous terrorist attack causing a large loss of civilian lives may lead policymakers to take a shortsighted and overconfident view of the ability of robust security measures to prevent terrorism.

The contributors to this volume agree that the effects of the response to terrorism have been costly to democracy in many ways, but that within certain broad outlines, policy consequences have differed in nature and severity. In general, policy changes since 2001 have been much more damaging to democracy than earlier counterterrorism measures, even as responses to the threat of Al Qaeda and its associated groups have usually not departed radically from counterterrorism policies of the past.

A key consideration in analyzing these issues is the possibility that a government's response to terrorism will diminish democracy more than the acts of terrorism themselves. Liberal democracies confront painful policy choices: terrorism is a threat that must be confronted in order to preserve the safety and security of the nation, but counterterrorist policies can diminish individual civil liberties and alter patterns of governance to the detriment of democracy. Measures designed to prevent terrorism often limit the basic rights and freedoms of citizens, invade their privacy, strengthen executive power, centralize police and intelligence bureaucracies, blur the distinction between domestic intelligence and law enforcement functions, expand the influence of the military in decisionmaking, cloak decisionmaking processes in secrecy, and encourage undemocratic shifts in public attitudes and political values (such as intolerance toward minorities or unquestioning acceptance of erosions of civil liberties).[4] In fact, as John E. Finn's chapter notes, it is not a simple matter even to determine what national counterterrorism policies are. Their scope goes well beyond specifically labeled antiterrorism legislation, and counterterrorism regimes are constantly changing. Internationally, common strategies against terrorism can lead to closed borders and reliance on military force over criminal justice, as well as infringements of individual rights. Disagreements over how to deal with terrorism spark controversy and partisanship within and between nations. The Bush administration's pursuit of a global war on terror frustrated many allies—and where governments were supportive of the United States, their publics often were not. Risk perceptions and conceptions of "homeland security" diverge (Föhrenbach 2006).

Many of the political consequences of counterterrorism efforts are unintended or secondary, although some cynical observers might suspect that governments, particularly officials of the executive branch, manipulate the threat of terrorism to expand their powers. The effects discussed here, however, seem frequently to have been unanticipated. In the heat of the moment of crisis, governments tend to act in haste without fully considering either the full scope of the alternative actions that are open to them or the consequences of that range of options. Lack of forethought and preparation produces decisions that are less than optimally rational, and publics have little chance to weigh in even if they have the inclination, expertise, and information to do so. There is insufficient check on what the government does. The question then is how enduring such changes are and whether they can be reversed if their effects are later judged harmful to democracy. This is a key element of the concept of proportionality of response to threat.

Experiences and perceptions of the threat of terrorism vary considerably among countries, not just between the United States and the rest of the world, and responses differ according to the threat and according to context. Before the 9/11 attacks, the consensus was that democracies confronting internal threats or "domestic terrorism" were more likely to adopt policies that undermine democratic principles than were democracies facing terrorism originating from outside, or "international terrorism" (Charters 1994, 213–14). That is, states presumably react more harshly to civil violence from groups composed of their own citizens acting within their borders than to violence organized by foreigners or occurring outside the country. The implications of violent dissent from within seemed much more serious than the external threat of terrorist attack, which before 9/11 was considered minor and was in fact extremely rare. In general, terrorism was not a national security issue, although the Reagan administration took international terrorism quite seriously, blamed Soviet "state sponsorship" of terrorism as part of the Cold War rivalry, and bombed Libya in 1986 in retaliation for Libyan complicity in terrorism directed against American targets in West Germany. Since the American declaration of a war on terror, however, the argument that internal terrorism is most provocative can certainly no longer be sustained. It is also interesting to note that the European Union (EU) list of terrorist organizations makes a distinction between domestic groups and those with foreign affiliations or transnational ambitions, and that the two types are subject to different levels of sanctions (see chapter 3).

Complicating matters, as we have come to recognize in the period since the 9/11 attacks, is the fact that many terrorist conspiracies are mixed in origin rather than exclusively internal or external, a point that Dirk Haubrich stresses in his chapter on the United Kingdom. Terrorist plots often involve a combination of citizens of the state and noncitizens or local operatives with external direction, resources, or inspiration.[5] Many such plots are rooted in social and family networks that are transnational. These groups are not directed by states, although their leaders may seek refuge in lawless areas, ally themselves with weak regimes such as the Taliban, or seek support from diasporas located abroad. National borders are increasingly blurred and permeable, especially as electronic communications make it easier to organize underground conspiracies across continents and to publicize a group's ambitions worldwide to mobilize support and inspire imitation.

Because some terror plots now emanate from sources formerly considered benign or inconsequential, expressions of religious faith or identity can seem alarming. Germany and Japan, for example, have removed protected religious status from some opposition groups charged with using or advocating terrorism. Britain also cracked down on mosques led by radical Islamist clerics who preached support for anti-Western terrorism, such as Abu Qatada, although Britain was relatively slow to act even after the 9/11 attacks. It has become harder to obtain such privileged status, but the long-term effects are still uncertain. One possibility is that radical activity will shift from mosques or on other public religious establishments to underground venues or onto the Internet.

Today, regardless of its form or source, terrorism has become a part of both national and international security debates. Those debates inevitably touch on other sensitive issues as well, such as the assimilation of minorities and immigration, asylum, and citizenship; since 9/11, all of these issues have been transformed into security problems and made part of the expanded security domain (see chapter 4). The response to terrorism has thus broadened conceptions of what constitutes national security and sensitized the public to the pervasiveness of insecurity.

The problematic political consequences identified by the authors in this volume, as well as by many other observers, are often presented as the price that must be paid for security from terrorism. Restriction of democracy is seen as unavoidable if the central objective of counterterrorism policy is to be achieved: protecting society from harm by preventing terrorist attacks.

Yet the assumption of an inevitable and necessary trade-off between safety and democracy may both underestimate the costs of the response to terrorism and overestimate its contribution to providing security (Donohue 2008; Zimmermann and Wenger 2006b). Citizens of democracies may be paying a high price for policies that fail to protect them from danger or that even put them at greater risk of terrorism. In the chapter on the use of terrorist designation lists, Chantal de Jonge Oudraat and Jean-Luc Marret make the important point that protecting democracy need not mean less security.

In the United States, the Obama administration repudiated most of the policies of George W. Bush's government and characterized what had been posed as a stark dilemma as a false choice between safety and democracy. The new administration distanced itself from the practices of its predecessor, particularly those that damaged the American reputation for upholding the rule of law. Enhanced interrogation techniques and preventative detention were particularly at issue. The Obama administration also promoted greater transparency with regard to the policymaking process and promised to set institutional limitations on executive power. Defenders of the necessity of the war on terror, led by former Vice President Richard B. Cheney, continued to insist that the measures that critics see as antidemocratic are required for American national security. They also contended that greater transparency only increases society's vulnerability by disclosing useful information to the enemy.

Many of the energetic efforts to prevent terrorism have led democratic governments to reach further and further back in the causal chain of the commission of acts of violence on their territories. Thus, governments try to interdict "precursor" activity, such as association or speech, which might indicate a willingness to support terrorism or preparation to engage in it. The perceived danger seems to lie as much in attitudes and beliefs as in behavior. In the pursuit of effective prevention, governments necessarily cast a broad net of suspicion. Dissent that was tolerable becomes intolerable if it appeals to violence and appears to be the first step down the path of a terrorist conspiracy. Surveillance becomes ever more intrusive as governments try to detect the early stages of planning for terrorist attacks. Governments collect more and more information on their citizens and on anyone who crosses their borders, whether immigrants or ordinary travelers. The information is gathered in centralized data banks and made available to a growing array of government institutions. Security and intelligence services are reformed to become more streamlined and efficient, with expanded powers of apprehension and arrest. The coercive capacity of states is strengthened at home and sometimes abroad. Domestic policing may be increasingly militarized.

A corollary is that the drive to prevent terrorism well in advance of the execution of the act can also prompt democracies to proceed with trials of suspected terrorists with weak evidence that was gathered at early stages of a plot and does not always stand up well in court. At the other extreme, the complicated nature of contemporary terrorist conspiracies and the desire to secure convictions often push security services to seek lengthened periods of preventive detention so that they have time to pursue investigations and bring charges that will in fact hold up in court. In addition to the United States, nations such as Britain, Spain, France, Italy, the Netherlands, Germany, and Denmark (among others) have tried many such cases since the 9/11 attacks. Advocates of democracy may think of a fair trial in a civilian court as the epitome of the application of the rule of law. The outcomes of these trials have been politically problematic, however, and their long-term effects on public opinion, regardless of whether they resulted in acquittal or conviction of the defendants, are as yet unknown. In addition, terrorism-related trials may result in loss of trust and confidence in the government and in the judicial system.

On the other hand, we should not automatically assume that all effects of counterterrorism measures are negative. Certainly some policies that are successful in reducing terrorism have decidedly adverse effects on political life, such as the stifling of dissent or increased surveillance of individuals. Other responses may have beneficial side effects, however, such as the recognition of genuine grievances and the need for socioeconomic reform and deeper cultural integration. Thus, the debates over radicalization in Europe following the bombings in London and Madrid may produce changes that will benefit society in the long run, despite their tragic origins. It is not necessarily bad that security institutions are reformed, that information gathering is coordinated, or that law enforcement is made more efficient.

Another complicating factor in analyzing the political consequences of counterterrorism policies is that it is often difficult to distinguish the effects of counterterrorism measures from the effects of terrorism itself. For example, are hardening public attitudes toward immigrants or toward religious or ethnic minorities the consequence of government actions and statements or of the fact that a number of post-9/11 terrorist plots were traced to small groups located in these communities? If publics are excessively fearful of terrorism, is it because of the actual danger or because of the government's framing of the threat?[6] Despite the catastrophic losses in the 9/11 attacks, terrorism causes far fewer casualties than other sources of death and injury, such as highway accidents. Do governments wittingly or unwittingly contribute to an exaggerated public perception of acute risk? How can governments respond to terrorism without stoking public apprehension and raising the salience of terrorism and the groups that practice it?

Setting the Stage

Before outlining the project presented in this volume, I want to sketch briefly the complex threat faced by European democracies, Japan, and Israel—the countries in question here—before the disastrous events of 9/11. This quick summary should aid readers in understanding the historical basis of the arguments proposed in the case studies, the different contexts within which terrorism occurs, and the connections between different experiences of the threat. This discussion accepts governments' identification of threats as "terrorism" rather than imposing an independent definition because it is governments' responses to perceived threat and the effects of those responses that interest us. Moreover, as Chantal de Jonge Oudraat and Jean-Luc Marret explain in chapter 3, national and international definitions of terrorism differ. Even within countries, definitions may vary. In fact, the United Nations has no definition of terrorism at all. De Jonge Oudraat and Marret suggest that official terrorist designation lists are actually a practical form of defining terrorism. In scholarly terms, terrorism is usually defined as involving deliberate attacks on civilians by nonstate actors with political objectives. The aim of such conspiratorial violence is not to destroy an adversary but to shift the attitudes of a watching audience. The aim may be to strike fear in the heart of the enemy, but also to mobilize support in sympathetic audiences. Targets are chosen for symbolic rather than utilitarian reasons. The use of force by governments to suppress resistance can also be called terror or terrorism, but this is not an issue we can address within the confines of this volume.

The short history outlined here shows that since the 1950s terrorism has consistently posed a serious security problem rooted in both domestic and international politics. Much about pre-9/11 terrorism is familiar. For example, attacks on the homeland of a great power in response to its foreign policy engagements, particularly military involvements, are not new. The Algerian national liberation movement mounted attacks in Paris in the 1950s, as did Iranian sympathizers in the 1980s and Algerian Islamist groups in the 1990s. Nor is it new to see terrorism by groups that are local in origin and composition but inspired by shared universalist ideologies;

the left revolutionary groups that emerged across Europe in the 1970s often acted in conscious imitation of "Third World" revolutionary movements, and cross-national collaboration among such groups was an early feature of the terrorist threat. Apparently autonomous national threats were often interconnected. International events consistently affected domestic developments. The reinvigoration of the Irish Republican Army (initially known as the Provisional IRA, in contrast to the older "official" IRA) in Northern Ireland in the early 1970s owed much to the spark of the Catholic civil rights movement, which in turn was inspired by the American civil rights movement. In an odd marriage of convenience, the IRA was later the recipient of weapons shipped from Libya.

Like most other groups accused of terrorism by governments, the IRA did not by any means consider itself a terrorist organization. Rather, it saw itself as an army fighting an unconventional war, or insurgency, against a foreign occupying power. The U.S. Department of State never listed the IRA as a "foreign terrorist organization," although it did list the Continuity Irish Republican Army and the Real IRA, which were breakaway factions that rejected the peace process that eventually ended the conflict in Northern Ireland.

In reviewing this history, which is only a partial one, I am struck by the proliferation and diversity of terrorist organizations in the pre-9/11 period. Organizations differed in size, ideology, structure, and consequentiality. It is clear that very small groups can pose large security problems for democracies. Impact has not been proportional to material resources or the extent of popular support. The sensitivity of the targeted polity to terrorism is critical.

It is also worth noting that, other than Israel, democracies have not commonly resorted to the use of military force to combat terrorism, especially outside national boundaries. Although the French attempted to crush the Algerian resistance by force, the British employed the military against the IRA in Northern Ireland, the United States launched retaliatory bombing raids against Libya, Iraq, the Sudan, and Afghanistan, and even West Germany used elite military units to rescue hostages abroad, these efforts were time-bound, and the dominant approach was law enforcement. The idea of launching a war against terrorism "of global reach," including overthrowing regimes that supported or were suspected of supporting terrorism, was new with the Bush administration.[7]

The story begins with the colonial period. In the 1950s and early 1960s, France faced urban terrorism in Algeria as well as terrorism in metropolitan France as part of the Algerian war for independence. Terrorism was an adjunct to a national liberation strategy that also involved guerrilla warfare and unconventional military combat. However, terrorist attacks were organized by both the resistance to French rule (Front de Libération Nationale, or FLN) and the opponents of Algerian independence, who appeared on the scene late in the war when France began to negotiate with the FLN. This "secret army" was the Organization de l'Armée Secrète (OAS), composed of Algerian settlers and renegade elements in the French military. Bombs exploded in the streets of Paris, and President Charles de Gaulle narrowly escaped multiple assassination attempts. The FLN even planned to bomb the Eiffel Tower. In the war zone, the "Battle of Algiers" in 1956–57 drew international attention to urban terrorism, particularly bombings of cafés and restaurants with large losses of life, attacks often carried out by women. The French army responded by using torture to break up the terrorist networks, sparking domestic controversy that has lasted over fifty years. The history of the Battle of Algiers served as the basis of the 1966 film by the same name, directed by Gillo Pontecorvo and starring none other than the chief terrorist of Algiers himself, Yacef Saadi. After the invasion of Iraq in 2003, the film was screened at the Pentagon.

The French may have won the war on the ground through the use of overwhelming military force against widespread insurgency, but Algeria gained independence in 1962. The FLN's victory inspired revolutionaries worldwide, especially in Latin America. The almost simultaneous Cuban revolution reinforced the expectation that revolutions of the weak and oppressed against a much stronger imperialist power could succeed. Many revolutionaries pitted themselves against military dictatorships supported by the United States, further bolstering the idea of a global struggle against Western hegemony. Revolutionary movements convinced of the prophetic quality of Marxist-Leninist ideologies, and sometimes aided by the Soviet Union or Cuba, emerged almost everywhere across Europe in the 1960s. Their relevance to the story of this volume lies in their influence on western European leftists, who were moved by sympathy for groups such as the Uruguayan Tupamaros to launch their own violent campaigns in the late 1960s and early 1970s. In fact, a German group designated itself the "Tupamaros West Berlin." Student opposition to the war in Vietnam as it escalated sharply in 1965 fed into an anti-imperialist movement that produced the Red Army Faction (Rote Armee Fraktion, RAF, established in 1970) and its various offshoots and successor generations in Germany, as well as the Red Brigades (Brigate Rosse) in Italy. In the United States, the Weathermen, or Weather Underground, similarly attempted to strike imperialism at its heart through "urban guerrilla" tactics.

The RAF and its companion, the June 2 Movement, were much more violent than their small numbers and lack of popular support would indicate. For example, in 1977 the original RAF leaders were sentenced to life imprisonment for four murders and twenty-seven attempted murders, and by late 1978 a total of twenty-eight deaths had been attributed to left-wing violence (Varon 2004, 197–98). The RAF was also remarkably persistent. Although overall probably only about one hundred people were involved, the organization lasted through three generations; its remaining members formally abandoned violence only in 1998, well after the end of the Cold War, although the 1970s were its most destructive years. Victims included a political candidate, a judge, a federal prosecutor, a bank chairman, and an industrialist, all of whom were seen as symbols of oppression and the Nazi past. As representatives of the imperial power, American military personnel were also favored targets. A notably brutal episode was the hijacking of a Lufthansa airliner and the killing of its pilot in 1977. The rescue of the passengers in Mogadishu, Somalia, was the first deployment of German military forces outside German borders since World War II.

The hijacking was carried out in collaboration with a small left-wing Palestinian faction. The RAF was notoriously sympathetic to the Palestinian cause, received military training in Palestinian camps in Jordan and Lebanon, and collaborated with Palestinians in several terrorist operations. This pattern of cooperation was part of the aftermath of the 1967 Arab-Israeli War; the Israeli occupation of the West Bank, Gaza Strip, Golan Heights, and Sinai Peninsula; and the organization of an external Palestinian resistance to Israel. It was not possible for Palestinian nationalist organizations to act effectively within Israel or the newly occupied territories, and since they were headquartered outside of the conflict zone in the surrounding Arab states, their international campaign was in many ways a matter of practical necessity as much as a deliberate strategy to widen the conflict (although not every Palestinian group favored international operations). International operations in the West or against Western interests in the Middle East were also a way of gaining the world's attention and forging a specifically Palestinian identity. In 1972 RAF leaders praised the murder of Israeli athletes at the Munich Olympics by the Black September organization, an offshoot of Yasir Arafat's Fatah, the central component of the Palestine Liberation Organization (PLO). In 1975 German leftists joined Palestinians to kidnap OPEC oil ministers meeting in Vienna. In 1976 they hijacked an El Al airliner to Entebbe, Uganda, where Israel subsequently succeeded in a spectacular military rescue of the passengers. Israel's first campaign of targeted assassinations was directed against Black September, in retaliation for the Munich Olympics attack, and Europe was the battleground for much of the campaign. Palestinian factions maintained a tolerated clandestine presence in France into the 1980s.

Attacks on civil aviation were an early part of the Palestinian international strategy. They began in 1968, when the Popular Front for the Liberation of Palestine (PFLP) hijacked an El Al jet and forced it to land in Algiers. Targets quickly expanded from Israeli planes to include American and European air carriers with service to Israel. In September 1970 the PFLP organized the first multiple hijacking, diverting three airliners to Jordan and one to Egypt. Terrorism against civil aviation also included armed assaults on passengers in airports, including a 1972 attack by the Japanese Red Army (JRA) at Lod airport in Israel. The attackers killed twenty-eight people and wounded seventy-eight, many of them Puerto Rican pilgrims traveling to the Holy Land.[8] Airport attacks spread to Europe and continued into the 1980s. For example, in 1983 an Armenian group bombed the Turkish Airlines ticket counter at Orly Airport near Paris. On December 27, 1985, in an early instance of the coordination of two geographically separated attacks, the Abu Nidal Organization, a Palestinian faction opposed to the PLO, used assault rifles and grenades to assault passengers waiting in line at both the Rome and Vienna airports.

The joint JRA-PFLP operation is another case of networking between leftist and Palestinian groups, especially the smaller organizations with a Marxist-Leninist orientation. Their collaboration also presents another strand of the history of terrorism: the appearance of a small underground revolutionary organization in Japan, parallel to those in Europe. The JRA was actually founded in Lebanon in 1970; it immediately adopted an international strategy, including cooperation with Palestinian groups. By 1972, it had been driven out of Japan and had effectively relocated to the Middle East, where it continued hijackings, embassy takeovers, and other armed assaults. Some of its members also fled to North Korea. In a similar pattern, some members of the RAF's successor generations fled to East Germany, under West German police pressure. The JRA was active into the 1980s, and some of its leaders were arrested in Lebanon as late as 1997.

Other strains of terrorism erupted in this critical historical juncture. In the 1970s, the United Kingdom and Spain faced campaigns of separatist or ethno-nationalist terrorism.[9] The IRA's campaign lasted until 1998 and the Good Friday Accords, and the Basque Freedom and Homeland Organization (ETA) has remained active at low levels into the twenty-first century. Splinters from the IRA continued sporadic terrorism even after the main body of the IRA had renounced violence. Both the IRA and ETA had deep local roots and particularistic territorial ambitions rather than universal grievances, but at the outset they too were moved by the revolutionary zeitgeist of the times. They cultivated an anticolonialist image and flirted with socialist ideas.

Both groups initially gained momentum because of a "democratic deficit," but they kept up the struggle well beyond its remediation. ETA was founded in 1959 under the Franco dictatorship when Basque identity was ruthlessly suppressed. Yet when Spain transitioned to democracy and granted substantial autonomy to the Basque provinces, ETA escalated, rather than decreased, its violence (see Shabad and Llera Ramo 1995). Numerous efforts to negotiate a compromise have failed, and ETA endures today at minimal but still lethal levels of violence. Rival Basque politicians and local police forces are frequently targeted. Over its history ETA has been responsible for over eight hundred deaths. Its campaign also has an international dimension, since the Basque territory extends into France and ETA leaders have often sought shelter there. Many have been arrested there as well, owing to the expansion of cooperation between French and Spanish law enforcement authorities after Spain's transition to democracy.

Few people other than terrorism experts know that in Spain a left revolutionary organization also emerged during the transition period. In 1976 the Grupos Armados Antifascistas Primero de Octubre (GRAPO) was established as a wing of the "reconstituted" Communist Party, with Maoist leanings; over its lifetime it killed eighty or ninety people (estimates vary), many in bank robberies. Spanish police arrested GRAPO members as late as 2007.

The IRA, whose history stretches back to the nineteenth-century resistance to British rule in Ireland, if not further, was resurrected in the context of Catholic protests against the inequities of the Protestant-dominated Stormont regime in Northern Ireland, which was instituted in 1920 when what is now the Republic of Ireland won independence from Britain. Britain instituted direct rule over the province of Northern Ireland, or Ulster, in 1972 and introduced significant reforms, but it took over twenty-five years and more than three thousand deaths before the IRA renounced violence. British military forces, introduced as a temporary measure to restore law and order in 1969, were withdrawn from an active role as the peace process was consolidated after 1998, and by 2008 only fifteen hundred nonoperational troops remained. British forces were at their peak strength of thirty thousand in the 1970s.

In both cases, democratic governments also had to contend with terrorism from supporters of the status quo who resisted change. In the Spanish case in the 1980s, this involved the complicity of some of the state security forces in an organization named Grupos Antiterroristas de Liberación (GAL). GAL activity between 1983 and 1987 involved death squads that targeted people who were thought to be ETA sympathizers, and at least twenty-eight people were killed. In 1998 two former senior government ministers were convicted of crimes in connection with GAL. In Northern Ireland, various Unionist or Loyalist terrorist groups nominally fought the IRA but mostly attacked Catholics at random. The Ulster Volunteer Force, for example, probably killed over four hundred people, most of them civilians.

France was largely spared internal violence in the 1970s, even though the May 1968 student uprising could well have been expected to spin off terrorist conspiracies.[10] Aspirant revolutionaries did not follow the examples of their peers in Germany and Italy. France's turn came in the 1980s. Left revolutionary terrorism appeared with the formation of the group Action Directe (AD), established in 1979, which frequently collaborated with other European groups of the times, such as the Belgian Cellules des Communists Combatants. When François Mitterrand was elected president in 1981, he pardoned AD's leaders, who perversely reciprocated by returning to violence. In 1982 AD split into domestic and international branches. It was responsible for at least thirteen deaths, including the assassination of a prominent industrialist. On at least one occasion, AD cooperated with the RAF in attacking the American military in Germany. It also assisted Middle Eastern groups acting in France.

Despite its acceptance of a clandestine Palestinian presence, France was vulnerable to the spillover of Middle Eastern politics: a combination of the 1979 Iranian revolution, the Lebanese civil war (after 1976), the Israeli invasion of Lebanon (1982), and the Iran-Iraq War (1980 to 1988) brought terrorism to French territory.[11] France joined the multinational force deployed to keep peace in Lebanon, and in 1983 its troops, along with those of the United States and Israel, were the victims of suicide bombings by Shi'ite factions affiliated with Iran. These groups coalesced into the Hezbollah organization, which is today a major player in Lebanese politics. French nationals were kidnapped and killed in Lebanon during the 1980s. French support for Iraq in the Iran-Iraq War further angered Iran. Thus, French involvement in conflicts in the Middle East attracted terrorism to France, including deadly bombings in Paris linked to Lebanon and Iran. For example, the Lebanese Armed Revolutionary Fractions

(FARL) assassinated an Israeli diplomat, an attack in which AD was implicated, as part of a campaign against Israeli, Jewish, and American targets.

With the end of the Cold War, left-wing terrorism began to fade. However, violence inspired by radical interpretations of Islam took its place. In the 1990s, France was once again exposed to the spillover of conflict in Algeria. In 1992, when it appeared certain that an Islamist party, the Front Islamique du Salut (FIS), would win parliamentary elections and it seemed possible that the FIS would then impose a strict religious program, the Algerian regime canceled the elections, banned the opposition, and returned to one-party rule. The result was a prolonged civil war that left over eighty thousand dead. It was principally conducted by an extremely violent Islamist faction, the Groupe Islamique Armée (GIA, Islamic Armed Group), which blamed France for aiding the Algerian government. In 1994 the GIA hijacked a plane from Algiers to Marseille and threatened to have it flown into the Eiffel Tower. A French commando squad intervened before they could carry out the threat. Yet again, in 1995 and 1996, Paris saw bombings of public transportation and commercial venues. In 2006 the successor to the GIA, the Salafist Group for Preaching and Combat (known by its French acronym, GSPC), formally merged with Al Qaeda.

Israel also faced an alarming and unexpected resurgence of terrorism in the 1990s. This threat similarly came from factions associated with Islamist movements. The mainstream Palestinian nationalist organizations mostly accepted the negotiated compromise formalized in the 1993 Oslo Accords, with the long-run aim of an independent and secular Palestinian state in the West Bank and Gaza Strip. The PLO was outflanked, however, by the religious organizations that had emerged in the context of the 1987 Intifada—the Palestinian popular uprising against Israeli occupation that set the stage for the Oslo peace process. Hamas (a branch of the Muslim Brotherhood) and the smaller group Palestinian Islamic Jihad (PIJ) rejected the two-state solution finally accepted by the PLO. Beginning in 1993, these two groups launched successive campaigns of suicide terrorism against the inhabitants of Israeli cities within the Green Zone. After 2000—when the second Al-Aqsa Intifada was initiated—they were joined by an offshoot of Fatah, the Al-Aqsa Martyrs' Brigade, and the still-active Popular Front for the Liberation of Palestine. There have been approximately 150 suicide bombings in Israel, the majority after 2000. Israel's emphatic response in 2002 is described in Ami Pedahzur and Arie Perliger's chapter. After the peace process broke down, the proposed date for a permanent status agreement was postponed indefinitely. Israel reoccupied most of the Palestinian-controlled areas of the West Bank and began building a security barrier, or wall, between the homeland and the Palestinian territories from which most of the suicide attacks were launched. In 2005 Israel withdrew from the Gaza Strip, which was then sealed off after Hamas won elections in 2006 and refused to recognize Israel, accept the peace process, or abandon violence. Suicide attacks declined sharply, with only three against civilian targets from 2006 to 2008. Rocket attacks from Gaza against Israeli towns, however, escalated. A ceasefire agreed to in June 2008 did not last—Hamas continued firing rockets across the border into Israel—and at the end of the year, when a temporary truce expired, Israel launched a brief but intense military campaign against Hamas.

In the post–Cold War world, Japan also confronted an indigenous "religious" group: Aum Shinrikyo, notorious for its 1995 sarin gas attack on the Tokyo subway system. Aum, founded in the 1980s by its charismatic leader, Shoko Asahara, was the first and so far the last terrorist group to develop and use so-called weapons of mass destruction (WMD). They experimented with anthrax as well as chemical weapons, which they employed on several occasions. Like Germany, Japan had permitted nominally "religious" organizations to operate with little official scrutiny; as a result, Aum's intentions were not detected until late in the game despite its millenarian goals, vast resources, broad international connections, and large membership (probably several thousand in Japan, and others abroad). In 1989 the Japanese government had designated Aum a religious organization, a status it had sought in order to gain exemption from taxes. Apocalyptic movements are not without a pragmatic streak.

This short overview shows that terrorism in diverse forms has posed a problem in democracies for many years. The countries and international institutions that have dealt with the threat have built up a reservoir of policies. Thus, European, Japanese, and Israeli reactions to the threat from Al Qaeda and its cohorts were grounded in long experience with terrorism. Most of these governments have tended to reject the popular American argument that twenty-first-century terrorism is entirely "new" and that old methods and old understandings should be tossed out in favor of a global war on terror.

A Guide to the Arguments

This volume focuses on the experiences of liberal democracies and the international institutions linking them. Part 1, "Governance, Civil Liberties, and Securitization," opens with thematic comparative analyses of counterterrorism policies as they affect constitutions and judiciaries, the creation of lists of designated terrorist organizations, and the relationship between counterterrorism and immigration policy in the European Union. In part 2, "National Counterterrorism Responses," we present case studies of Britain, France, Germany, Spain, Japan, and Israel. These analyses offer distinctive emphases on the political issues common to all democracies. The case studies stress both change and continuity in patterns of governance and the relationship between citizens and the state.

John E. Finn's overview chapter on the effects of counterterrorism policies on constitutional principles and norms introduces many of the themes that appear later. Finn explains that liberal democracies had much in common as they embarked on post-9/11 legislative packages. All responded not by starting from scratch to deal with an unprecedented "new" terrorism, but by revising existing antiterrorism legislation built up over their years of hard experience. They also borrowed freely from each other, although it is by no means certain that they learned anything in the process. Reactions were similar. Many governments were tempted to narrow freedom of expression and association, restrict privacy, and expand immigration law into the realm of criminal justice.

Finn contends that legislation adopted in haste and under crisis conditions undermines democratic norms of transparency and deliberation. A grave danger is that the possibility of informed and involved public debate is closed in the rush of an understandably urgent reaction to shocking violence against citizens. Secrecy becomes paramount, and an inclination to concentrate political and legal authority in the executive branch comes to the fore. (This consolidation of authority has occurred at the supranational level as well: the power of the European Union over its component national governments in the area of migration policy has been strengthened.) Finn notes that this tendency to concentrate executive power was not restricted to the United States (where it was taken to the extreme in the Bush administration). In some settings, the consolidation of authority has been countered more systematically than in others, but in general this development has shifted the balance of power between executive, legislative, and judicial branches. In Finn's view, the consequences have been more damaging for the rule of law than for civil liberties. Liberal governments are tempted to relax mechanisms for governmental accountability and to resist judicial oversight, which can provide a critical bulwark against the expansion of executive power and the dilution of civil liberties protections. Courts sometimes push back, but not always, and thus the record is mixed.

In Germany, Britain, and Israel, national courts took different positions that were effective in limiting the government in the first two cases, but less effective in the last case. In the spring of 2008, for example, the U.K. Home Office suffered an embarrassing setback when courts first prevented the deportation of the radical cleric Abu Qatada to Jordan (where it was said he would face torture as well as lack of a fair trial) and subsequently ordered him released from prison on bail, albeit under very restrictive conditions. Abu Qatada, who had been granted asylum in Britain in 1994, was charged with having links to Al Qaeda, although he denied any connection. Human Rights Watch was strongly critical of the deportation proposal. In February 2009, the European Court of Human Rights granted Abu Qatada's request and ordered the U.K. government not to proceed with deportation until the court had given due consideration to the matter. (Increasingly reluctant to grant political asylum, countries often prefer deportation to unpredictable trials.)

In Germany, the division of power between the national and state levels of government has also constrained the expansion of executive authority in counterterrorism. Lack of coordination between national and state security institutions may lead to jurisdictional struggles and impede counterterrorism efficiency, but it also places a check on overreaching. Spain and France exhibit a different pattern: rather than limiting executive power, judicial authorities in those countries are autonomous drivers of counterterrorism policy in their own right. Specialized terrorism magistrates presiding over special courts have enormous independent powers to conduct investigations and make arrests and have close connections with security and intelligence services. Yet there appears to be little oversight or accountability (as Jeremy Shapiro notes in chapter 7).

Another risk of hastily constructed counterterrorism policy is that what is anticipated as a temporary emergency change in the administration of criminal justice becomes permanent. Counterterrorism provisions also tend to "bleed over" into ordinary criminal justice, as the chapter on the United Kingdom emphasizes, with effects that are difficult to reverse in part because they are so gradual and incremental. It is hard to contest something that is taken for granted. What was originally a crisis response becomes normalized and incorporated into routine practices.

In general, however, most publics seem not to resist the antidemocratic implications of counterterrorism policy in their willingness to countenance, and in some cases even demand, robust measures against terrorism. This supportive reaction is seen not just in Israel but also in Germany, Britain, France, and Japan. In France, in particular, it is noteworthy that what are the strictest counterterrorism measures among Western countries do not provoke public dissent.[12] In addition to the courts, including the European

Court of Human Rights, interest groups such as human rights organizations appear to be the main critics of counterterrorism measures, not the public at large. What appears to be popular apathy, however, is probably due to the complexity of the issues as well as the belief that restrictions on democracy are both necessary and effective.

Chantal de Jonge Oudraat and Jean-Luc Marret focus on the impact of counterterrorism on civil liberties in criticizing the rapidly proliferating use of terrorist designation lists; this counterterrorism measure with potentially long-term political consequences has been adopted by both international and regional institutions. In evaluating the use of these lists by the UN, the EU, the United States, the United Kingdom, Russia, and China, the authors note their serious drawbacks. The individuals and groups listed—including charitable organizations as well as opposition groups—are subject to sanctions and judicial prosecution, are put in a generally suspect category, and have little recourse or access to due process.[13] The process of making the lists is far from transparent, and once an individual or a group is on a list, it is very difficult to get off. In Britain, for example, it took the People's Mujahidin of Iran seven years of legal effort to appeal successfully its designation as a proscribed terrorist organization.[14] Some changes are being made in response to criticism from human rights organizations (for example, in the EU), but nevertheless, we know very little about the practical effects of being listed beyond the observation that charitable giving to Islamic organizations has decreased. Moreover, the effectiveness of the lists in reducing terrorism is mixed. De Jonge Oudraat and Marret argue that improved democratic safeguards, such as the transparency and accountability that John E. Finn advocates, would make terrorist designation lists a much more useful policy instrument in counterterrorism. Democratic due process and counterterrorism effectiveness can be compatible. There need not be a trade-off between values and security.

In the post-9/11 world, the regulation of migration and borders has become part of a new security framework, although the issues themselves are far from new. Gallya Lahav analyzes immigration policy as a tool of counterterrorism in the EU, where its incorporation into counterterrorism policy in turn has strengthened the EU's role as an actor in foreign and security policy. The impact of counterterrorism on migration control is "formidable," in Lahav's view. Migration is no longer "low politics" but "high politics." Securitization has also become "Europeanization," but as we see at the level of the nation-state (Japan is the exception), these developments are not departures from the past. A move to shift issues such as asylum and policing from the national to the EU level was already under way before 9/11. Policing has now been "unhitched" from the nation-state. Lahav notes another surely unintended effect of counterterrorism in the deepening cooperation between the EU and the United States, despite the contrast between a general European view of terrorism as a problem for law enforcement and the American war model. The new security emphasis in the EU has provoked contentious debate over formerly narrow technical issues such as biometric identifiers. Lahav explains that EU policy linking migration to security accelerated, not in response to the 9/11 attacks, but after the 2004 assassination of Dutch filmmaker Theo van Gogh by an Islamist extremist who was a Dutch citizen. The EU's risk perception, like that of most European national governments, differs substantially from the American perception. For the United States, the threat is still largely external, but to the EU internal controls are more important than protecting external borders.[15] The British experience with terrorism may confirm this judgment on the national level, although Dirk Haubrich sees the current threat as a mixed one, not exclusively internal. It is easier to implement internal controls within the EU, however, than to prevent travel and exchanges of ideas and information, especially in the age of the Internet. The end result is a retreat from core liberal values.

In the first of the country case studies, Dirk Haubrich identifies three types of threats that the United Kingdom has faced: domestic, transnational, and "compounded" terrorism. Haubrich employs social contract theory to explain differences in the willingness to compromise democratic principles evoked by each variety of threat. In his view, Britain's early coercive policies toward the IRA were unsuccessful and counterproductive. The policy of internment, for example, was disastrous because it alienated Catholic opinion. The British government eventually learned that its response to the IRA undermined the state's legitimacy because the state was competing with the IRA for the same public constituency in Northern Ireland. Thus, the government switched to the more conciliatory measures that eventually led the IRA to abandon violence—although the process was long and arduous. (Rogelio Alonso, in chapter 6, criticizes the British government's leniency toward the IRA during this process.)

The 9/11 attacks on New York and Washington posed another challenge for the United Kingdom. Although the British homeland was not attacked, the government identified closely with the United States and felt similarly threatened, especially as the number of failed and foiled plots increased. The government responded accordingly, both at home and abroad.[16] The government's fears were realized when suicide bombers struck public transportation targets in London in July 2005. The perpetrators of the attacks were citizens, but their stated cause was transnational. It was suspected that some of the leadership benefited from training in Al Qaeda camps in Pakistan. This attack thus represented compounded terrorism. Social contract theory predicts that the state's reaction would be less repressive than in cases of transnational terrorism, but more severe than in cases of domestic terrorism. Such has not been the case. Lack of a clearly definable enemy has led the authorities to focus their counterterrorist operations against domestic targets. Based on data he collected, Dirk Haubrich notes skeptically that of 895 terrorist suspects arrested between 2001 and 2005, only twenty-three were eventually convicted. More than half of 130 terrorism-related trials did not lead to convictions. A U.K. Home Office report in 2009 stated that, as of March 31, 2008, 125 persons were in prison for terrorism-related offenses, most of them citizens of the United Kingdom.[17] It noted that 1,471 arrests had been made, with 35 percent resulting in a charge and a 60 percent conviction rate for those persons charged. Putting these figures into a contemporary European context, in 2009 Europol reported that in 2008 over one thousand individuals were arrested in thirteen European countries, with 359 of them brought to trial in 187 cases. Twenty-nine percent of these defendants were acquitted.[18]

Counterterrorism policy in Britain has been highly controversial. In June 2008, the debate in Britain over extending the period of preventive detention for terrorist suspects from twenty-eight to forty-two days was extremely polarized.[19] More than thirty Labor Party members voted against the government of Prime Minister Gordon Brown, for whom the vote was a test of leadership of the Labor Party. The Conservative and Liberal Democratic Parties, civil liberties groups, and organizations representing Britain's Muslim population all opposed the legislation. Although polls showed that the public supported the measure, the government won only because the nine Democratic Unionists in Parliament voted for the measure when concessions were made to them on local issues in Northern Ireland. Following the vote, the shadow home secretary resigned his seat in Parliament to seek reelection independently on an antidetention platform. He explained the extraordinary move as a protest against the government's "strangulation" of British freedoms.[20]

Rogelio Alonso focuses on ethno-nationalist challenges to democracy and approaches the security-versus-democracy puzzle from a new direction. He compares Spain's response to ETA to the campaigns against the IRA in the United Kingdom and the Republic of Ireland. Alonso's position is that banning political parties and censoring the news media are actually democratic responses when the "democratic deficit" that contributed to the original formation of violent opposition movements has been made up. Governments that have provided violent oppositions with a democratic opening—that is, the opportunity to participate freely in the political process—should not condone continued violence. They should insist on disarmament and disbandment of the extremist organization before negotiating concessions such as prisoner releases. Doing otherwise undermines moderate nationalist parties and their supporters who are loyal to the state, accept majority rule, and favor nonviolence. Tolerance of terrorism during "peace processes" deprives citizens of their rights to political participation and equality before the law and legitimizes the resort to violence to influence the political process. The process of democratic representation is distorted. Coercion and intimidation by underground organizations, even if they claim to be committed to a peaceful transition, is undemocratic. Thus, Spain was right to proscribe Batasuna, the political wing of ETA, and Ireland and the United Kingdom were right to forbid the transmission on television or radio of interviews with members of illegal organizations, such as the IRA.

Spain's decision to ban ETA was supported by both the executive and the courts. The Spanish government initially banned Batasuna in 2003. The courts then reaffirmed the decision in 2007, when Batasuna members tried to establish a new party to compete in municipal elections. Again in 2008 the courts cut off funding for parties associated with Batasuna and prevented them for presenting candidates in the general election.

What happens if parties are banned because they will not renounce violence? Tim Bale of the University of Sussex reviewed the experiences of Turkey, Spain, and Belgium (Bale 2007, 2008). He found few negative consequences, but noted that the European Court of Human Rights (ECtHR) agreed in December 2007 to hear Batasuna's claim that the Spanish government had violated its rights to freedom of expression and association. In Bale's view, however, banning Batasuna did not seem to make ETA more violent. In 2009, the ECtHR upheld the ban.

As in Britain, the Spanish government's response to terrorism aroused dissent, but of a different sort, as Rogelio Alonso notes. Policy toward ETA was a major issue in the March 2008 elections that returned the Socialist Party and Prime Minister José Zapatero to power. (The other two key issues were the economy and immigration, the latter also a terrorism-related issue.) The salience of counterterrorism was reinforced when ETA assassinated a former Socialist local government official on the eve of the elections. Zapatero's earlier policy of negotiations with ETA had been widely unpopular, particularly with the powerful Association of Victims of Terrorism, and huge popular demonstrations opposed the initiative. The opposition People's Party constantly accused the government of being "soft on terrorism" and betraying ETA's victims. The policy became even more unpopular after ETA placed a bomb at the Madrid airport in December 2006 that killed two people, although the group was supposed to be observing a ceasefire. In March 2007, the government's decision to release an imprisoned ETA militant whose health had deteriorated because of a hunger strike unleashed what the *London Times* called a "storm of outrage" (March 2, 2007). When the Zapatero government finally broke off negotiations after ETA officially renounced the ceasefire in June, the Socialist Party's approval rating immediately went up, and the government then stuck to a hard line. It should be recalled that Zapatero was originally elected after the disastrous March 2004 Madrid bombings by an Islamist cell. His predecessor, People's Party leader José María Aznar, initially blamed ETA for the bombings, a blunder that may have cost him the election.

Jeremy Shapiro analyzes the French case. Like Dirk Haubrich, Shapiro sees the state as confronting a series of specific terrorist threats over time with correspondingly different countermeasures. France confronted no single terrorist threat and had no uniform counterterrorist policy; the government adapted to a shifting landscape. From the 1950s on, France moved sequentially from treating terrorism as an emergency (in the context of the Algerian war) to providing sanctuary for international terrorist groups (for example, some of the nationalist Palestinian factions) as long as they did not target France, to accommodating the demands of terrorist groups and their state patrons in the 1980s, to suppressing terrorism, and on to preventing it in the post-9/11 era. Having dealt with terrorism for over fifty years, France accepts it as an inevitable fact of modern life, not an existential threat. Shapiro argues that the French experience highlights the importance of responding to terrorism through normal channels, particularly judicial institutions, in order to preserve the legitimacy of the state. Unlike John E. Finn and Dirk Haubrich, Shapiro is optimistic that antiterrorist measures that lack public support will wither away when the threat has passed. He notes that France may be the exception among Western democracies: some well-established French counterterrorism measures, such as lengthy detention without charges and pervasive surveillance, would be unacceptable to other liberal states.[21] Although French political culture may easily tolerate such infringements on civil liberties, the Muslim and Arab population of France (the largest Muslim minority in Europe) suffers the brunt of the policy's repressive effects. France will eventually have to reckon with their frustration.

The case of France illustrates another general point: old debates do not fade away, and memories are long. The use of torture by French forces during the Algerian war reached the national political agenda yet again some forty years later when General Paul Aussaresses published his wartime memoirs in 2001, as Jeremy Shapiro recounts. The general and his publishers were subsequently fined by the courts for justifying torture. The year before the publication of Aussaresses's book, an Algerian woman accused other prominent French military figures of torture, a charge that generated a spate of press commentary on the various denials and admissions that followed. In 2005 and 2006, the Ligue des Droits de l'Homme vigorously protested public commemorations of OAS's forty-fifth-year anniversary. The United States may also find that controversy over enhanced interrogation after 9/11 will persist well into the future, even though the practices were halted by the Obama administration.

Like France, Germany may also be an exception in resisting deep change in counterterrorism policies and institutions, although its policies might shift if Germany experienced a major terrorist attack on its territory. So far all attempts have been foiled. Giovanni Capoccia argues that norms and institutions did not change in the 1970s, when the Federal Republic faced terrorism from the left, or after the shock of 9/11. Although the German state has adapted, it has done so incrementally and gradually. One important constraint is the federal system: the Länder and the judicial institutions have firmly resisted the growth of executive power. Second, for historical reasons, democracy is not taken for granted in Germany, and the principles of the Basic Law of 1949 are deeply respected. On the other hand, the German public is willing to countenance harsher policies than the government has advocated or implemented. Attitudes toward Muslims have hardened, although concerns about the protection of civil liberties remain paramount. It is also worth noting that a key German counterterrorist measure is the withdrawal of legal exemptions for religious organizations, a development resembling those in Japan after 1995 and in the United Kingdom in the wake of 9/11.

It is an understatement to say that Israel is an extreme case. Israel has faced terrorism throughout its existence, and terrorism has always been linked to the hostile intentions of neighboring states that were adversaries in major wars. One could say that Israel has been at war with terror since 1948. It is not surprising that Israel's response to terrorism has been much more consistently coercive than elsewhere (although some critics of U.S. policy may disagree). Ami Pedahzur and Arie Perliger argue that Israeli policy does not score high in terms of either effectiveness or democratic acceptability. In their view, adopting a war model to deal with terrorism has completely failed. This approach is the result of the influence of the military elite on the institutions of the state, uncritical public support for the military establishment, and the reluctance of the Supreme Court to counter executive power. Severe policies such as house demolitions, targeted killings, restrictions on citizenship, and the building of the "security fence," or wall, have not received the public scrutiny they should have, a finding that confirms John Finn's warning about the undemocratic effects of lack of transparency in executive decisionmaking. The consequence, in the authors' judgment, is a tragic decline in Israeli democracy, without a corresponding increase in security for its citizens. The war model, they conclude, is not one to be imitated.

Like Spain, Israel also considered disqualifying pro-Palestinian political parties, but unlike the Spanish courts the Israeli Supreme Court blocked the initiative. The victory of Hamas in the Gaza Strip raised another set of problems, as Israel and its allies, including the United States, refused to deal with Hamas until it renounced violence and recognized Israel's right to exist. It is not clear how democracies should proceed when violent extremist parties are democratically elected. There is also an international dimension to the problem: as de Jonge Oudraat and Marret explain, Hamas is on the EU's list of terrorist organizations as well as the U.S. list (although the latter does not include Hezbollah). Such designations, which are contested, can close off possibilities of negotiations or third-party involvement in peace processes because the designated parties are thereby stigmatized.

As in Ami Pedahzur and Arie Perliger's analysis of Israel, the implications of counterterrorist policy for the role of the military are at the center of David Leheny's analysis of Japan. Here too the response to terrorism has enhanced military institutions. Before 9/11, Japan considered terrorism a law enforcement issue, which was the dominant international framing at the time as well as the way in which Japan had traditionally approached internal threats such as the Japanese Red Army in the 1970s and Aum Shinrikyo in the 1990s. After the United States launched the war on terror, however, Japan came to agree with the American position that terrorism was a momentous threat to national security that justified a military response. Leheny regards the changes in Japanese security policy after 9/11 as "breathtaking." He notes that before 9/11 the ideas of democracy and a restricted role for the military were inextricably linked. This linkage ensured that the use of force would always be an acutely contested domestic political issue. After 9/11, the threat of terrorism (typically conflated with the traditional security threat posed by North Korea) was used to justify dramatic changes, including the first use of Japanese troops in support of combat operations since World War II. The boundaries between policing and military action are increasingly blurred in Japan.

In the post–World War II period, Japan and Germany have typically been regarded as similar "civilian" powers, for similar historical reasons, yet their reactions to post-9/11 security challenges differ considerably. In contrast to Japan, in Germany a restricted role for the military is still considered fundamental to democracy. All German military deployments must be individually approved by the Bundestag. The German Bundeswehr supported the NATO mission in Afghanistan, but agreed only to train Iraqi forces outside of Iraq.

Counterterrorism in the Post-9/11 World

Liberal democracies remain split between the criminal-justice or law-enforcement approach to terrorism and the war model, even though counterterrorism policing may be shifting in a military direction. Israel adopted a war model well before 2001, but it did not create an international precedent. Support for the American war model—the post-2001 global war on terror as it extended to intervention in Iraq—was deeply unpopular in both Britain and Spain, even though political elites favored it. The bombings in London and Madrid reinforced popular antagonism, since they were interpreted as reprisals against British and Spanish participation in the occupation of Iraq. Neither the French nor the German government, nor their citizens, supported the U.S. mission in Iraq. Other American counterterrorism actions—especially the prison at Guantánamo Bay, the secret prisons in Europe, the covert operations, and the extraordinary renditions—further troubled allied relationships. Nevertheless, disapproval of American actions and policies was far from universal. For instance, while there was public concern among Germans about the consequences of their country's role in Afghanistan, Japan has seized the opportunity of the American war on terror to reframe conceptions of national security and build a role as a military power. Reactions to the Obama administration's shift away from the war on terror model were generally positive, especially in western Europe, although the administration's emphasis on the war in Afghanistan met with reservations. Israel remained suspicious of the new administration's efforts to restrict settlements as part of a renewed peace process. The Israeli government also feared that the United States would not take a sufficiently hard line with Iran, a threat because of its nuclear aspirations as well as its support for both Hamas and Hezbollah.

With the exception of Japan, we see few abrupt post-9/11 changes in the national policies studied here, in the EU policy on immigration, or in the establishment of terrorist designation lists. In general what political scientists call "path dependency" is very much in evidence. The momentum toward adopting stricter measures has typically been gradual. Outside the United States, Britain has shown the most change. France had developed a robust counterterrorism stance earlier than other liberal democracies, and Germany has resisted the erosion of democratic norms. Given this solid and deep historical base and the steady accretion of counterterrorist policies, it is unlikely that there will be major reversals. European fears of domestic radicalization and the persistence of terrorist attacks and interrupted plots will encourage the maintenance in these countries of existing systems of prevention.

From our analysis of post-9/11 counterterrorism policy we can project a number of short-term consequences—for instance, lengthened periods of preventive detention will keep more people in jail before charges are brought against them, and increased surveillance and the establishment of large databases on individuals will reduce privacy. It is much harder, however, to foresee the long-term political effects or to understand variations among countries. There is much that we do not know. The chapters in this volume thus suggest a rich research agenda for an uncertain future. Terrorism will continue to present a variety of complex threats resulting from a mixture of local, national, and international politics. Creating disruption by killing civilians in surprise attacks is unfortunately all too easy. Governments and international institutions will respond according to their perceptions of the threat and their distinctive norms and institutions.

The analysis and arguments presented here should help inform public debate over counterterrorism policy in democracies. Accountability and transparency are as essential to democracy as the protection of civil liberties, democratic institutions, and processes of governance. Security policy inevitably requires some secrecy, but democratic governments have to explain and justify their actions to their constituencies. Government leaders must anticipate and be prepared for contingencies and surprises, but good judgment requires thinking beyond the immediate moment of crisis. This volume should assist these government decisionmakers as they identify and evaluate the potential consequences of a range of policy alternatives. The studies presented here should also encourage democratic governments to learn from one another, as well as from their own experiences, the ways in which they can better anticipate the political impact of their policy choices and to take that potential impact into account in their decisionmaking.

Notes

1. Most comparative analyses of non-American counterterrorist policies describe the policies of different states, explain how they have changed, and evaluate their current effectiveness (see, for example, Von Hippel 2005; Alexander 2002; von Knop, Neisser, and van Creveld 2005; Jacobson 2006; Zimmermann and Wenger 2006a). Some analyses consider specifically the effectiveness of democracies in reducing terrorism (for example, Art and Richardson 2007, a volume that includes case studies of Britain, France, Japan, and Israel). European lessons for homeland security in the United States are considered in Hamilton, Sundelius, and Grönvall (2005), a volume that includes studies of European states not considered here: Sweden, Finland, Norway, Switzerland, and Austria.
2. For a small sample of the critical appraisals of American policies under the Bush administration, see Cole and Lobel (2007) and Goldsmith (2007).
3. On this need, see Krebs (2009).
4. Some authors (for example, Mueller 2006 and Lustick 2006) argue that it would be best for governments to do nothing, but passivity does not seem to be a politically acceptable option.
5. It is well to remember, however, that a number of ostensibly domestic left-wing groups in the 1960s and 1970s (such as the Red Army Faction in Germany and the Weather Underground in the United States) took their inspiration from revolutionary movements in the Third World, particularly Latin America. The Uruguayan Tupamaros were particularly influential, as I note later in this chapter.
6. The German Marshall Fund's Transatlantic Trends 2007 public-opinion survey found that 66 percent of Europeans felt personally affected by international terrorism (versus 74 percent of Americans). This was a sixteen-percentage-point increase over 2005. Perceptions of Islamic fundamentalism and immigration as threats also increased. In 2008, however, attitudes shifted slightly: 62 percent of Europeans and 69 percent of Americans thought they would be personally affected by international terrorism in the next ten years. A little over 40 percent of Europeans and Americans agreed that international terrorism should be at the top of the policy agenda, along with economic issues. Interestingly enough, in 2009 European publics expressed more confidence in President Obama's counterterrorism policies than Americans did. See "Transatlantic Trends: Key Findings 2007," available at: http://www.transatlantictrends.org/trends (accessed September 14, 2009). Nevertheless, some experts point to divergent risk perceptions as a divisive factor in transatlantic relations (Föhrenbach 2006).

7. The case studies in Cohen (2008) deal with democracies engaged in military conflicts against armed groups defined as terrorist. They consider the difficulties of conducting such warfare without violating international law.
8. See U.S. Department of Homeland Security, National Consortium for the Study of Terrorism and Responses to Terrorism (START), "Global Terrorism Database," available at: http://www.start.umd.edu (accessed September 14, 2009).
9. Even in 2008, Europol was still reporting that separatist terrorism was the area of terrorism that most affected the European Union. See Europol, "European Union Terrorism Situation and Trend Report," TE-SAT 2009, available at: http://www.europol.europa.eu/publications/EU_Terrorism_Situation_and_Trend_Report_TE-SAT/TESAT2009.pdf (accessed September 14, 2009).
10. This leaves aside the Breton National Liberation Movement and the much more serious Corsican National Liberation Front, founded in 1976 and still in existence. The latter has mainly been active in Corsica rather than on the French mainland, but there have been attacks in the south of France.
11. The provocative power of terrorism is evident in the fact that the Israeli invasion of Lebanon was ostensibly a reaction to a terrorist attack on the Israeli ambassador to the United Kingdom by the PFLP.
12. See Craig Whitlock, "French Push Limits in Fight on Terrorism: Wide Prosecutorial Powers Draw Scant Public Dissent," *Washington Post*, November 2, 2004.
13. See Molly Moore, "Panel Decries Terrorism Blacklist Process," *Washington Post*, November 13, 2007.
14. In January 2009 the EU also removed the group from its list of terrorist organizations. See John F. Burns, "Iranian Exiles Aren't Terrorist Group, British Court Says," *New York Times*, May 8, 2008, and Stephen Castle, "Europe Takes Terrorist Label Off Iranian Resistance Group," *New York Times*, January 26, 2009.
15. Similarly, Daniel Hamilton and his colleagues (2005) refer to a changing conception of security in Europe from defense of territory and borders to "societal security."
16. The cascading effect of counterterrorism measures is neatly illustrated as follows. One provision of the quickly enacted legislative package was to permit the detention without trial of suspected foreign terrorists who could not be deported to their home countries owing to the risk of torture. Since the European Convention on Human Rights prohibits imprisonment without trial, the United Kingdom had to declare a state of public emergency in order to meet its treaty obligations.
17. See U.K. Home Office, "Statistical Bulletin: Statistics on Terrorism Arrests and Outcomes in Great Britain, 11 September 2001 to 31 March 2008," May 13, 2009.

18. See Europol, "Situation and Trend Report" (see note 9); see also Jacobson (2006) on terrorist prosecutions in Europe.
19. See John F. Burns, "Vote Favors Terrorism Bill and Premier in Britain," *New York Times*, June 12, 2008.
20. See Philip Webster and David Byers, "Shadow Home Secretary David Davis Resigns to Force By-Election," *Times Online*, June 12, 2008. Available at: http://www.timesonline.co.uk/tol/news/politics/article4120459.ece (accessed September 14, 2009).
21. "France permits prosecution under a crime called association de malfaiteurs (criminal association), which allows charges to be brought when there is an 'understanding' between two or more people to carry out a crime and the group has taken at least one material step toward its goal. This resembles U.S. conspiracy law but is harsher because it allows charges to be lodged on the basis of information gained through interrogation without the presence of a lawyer—often supplemented by hearsay evidence—and a suspect can then be held in pretrial detention for more than three years. In terrorism cases, such detention has been common. France thus stays within a criminal justice paradigm but requires far less evidence before allowing the state to place a suspect in long-term detention" (Roth 2008, 2).

References

Alexander, Yonah, ed. 2002. *Combating Terrorism: Strategies of Ten Countries.* Ann Arbor: University of Michigan Press.

Art, Robert J., and Louise Richardson, eds. 2007. *Democracy and Counterterrorism: Lessons from the Past.* Washington, D.C.: United States Institute of Peace Press.

Bale, Tim. 2007. "Are Bans on Political Parties Bound to Turn Out Badly? A Comparative Investigation of Three 'Intolerant' Democracies: Turkey, Spain, and Belgium." *Comparative European Politics* 5(2): 141–57.

———. 2008. "Will It All End in Tears? What Really Happens When Democracies Ban Parties." Paper presented to the international conference on "Democracy and Extremism." Georgia State University (June 11–13).

Brimmer, Esther, ed. 2006. *Transforming Homeland Security: U.S. and European Approaches.* Washington, D.C.: Center for Transatlantic Relations.

Charters, David A., ed. 1994. *The Deadly Sin of Terrorism: Its Effect on Democracy and Civil Liberty in Six Countries.* Westport, Conn.: Greenwood Press.

Cohen, Samy, ed. 2008. *Democracies at War Against Terrorism: A Comparative Perspective.* New York: Palgrave Macmillan.

Cole, David, and Jules Lobel. 2007. *Less Safe, Less Free: Why America Is Losing the War on Terror.* New York: New Press.

Donohue, Laura K. 2008. *The Cost of Counterterrorism: Power, Politics, and Liberty.* Cambridge: Cambridge University Press.

Föhrenbach, Gerd. 2006. "Transatlantic Homeland Security and the Challenge of Diverging Risk Perceptions." In *Transforming Homeland Security: U.S. and*

European Approaches, edited by Esther Brimmer. Washington, D.C.: Center for Transatlantic Relations.

Goldsmith, Jack. 2007. *The Terror Presidency: Law and Judgment Inside the Bush Administration.* New York: W. W. Norton.

Hamilton, Daniel, Bengt Sundelius, and Jesper Grönvall, eds. 2005. *Protecting the Homeland: European Approaches to Societal Security—Implications for the United States.* Washington, D.C.: Center for Transatlantic Relations.

Jacobson, Michael. 2006. *The West at War: U.S. and European Counterterrorism Efforts, Post–September 11.* Washington, D.C.: Washington Institute for Near East Policy.

Krebs, Ronald R. 2009. "In the Shadow of War: The Effects of Conflict on Liberal Democracy." *International Organization* 63(Winter): 177–210.

Lustick, Ian S. 2006. *Trapped in the War on Terror.* Philadelphia: University of Pennsylvania Press.

Mueller, John. 2006. *Overblown: How Politicians and the Terrorism Industry Inflate National Security Threats, and Why We Believe Them.* New York: Free Press.

Roth, Kenneth. 2008. "After Guantánamo: The Case Against Preventive Detention." *Foreign Affairs* 87(3, May–June). Available at: http://www.foreignaffairs.org/20080501facomment87302-p10/kenneth-roth/after-guant-namo.html (accessed June 14, 2008).

Shabad, Goldie, and Francisco José Llera Ramo. 1995. "Political Violence in a Democratic State: Basque Terrorism in Spain." In *Terrorism in Context*, edited by Martha Crenshaw. University Park, Penn.: Penn State University Press.

Varon, Jeremy. 2004. *Bringing the War Home: The Weather Underground, the Red Army Faction, and Revolutionary Violence in the Sixties and Seventies.* Berkeley: University of California Press.

Von Hippel, Karin, ed. 2005. *Europe Confronts Terrorism.* New York: Palgrave Macmillan.

Von Knop, Katharina, Heinrich Neisser, and Martin van Creveld, eds. 2005. *Countering Modern Terrorism.* Bielefeld, Germany: W. Bertelsmann Verlag.

Zimmermann, Doron, and Andreas Wenger, eds. 2006a. *How States Fight Terrorism: Policy Dynamics in the West.* Boulder, Colo.: Lynne Rienner.

———. 2006b. "Conclusion: Toward Efficiency and Legitimacy." In *How States Fight Terrorism: Policy Dynamics in the West*, edited by Doron Zimmermann and Andreas Wenger. Boulder, Colo.: Lynne Rienner.

Part I

Governance, Civil Liberties, and Securitization

CHAPTER 2

COUNTERTERRORISM REGIMES AND THE RULE OF LAW: THE EFFECTS OF EMERGENCY LEGISLATION ON SEPARATION OF POWERS, CIVIL LIBERTIES, AND OTHER FUNDAMENTAL CONSTITUTIONAL NORMS

JOHN E. FINN

In this chapter, we consider the long-term effects of post-9/11 counterterrorism policies on judiciaries and national constitutions. Our emphasis is on counterterrorism regimes in Europe and Canada, with occasional comparisons to Israel, Japan, India, and Australia. My approach is broadly comparative: I first identify general themes and trends, and my use of examples from specific countries is directed to highlighting and emphasizing these themes and trends.[1] I then appraise the effects of antiterrorism legislation on the protection of civil liberties, which I take to be among the fundamental objectives of any constitutional democracy. Finally, I consider the impact of such policies on three other and equally fundamental constitutional norms—the norm of accountability, the norm of transparency and deliberation, and the norm of proportionality.

To fully appreciate the effects of counterterrorism policies on civil liberties and other constitutional norms, we must first settle on what those policies are. This is not as simple as it might seem. Most readers would name the USA Patriot Act as one such policy. Other prominent examples include Canada's Anti-Terrorism Act (ATA) and the United Kingdom's Anti-Terrorism, Crime, and Security Act (ATCSA) of 2001. In the countries we consider, however, there are additional policies and statutes that have some bearing on antiterrorism policy, and many of them also raise issues with respect to judicial power and the rule of law. Counterterrorism regimes include changes in the administration of criminal justice and procedure but extend also to state policies on immigration and asylum and to regulations governing international banking and finance. In addition, counterterrorism regimes commonly include reorganization of what is sometimes called the "security architecture," examples of which would include the Department of Homeland Security and the reorganization of intelligence agencies in the United States under the Intelligence Reform and Terrorism Prevention Act of 2004. Other examples include the ongoing restructuring of German intelligences agencies following 9/11, as well as changes in the structure and procedures of the Japanese executive branch. Many of these changes are beyond the scope of this chapter, but a complete understanding of how counterterrorism policies affect civil liberties and constitutions should address them.

In the first section, I provide an overview of the counterterrorism regimes adopted by specific countries; this review of necessity is wide-ranging, and many of the policies and statutes are covered in more detail in other chapters of this book. It is important to remember, too, that counterterrorism regimes are not static. In most of the countries we take up—the United Kingdom and Germany are two especially good examples—the statutory frameworks governing antiterrorism efforts are continually changing. My primary aim in this section, therefore, is to foreshadow issues that transcend country-specific acts of legislation. Among these common issues are:

1. Questions regarding the reasons why countries adopted emergency legislation
2. Similarities and differences in legal definitions of terrorism, especially concerning the statutory elements of intent and motive
3. The use of specialized courts
4. The use of so-called sunset or expiration provisions in emergency legislation

In the second section, I consider the effects of counterterrorism regimes on specific constitutional liberties, such as freedom of expression, criminal due process, and privacy rights. I take up these issues by topic or category, not by country. At this level of abstraction, however, the categories often mask important, substantive differences in meaning. Freedom of expression, for example, is best understood, not as a uniform guarantee with a precise or common core of meaning, but rather as an umbrella term that covers a set of interests and rights that vary in breadth and depth across constitutions. As a consequence, it is difficult to engage in direct comparisons. The comparisons we do draw may mask important differences in the structural and institutional mechanisms designed to protect these specific liberties, which can vary dramatically across specific cases.

Even with such qualifications, the counterterrorism policies embraced in most of the countries we consider have substantially narrowed rights of speech and association. Privacy rights have been similarly limited, especially through provisions that expand the state's authority to gain access to telephone, Internet, and other electronic records. In most of the countries we examine, counterterrorism statutes have expanded the authority of the state to arrest suspects and to detain or hold them without charge. Foreign nationals are typically the subject of additional restrictions, and in many cases laws and regulations regarding asylum and immigration are important parts of national counterterrorism regimes.

In the third section, I consider how antiterrorism legislation affects three other fundamental constitutional norms. First, I examine the effects of counterterrorism regimes on the constitutional norm of *accountability*, or the requirement that governmental action be subject to review by other actors. As I have written elsewhere, the fundamental project here (which dovetails with the second norm) is one of public justification (Finn 1991; see also Ramraj 2005a, 6). The norm of accountability requires that governments seeking far-reaching and fundamental changes in the rule of law produce, in public, a justification for such changes, especially when they challenge the very desirability of the rule of law as a governing norm in times of crisis (Finn 1991).[2] The norm of accountability is what animates the separation of powers doctrine, especially with regard to the relationship between executive power, legislative oversight, and judicial review. In applying the norm to counterterrorism regimes, we want to ask whether antiterrorism regimes always increase the authority of the executive, or whether there are times when such policies expand or enhance legislative or judicial power. Concerns about the kinds of constitutional review that attach to security legislation—whether judicial, legislative, or administrative—likewise fall within this broad norm.

In most of the states we consider, counterterrorism policies concentrate authority in the executive, resulting in a profound shift in the balance of power between the executive and the other branches. One example of expanded executive power is the authority to compile lists of terrorist organizations and to proscribe them (see chapter 9). Another challenge to the separation of powers is the concentration of power in state bureaucracies found in most counterterrorism regimes, and not just at the national level. In many countries, judicial oversight has been weakened or at least challenged, but some national judiciaries have resisted; courts play a stronger role in some countries than others. Moreover, other types of review mechanisms, such as those that rely on legislative or parliamentary committees, have not worked well. In practice, then, many aspects of antiterrorism legislation pose a direct and substantial test to the separation of powers.

Second, counterterrorism legislation must be measured against the constitutional norm of *transparency and deliberation.* This principle holds that changes in the rule of law must be undertaken publicly and must conform to published (that is, constitutional or statutory/public law) standards. Such a requirement leads us to consider the processes involved in the post-9/11 adoption of counterterrorism laws. In most cases, the consideration of specific antiterrorism statutes was rapid and rushed. Often such changes were implemented with no sustained consideration of their potential long-term effects. Similarly, these statutes and policy changes were often adopted with no consideration of how they might affect the rules of criminal procedure or the legal system more generally. On the other hand, in most cases the new antiterrorism statutes and rules were not entirely novel or unprecedented. Most of these laws were enacted against a statutory backdrop that already included antiterrorism laws or rules of criminal procedure specially crafted to deal with terrorism-related offenses.

The sense of urgency surrounding the adoption of security legislation and the consequent breakdown of the ordinary processes of democratic dialogue have undermined basic constitutional norms of transparency and deliberation. This has substantially reduced the possibility of informed and involved public debate. Furthermore, the sunset provisions designed in part to remedy such consequences are not always effective.

Another question is whether there is evidence that states borrow antiterrorism legislation or learn from the experiences of other countries (see, for example, Art and Richardson 2007, 564). As we shall see, the rush to legislation after September 11, 2001, sometimes led policymakers to search for models of counterterrorism legislation in other countries. The United Kingdom's ATCSA, for example, has served as a template for antiterrorism legislation in many other jurisdictions, including Canada and other Commonwealth countries, and, more recently, the United States.[3] But there is less evidence that the continued adjustment and improvisation of counterterrorism legislation is actually informed by the successes and failures of similar legislation in other countries.

Third, I consider the constitutional norm of *proportionality*, or the demand that counterterrorism policies be not only consonant with other constitutional norms and rules but also proportionate to the degree and the nature of the threat. Concerns about proportionality lead to questions about whether counterterrorism legislation is a temporary response to an emergency or a permanent change in the administration of justice. An associated inquiry concerns the long-term and systemic constitutional effects of counterterrorism policies, such as "normalization," or the process by which changes made in counterterrorism policies begin to influence the administration of justice in ordinary criminal cases. Hence, an assessment of counterterrorism regimes must include a consideration of how such regimes impinge on the administration of justice and the rule of law more generally.

An Overview of Counterterrorism Regimes in Selected Countries

Although there are significant differences in their responses, all of the countries included in our study enacted antiterrorism legislation in the immediate aftermath of 9/11. In North America, the United States embraced a counterterrorism regime that included not only the well-known USA Patriot Act but a wide variety of supplementary legislation, such as the Homeland Security Act (2002), which created the Department of Homeland Security, and a series of executive orders (including those regarding military tribunals) and administrative regulations (including Department of Justice regulations regarding the detention and questioning of suspected terrorist offenders). Other elements of the counterterrorism regime in the United States include the Terrorist Information Awareness Program (2002) and ongoing reorganizations of the intelligence community (Wong 2005, 201–2).

In Canada, the government responded to 9/11 quickly. On October 15, the government introduced Bill C-36, the Anti-Terrorism Act (ATA), in the House of Commons. The act was finalized on December 18, 2001. In general, the ATA creates new terrorism crimes, including offenses regarding membership in and the financing of terrorist organizations. The act also authorizes the executive to designate terrorist groups and creates new and expanded powers of criminal investigation, which include the power of preventive arrest and the power to conduct investigative hearings. In addition to the ATA, Canada's counterterrorism regime includes the Public Safety Act (introduced in November 2001 but not passed until May 2004). The act includes provisions designed to protect Canadian infrastructure, such as seaports and airports. In 2003 Canada also created the Ministry of Public Safety and Emergency Preparedness, which is in some ways analogous to the Department of Homeland Security in the United States.

Like the United States (and the United Kingdom), Canada responded to 9/11 by making aggressive use of immigration laws, in particular the Immigration and Refugee Protection Act (IRPA) of 2001. Parts of IRPA, such as those regarding investigative detention, are substantially more far-reaching than similar provisions in the ATA.

Many members of the European Union (EU) also enacted far-reaching counterterrorism regimes, both as individual member states and as a collective.[4] On the day after 9/11, the General Council of the EU condemned the attacks. The EU followed this with a "United Action Plan" on September 21, designed to enhance a coordinated European response to terrorism.[5] Also included were proposals for a common European arrest warrant and the creation of Eurojust, an agency designed to improve judicial and prosecutorial cooperation within the EU. In June 2002, the EU adopted two resolutions under a "Framework Decision on Combating Terrorism," which included a common definition of terrorist acts and a common schedule for criminal sanctions. A second round of common European Union action followed the March 2004 bombings in Madrid. Nevertheless, individual states remain responsible for the implementation of specific legislation, and as a consequence there are important differences in the resulting legislation adopted by individual countries.

In the United Kingdom, the government quickly adopted the Anti-Terrorism, Crime, and Security Act (ATCSA) of 2001, which runs 118 pages, notwithstanding the passage just the year before of the comprehensive Terrorism Act (TA) 2000. Parts 1 and 2 of ATCSA work important changes on TACT, and TACT itself built on a long history of antiterrorism legislation in the United Kingdom (such as the Northern Ireland Emergency Provisions Act and the Prevention of Terrorism Acts). However, unlike those earlier acts, which were designed chiefly to respond to terrorism associated with Northern Ireland, TACT and ATCSA were designed to account for "the changing threat from international terrorism" (Art and Richardson 2007, 97).

TACT provided for the proscription of certain terrorist organizations, included expansive powers of investigation, arrest, and detention, and utilized an expanded definition of "terrorism." In turn, ATCSA expands TACT in several important ways. Part 3 of ATCSA concerns foreign property held by U.K. financial institutions. Part 4 substantially alters the laws governing immigration and asylum by authorizing the indefinite detention of noncitizen suspected terrorists who cannot be deported. (Subsequently, the Prevention of Terrorism Act of 2005 implemented a number of significant changes to this system, replacing the original indefinite detention provisions with an elaborate system of "control orders.") A later act, enacted in the aftermath of the London bombing attacks in the summer of 2005 (the Terrorism Act of 2006), includes provisions that criminalize the "encouragement" or "glorification" of terrorism and certain kinds of "terrorist publications." It also addresses nuclear terrorism, including the possession of nuclear materials and trespass at nuclear facilities.

In Germany, the government responded to the World Trade Center attacks by asking for new legislation on September 12. Two major acts, or "security packages," followed shortly thereafter. The first, enacted on September 19, includes provisions criminalizing the creation of and demonstrations of support for terrorist organizations. It also eliminates the so-called religious provision in German law, which had provided that German laws authorizing the prohibition and proscription of certain associations could not be applied to religious associations and communities.[6] A third part of the first security package provides for mandatory security checks for all airport personnel.

The second security package, passed on January 1, 2002, produced changes in seventeen different statutes. Generally speaking, these changes tend to increase the powers of the German security forces (Lepsius 2004, 435). They include the authority to gain access to information held by banks and telecommunications companies. In addition, the second security package substantially changes the law governing aliens and asylum. These provisions include the authority to expel persons who constitute a threat to the democratic order or national security.

Although the two security packages constitute the core of the German counterterrorism regime, altogether there are approximately fifty counterterrorism statutes, including, for example, the Air Transport Security Act (Luftsicherheitsgesetz), enacted by the Bundestag in June 2004.[7] In 2006, following an attempted train bombing in western Germany, German authorities created an antiterrorism database that permits both the police and intelligence services to gain easier access to a wide range of information on suspected terrorists, including information concerning Internet and telecommunications usage, bank account and safety deposit information, religious and family information, and information about travel patterns.

In contrast, the French counterterrorism regime is still centered largely on legislation passed in 1986, which "attempted to centralize all judicial and investigative proceedings relating to terrorism" (Shapiro 2007, 138). The government did respond to the 9/11 attacks in December 2001, however, by expanding police powers to search private property (including cars, which under French law are traditionally private and require a warrant to be searched) and extending the time given to authorities to question suspected terrorists from four to six days. According to one estimate, however, "the legislation in fact contained only minor updates to the powers of the French police, as well as a lot of non-terrorism-related regulations" (Shapiro 2007, 161). The acts also include a new offense, "association with terrorists," and authorize courts to imprison suspects on the basis of suspicion. Like the Prevention of Terrorism Act of 2005 in the United Kingdom, the French counterterrorism regime includes a system of control orders, under which the movements of suspected terrorists can be monitored and restricted, even in cases where there is insufficient evidence to bring the person to trial. The bill also authorizes the installation of surveillance cameras in mosques, department stores, malls, and other places.

In Japan, Prime Minister Junichiro Koizumi's government reacted quickly to 9/11. The Diet passed the Anti-Terrorism Special Measures Bill in October, which permits the use of Japanese forces to provide noncombat support to U.S. military forces in areas "surrounding" Japan (importantly, such areas were not defined in geographical terms). This change in policy, a substantial departure from Japan's response to the first Iraq war, occurred against the background of article 9 of the Japanese Constitution, which prohibits the use of force as a means to settling international disputes. It also forbids Japan from maintaining an army, a navy, or an air force.

Additional security legislation in Japan predates 9/11, including the Telecommunications Intercept Law (1999) and the Subversive Activities Prevention Law (1952) and its follow-up, the Group Regulation Act (1999), which authorizes authorities to "monitor and inspect without warrant facilities of groups found to have committed 'indiscriminate mass murder during the past ten years and to uncover assets of companies associated with these groups" (as quoted in Parachini and Furukawa 2007, 545). For the most part, however, there was no significant effort in Japan to alter the criminal code of 1907 (although under the code, specific crimes, such as kidnapping, insurrection, and homicide, may be prosecuted as acts of terrorism) or to expand police powers, save for new regulations regarding the financing of terrorist activities. As Mary Fenwick explains, there are several reasons why Japan chose not to introduce comprehensive antiterrorism laws, including the lack of domestic pressure in the form of public outcry or pressure from the United States (gaiatsu), as well as a sense that existing criminal law was sufficient (Fenwick 2005; see also Ramraj, Hor, and Roach 2005, 333). Nevertheless, as David Leheny stresses in chapter 10, the 9/11 attacks have had profound consequences for the Japanese constitutional order, and in particular for the understanding of article 9 (Fenwick 2005, 347).

Most of the major components of the Israeli counterterrorism regime precede 9/11. Antiterrorism legislation includes the Defense Regulations (State of Emergency) of 1945, the Terrorism Prevention Ordinance of 1948 (which includes provisions that prohibit financial assistance and other kinds of material support for terrorist organizations), the Penal Law of 1977 (which includes provisions that define and prohibit "unlawful associations"), and the Detention of Illegal Combatants Act of 2002. In addition, there are specific provisions relevant to the war on terrorism in other legislation, such as the Firearms Law of 1949 and the Air Navigation (Security in Civil Aviation) Law of 1977. Moreover, the Prohibition of Money Laundering Law of 2000 requires financial institutions to report suspicious transfers of funds and requires the reporting of movements of cash and other monetary instruments in and out of Israel.

Why Did These Countries Adopt Counterterrorism Legislation?

The reasons why so many countries enacted emergency legislation following 9/11 are not difficult to determine. First, in many of the states we consider in this chapter, there were tangible connections to the 9/11 attacks. In some cases, the countries had nationals killed in the attacks, and in others (such as the United Kingdom, France, and Germany), individuals who played a part in planning and carrying out the attacks were arrested in their jurisdiction. These tangible, physical connections to the 9/11 attacks helped to underscore the judgment that existing antiterrorism statutes were inadequate. The very existence of terrorist attacks was sometimes claimed to be evidence of such inadequacy, but more generally criticisms tended to center on limitations on the state's authority to gather intelligence, to apprehend and arrest, and to try and convict suspected terrorists under existing criminal rules of evidence and procedure.

Another reason why states embraced antiterrorism legislation was for its symbolic value. Especially in democratic states, there is reason to think that governments feel the need to adopt legislation as a visible sign of their commitment to protect the public (Richardson 2007, 84). In Germany, for example, "the suggestive images of the terrorist attacks channeled the development of political opinion and fuelled legislative activism. . . . Whether a need for legislative regulation existed was never in doubt" (Lepsius 2004, 437). Oliver Lepsius (2004, 437) further argues that the security legislation in Germany was not a reaction "to the attacks as such but constitute[s] a political symbolic act." The symbolic importance of antiterrorism legislation is partly explained by the perceived sense that some kind of action was necessary, both because it was useful politically and because states do have a duty to protect their citizens. As Laura Donohue (2005, 24) has noted, "counter terrorism, like terrorism, is ultimately about political power. It is the state reasserting its claim over the coercive mechanisms of government."

A third reason why some states hurried to adopt emergency legislation was United Nations Resolution 1373, adopted on September 28, 2001. The resolution required member states to adopt a series of steps against terrorism, including measures that criminalized participation in terrorist attacks, criminalized the financing of terrorism, and prohibited the use of state territory as a safe haven for terrorist organizations. The resolution also created a special body, the Counter-Terrorism Committee (CTC), which receives reports from member states about the steps they have taken to comply with the resolution.[8]

Finally, one might also argue that the attacks, coupled with Resolution 1373, gave some advocates of security legislation an opportunity to further a legislative agenda that preceded 9/11. Some critics of post-9/11 counterterrorism statutes have thus charged that governments used the attacks to press for legal changes that were already in the works or that had stalled politically.[9] At the very least, in most states, post-9/11 security statutes can only be fully understood against a background that acknowledges the preexistence of antiterrorism legislation (see Haubrich 2003, 3, n. 3). In the United States, for example, many of the provisions included in the Patriot Act had been proposed and rejected during the Clinton administration. The attacks provided an occasion to revisit the need for additional security legislation in a more favorable political environment.[10] Moreover, as Dirk Haubrich argues in chapter 5, the transnational character of the 9/11 attacks precluded any need to gain the support of a domestic population, and hence the perpetrators had little incentive to moderate their attacks (as might be the case, for example, in domestic terrorism). In such cases, "where the probability of an alliance between the terrorists and the public is low or nonexistent, governmental reactions to terrorism are much less constrained."

Similarities and Differences in Counterterrorism Legislation

In this section, we consider similarities and differences between various counterterrorism regimes. Where possible, we also want to look at evidence of "borrowing," or efforts to learn from the experiences of others. One well-publicized comparative effort is the so-called Straw Review, a summary of counterterrorism statutes adopted by Western democracies that was conducted at the behest of U.K. Secretary of State for Justice Jack Straw in October 2005 in the midst of an extensive debate in the United Kingdom over indefinite detention and control orders. As we shall see, there is some evidence that states do borrow from one another (especially when they seek to justify the adoption of extraordinary powers, typically by arguing that departures from the rule of law are common in other democracies), but somewhat less evidence that they learn or profit from the experiences of other countries.

The Definition of Terrorism We noted earlier that UN Resolution 1373 called upon states to criminalize terrorism, but failed to define the term or the offense.[11] Whether antiterrorism statutes should include such a definition is a major point of divide when we consider domestic statutory efforts. To some extent, those statutes that fail to include a definition follow the example of Resolution 1373. Among those countries that do not include a definition of terrorism in their statutes are Israel, Italy, France, Germany, Spain, and Japan.

The United States, the United Kingdom, Australia, Greece, Norway, and South Africa, on the other hand, do include definitions of terrorism as part of the statutory framework (see James 1997, 450, n. 2). These definitions vary, especially in scope and breadth. As Kent Roach (2006, 2174) has noted, "A common feature of post 9/11 anti-terrorism laws has been the very broad definitions of terrorism that go beyond the murder and maiming of civilians." The definitions advanced in the U.K. legislation and in South Africa are expansive examples of this trend (Ramraj, Hor, and Roach 2005, 630). In addition, some of the strongest evidence of borrowing concerns the efforts of various states to define terrorism. For example, the definition of terrorism adopted by the United Kingdom's Anti-Terrorism Act of 2000 has been influential in several other states, especially in Australia, Canada, and South Africa (Ramraj, Hor, and Roach 2005, 630).

Does the Definition Include Motive? Another point of division concerns the element of motive as a part of the definition of the offense. Motive is not included as an element in the U.S. legislation, in Indonesia, or, in general, in the antiterrorism legislation enacted in the Middle East countries (Ramraj 2005a, 3).

Motive is an element in the United Kingdom, Canada, France, Norway, Spain, and Australia. In the United Kingdom, the Terrorism Act 2000 defines terrorism as the use or threat "for the purpose of advancing a political, religious or ideological cause, of action designed to influence a government or to intimidate the public, which involves serious violence against any person or serious damage to property, endangers the life of any person, or creates a serious risk to the health or safety of the public" (Fenwick and Phillipson 2005, 460). In Australia, the Security Legislation Amendment (Terrorism) Bill of 2002 defines terrorism in broad terms, so that a terrorist "act" is an act or a threat intended to coerce, or influence through intimidation, a government, the public, or a section of the public.

Initial drafts of the ATA in Canada borrowed extensively from the United Kingdom's TACT, defining terrorism as acts intended "to cause serious interference with or serious disruption of an essential service, facility, or system, whether public or private, other than as a result of lawful advocacy, protest, dissent or stoppage of work." Many scholars and civil libertarians objected that such a comprehensive definition might easily extend to acts of civil disobedience. In subsequent drafts, the definition was narrowed (to exclude unlawful, and lawful, "advocacy, protest, dissent, or stoppage of work"; see Mazer 2002) and to make clear that the expression of religious, political, or ideological opinions did not necessarily constitute terrorism (Mazer 2002, 10; Roach 2005a, 513).

Permanent or Temporary?

In some states, the antiterrorism legislation enacted after September 11 was introduced as a permanent part of the public law armature. Such was the case with the Canadian ATA—in contrast, for example, with the temporary legislation enacted in the 1970s to deal with the October crisis.[12] Similarly, the USA Patriot Act was passed as a permanent fixture (although, like the ATA, certain sections were coupled with sunset clauses), as was the antiterrorism legislation enacted in the United Kingdom in 2000 and 2001. The U.K. case is especially interesting because this permanent legislation built on a long history of "temporary" antiterrorism legislation prompted by the troubles in Northern Ireland. The Prevention of Terrorism (Temporary Provisions) Act (PTA) of 1974 is one such example (Fenwick and Phillipson 2005, 459; see also the PTA 1989 and the Northern Ireland

Emergency Provisions Act [NI (EPA)] 1996). After a series of one-year renewals, the government passed the Prevention of Terrorism Act 1984, which was set to expire after five years. In 1988 the government announced its intention to make the act permanent, which it accomplished with the PTA 1989.

Whether antiterrorism legislation should be permanent or temporary is typically caught up with questions about whether the legislation, or parts of it, should be coupled with "sunset clauses." Perhaps the clearest example of such coupling can be found in the debate over the Canadian legislation. Initial drafts included provisions for parliamentary review after three years. Critics of the bill argued for stricter forms of expiry, suggesting, as did the Canadian Bar Association, "when governments seek to impose . . . restraints on fundamental rights and freedoms, particularly with limited time available for study and debate, those restraints must be limited in duration" (Mazer 2002, 12). In contrast, Prime Minister Jean Chrétien argued against such clauses on the ground that as the threat was permanent, so must be the response (Mazer 2002, 12). The final version of the ATA attached a five-year sunset clause, but only to provisions concerning investigative hearings and preventive arrest (Roach 2006, 2151). Similarly, in Germany, the provisions in the second security package regarding privacy rights and data exchange are also governed by a five-year sunset (Zoller 2004, 486). In Australia, the Anti-Terrorism Bill (no. 2) 2005 states that the provisions allowing for the issuing of control and preventative detention orders are subject to a ten-year sunset clause.

As most readers know, some provisions in the USA Patriot Act expanding the search and surveillance powers of authorities were scheduled to sunset on December 31, 2005. President George W. Bush called for the renewal of these provisions in his State of the Union address in January 2003, well in advance of the scheduled expiration. On July 21, 2005, the House of Representatives voted to extend these provisions indefinitely, and the Senate followed on July 29, 2005. (It is worth noting that, for reasons I elaborate upon later, the House voted on the extension immediately after a series of terrorist attacks in London, which also led to additional antiterrorism legislation in the United Kingdom.)

Ordinary or Specialized Courts?

Australia, Canada, Germany, Israel, and Japan use regular courts to hear cases involving acts of terrorism, which is also the standard practice throughout much of the European Union.[13] In Italy, for example, ordinary judicial tribunals, known as the Corte d'Assise, hear terrorism crimes. Some counterterrorism regimes, however, use a separate system of courts with exclusive jurisdiction over terrorist offenses. For instance, specialized courts have a long history in Spain (Reinares and Alonso 2007, 115), which has used them at least since 1977. Cases involving terrorism-related offenses (and organized crime) are heard in Madrid at the National High Court, which has exclusive jurisdiction over such cases with special security features. This represents a substantial change from earlier practice, when such cases were heard in military courts (Reinares and Alonso 2007, 115).

In India, the Prevention of Terrorist Activities Act (POTA), a counterterrorism statute passed in 2002 and repealed in 2004, worked in tandem with specialized courts (for an overview of antiterrorism legislation in India, see Wallace 2007, 452–54). Run by a single judge appointed by the central government, these courts operated under highly relaxed rules of evidence, especially concerning when the court could draw an "adverse inference" from a defendant's silence (Krishnan 2004, 238–85).[14]

France also uses specialized terrorism courts. Since 1986, there has been a special bench in Paris—the Cour d'Assises—for terrorism-related crimes (defined as "acts committed by individuals or groups that have as a goal to gravely trouble public order by intimidation or terror"). A local prosecutor first determines if a crime is related to terrorism; if so, the case is referred to a special section of the court, which has "led over time to the establishment of a specialized and expert corps of counter terrorism magistrates" (see Foreign and Commonwealth Office 2005, 9). Even in cases that do not involve terrorism, the magistrate has a broad and expansive mix of powers (including authority to monitor suspects) that would be separated between prosecutor and judge in common law jurisdictions. The decisions of these magistrates are subject to very limited review by the Chambre d'Accusation (Shapiro 2007, 155). In addition, terrorists may be tried without juries.

In Greece, a special prosecutor has jurisdiction over all terrorism-related offenses. All terrorism crimes are under the jurisdiction of the Criminal Court of Appeals instead of "mixed jury courts," as would otherwise be the case under article 97 of the Greek Constitution (Kallergi 2005, 12–13).

Finally, in the United States, most offenses under the USA Patriot Act are heard by ordinary criminal courts. However, on November 13, 2001, President Bush issued an executive order that created a system of military tribunals to try non-U.S. citizens (aliens resident in the United States for many years as well as those captured in combat) who are suspected of terrorism.[15] The order authorizes these tribunals to try non-

U.S. suspects at the president's discretion (see further discussion later in the chapter).[16]

Separate courts are sometimes justified by the claim that terrorism cases present unique risks, whether to witnesses or to court personnel, or that separate courts are necessary to protect the workings of intelligence agencies and sensitive information. In addition, the existence of separate courts is said to enable such actors to develop an expertise in the management and resolution of terrorism cases. In addition, some argue that special courts are better equipped to reach verdicts not tainted by fears of reprisal or threats against witnesses and court personnel. (Similar arguments were advanced in favor of the Diplock Courts in Northern Ireland.) Critics charge that the creation of such courts is a tool that executive branch officials use to escape the kind of independent scrutiny that an autonomous and fully independent judiciary could bring to the oversight of counterterrorism policies. Human rights organizations in the United Kingdom, for example, have condemned proposals for special courts "as an attempt at co-opting judges into administrative detention policy" (see Zedner 2005, 528, n. 102). Some evidence for this claim can be found in instances where appeals from specialized courts to ordinary appellate courts have been disallowed or severely circumscribed, or in cases where the appointment and removal of judges and other personnel have largely occurred within the discretion of executive branch officials.

Counterterrorism Legislation and Civil Liberties

One of the principal dangers of antiterrorism legislation is the threat it poses to civil liberties.[17] In this section, I take up these issues by topic or category, not by country. At this level of examination, however, the categories often mask important, substantive differences in meaning. Freedom of expression, for example, is best understood not as a uniform guarantee with a precise shared meaning, but rather as an umbrella term that covers a set of interests and rights that vary in breadth and depth across national constitutions. Similarly, the comparisons mask important differences in the structural and institutional mechanisms designed to protect liberty in each country. In some but not all of the countries under review, there are formal bills of rights, often but not always coupled with institutionalized mechanisms for judicial review. In other countries, civil liberty protections may be grounded in statutory instruments and various international treaties and conventions, and responsibility for enforcing these protections may be shared by legislative and judicial actors.

Freedom of Expression and Association

Freedom of Expression Threats to freedom of expression in antiterrorism legislation ordinarily appear in one of two forms. First, some statutes implicate freedom of expression values in the process of defining terrorism as a criminal offense. In cases where the term is left undefined, such as in UN Resolution 1373, critics have complained that the term is too easily extended to cover otherwise peaceful and constitutionally protected expressions of political criticism and dissent, including peaceful forms of public protest. The difficulty is that the line between advocacy and incitement is sufficiently elastic to permit criminal prosecutions based solely on speech and expression, without any accompanying criminal activity.

The problem is similar where there is a statutory definition of terrorism but the definition itself is sufficiently elastic or expansive to comprehend speech and activity that would otherwise be constitutionally protected. This is arguably the case in Canada, where, for example, the broad definition of terrorism in early versions of the ATA brought forth immediate protests that the ATA would criminalize legitimate social protests (Roach 2006, 2160; see also Roach 2005a, 513).[18] In subsequent drafts, the definition was narrowed to exclude certain kinds of political protests and strikes and to provide that the expression of religious, political, or ideological opinions would not necessarily constitute terrorism (Roach 2006, 2160; see also Roach 2005a, 513). Other parts of the ATA also implicate speech and expression values, especially those that create the new offense of "hate-motivated" mischief against religious property.

The second form in which threats to freedom of expression may arise is through legislation that directly targets "extremist" expression. One example is Security Council Resolution 1624 (2005), introduced by the British government (Roach 2006, 2176), which requires UN member states to make efforts to prevent "incitement" to commit terrorist acts and provides that members "have obligations under international law to counter incitement of terrorist acts motivated by extremism and intolerance and to prevent the subversion of educational, cultural and religious institutions by terrorists and their supporters."

The resolution directs states to "continue dialogue and broaden understanding," but its call for states to prohibit "incitement" may lead to statutory efforts to control or prohibit speech and dissent. Britain acted on its own resolution in the Terrorism Act 2006, which has provisions that prohibit speech that "directly or indirectly encourages" terrorism. Section 1 of the act creates the offense of "encouraging terrorism," subject to a penalty of seven years' imprisonment. The new offense extends to "a statement that is likely to be understood by some or all of the members of the public to whom it is published as a direct or indirect encouragement or other inducement to them to the commission, preparation or instigation of acts of terrorism." Similarly, the 2006 antiterrorism legislation includes a provision that prohibits "a statement that is likely to be understood by some or all of the members of the public to whom it is published as a direct or indirect encouragement or other inducement to them to the commission, preparation or instigation of acts of terrorism." Indirect encouragement is defined by the act as:

> every statement which (a) glorifies the commission or preparation (whether in the past, future or generally) of such acts or offenses; and (b) is a statement from which those members of the public could reasonably be expected to infer that what is being glorified is being glorified as conduct that should be emulated in existing circumstances.

The speech may be prohibited as long as it advocates terrorism, even if the terrorism does not include an element of violence.[19]

The 2006 legislation builds on provisions in the Terrorism Act 2000 that criminalized the acts of arranging or speaking at a meeting of three or more persons that would encourage support for a proscribed group, and on section 59, which criminalized the act of "soliciting acts of terrorism" outside of the United Kingdom. (This section in turn built on a much longer history of speech regulations in British counterterrorism laws, including proscription and the broadcasting ban in Northern Ireland that Rogelio Alonso defends in chapter 6.[20]) Sections 2 and 3 address related offenses concerning terrorist publications, defined broadly as publications that directly or indirectly encourage terrorism or that "are useful in the commission or preparation" of terrorism. A related provision authorizes police officers to notify individuals that "there is terrorist material on a website and to give them two days to remove it."

Freedom of Association Antiterrorism laws typically implicate not only freedom of speech but also freedom of association. The power to proscribe organizations bears directly on freedom of association, and in most regimes the power of proscription includes not only the ability to ban certain terrorist organizations but also defines a series of complementary offenses, such as membership in or providing support for banned organizations (Ramraj 2005a, 4). In Canada, for example, the executive branch may designate certain organizations as "terrorist" groups. Similar powers of proscription in the United Kingdom outline a series of related "proscription offenses," including the criminalization of membership in or support for such organizations.[21]

In the United States, the authority to proscribe "foreign terrorist organizations" reaches at least as far back as the Antiterrorism and Effective Death Penalty Act of 1996 (see Finn 2001, 70–74). The United States also maintains a "Terrorist Exclusion List" under the USA Patriot Act of 2001.[22] Section 219 of the Immigration and Nationality Act permits the secretary of state to designate as a terrorist organization any foreign group that he or she finds to have engaged in terrorist activities. In Australia, the Security Legislation Amendment (Terrorism) Bill of 2002 also permits in some narrow instances the proscription of organizations (Williams 2002, 4). Similar legislation exists in Germany and Norway, but not in Italy or Spain, which simply follow lists maintained by the European Union.

Post-9/11 legislation in France includes a new offense—"association with terrorists." Under this charge, arrests may be based on intelligence alone instead of on concrete evidence that must be produced in a court of law. Sometimes called the "pimping for terrorism" provision (see Scheppele 2006, 9), it provides that a person who cannot substantiate the source of his income may be charged if he also associates with persons suspected of terrorist activity. The new provision plainly implicates freedom of association values.

In Germany, section 129a of the criminal code makes terrorist organizations illegal; coupled with the absence of a definition of terrorism, these provisions may cover a wide variety of associations and organizations, although limits have been suggested by some judicial decisions (Zoller 2004, 477). In addition, section 129a criminalizes support and recruitment for terrorist organizations. The definition of support is not included in the criminal code. As a consequence, "it may manifest itself in financial, practical/logistical or written and oral support" (Zoller 2004, 478). Enacted in the aftermath of 9/11, section 129b goes further by encompassing "the creation of foreign organizations" and permitting the state to punish certain demonstrations of support for such organizations.[23] Section 129b also eliminates the religious privilege exception to section 3 of the Vereinsgesetz, under which associations can be prohibited if they are antithetical to the constitutional order "or the spirit of understanding among the peoples of the world." Before section 129b was enacted, religious organizations fell outside of section 3.

Personal Liberty: Arrest and Detention

A preventive arrest or detention refers to the authority of the state to detain suspects, short of arrest, based on mere suspicion of terrorist activity. As a general rule, the security legislation adopted after 9/11 greatly expands the authority of security officers to arrest suspects or to hold them without formal charge, often without access to legal counsel, for extended periods of time (Reinares 1998, 363). Beyond this, however, the provisions vary in the details. The maximum period a suspect may be held without charge varies from country to country (for a useful review, see FCO 2005; see also Roach 2006, 2176).

In France, the normal custodial period of forty-eight hours for criminal arrests may be extended for two additional periods of twenty-four hours, and a person held in custody may speak to legal counsel only after seventy-two hours. Once charged, suspects can be held for up to four years before trial. In Italy, a suspect may be held in custody during preliminary investigations for a period of twenty-four months (extended from eighteen months in May 2001). In Australia, the Anti-Terrorism Act of 2004 extended the time permitted for questioning suspects to twenty-four hours (Williams 2002, 543). In India, emergency legislation enacted in 1980 (the National Security Act) authorized detention without charge or trial for one year and "was extended to two years for Punjab in 1984" (Wallace 2007, 453).

In Spain, terror suspects can be held for three days, but a judge may extend the period for an additional forty-eight hours. Changes enacted after the March 2004 attacks in Madrid permit judges to hold suspects incommunicado if they think that publicizing the suspect's detention will harm an ongoing investigation. An order imposing such a condition is valid initially for seventy-two hours, but it may be extended an additional forty-eight hours. Thereafter, the magistrate may initiate criminal proceedings and place the suspect in preventive detention, which may last up to two years.

Until just recently, the Canadian ATA permitted preventive arrests, for up to seventy-two hours, where there are "reasonable grounds" to suspect that a terrorist act is imminent and reasonable suspicion that detention is necessary to prevent it. The detainee must be brought within twenty-four hours before a court, where the state must then demonstrate that continued detention is necessary. The initial period of detention may be extended to seventy-two hours at a judge's discretion. Similarly, under a set of rules regarding "investigative hearings," the police can compel a person to answer questions regarding suspected terrorist activities, although such statements may not be used against them in later criminal proceedings (Roach 2005a, 518). In February 2007, both of these provisions in the ATA were allowed to lapse, in part because neither had been used.

In the United Kingdom, section 4 of the ATCSA (2001) authorized the government to detain foreign nationals without trial indefinitely, upon certification by the home secretary that the person detained is a risk to national security and that there is a reasonable ground for suspecting the person is a terrorist, defined elsewhere in the act as a person who is or has been concerned in the commission, preparation, or instigation of an act of international terrorism, is a member of such a group, or "has links" with such a group.[24]

Under the Prevention of Terrorism Act 2005, designed to replace section 4 in light of the decision by the House of Lords in *A. v. Secretary of State for the Home Department* (2004), the government may, upon reasonable suspicion of either a citizen or a noncitizen of involvement in terrorist activities, apply for a control order for a renewable twelve-month period of time. A control order, or a deprivation of liberty just short of an arrest, may include requirements that the individual not associate with others, possess certain substances, or travel to certain places and that he must wear an electronic monitoring device. As we will see, the control orders provisions have been the subject of extensive litigation and revision in the past two years (see Lepsius 2006, 776–77; Israel Ministry of Foreign Affairs 2005; Mersel 2006, 67; Grebinar 2003, 269; Gross 2002, 1161; Rosenfeld 2006, 2120).

Extensive controversy likewise surrounded the government's proposal in a counterterrorism bill, submitted in 2008, to extend periods of detention from twenty-eight days, as established in the Terrorism Act 2006, to forty-two days without charge; the proposal was defeated in the House of Commons in October 2008.

Like the Prevention of Terrorism Act 2005 in the United Kingdom, the French counterterrorism regime also includes a system of control orders under which the movements of suspected terrorists can be monitored and restricted, even in cases where there is insufficient evidence to bring the person to trial.

Persons arrested in Germany must be brought before a judge by the "termination of the day following the arrest." A judge may authorize further detention, but the detention must be reviewed every six months. No special rules govern the arrest and detention of suspected terrorists, but the first security package does grant the police expanded investigative powers. In particular, any person may be subjected to questions about his or her identity while traveling by train or air, even without prior suspicion (Lepsius 2004, 450).

In Israel, military commanders are empowered to detain individuals for periods of up to six months. They may extend detentions for an unlimited number of additional six-month periods. Civilian courts provide a limited mechanism for oversight by "confirming" the initial detention order and then by reviewing the status of each detainee every three months, overlapping with the review, every six months, by the minister of defense. Israeli law also provides that detainees have the right to an attorney and the right to be present at their confirmation hearing and at all subsequent judicial proceedings. On March 4, 2002, Israel adopted the Imprisonment of Illegal Combatants Law, which allows the chief of staff of the Israeli Defense Force to detain anyone if there is a basis to assume that he or she "takes part in hostile activity against Israel, directly or indirectly," or "belongs to a force engaged in hostile activity against the State of Israel."[25] All detainees held under the law are automatically assumed to be a security threat and can be held without charge or trial as long as hostilities against Israel continue.

There are no policies that explicitly authorize indefinite detention in the United States. On November 13, 2001, however, President Bush issued an executive order that created a system of military tribunals to try non-U.S. citizens suspected of terrorism at the president's discretion.[26] In *Rasul v. Bush* (2004), the U.S. Supreme Court ruled that detainees at the Guantánamo Bay detention camp could file habeas petitions in a federal court. Congress responded with the Detainee Treatment Act of 2005, which in effect restored the status quo. Similarly, in *Hamdan v. Rumsfeld* (2006), the Supreme Court ruled that military commissions violate both the Uniform Code of Military Justice (UCMJ) and the Geneva Conventions. Shortly thereafter, Congress passed the Military Commissions Act (MCA) of 2006 to "facilitate bringing to justice terrorists and other unlawful enemy combatants through full and fair trials by military commissions, and for other purposes."[27] In *Boumediene v. Bush* (2008), the Court considered the constitutionality of the Military Commissions Act. Writing for a divided Court, Justice Anthony Kennedy concluded that, the MCA notwithstanding, the writ of habeas corpus does apply to the detainees at Guantánamo. Following the decision, a lower federal court ordered the release of several men, including Lakhdar Boumediene, a naturalized citizen of Bosnia and Herzegovina, who had been held at Guantánamo for several years.

Privacy

In several countries, including France, Germany, Italy, Spain, the United Kingdom, and the United States, antiterrorism legislation includes provisions that permit authorities to wiretap phone conversations or to obtain access to records from Internet service providers. In Europe, such legislation must be set against the backdrop of article 8 of the European Convention, which guarantees the right of respect for privacy with regard to the individual, family life, the home, and correspondence. Section 8(2) provides, however, that such rights may be compromised if they are "necessary" and "proportionate" for the protection of national security.

Legislation passed in 2005 in France substantially expanded the state's powers of electronic surveillance, including the recording and monitoring of Internet activity. For example, article 29 in the French antiterrorism legislation requires Internet service providers to hold information on their clients for one year. Article 59 provides that the state may monitor the bank accounts of suspected terrorists. Similar legislation in Greece authorizes authorities to oversee transport and communications information and to get access to records at financial institutions.

In Germany, the second security package passed in 2001 states that Internet providers and phone companies must maintain records for six months and that authorities may access information held in bank accounts, as well as postal and airline data (Haubrich 2003, 12). There is also a requirement that the individual not be notified of such surveillance. In addition, the second security package makes it easier for various security authorities to exchange information, and it enlarges the authority of the Bundesverfassungsgericht (BVerfGE, or the Federal Constitution Court) to include the power to gather information on individuals and groups who "disturb the international understanding or peaceful cohabitation of peoples." Other sections of the second security package authorize a central database for use in tracking foreigners, which might include such information as fingerprints and religious affiliation (Zoller 2004, 483).[28] In 2006, following an attempted train bombing in western Germany, authorities created an antiterrorism database that permits both the police and intelligence services to gain easier access to a wide range of information on suspected terrorists, including information concerning Internet and telecommunications data, bank and safety deposit account information, information about family and religious practices, and data about travel.

In February 2008, the Federal Constitutional Court ruled that law enforcement authorities must receive permission from a judge before uploading spyware to a suspect's computer by e-mail. Such permission should be granted, the court noted, only if there is evidence that "legally protected interests," such as human life or state property, are at risk. In determining that the Basic Law creates a "basic right to the confidentiality and integrity of information-technological systems," the court struck a provision that had permitted authorities to conduct secret online searches of personal hard drives and other forms of storage media (BVerfGE, 1 BvR 370/07; for an account, see European Digital Rights 2008). Chancellor Angela Merkel's government subsequently introduced legislation that would permit law enforcement officials to conduct surveillance of home computers (through "remote forensic software") in cases of identifiable, concrete threats but that would prevent federal police officers from entering a suspect's home. The bill passed the lower house but was rejected by the upper house of the Bundestag in November 2008.

In the United Kingdom, the ATCSA 2001 requires that communication service providers keep data about their customers' communications for two years. As Mary Wong (2005, 218) has noted, "ATCSA's data retention provisions [cover] data relating to mobile text messages as well as web activity." The state may also demand that financial institutions provide information about bank accounts for ninety days, and the act facilitates the disclosure of confidential information from public authorities to agencies involved in criminal investigations and proceedings.[29] Changes in 2004 led to a "voluntary code" of practice under the ATCSA that specifies in detail the kinds of information that must be retained, how long it must be retained, and the legitimate reasons for the government to gain access to this information.

The direction of these legislative changes seems to support Dirk Haubrich's suggestion in chapter 5 of this volume that the British government seeks "to introduce additional legal measures and policies to help control, track, and monitor the domestic population." Similarly, some critics of German antiterrorism legislation have argued that one of its central purposes—and among its chief defects—is the "de-individualization" of the criminal law and its replacement with a system in which "individual rights are replaced by collective interests" (Lepsius 2004, 455). This is part of the justification for new antiterrorism databases in Germany, as well as the philosophy behind Interior Minister Wolfgang Schäuble's recent remarks suggesting that the presumption of innocence ought not to apply to suspected terrorists.

In the United States, the Patriot Act includes several provisions that impinge on the right to privacy, including changes to preexisting legislation regarding wiretapping, pen traps, and the application of the Foreign

Intelligence Surveillance Act (FISA) (Wong 2005, 200). In particular, the Patriot Act greatly expands the number of crimes covered by the wiretapping laws. It also authorizes "sneak-and-peak" searches and substantially lowers the legal standards necessary to obtain a tap under FISA. Other post-9/11 developments that touch privacy concerns include the establishment of the Department of Homeland Security and the creation of the Terrorist Information Awareness (TIA) program, which authorizes both data mining and automated data analysis (Wong 2005, 209). An act passed in 2004 authorizes the FBI to obtain records from financial institutions, which are broadly defined as including not only banks but also real estate brokers and automobile dealers. The legislation addresses privacy concerns by creating the Privacy and Legislative Oversight Board. The board has little authority, however, and it has been subject to criticism because its members are appointed by the president and because its powers to obtain documents and testimony are subject to a veto by the attorney general.[30]

Asylum and Immigration

Rules and regulations governing immigration and asylum often overlap and function in tandem with changes in the administration of criminal justice. Although many of the specifics of these issues are taken up by Gallya Lahav in chapter 4 of this volume, it is important to note here that "asylum, immigration and nationality law have all been used in the 'war against terrorism' in, for example, the U.K., the U.S. and Canada" (Harvey 2005, 152). In the United Kingdom, section 4 of the ATCSA substantially expanded the power of the home secretary to detain and deport suspected non-national "international" terrorists, and this included the authority to detain suspects indefinitely, with limited rights of appeal to a special immigration appeals commission. These provisions required the United Kingdom to formally derogate from article 5 of the European Convention of Human Rights (ECHR).

At least one survey of Canadian counterterrorism efforts likewise concludes that the Immigration and Refugee Protection Act (IRPA) has been of far greater consequence than the ATA. Under IRPA, a noncitizen suspected of an act of terrorism may be excluded, but IRPA itself does not include a definition of terrorism. In the leading case of *Suresh v. Canada* (2002), the Canadian Supreme Court defined terrorism as "an act intended to cause death or serious injury to a civilian, or to any person not taking an active part in the hostilities in a situation of armed conflict, when the purpose of such act by its nature or context is to intimidate a population or to compel a government or an international organization to do or abstain from doing any act."

Although this definition appears to be somewhat narrower than the one adopted in the ATA, the provisions under IRPA that authorize preventive detention are substantially broader (for a detailed description of the differences, see Roach 2005a, 523). Consequently, "immigration law has been attractive to the authorities because it allows procedural shortcuts and a degree of secrecy that would not be tolerated even under an expanded criminal law" (Roach 2005a, 521). In the recent case of *Charkaoui v. Canada (Citizenship and Immigration)* (2007), however, the Supreme Court of Canada ruled that the detention and security certificate procedures violated section 7 of the Charter of Rights and Freedoms.

In summary, counterterrorism regimes have had a considerable, if difficult to measure, effect on civil liberties. Most schemes significantly narrow freedom of expression and association. In addition, antiterrorism legislation often impinges on privacy rights, especially insofar as authorities can gain access to financial data and communications records. Finally, in most countries the power of the state to arrest individuals and hold them without charge has been extended dramatically, and foreign nationals are particularly vulnerable, often under the separate immigration and asylum statutes and rules that constitute an important part of many counterterrorism regimes.

The Effects of Counterterrorism Legislation on Constitutions and the Rule of Law

The effects of counterterrorism statutes and policies on the rule of law extend far beyond their impact on civil liberties. In this section, we consider the effects on national constitutions and on constitutionalism itself. To that end, I organize what follows around three constitutional norms, or values,[31] that are constitutive of the rule of law in any constitutional democracy.[32] These are:

1. The norm of *accountability*, by which I mean the structures, institutions, and constitutional rules necessary in a constitutional democracy to discipline public authorities by prohibiting unilateral and arbitrary (or unaccountable) exercises of power. These mechanisms of public accountability include the separation of power, especially horizontally, and some means of constitutional appraisal, such as judicial review, or parliamentary review in instances where judicial review does not exist or is extremely narrow.[33] Among the questions we must ask in considering separation-of-powers issues is whether antiterrorism regimes always concentrate authority in the executive, or whether there are

instances when such policies augment, or at least do not circumscribe, legislative or judicial power.

2. The norm of *transparency and deliberation*, by which I mean the requirement that state action be public and conform to published standards (that is, standards that are constitutional or statutory/public law). Among the concerns raised by the norm of transparency is the near-universal tendency in the states under review to adopt antiterrorism legislation in extreme haste and without extensive legislative or public deliberation.

3. The norm of *proportionality*, by which I mean the general requirement that state counterterrorism regimes be consonant not only with other constitutional norms but also with the degree and the nature of the emergency. I include as threats to the principle of proportionality the "normalization" of counterterrorism policies and the tendency of temporary changes in the administration of criminal justice to become permanent legal fixtures, sunset clauses and fixed schedules for parliamentary or legislative review notwithstanding.

Separation-of-Powers Issues

A constitutional democracy must be committed to the separation of powers, and the horizontal separation of power is an essential component of constitutional design. Typically the separation of powers takes the form of the tripartite distinction between executive, legislative, and judicial powers. The precise division and assignment of these powers varies across states and depends heavily on other aspects of democratic design, such as whether the system is parliamentary or presidential in nature. As a rule, for example, we can posit that parliamentary regimes are less likely to envision strict separations between legislative and executive power (Rosenfeld 2006, 2079, n. 259).

There are a number of reasons why constitutional democracies separate powers, including the desire to protect civil liberties. In the context of counterterrorism legislation, the doctrine is best understood as a mechanism for disciplining the exercise of power by one branch by making it accountable—first to other branches, and second to the public. Antiterrorism statutes typically threaten separation-of-powers values and the constitutional norm of accountability, in one of three ways.

1. The Concentration of Power in the Executive Branch Appeals for antiterrorism legislation are ordinarily predicated on a claim that is fundamentally antithetical to the separation of powers—that there is an urgent need for extraordinary powers to deal with extraordinary or unusual threats. Such claims see the separation of power as an impediment to the efficient and rapid response that governments need to be able to make when they face unconventional threats (Zoller 2004, 477; Lepsius 2004, 447). Similarly, proponents of antiterrorism legislation occasionally argue that enforceable mechanisms of accountability may endanger the state by requiring the government to disclose information and intelligence that should be kept secret (Roach 2005b, 145).[34]

Sometimes the tension between separation-of-powers values and counterterrorism legislation involves a rejection of the value of accountability that is at the center of the separation-of-powers doctrine. This is especially the case insofar as counterterrorism legislation eliminates the institutional and structural mechanisms designed to make regimes accountable; in such instances, antiterrorism legislation is fundamentally incompatible with the separation of powers.

More often, however, antiterrorism legislation threatens separation-of-powers values by substantially relaxing ordinary mechanisms for accountability. One way in which many such statutes disrupt the separation of power is by concentrating power in the executive branch.[35] In nearly every case we study in this chapter, antiterrorism legislation has profoundly shifted the balance of power between executive, legislative, and judicial authorities.[36] Such reallocations are based on claims that the executive branch is better suited functionally to conduct the war on terrorism, in large measure because of its ability to mobilize resources, including intelligence, quickly and efficiently. Three basic arguments are advanced to support this shift in favor of executive power. First, proponents of executive power argue that the institutional design of executive branches makes them better at gathering information about and assessing risk.[37] This is partly an argument based on institutional design, but it is also partly premised on deference to policy expertise.[38] Second, arguments in favor of the expansion of executive power sometimes depend on the related claim that the executive is more likely to maintain the trust of the population.[39] Third, arguments in favor of executive power sometimes are based on history and political theory, and in particular on the claim that in the Western tradition, at least, the executive is invested with the power of prerogative. The prerogative power, as Locke (1690/1960, 159–61, 163, 168) once wrote, is the power to act outside the law when the common good demands it (see also Rossiter 1948). In the United States, for example, advocates of presidential authority sometimes make the case for a theory of presidential power that relies on the prerogative, or the claim that the president possesses an inherent authority to use whatever force is necessary to conduct the war on terrorism.[40]

Antiterrorism legislation usually expands executive power in several ways. One way is expanding the power to proscribe certain organizations. In most regimes, proscription includes not only a ban on certain terrorist organizations but also a series of complementary offenses, such as membership in or providing support for banned organizations (Ramraj 2005a, 4). In Canada, for example, the executive branch may designate certain organizations as "terrorist" groups. The United Kingdom has similar powers of proscription, which include a series of related "proscription offenses," including the criminalization of membership in or support for such organizations.

In the United States, section 219 of the Immigration and Nationality Act permits the secretary of state to designate as terrorist organizations any foreign group that he or she finds to have engaged in terrorist activities (but see Zoller 2004, 477). Similar legislation exists in Australia, Germany, and Norway, but not in Italy or Spain (which simply follow lists maintained by the European Union) or in France. The establishment of these lists is discussed further in chapter 3.

Another way in which security statutes disrupt the separation of powers is by reassigning and concentrating power in various state administrative agencies and bureaucracies. For example, in Germany the concentration-of-power issues are less about the division of power between legislative and executive authorities and more about the division of power between the national government and the Länder. The Basic Law provides that the Länder are primarily responsible for the criminal law and police powers; intelligence matters, however, typically fall within the competence of the federal government. This division of authority "is meant to prevent that jurisdiction and competences are concentrated on one level" (Lepsius 2004, 445). Concerns about the division of authority between the Länder and the central government were a significant part of the controversy surrounding the Merkel government's proposed antiterrorism legislation in 2008.

Under the second security package, the Military Counterespionage Service (MAD) and the Federal Intelligence Service (BND) were given "enlarged competences" to gather information from telecommunications services and financial institutions (Lepsius 2004, 447). In addition, the federal Office for the Protection of the Constitution (BVerfGE) now has additional authority to investigate "attempts to disturb the international understanding" (Lepsius 2004, 447).[41]

In Japan, the enhancement of executive power is less a consequence of specific provisions in security legislation than of the political dynamic that surrounded passage of the legislation. As many commentators have observed, perhaps the most salient feature of Japan's post-9/11 response was the extraordinary role played by Prime Minister Junichiro Koizumi's government in securing a rapid response, which resulted in legislation that authorized the use of "Japan's Self-Defense Forces in wartime conditions for the first time in the country's postwar history" (Shinoda 2003, 19; see also Midford 2003, 329; Leheny, this volume).[42] According to some of the same observers, the process speaks to a new and more expansive conception of executive leadership (Shinoda 2003).

2. Constitutional and Judicial Review The concept of constitutional review is an essential part of the separation-of-powers doctrine. In presidential systems, such as the United States, the most familiar form of constitutional review is the more specialized practice of judicial review. Judicial review channels the larger mechanism of constitutional review into a single branch—the judiciary. But there is no reason why constitutional assessment must be the sole or even the primary prerogative of judges and courts. Especially in parliamentary systems, other mechanisms of constitutional review may include oversight by standing or ad hoc parliamentary committees or by administrative agencies. In France, constitutional review is entrusted largely to the Constitutional Council, which is not a judicial institution. In the United Kingdom, constitutional review is likewise essentially a parliamentary function, although the Human Rights Act (1998) envisions a very limited power of judges to declare legislation "incompatible" with the European Convention on Human Rights.

It is also conventional wisdom that antiterrorism legislation, insofar as it tends to concentrate power in the executive branch, undermines judicial power by reducing opportunities for constitutional review.[43] In many countries, this concentration of executive power has resulted in the weakening of judicial oversight over key parts of the administration of criminal justice and civil liberties more generally. The reasons advanced for loosening or relaxing judicial control over antiterrorism policies typically mirror those advanced for concentrating power in the executive. First among them is the claim, often advanced by judges themselves, that they lack the necessary institutional competence and expertise in areas of national security and foreign policy.[44]

Arguments in favor of judicial review, on the other hand, concentrate on the checking function of review by judicial authorities. As Lucia Zedner (2005, 529) has argued, "Openness and accountability are central to the rule of law." This checking function encompasses a review of the factual claims made by authorities. In detention proceedings, those claims of fact may well be subject to limited review of alleged security risks. For example, in her opinion for the U.S. Supreme Court in *Hamdi v. Rumsfeld* (2004), Justice Sandra Day O'Connor argued that "'security considerations' are not magic words. The court must insist on learning the specific security considerations that prompted the government's actions. The court must be persuaded that these considerations . . . were not merely pretextual."

The checking function of judicial review is important, but as I have argued elsewhere (see Finn 1991, 28–37), the great contribution of constitutional review to the rule of law and to the constitutional norm of accountability is that it compels authorities to produce reasons in support of their public policy choices. Moreover, the same considerations of comparative institutional advantage that assign expanded powers to the executive based on its superior capacity to assess risk and to act with dispatch might lead us to conclude that there are institutional advantages attached to courts as well. Courts may be especially well suited to the dispassionate review of public policy in light of overarching constitutional norms.[45] As Victor Ramraj (2005b, 121) argues, "Judicial review allows for a careful and sober consideration of risks and responses in a forum in which limitations on liberty are given their due and where the effectiveness of antiterrorism policies can be assessed against its impact on fundamental freedoms." A requirement of "reason giving" is what makes informed criticism of policy decisions possible and is thus a prerequisite of discourse and deliberation as well as of accountability. Reason giving is, in other words, a necessary precondition for satisfying the norm of accountability.

Whether the concentration of power in the executive has in fact resulted in the diminution of judicial power is not easy to determine. Even in the United States, often said to be the paradigmatic example of strong judicial review, recent cases suggest a more mixed picture. As we saw earlier, immediately after 9/11 the Bush administration created a set of military tribunals for certain kinds of defendants, under which the normal rules of criminal procedure would not apply. In *Rasul v. Bush* (2004), the Supreme Court held that detainees at Guantánamo could file habeas petitions in a federal court. Justice John Paul Stevens wrote that what is "at stake in this case is nothing less than the essence of a free society. Even more important than the method of selecting the people's rulers and their successors is the character of the constraints imposed on the Executive by the rule of law." Congress responded with the Detainee Treatment Act of 2005, which in effect restored the status quo.

Similarly, in *Hamdi v. Rumsfeld* (2004) and *Rumsfeld v. Padilla* (2004), the Court ordered a lower federal court to begin new proceedings in the cases of Yaser Hamdi and José Padilla—two American citizens charged as "enemy combatants" and held without charge or access to legal counsel. In Justice O'Connor's opinion for the plurality in *Hamdi*, Hamdi's detention was authorized by the Authorization for Use of Military Force Against Iraq Resolution passed in 2001, but she also found that certain conditions surrounding Hamdi's detention violated the due process clause of the Fifth Amendment. In particular, the plurality held that Hamdi had to be given the factual basis for his detention and an opportunity to rebut that evidence before "a neutral decision maker." In response, the Pentagon announced the creation of a "combatant status review tribunal," which permits detainees to challenge their status in front of a commission staffed by military officers.

In *Hamdan v. Rumsfeld* (2006), the Supreme Court ruled that the military commissions created to try detainees at Guantánamo did not have "the power to proceed because its structures and procedures violate both the Uniform Code of Military Justice and the Geneva Conventions signed in 1949." Passed in response to *Hamdan v. Rumsfeld* (2006), however, the Military Commissions Act (MCA) of 2006 specifically stripped federal courts of jurisdiction to hear habeas appeals by aliens detained by the U.S. government.

The Supreme Court took up the constitutionality of the MCA in the recent case of *Boumediene v. Bush* (2008). Writing for the majority, Justice Anthony Kennedy held that the MCA's suspension of the writ of habeas corpus for detainees at Guantánamo was unconstitutional. In reaching this conclusion, the Court first determined that the writ of habeas corpus does apply to Guantánamo, thus rejecting the government's argument, following the earlier case of *Johnson v. Eisentrager* (1950), that the writ does not run to areas outside the sovereignty of the United States. The second component of the Court's opinion concerned the constitutionality of those provisions in the Detainee Treatment Act and the Military Commissions Act that provided alternatives for ordinary judicial review of the detainee's status. The Court concluded that these alternatives were not an adequate substitute for habeas proceedings. In a sharply worded dissent, Justice Antonin Scalia asked: "What competence does the Court have to second-guess the judgment of Congress and the president . . . ? None whatsoever." In response, Justice Kennedy argued that judicial involvement "does not undermine the Executive's power. . . . On the contrary, the exercise of those powers is vindicated, not eroded, when confirmed by the Judicial Branch." In the majority's view, cases like *Hamdan* and *Boumediene* are part of an "ongoing dialogue" with the political branches and not simply unwarranted judicial "second-guessing."

The import of these decisions is that U.S. courts may play a limited role in the oversight of some counterterrorism policies. Some observers have lauded the Supreme Court's work, especially in *Boumediene*, calling it a "great victory" (Dworkin 2008, 13). But what some critics wrote of *Hamdan* might apply with equal force to *Boumediene:* "The 'balance' struck by the plurality imposes little additional burden on the Government. . . . In the last analysis, whereas the plurality rejected Executive unilateralism, when one considers where the balance was struck, the departure from unilateralism was limited" (Rosenfeld 2006, 2113).

Consequently, in the United States the record is mixed. Although the Court appears to have insisted on some measure of judicial accountability, it has also authorized important and far-reaching departures from what the rule of law requires in ordinary criminal cases. None of these decisions support the president's claim that he has inherent authority to create special courts or military commissions, but neither are there clear and unambiguous prohibitions on their use based on constitutional principles. Instead, recent decisions point to a different, but significant, judicial role—that of insisting that the president work within a statutory and regulatory framework authorized by Congress. This is an important qualification and a significant contribution, but a limited one. The overall import of the decisions is to authorize a separate system of jurisprudence and court procedures for offenders designated by the government as enemy combatants.

In contrast to the United States, there is no long-standing tradition of judicial review in the United Kingdom. The Human Rights Act (HRA, 1998) does give British courts some power to appeal to the terms of the European Convention on Human Rights in specific cases. This power does not include the authority to strike legislation, but instead limits the court to a declaration of incompatibility. Moreover, the act's derogation provisions, coupled with section 3 of the HRA, severely limit the breadth of the power.

Under ATCSA 2001, the home secretary may detain or exclude a person who is suspected of terrorism or presents a risk to national security. In 2004 the secretary issued such a "certificate" against a Libyan national (known as "M") in the United Kingdom, who was then taken into custody. The only real mechanism for challenging a decision rests with the Special Immigration Appeals Committee (SIAC). Although it may be characterized as an administrative tribunal, the normal common-law rules governing the burden of proof and evidence do not apply to the SIAC. M appealed to the SIAC, which granted the appeal, and the home secretary appealed that decision to the Court of Appeal.

In *Secretary of State for the Home Department v. M* (2004), Lord Chief Justice Harry Woolf rejected the home secretary's appeal. In rejecting the appeal, the court advanced the requirement that the home secretary's suspicion—upon which the certificate order is based—must be reasonable, although it appears that this requirement is "a standard below that of the civil standard of proof" (Fenwick and Phillipson 2005, 470). But it also affirmed the legality of the streamlined procedures generally: they may include closed, secret hearings (indeed, some of the court's proceedings were closed), as well as nondisclosure to the defense of information that might compromise national security. Those procedures, however, also provide for a "special advocate" in such cases. The court observed:

> The involvement of a special advocate is intended to reduce (it cannot wholly eliminate) the unfairness which follows from the fact that an appellant will be unaware at least as to part of the case against him. . . . We feel the case has additional importance because it does clearly demonstrate that, while the procedures . . . are not ideal, it is possible by using special advocates to ensure that those detained can achieve justice.

The decision does suggest some measure of judicial oversight in such cases. On the other hand, one study concluded, "in the eleven cases determined by the SIAC following appeal against certification, the Home Secretary's decision to certify [was] upheld in all but one of them" (Fenwick and Phillipson 2005, 472).

In another case, *A. v. Secretary of State for the Home Department* (2004), the House of Lords considered whether indefinite detention without charge violated provisions of the ECHR. This required derogation from article 5(1), but derogations are permitted only in times of war or other public emergencies and must be "strictly required by the exigency of the situation." In November 2001, the United Kingdom had filed a derogation based on the September 11 attacks.

In *A. v. Home Secretary*, the House of Lords first concluded that they should defer to the executive's finding that such a crisis existed. The Law Lords also concluded, however, that the part IV certification scheme was unconstitutional because it was "disproportionate" and discriminatory against noncitizens.[46] The House of Lords thus quashed the order of derogation and issued a declaration stating that section 23 was incompatible with article 14 of the European Convention. In response, the government repealed the provisions, but in 2005 it passed the Prevention of Terrorism Act (PTA, 2005), which instead authorized a system of "control orders" for citizens and noncitizens that can be issued by the home secretary and imposed without a judicial hearing. Those served with an order are electronically tagged at all times, must be at home from 7:00 PM to 7:00 AM, are deprived of their passports, and have their phone lines cut.

In July 2006, Justice Jeremy Sullivan of the High Court ruled that the new control orders scheme was incompatible with the Human Rights Act, finding it "conspicuously unfair" and a contravention of the European Convention's restrictions on detention without trial. In August, the Court of Appeal upheld the high court decision by Justice Sullivan, finding in *Secretary of State for the Home Department v. JJ, KK, GG, HH, NN, and LL* (2006) that "the orders amounted to a deprivation of liberty contrary to Article 5. For that reason the appeal against the decision of the judge on the first issue is unsuccessful." On the same day, however, the same Court of Appeal also ruled that a lower court judge "was in error in holding that the provisions for review by the court of the making of a non-derogating control order by the Secretary of State do not comply with the requirements of [ECHR] Article 6." The court wrote:

> If one accepts, as we do, that reliance on closed material is permissible, this can only be on the terms that appropriate safeguards against the prejudice this may cause to the controlled person are in place. We consider that the provisions of the PTA for the use of a special advocate, and of the rules of court made pursuant to paragraph 4 of the Schedule to the PTA, constitute appropriate safeguards, and no suggestion has been made to the contrary. . . . The [lower court] judge was in error in holding that the provisions for review by the court of the making of a non-derogating control order by the Secretary of State do not comply with the requirements of Article 6.

Following the 2004 decisions, one observer predicted that "the dialogue between the government and the judiciary . . . seems destined to continue indefinitely" (Ramraj, Hor, and Roach 2005, 627). The decisions in 2006 support that prediction. This kind of democratic dialogue, which we saw in the United States as well, is a critical part of the constitutional norm of separation of powers. On the other hand, as we noted earlier, many proponents of security legislation argue that such qualifications are inadvisable in the fight against international terrorism. One member of Parliament, for example, responded that the dispute between England's judges and its elected representatives might lead to a constitutional crisis.

In *Charkaoui v. Canada* (2007), the Canadian Supreme Court struck down the security certificate system as a violation of section 7 of the Charter of Rights and Freedoms. Under that system, the executive could detain non-nationals indefinitely, using secret evidence and without bringing charges. The court did not argue that a security certificate system by definition is unconstitutional, but it did conclude that some of the procedures violate fundamental notions of constitutional fairness. In particular, the court concluded that the detainees must be informed of the evidence against them, and it pointed to the British system that allows attorneys (but not their clients) limited access to sensitive materials. Under the court's ruling, Parliament had one year to restructure the security certificate system.

In an earlier case, *Application Under S. 83.28* (2004), the Canadian Supreme Court upheld the constitutionality of the controversial investigative hearing provisions of the Anti-Terrorism Act (ATA). The court ruled that the investigative hearing provisions do not violate section 7 of the Canadian Charter, though it did find that the procedure would violate the Charter if investigative hearings are used primarily to determine penal liability or if such information is used in subsequent extradition and deportation hearings.

More generally, in *Canada (Justice) v. Khadr* (2008), the Canadian Supreme Court considered the case of Omar Ahmed Khadr, a seventeen-year-old Canadian citizen detained by American authorities at Guantánamo Bay in 2002. Canadian officials had interrogated Khadr at Guantánamo and shared the content of those interviews with American officials. Khadr challenged the constitutionality of these interviews, claiming that Canadian officials had not advised him of his rights to silence and counsel under the Canadian Charter. The Canadian Supreme Court, relying on the U.S. Supreme Court's decisions in *Rasul v. Bush* (2004) and *Hamdan v. Rumsfeld* (2006), concluded that "the regime providing for the detention and trial of Mr. Khadr . . . constituted a clear violation of fundamental human rights protected by international law," and thus of Canada's international obligations.

German courts also appear to play a significant role in the oversight of antiterrorism legislation. For example, in two cases involving trials of men arrested for participation in the 9/11 attacks, German courts refused to convict the defendants, in part because the judges' requests for potential exculpatory evidence was refused by the American government (Scheppele 2004, 116). As we saw earlier, in 2008 the Federal Constitutional Court (BVerfGE) ruled that law enforcement authorities must receive permission from a judge before uploading spyware to a suspect's computer by e-mail. In 2004 the Federal Constitutional Court had similarly declared unconstitutional parts of a pre-9/11 antiterrorism law concerning wiretapping in cases involving organized crime and terrorism.[47]

In another case, decided in 2006, the German court found unconstitutional a controversial provision of the Air Transport Security Act (2004). Section 14(3) authorized the minister of defense to order a passenger airplane shot down if it could be assumed that the aircraft was going to be used to destroy the lives of others and if doing so was the only means of preventing this present danger.[48] The court concluded that the provision violated the fundamental right to human life in article 2(2) of the Basic Law, as well as the human dignity clause in article 1. Lepsius (2006, 776–77) concludes that, "in general, the Constitutional Court proved to be a reliable guardian of the constitution both in civil rights issues and competencies (enumerated powers, federalism)."

In Israel, the Supreme Court has considered several cases involving different aspects of Israeli counterterrorism policies (for an overview of the Supreme Court's work, see Israel Ministry of Foreign Affairs 2005; see also Mersel 2006). Recent commentary suggests that the Supreme Court is "more willing to intervene than it used to be when ruling on a security decision" (Grebinar 2003, 269; see, generally, Gross 2002, 1161). The court took up the issue of preventive (administrative) detention in the case of *Anon v. Minister of Defence* (2000) and found that the term "reasons of state security" required a showing that the person detained represents a "direct threat and real danger to the state." In two recent cases, the Israeli Supreme Court has considered the legality of the Israel Defense Forces (IDF) fence on the West Bank and IDF operations in Gaza. In both instances, the court's rulings have had a substantial effect on governmental policy, although Ami Pedahzur and Arie Perliger (this volume) are generally critical of the court's role.

In *Beit Sourik Village Council v. Israel* (2004), the court ordered the military to make certain changes in the placement of the barrier, finding that the requirement of proportionality must be weighed against the recognition that "we, Justices of the Supreme Court, are not experts in military affairs" (Rosenfeld 2006, 2120). In the second case, *Physicians for Human Rights v. Commander of the IDF Forces in the Gaza Strip* (2004), the court considered the legality of several military operations in Gaza. Here, too, the court emphasized that it does not have the authority or the expertise to second-guess military decisions, especially when those decisions place the lives of Israeli soldiers in immediate danger. "But when they are not in danger, courts are empowered to review military decisions to make sure they comply with applicable law" (Rosenfeld 2006, 2126). According to some critics, the court's apparent willingness to conduct this review contemporaneously, "rather than *ex post*," comes exceptionally close to "bringing the Court in on every step of an ongoing military mission" (Rosenfeld 2006, 2126). On the other hand, as Michel Rosenfeld (2006, 2120) observes, "Close examination of what the Court does rather than what it says it does, leads to a much more nuanced conclusion." In another case, however, *Ajuri v. IDF Commander in the West Bank* (2002; regarding the residences of Arabs in the West Bank), Chief Justice Aharon Barak again noted, "In exercising judicial review . . . we do not make ourselves into security experts. We do not replace the military commander's security considerations with our own. . . . Our job is to maintain boundaries . . . [and to insist that those decisions] fall into the range of reasonableness." At least one observer thus concludes that the "Israeli High Court . . . served as a constraint and ensured greater discrimination in the application of force in the West Bank and Gaza strip" (Art and Richardson 2007, 572, summarizing Boaz Ganor).

In India, the Supreme Court has sustained the constitutionality of a long line of antiterrorism statutes, beginning with the decision in *A. K. Goplan v. State of Madras* (1950) upholding the Preventive Detention Act (1950). The court considered and upheld the 1987 Terrorist and Destructive Activities (Prevention) Act (TADA) legislation in *Kartar Singh v. State of Punjab* (1994). The Indian courts also heard several challenges to the 2002 Prevention of Terrorism Act (POTA) legislation. In general, such challenges were unsuccessful (see, for example, the decision by the Division Bench in *People's Union for Civil Liberties v. Union of India* [2004]), but in some instances the court narrowed the reach of certain provisions. For example, the court read a requirement of "knowledge" in *Sanjay Dutt v. State (II)* (1994) and imposed a mens rea requirement for sections 20 to 22 (concerning support for terrorism). "Thus the Supreme Court followed the tradition of upholding the constitutional validity of POTA, like the previous detention and terrorism laws" (Vijayakumar 2005, 364). It remains to be seen whether the Indian Supreme Court's general unwillingness to challenge Indian antiterrorism legislation will continue with respect to the Unlawful Activities (Prevention) Amendment Ordinance (2004).

Overall, the record concerning judicial superintendence of counterterrorism policy is mixed. In many instances, the desire to evade judicial supervision has resulted in legislation that either immunizes key provisions from judicial review or creates an alternative system of courts with rules of procedure and evidence that differ markedly from those of ordinary courts. The arguments for such courts, we have seen, are typically predicated on claims by the government that they are necessary because of the unique kinds of security threats that such trials pose, as well as claims about the need to protect information necessary to national security. When courts do exercise the power of judicial review, they often use relaxed rules of oversight and are willing to permit significant departures from what the rule of law would ordinarily require. On the other hand, we do see some courts—in the United Kingdom, Canada, Germany, and the United States, for example—that have attempted to exercise some constitutional oversight of antiterrorism legislation, often by insisting on various forms of interbranch and interagency dialogue.

The key to evaluating the success of these efforts is clarity about what "success" means. One way to define success is to measure it by the ability of courts to process terrorism cases without overly hindering the executive's ability to conduct counterterrorism efforts. The limited charges of specialized courts, for example, in the sense that their jurisdictional authority rarely extends to the power to challenge the underlying legality or constitutionality of the counterterrorism laws themselves, indicate that they are essentially extensions of executive power—a finding furthered by the frequency with which appointments to such courts are handled as essentially an executive function.

Alternatively, success might be defined as the capacity of courts to advance the values of accountability and reason that underlie the separation-of-powers doctrine. In this sense, success is a function of the facility with which such courts advance and promote the second constitutional norm of transparency and deliberation. On this measure, we would want to ask whether courts promote the separation of powers by having executive branch officials and other officials explain their decisions and policies to a neutral third party, thus making them accountable. In some cases, such as Germany, Israel, and more recently the United Kingdom and the United States, there is evidence that courts have begun to insist that the executive branch identify and explain the kinds of policy considerations that animate particular counterterrorism policies and decisions. In these cases, judicial review "may stimulate public debate and provide civil society groups with the means to ask critical questions about anti-terrorism policies" (Ramraj, Hor, and Roach 2005, 125). In other words, to some extent judicial review may create, or at least reinforce, the structural conditions that make democratic deliberation possible.

3. Separation of Powers and Parliamentary and Administrative Review

Constitutional review need not occur in the judiciary. Many of the counterterrorism regimes described in this volume provide for review through parliamentary or administrative law mechanisms, or they combine them with judicial review. In principle, there is no reason why administrative or legislative mechanisms for review cannot advance the fundamental norms of accountability and deliberation at least as well as judicial review. Indeed, one can imagine instances in which such mechanisms would be more likely to advance these goals—in part, for example, because governments may be more willing to share intelligence and confidential information in a non-adversarial and less public setting than in a judicial arena. On the other hand, one immediate concern with parliamentary or administrative review must be whether such agencies and actors can be independent in fact, or whether they can serve as a neutral, objective third party willing to engage and critically review governmental policy. A related question concerns whether such agencies or legislative committees have the statutory or legal authority to compel the government to provide them with relevant information, and also whether they have the authority to make policy or can only conduct reviews and issue findings or recommendations.

In Britain, reviews of counterterrorism policy have traditionally been the province of parliamentary committees. Currently, for example, the activities of Britain's security services are overseen by the Intelligence and Security Committee. The Northern Ireland Emergency Provisions Act (1978, 1987) and the Prevention of Terrorism Act (1976, 1984) were both subject to parliamentary reviews, such as those conducted by the Diplock and Jellicoe Committees. However, these reviews were always limited in nature and scope. In none of them, for example, did the committee's charge extend to the most important or fundamental questions raised by such legislation: whether it was necessary.

This tradition has continued under TACT (2000), ATCSA (2001), and subsequent legislation. There have been reviews of ATCSA by Lord Carlile of Berriew and by a group of privy councilors (the Newton Report). The latter review was required by the terms of ATCSA itself. Section 122 provides that the entire act is subject to a single, comprehensive review by a committee of privy councilors appointed by the secretary of state, a group that was to report to the secretary of state no later than December 13, 2003, two years after the act was passed. (After taking evidence and deliberating through much of 2003, the committee reported to Parliament on December 18, 2003.) Part 4 was subject to additional annual review by Lord Carlile, a member of the House of Lords and former judge, as well as periodic consideration by Parliament. As was the case with earlier reviews, Carlile's charge was limited to the question of whether the detention powers under part 4 were exercised in a manner consistent with the act

(Human Rights Watch 2004). The utility of such reviews is limited. For example, the government dismissed many of the recommendations issued by the privy councilors on the same day the report was issued (Fenwick and Phillipson 2005, 480).

In Canada, the ATA "contained no enhanced powers and resources for review of new powers given to the police," and the "independent Privacy Commissioner of Canada has also raised concerns that she may not have the necessary legal powers or resources to review incursions on privacy caused by the new anti-terrorism powers" (Roach 2006, 2168). On the other hand, the 2004 national security policy study concluded that "it is vitally important that we ensure that review mechanisms keep pace" (Roach 2006, 2168), and in 2005 a bill was introduced that would give a committee of members of Parliament and senators the authority to review national security activities in secret (Roach 2006, 2168–70).[49] In addition, there are parts of the ATA that are subject to modest types of judicial review. For example, the provisions that authorize the government to designate certain groups and persons as terrorists may be challenged as unreasonable in a court, but the hearings may be closed to the public, and the challenging party may be denied access to evidence, or even to a summary of the evidence.

Administrative reviews are partly anticipated in Canada under the preventive arrest and investigative hearing provisions as well. The government is required to report on the use of these provisions. As we saw, the investigative hearing provisions were upheld as constitutional in the important case of *Application Under S. 83.28* (2004). A form of review is established by requirements that the use of the new powers in specific cases first be authorized by a provincial or federal attorney general (Roach 2005a, 519). Nevertheless, as Kent Roach has noted, the act itself is primarily administered by the Royal Canadian Mounted Police (RCMP), which has a history of misconduct in terrorism investigations (following the October 1970 crisis; Roach 2006, 2168; see also Roach 2005a, 519–20). Although the activities of the RCMP are subject to parliamentary review, there is doubt about the effectiveness of such review in light of the expanded authority given to the police in the ATA. The government, however, has "announced its intention to create 'an independent arms' length review mechanism" for the RCMP with respect to national security (Roach 2005a, 520).

In addition to the oversight provided by courts, Germany also provides for a set of parliamentary checks regarding the intelligence services. The Parliamentary Control Commission—comprising nine members from the lower house, five elected from the governing coalition and four from the opposition—receives reports from the government concerning intelligence activities. It in turn must report to the Bundestag once every two years. Moreover, amendments to article 10 of the Basic Law created two committees to review the surveillance activities of the intelligence services and the police.

In the United States, the USA Patriot Act includes a section that requires the Department of Justice to review complaints about civil liberties violations and to report on a semiannual basis to Congress.[50] Section 215 requires the Justice Department's independent inspector general to conduct an audit of each use of section 215 orders. Other sections require similar audits of national security letters (NSLs). In addition, legislation enacted in 2004 created the Privacy and Civil Liberties Oversight Board, which has five members, appointed by the president, and is a part of the executive branch. Through March 2006, the board had no budget and no staff.[51] The terms of the original board members expired in January 2008, and as of February 2008 the president had not acted to fill the vacancies.

The Norm of Transparency and Deliberation

The constitutional norm of transparency and deliberation holds that state action must be public and must conform to published (that is, constitutional or statutory/public law) standards. As a practical matter, this norm requires that the procedures used by governments to adopt counterterrorism regimes must conform as nearly as possible to the ordinary processes of lawmaking. In practice, however, the adoption of counterterrorism laws almost invariably departs from these ordinary procedures. In nearly every case, the antiterrorism legislation in question was adopted with alarming speed and a consequent lack of democratic deliberation.[52]

We saw earlier that there are several reasons why states hurry to enact emergency legislation. First, security legislation may offer some symbolic reassurance that the government is committed to protecting the public. In addition, the sense of urgency may be compounded by the judgment that existing legislation and policies, having failed to prevent the attacks, must be inadequate. The rush is a consequence also of UN Resolution 1373, which required states to establish terrorism as a crime and called them to report back to the Counter-Terrorism Committee within ninety days (Roach 2005b, 133). It is important to recall that the resolution was passed on September 28, 2001—less than three weeks after 9/11. The European Union acted on September 12, when a special meeting of ministers "reaffirmed its determination to combat all forms of terrorism."

In the United States, a joint resolution for the Authorization for Use of Military Force (AUMF) was passed by Congress on September 18 and signed by President Bush on the same day. It authorized the president to "use all necessary and appropriate force" against the perpetrators of the attacks.[53] The USA Patriot Act was introduced on October 23 and signed into law by the president on October 26, just about six weeks after the September attacks.[54] Given the telescoped time frame, the 352-page bill was enacted with few hearings and limited opportunity for congressional or public debate.

In Canada, the government introduced the ATA on October 15, 2001, or just over a month after 9/11. As Alex Mazer, Kent Roach, and many others have noted, the Canadian legislation is complex and comprehensive, reaching 175 pages and working changes in at least ten other public laws. In Mazer's (2002, 18) words, "Bill C-36 was legislated under severe time constraints. The Bill was drafted in mere weeks . . . and was given Royal Assent only two months (on December 18) after being tabled in the House." At one point in the deliberative process, the government moved for restraints on discussion because, according to Minister Anne McLellan, it was "clear to the government House leader that opposition members would not cooperate in the expeditious passage of the legislation" (Mazer 2002, 18).

In December 2001, the United Kingdom enacted the Anti-Terrorism, Crime, and Security Act (ATCSA), 124 pages long, after just sixteen hours of debate; only eighty-six of the bill's 135 clauses were the subject of debate at all. Substantive changes were made as the bill progressed, but as Dirk Haubrich (2003, 9) has argued, parliamentary committees "had little opportunity to amend the substance of the text." Helen Fenwick and Gavin Phillipson (2005, 131) likewise observed that Parliament's role "reveals not only the absence of any effective *democratic* opposition . . . but also a lack of willingness to subject [the bill] to the kind of sustained, careful scrutiny that might be expected of a country with (purportedly) a strong allegiance to the rule of law and basic human rights values."[55] The pattern was repeated following the July 2005 attack in London, when the government introduced new legislation within just a few days; it was passed in December.

Japan enacted its security legislation on October 29, 2001, following an aggressive campaign by Prime Minister Junichiro Koizumi. France, too, adopted legislation by the end of October, following just two weeks of parliamentary debate. Germany's minister of the interior asked for new security legislation on September 12, and the legislature ratified the first security package only eight days later, on September 19. The second, perhaps more far-reaching, security package was passed in December and took effect on January 1, 2002. As Lepsius (2004, 437) has observed, "Time pressure . . . became a predominant element in the ensuing legislative process."

It is important to identify why and how the demand for immediate legislation threatens constitutional values and to be particular about what those values are. First, the urgency to enact new legislation implicates a basic constitutional norm and perhaps the ultimate constitutional value—transparency in government and the possibility of earnest, impassioned public debate. This urgency privileges the desire for *some* law, *any* law, over the kind of dispassionate and sober inquiry that produces wise and effective laws.[56] This does not mean that speed in the legislative process is necessarily inimical to the constitutional norm of transparency and deliberation. As some commentators have suggested about the Canadian experience with Bill C-36, sometimes parliamentary and public debate over counterterrorism legislation can be both sophisticated and raucous, an observation reaffirmed in recent parliamentary debates over the sunset provisions in the ATA (discussed later in the chapter).[57]

Second, and relatedly, there is the risk that impressing emergency statutes in the immediate aftermath of crisis will lead to legislation that is unnecessarily draconian and disproportionate to the actual threat. This raises concerns about the constitutional norm of proportionality, but it also forces us to consider whether in their haste to adopt legislation—and in particular legislation that dramatically alters the criminal law—governments may "produce high profile laws that fail to use all of the policy instruments that can be used against terrorism" (Roach 2005b, 132). Similarly, the sense of exigency means that legislators are unlikely to have the time or resources to consider whether such laws are necessary correctives to existing law or whether they are likely to have any practical effect on the war on terrorism. In the United States, for example, there was little or no legislative discussion about whether the provisions of the USA Patriot Act would have been necessary to prevent the 9/11 attacks.[58] Here again, exigency seems to overcome deliberate and dispassionate inquiry into the necessity of the legislation in the first instance. Urgency helps to create an environment in which such questions either are not asked or are secondary.

Sunset Provisions Advocates of counterterrorism legislation often suggest that the excesses and mistakes occasioned by the alacrity with which it is passed can be partially offset by the inclusion of sunset provisions. Most of the legislation we have considered in this chapter includes sunsets. In the United States, several provisions in the USA Patriot Act were initially subject to sunset clauses. Under section 224, for example, several of the surveillance portions (the 200-level sections) of the act were originally set to expire on December 31, 2005; President Bush, however, called for the renewal of these provisions as early as January 2003, in his State of the Union address. The original date was later extended to February 3, 2006, and then extended again to March 10, 2006. The Senate voted to renew the act on March 2, 2006, and on March 7 the House also voted to renew it; importantly, the renewals make all but two provisions permanent.[59] Bush signed the reauthorization of the act on March 9, 2006 (Gross 2006, 79–80).

In Germany, the provisions in the second security package regarding privacy rights and data exchange were governed by a five-year sunset clause (Zoller 2004). Recent judicial decisions concerning data retention and computer privacy rights have prompted legislative efforts to revise the statutory framework governing these issues.[60] In Canada, the ATA required that a committee of Parliament review the act after three years, and it included a five-year sunset on the provisions concerning special investigative hearings and preventive arrests (Roach 2006, 2151, n. 49). In March 2007, following a spirited debate in Parliament, both provisions were permitted to lapse. The Conservative Party, which was in power, pushed for a three-year renewal, while the Liberals, under the new leadership of Stéphane Dion, and two minor parties (the New Democratic Party and the Bloc Québécois) were opposed to the extension. The Liberal Party's opposition is all the more interesting because the measures were passed while it controlled the government. According to some observers, the debate is best understood as a reflection of the "fractious politics of Canada's parliament" and an anticipated upcoming election, as much as a national reassessment of antiterrorism politics.[61] Hence, Prime Minister Stephen Harper warned that "any party that doesn't take the national security of Canadians seriously will never be chosen by Canadians to form the government of Canada." Some members of the Liberal Party noted in turn that neither provision had ever been used. As Dion observed, "These two provisions especially have done nothing to fight against terrorism, have not been helpful, and have continued to create some risk for civil liberties." In turn, Prime Minister Harper suggested that he might propose new legislation to restore the provisions. The debate may also have been influenced by the Canadian Supreme Court's decision in *Charkaoui*, which came just two days before the vote.

The history of sunset clauses in India also underscores the importance of electoral politics in assessing the utility of sunset clauses. The Terrorist and Disruptive Activities (Prevention) Act of 1985 included a two-year sunset. In 1987 it was replaced by a similar ordinance that also included a sunset clause. That act (TADA 1987) was renewed three times; hence, "a law that should have existed only for two years, continued for eight years" (Vijayakumar 2005, 353). On the other hand, the Prevention of Terrorist Activities Act (POTA) of 2002 included a sunset period of three years. The act expired in 2004, thus making it "probably . . . the first law to be repealed even before the operation of the sunset clause built into it" (Vijayakumar 2005, 353). Nevertheless, the reasons for its repeal underscore why sunsets usually provide more of an illusory safeguard than a practical one. Those reasons, essentially political in character, centered on a change in ruling parties and the ascension of a new government that had campaigned, in part, on its promise to repeal the act. It is also important to note that the repeal of POTA was premised partly on a decision to augment a preexisting antiterrorism law, the Unlawful Activities (Prevention) Act 1967, which has no sunset provision. Two additional statutes passed in 2004 effected those changes.

Whether sunsets are in fact a useful tool for oversight thus depends largely on the particulars of parliamentary and legislative politics, as the recent debate in Canada demonstrates. Absent unusual conditions, such as those that prevailed in Canada and India, the logic of electoral accountability, as well as most of the historical record, strongly tends toward the renewal of such legislation. The nature of the democratic process suggests that most congressional or parliamentary representatives think their constituents will punish them if they appear weak on the war on terrorism. Similarly, many representatives hesitate to repeal antiterrorism legislation for fear that a subsequent attack will then make that decision look foolish. I do not mean to suggest that sunsets never result in lapsed legislation, but experience suggests that there are strong political pressures that counsel representatives to renew antiterrorism legislation. Moreover, the expiration of specific acts of emergency legislation is often accompanied by calls for new legislation to replace the provisions that have been permitted to sunset.

In addition, history suggests that sunsets rarely lead to a decision to repeal antiterrorism legislation, Canada and India notwithstanding. Recall that the Prevention of Terrorism (Temporary Provisions) Act of 1939 was introduced by the British government for a period of two years. Notwithstanding the act's "temporary provisions," it "was renewed annually until 1954, even though IRA terrorism had declined substantially by 1940, and was not to see a substantial resurgence until the 1960s" (Lal 1994, 5).

For the most part, then, claims that sunsets are an important safeguard for the protection of civil liberties are unfounded. In most instances, sunsets have failed to result in the expiration of the attached provisions. The "failure" of these provisions is highly predictable. On the other hand, how we assess the success or failure of these provisions is a more complicated task than counting how often they lead to the expiration of emergency legislation or specific provisions therein. Insofar as they mandate public debate, sunset clauses may advance the constitutional norm of transparency and deliberation, independent of the result. In some cases, deliberation may yield a decision that the provisions in question should be renewed or extended as a matter of sound public policy. In theory, then, sunsets can advance the goals of transparency and deliberation, in part by structuring the deliberative process to call for periodic debate in the legislative branch, even if they do not routinely lead to nonrenewal. In some cases, however, there is no requirement that legislative debate occur in public, and often such debate occurs in closed and secret committee meetings owing to the felt need to protect intelligence and sources. In these cases, the sunset requirements may advance the goal of deliberation, but only in a small sense, and they do not much advance, if at all, the goal of transparency and the public debate that is an essential part of constitutional self-governance.[62]

The Norm of Proportionality

The principle of proportionality requires that counterterrorism policies be consonant not only with other constitutional norms and rules but also with the degree and the nature of the threat or danger. As we saw in earlier sections, courts have sometimes used the norm of proportionality in assessing the constitutionality of counterterrorism policies; examples include cases decided by the Israeli and German courts and, to a lesser extent, some of the recent decisions of the U.S. Supreme Court. Proportionality is therefore a principle of judicial decisionmaking, but it has a larger dimension as well (Rosenfeld 2006, 2081–84, 2088–95).

I include as threats to the principle of proportionality the "normalization" of counterterrorism policies and the tendency of temporary changes in the administration of criminal justice to become permanent fixtures, sunset clauses and fixed schedules for parliamentary or legislative review notwithstanding. As we saw in our review of antiterrorism legislation in the United Kingdom, legislation such as the Prevention of Terrorism Act, intended to be temporary and formally scheduled for periodic review, is often eventually made permanent. The trend is likely to continue in other democracies for a variety of reasons, many of which we discussed in our earlier consideration of the efficacy of sunset clauses.

Permanent Versus Temporary Changes in the Administration of Justice As one commentator has noted, "It is true that in most jurisdictions . . . anti-terrorism laws are usually introduced on a temporary basis."[63] Frequently, however, these temporary changes become permanent (Richardson 2007, 95; see also Finn 1991, 134). In practice, we can expect that even the temporary counterterrorism regimes put in place after 9/11 will become permanent legal fixtures, and we should understand most of them as neither sudden and new nor of temporary or limited duration.

There are several reasons for this conversion. Even when the need cannot be established, there are reasons why we should predict that antiterrorism legislation will outlive the emergency that occasioned it. Such changes are permanent first because governments find such changes advantageous in the prosecution of criminal conduct more generally. The inroads on civil liberties and rules of criminal procedure made in cases involving terrorism invariably begin to apply to the ordinary criminal process, chiefly because they make it easier for the state to secure convictions. "In this sense, effective emergency legislation threatens constitutional values even when it succeeds, for then the temptation to make such powers permanent increases" (Finn 1991, 134).

Second, if such legislation is a necessary response to an authentic threat, then the life span of the threat is directly related to the duration of the legislation adopted to counter it. There will always be a case to be made that the war on terrorism, unlike conventional conflicts, has no foreseeable end.[64] The changes that such policies work in the administration of criminal justice are likely to be permanent because the "war" on terrorism is of indefinite duration, and so long as the perceived need persists, so must the response. Moreover, if the need is genuine, then the durability of antiterrorism legislation is not only predictable but arguably desirable.

This suggests a breakdown in the dichotomy between ordinary and emergency legislation at the level of both constitutional theory and practice. As Oren Gross (2006, 74–75) has observed, "The advent of the 'war on terrorism' has . . . led to questions about the relationship between normalcy and exception in the face of a 'war' that may well be endless."

The Normalization of Antiterrorism Changes A second and related threat to the constitutional norm of proportionality consists in the tendency of antiterrorism legislation to apply to other types of criminal behavior. The USA Patriot Act, for example, has been used to initiate legal proceedings in child pornography cases. As Oren Gross (2006, 81–82) has observed, "The government is using its expanded authority under the far-reaching law to investigate suspected drug traffickers, white-collar criminals, blackmailers, child pornographers, money launderers, spies, and even corrupt foreign officials." The Department of Justice acknowledged as much when the act was passed (O'Connor and Rumann 2003, 1706).

The pattern is evident in the other countries under our consideration. Complaints about the use of emergency powers to arrest individuals not involved with terrorism were recurrent under the Prevention of Terrorism Acts in Britain. Certainly the great majority of persons detained under those acts were not formally charged, and one study concluded that "the emergency powers were far more frequently used to combat offenses not listed under the Acts, that is, 'normal' street crime" (O'Connor and Rumann 2003, 1682). Another example concerns restrictions on a suspect's right to silence (Finn 1991, 107, 125). First included as a part of the security legislation intended for Northern Ireland, such restrictions have since been extended to the ordinary criminal law (Roach 2005b, 139). Similarly, a recent study in India suggested that key elements of POTA ought to be incorporated into the Indian Penal Code more generally (see Krishnan 2004, 299, and n. 245).[65] This followed an observation by the Indian Supreme Court in *Kartar Singh v. State of Punjab* (1994) that the state had used terrorism laws to circumvent the ordinary criminal law even "when the offence fell outside the scope" of those laws (Vijayakumar 2005, 353).

Part of the problem goes back to the definitional issues we addressed earlier. In cases where security legislation fails to define the term or the offense of terrorism, the special powers and procedures initially intended to govern terrorist activities quickly encompass other forms of criminal behavior because the underlying definition of the offense cannot serve as a jurisdictional limit to those powers. Many of the offenses listed in the U.K. legislation of 2000, for example, are not limited to terrorism (Fenwick and Phillipson 2005, 460). Similarly, ATCSA 2001 makes it quite clear that its powers do not limit their reach to terrorism offenses (Zedner 2005, 515). Thus, "while on the surface this newly refined definition of terrorism may appear more precise than its predecessors; in actuality it is extremely vague. It opens the concept of terrorism to include a variety of different behaviors which would not have previously been considered 'terrorist.'"[66]

There is a second kind of "normalization" problem: each extension of emergency powers, after a time, becomes accepted as the norm. Additional crises justify yet another departure from the norm, both domestically, as states draw on their own experience, and internationally, as they cite the experiences of other states (Gross 2006, 82). As Vinay Lal (1994, 9) wrote in an article on British antiterrorism legislation predating 9/11, "More significantly, we must consider that, as a consequence of the Prevention of Terrorism Acts, what was once considered exceptional has come to be viewed as normal" (see also Sim and Thomas 1983, 71). Laura Donohue (2000, 40), in making the same argument about British antiterrorism legislation, concludes that such legislation became normalized and was eventually accepted as the standard. Another scholar observes that, "put another way, what was classified as extraordinary powers had been subsumed by ordinary police powers, thus normalizing the extraordinary by pushing back the threshold of what constitutes repression" (Cobane 2003, 370). "Powers previously described as 'extraordinary,' 'draconian,' 'special' and 'temporary' were now a normal part of the ordinary criminal justice system" (Cobane 2003, 372). The process of normalization muddies the distinction between normalcy and emergency and in so doing undermines the concept of proportionality as a constitutional norm.

Conclusion

What the rule of law requires in the war on terrorism, I have argued elsewhere, is not invariance from basic constitutional norms but rather robust and public justifications for those departures (Finn 1991, ch. 1). The question of how the war on terrorism has affected national judiciaries and constitutions necessarily leads us therefore to consider how counterterrorism regimes impinge upon the most basic and important of constitutional norms. One of those norms is the commitment to civil liberties; I have suggested that the counterterrorism regimes constructed after 9/11 have had a pronounced effect on the protection of civil liberties. I have argued also that these regimes implicate three other fundamental constitutional norms—accountability, transparency and deliberation, and proportionality. Our study raises issues that are fundamental not only to understanding these specific norms but also to understanding how counterterrorism regimes affect constitutional democracy writ large. These issues include questions about the meaning of the rule of law, about the relationship of the individual to the state, and about the impact of shifts in the allocation of power on liberal democratic norms more broadly.

Notes

1. There are, however, some country-specific issues that deserve comment. In Japan, for example, counterterrorism policies have refocused attention on article 9 and helped to reopen debate about the desirability of the "peace" Constitution. Similarly, in Australia, debates over security legislation have

reinvigorated discussions about the desirability of a bill of rights. In Germany, remarks by Interior Minister Wolfgang Schäuble in the summer of 2007 ("The old categories no longer apply. We have to clarify whether our constitutional state is sufficient for confronting the new threats") indicate that the challenges posed by the threat of international terrorism are not specific to constitutional institutions and norms but to the viability and desirability of constitutional democracy itself.

2. See also Ramraj (2005a, 6) and the very valuable interchange between David Dyzenhaus and Oren Gross in Ramraj, Hor, and Roach (2005, 65–106).
3. On August 14, 2006, Attorney General Alberto R. Gonzales ordered a "side-by-side" review of American and British antiterrorism laws. In particular, both Gonzales and Homeland Security secretary Michael Chertoff pointed to the ability of British authorities to detain suspects for up to twenty-eight days as a policy that American authorities might want to adopt as well; see Eric Lichtblau, "In Wake of Plot, Justice Dept. Will Study Britain's Terror Laws," *New York Times*, August 14, 2006.
4. However, not every European state adopted antiterrorism legislation after 9/11. In the European Union (EU), for example, there are several states, including Austria, Belgium, Denmark, Finland, Luxembourg, the Netherlands, and Sweden, that do not have specific statutes regarding terrorism and instead treat terrorist offenses as ordinary criminal offenses.
5. On the EU response, see European Commission, "Freedom, Security, and Justice: Strategies and Action Plan," available at: http://ec.europa.eu/justice_home/fsj/terrorism/strategies/fsj_terrorism_strategies_en.htm (accessed September 14, 2009).
6. Section 129b builds on an earlier provision in the German Criminal Code, section 129a (enacted in 1976), which criminalized terrorist organizations and support and recruitment for them.
7. The Air Transport Security Act (2004) authorizes the minister of defense to order a passenger plane shot down if it can be assumed that the aircraft will be used to harm others and if the action is the only means of preventing the danger. The Federal Constitutional Court declared this provision unconstitutional in 2006. See Art and Richardson (2007, 572, summarizing Ganor).
8. Resolution 1373 is flawed in several respects. First, although it requires states to prohibit terrorism, it provides no definition of terrorism. Second, the resolution does not require that states comply with international human rights agreements. Together, these omissions have led many critics to argue that states will use their 1373 obligations to criminalize not only acts of terrorism but also routine forms of political dissent and opposition (see the discussion later in this chapter).
9. See, for example, the remarks by Marjorie Cohn (2004): "Many of the new anti-terrorism laws in Europe, as in the United States, were in the works before September 11. The 342-page Uniting and Strengthening America by Providing Appropriate Tools Required to Intercept and Obstruct Terror-

ism Act, or USA Patriot Act, rushed through Congress a month after September 11, contains detailed provisions that had to have been a long time in the drafting." Available at: http://www.commondreams.org/views04/0317-12.htm (accessed September 14, 2009).

10. Other critics echoed these complaints; see Zoller (2004, 474): "The Government used the opportunity to adopt legislation, which had already been planned before 9/11 but had lacked political support."
11. As one report summarizes the legislation, "An act may be defined as an act of terrorism if: it constitutes a threat to law and order and public peace (France, Italy and Spain); it affects the proper functioning of government and institutions (Portugal, Spain and the United Kingdom); it intimidates persons or groups of persons (Portugal and the United Kingdom). The British and Italian laws aim, moreover, to target the preparatory activities of terrorists by extending their very definitions of terrorist activity to include foreign and international terrorist organizations and States." See NATO Parliamentary Assembly, "General Report: Fight Against Terrorism: Achievements and Questions," available at: http://www.nato-pa.int/default.asp?SHORTCUT=241 (accessed September 14, 2009).
12. The "October Crisis" was precipitated by two kidnappings of governmental officials, U.K. Trade Commissioner James Cross and Quebec Justice Minister Pierre Laporte, in October 1970, by the Front de Libération du Québec (FLQ), a revolutionary organization promoting an independent and socialist Quebec. In response, the Canadian government invoked the controversial War Measures Act, which authorized the government to deploy Canadian military forces in the province of Quebec.
13. There is, however, an elaborate system of military courts in the Occupied Territories that try only West Bank and Gaza residents. For an overview, see Hajjar (2005).
14. The Prevention of Terrorist Activities Act (POTA) was repealed in 2004, but many provisions were effectively restored in the Unlawful Activities (Prevention) Amendment Ordinance of 2004.
15. See "Detention, Treatment, and Trial of Certain Noncitizens in the War Against Terrorism" (military order), November 13, 2001, 66 Fed. Reg. 57,833 (2001).
16. In 2002 the Bush administration claimed that it had a similar authority to detain indefinitely two American citizens, grounded not in this military order but rather on the strength of the Authorization for Use of Military Force Against Iraq Resolution of 2002 (the Iraq War Resolution) and the president's authority as commander in chief.
17. As a general matter, there has been widespread criticism of post-9/11 statutes by prominent international human rights organizations, such as Amnesty International and Human Rights Watch. In addition, specific legislation in the countries under consideration has also been criticized by domestic human rights and civil libertarian organizations.

18. Similar complaints have been directed against the Security Legislation (Amendment) Bill 2002 in Australia. For an excellent summary, see Hocking (2003, 362–63).
19. See the review by Lord Carlile upholding the provision against the Human Rights Act (Roach 2006, 2181). Under the terms of the 2006 legislation, the definition of terrorism includes not only acts of serious violence or danger to life but also serious damage to property or "an electronic system" if such acts "are designed to influence the government or to intimidate the public or a section of the public, and the use or threat is made for the purpose of advancing a political, religious or ideological cause."
20. Under the Northern Ireland Emergency Provisions Act, there were prohibitions on broadcasting by members of terrorist organizations such as Sinn Féin and the Ulster Freedom Fighters, as well as provisions that permitted authorities to proscribe such organizations. The Anti-Terrorism Act 2000 similarly criminalized membership in a proscribed organization and also made it illegal to arrange or speak at a meeting of three or more persons that would encourage support for such a group; upheld in *Sheldrake v. DPP*, 1 A.C. (H.L.; 2003), p. 54 (U.K.).
21. Proscription offenses in the United Kingdom, of course, long predate TACT 2000 and the ATCSA 2001. For a general treatment of proscription, including in the United States, see Finn (2001).
22. In 2006 a federal district court judge ruled that a similar executive order was unconstitutionally vague because it appeared not to put any limitations on the president's authority to put groups on the list. See *Humanitarian Law Project v. U.S. Department of Treasury*, 463 F. Supp. 2d 1049 (2006).
23. As Lepsius (2004, 440) notes, "the enactment of s. 129b Criminal Code was primarily motivated by the fight against cross border, regional terrorist activity in Europe."
24. See NATO Parliamentary Assembly, "General Report: Fight Against Terrorism: Achievements and Questions," available at: http://www.nato-pa.int/default.asp?SHORTCUT=241 (accessed September 15, 2009). Preventive detention in the United Kingdom is not limited to noncitizens who are suspected terrorists. Under the Prevention of Terrorism Act 1985, for example, the government could utilize a similar power, though the provisions authorizing such were declared in violation of article 5(3) of the European Convention in *Brogan v. the United Kingdom* (1989) (Roach 2006, 2198). Parliament in turn filed a notice of derogation, which was upheld in *Branigan v. United Kingdom* (1994). Under the Terrorism Act 2000, the derogation was suspended; the new provisions permit seven-day preventive arrests upon "reasonable suspicion" that a person is a terrorist. In 2003 the detention period was extended to fourteen days. The Terrorism Act 2006 proposed extending the period to ninety days; the controversial proposal was subsequently reduced to twenty-eight days.

25. The law was passed in response to the Israeli Supreme Court's April, 12, 2000, ruling that the indefinite detention of Lebanese captives as "bargaining chips" could not be justified under the country's administrative detention law; see CrimA 7048/97 (2000), *Anonymous Persons v. Minister of Defense*, 54(1) P.D. 721 (ISR.).
26. See note 15.
27. In June 2007, a federal appeals court ruled that the MCA did not strip a defendant, legally in the United States, of a constitutional right to habeas corpus even though the president had declared him an enemy combatant. The defendant, Jarallah al-Marri, had been imprisoned without charge in a military jail. Also in June 2007, two military judges dismissed charges against detainees who had been declared by military tribunals to be "unlawful enemy combatants." But they said the tribunals held at Guantánamo, known as combatant status review tribunals (CSRTs), had determined only that the detainees were enemy combatants, without making the added determination that their participation was "unlawful"; see Roach (2006, 2176).
28. Recently, the Federal Constitutional Court declared unconstitutional a section of a law passed in 1998 that greatly expanded the power to eavesdrop in private homes, finding that parts of it violated article 13 of the Basic Law regarding the inviolability of the home; see BVerfGE, 1 BvR 2378/98 (March 3, 2004).
29. See note 15.
30. Such criticisms are reminiscent of complaints about executive control over special courts whose judges are appointed by the executive branch, as discussed earlier.
31. As was the case when we considered specific liberties, we must remember that the precise articulation of these norms and principles varies from one constitutional text to another.
32. Here I do not defend the claim that they are superordinate, or constitutive of constitutionalism. For a defense of that claim, please see Finn (1991, ch. 1). Nor do I want to suggest that these three norms are the only such norms. For example, I have proposed a fourth—that of human dignity. This principle requires that all exercises of state power recognize that all constitutional norms and principles reflect our commitment to the equal moral worth and standing of the individual person (Finn 1991, 36–38). Several of the antiterrorism policies we have considered, such as the loss of civilian control over military authorities (Haubrich, this volume) and the process of deindividualization in Germany (see Lepsius 2004, 450), as well as policies that authorize torture and cruelty, would violate this norm; see also Donahue (2005).
33. It should be obvious that these are not mutually exclusive. Even in "pure" systems of judicial review, there are typically devices that allocate constitutional review to nonjudicial actors, and even in cases of "pure" parliamentary review, such as the United Kingdom, developments such as the Human Rights Act seem to carve out at least a limited form of judicial review.

34. The United States has sometimes been willing to forgo criminal convictions in favor of keeping certain intelligence information classified, and of course one of the central justifications for extraordinary courts—such as military tribunals—is the necessity of confidentiality and secrecy.
35. The concentration of power in any single branch, not just in the executive branch, might threaten separation-of-powers values. See, for example, Shapiro's comments on the concentration of power in France in the magistrates, in Shapiro (2007, 155).
36. The claim that the war on terror has facilitated the rise of an imperial presidency in the United States is common in reviews critical of the USA Patriot Act and the Bush administration's establishment of military tribunals.
37. See, for example, the Court in *United States v. Curtiss-Wright Exp. Corp.* (1936): "[The president] has . . . confidential sources of information. He has his agents in the form of diplomatic, consular and other officials. Secrecy in respect of information gathered by them may be highly necessary, and the premature disclosure of it productive of harmful results."
38. Consider the following quotation by Justice Clarence Thomas: "It is crucial to recognize that judicial interference in this domain destroys the purpose of vesting primary responsibility [to protect national security] in a unitary executive"; *Hamdi v. Rumsfeld* (2004) (Thomas, J., dissenting). See also Sunstein (2002, 1119) and Ramraj (2005b, 116).
39. A similar argument sometimes appears in the literature on the "unitary presidency" in the United States. Advocates of the unitary theory of the presidency argue that the president has expansive powers in times of crises, powers that trump ordinary constitutional or legal constraints on presidential power. One of the arguments in favor of this understanding of the presidency is that it is said to encourage democratic accountability by centering responsibility in a single, identifiable location. See, for example, Calabrisi and Yoo (2008) and Yoo (2005).
40. Perhaps the most expansive proponent is John Yoo (2005). For a response, see Duffy (2005).
41. As Lepsius (2004, 449) has observed, "civil liberties are limited by new regulations concerning organizational competences."
42. Paul Midford (2003, 329) acknowledges the weight of Koizumi's leadership, but explains Japan's change of course as a response "to a significant reduction in Asian *gaiatsu*."
43. For an insightful and nuanced discussion of national security and executive power, see Ramraj (2005b, 114–18). For an insightful review of the problems engendered in controlling executive power, see Tushnet (2005).
44. See the remark by Justice Thomas in note 38. In the United Kingdom, see *Liversidge v. Anderson* (1942). In Israel, see *Ajuri v. IDF Commander in the West Bank* (2002; regarding the residences of Arabs in the West Bank), where Chief Justice Aharon Barak noted, "In exercising judicial review . . . we do

not make ourselves into security experts. We do not replace the military commander's security considerations with our own. . . . Our job is to maintain boundaries . . . [and to insist that those decisions] fall into the range of reasonableness."

45. See, for example, Ronald Dworkin's (1986, esp. ch. 2) suggestion that courts may be forums of principle, in part because of their institutional insulation from direct electoral accountability, a point that coincides in part with our earlier reference to Sunstein (2003) and risk perception in democracies.
46. See *A. v. Secretary of State for the Home Department* (2004) UKHL 56 (2005), 2 A.C. 68 (U.K.).
47. See BVerfGE, 1 BvR 2378/98 (March 3, 2004). Under article 10 of the Basic Law, every person has a right to the confidentiality and secrecy of mail and communications, but in cases where there may be a threat to the constitutional order or the safety and security of the Länder, the government may replace judicial review with a system of review by a parliamentary committee. Moreover, in such cases the subject of the investigation does not need to be told of the infringement (Lepsius 2004, 445). In *Klass v. Germany* (1978), the court ruled that a constitutional amendment that permitted inroads on the privacy of communications was constitutional, in part because the provision included a limited form of parliamentary review (30 BVerfGE 1 [1970]).
48. As Lepsius (2006, 762) notes, "Section 14 (3) was clearly drafted with the attacks of 9/11 in mind. The Bundestag framed the statute as a response to 9/11 and as an effort to prevent attacks patterned after those that occurred on 11 September 2001."
49. But note that the bill also states that ministers may sometimes withhold information from the committee.
50. In addition, the Gilmore Commission (U.S. Congressional Advisory Panel to Assess Domestic Response Capabilities for Terrorism Involving Weapons of Mass Destruction), chartered by Congress in 1999, issued a series of five annual reports on American antiterrorism policy.
51. In May 2007, news reports indicated that the White House played an active role in vetting the commission's report to Congress. "One of the panel's five members, Democrat Lanny J. Davis, resigned in protest Monday over deletions ordered by White House lawyers and aides"; see John Solomon and Ellen Nakashima, "White House Edits to Privacy Board's Report Spur Resignation," *Washington Post*, May 15, 2007, available at: http://www.washingtonpost.com/wp-dyn/content/article/2007/05/14/AR2007051402198.html (accessed September 15, 2009).
52. In the words of Oren Gross (2006, 76), "Violent emergencies tend to bring about a rush to legislate."
53. It is important to note that the AUMF is an important part of the counterterrorism regime, for it includes no time limit or limitations based on jurisdiction.

54. As we saw, the counterterrorism regime in the United States extends well beyond the USA Patriot Act. See Finn (1991); see also Ramraj (2005a, 6); Wong (2005, 201).
55. See Fenwick and Phillipson, "Fundamental Rights," in Ramraj, 2005a, p. 247; Similarly, the PTA 1974 was enacted after only seventeen hours of legislative debate (Roach 2005b, 131).
56. But contrast this with James Kelly (2006), who argues that the democratic dialogue surrounding the act was vociferous and informed; see also Mazer (2002, 6–7).
57. There is probably a relationship between the kind of public and legislative debate following terrorist attacks and the underlying nature of the polity, such as whether our conception of democracy is thin and populist or deliberative. Victor Ramraj (2005b, 113–14) notes that "social forces amplify and distort our judgments about risk. . . . Only on a thin, *populist* conception, could democracy be seen simply as an aggregating mechanism for mere popular opinion, rather than as a sophisticated system to promote public deliberation." I would add that the kind of democratic deliberation and public dialogue that Ramraj describes is subsumed within the constitutional norms I describe here.
58. Some critics, for example, have argued that "the failure was not in the provisions of the criminal law, but rather with the investigative bureaucracy that enforces those laws"; see O'Connor and Rumann (2003, 1734).
59. The provisions in question are the authority to conduct "roving" surveillance under the Foreign Intelligence Surveillance Act (FISA) and the authority to request the production of business records under FISA (USA Patriot Act, sections 206 and 215, respectively). These provisions will expire in March 2010.
60. See, for example, the decision on computer privacy cited earlier (BVerfGE, 1 BvR 370/07) and the court's preliminary decision on data retention (BVerfGE, 1 BvR 256/08, March 11, 2008).
61. See Ian Austen, "Canadian Parliament Decides to Let Two Measures Passed After 9/11 Expire," *New York Times*, February 28, 2007.
62. See John E. Finn, "Sunset Clauses and Democratic Deliberation: Assessing the Significance of Sunset Provisions in Antiterrorism Legislation," *Columbia Journal of Transnational Law* 48 (forthcoming 2010).
63. See Nazia Ali and Saurabh S. Sinha, "Terror Laws: A Comparative Overview." Available at: http://www.indlaw.com/legalfocus/focusdetails.aspx?ID=74 (accessed September 17, 2009).
64. Consider the following statement from President George W. Bush in his State of the Union address of January 23, 2007: "The war on terror we fight today is a generational struggle that will continue long after you and I have turned our duties over to others."
65. In part this recommendation was issued to avoid "having to re-enact the legislation every so many years" (Krishnan 2004, 300, n.245).
66. See http://homepages.strath.ac.uk/~cias19/teaching/misc/anti-terrornew.pdf (accessed September 17, 2009).

REFERENCES

Art, Robert J., and Louise Richardson. 2007. "Conclusion." In *Democracy and Counterterrorism: Lessons from the Past,* edited by Robert J. Art and Louise Richardson. Washington, D.C.: United States Institute of Peace Press.

Calabrisi, Steven G., and Christopher S. Yoo. 2008. *The Unitary Executive: Presidential Power from Washington to Bush.* New Haven, Conn.: Yale University Press.

Cobane, Craig T. 2003. "Terrorism and Democracy: The Balance Between Freedom and Order: The British Experience." Ph.D. diss., University of Cincinnati. Available at: http://www.ohiolink.edu/etd/send-pdf.cgi?ucin1070571375 (accessed September 15, 2009).

Cohn, Marjorie. 2004. "Spain, EU, and US: War on Terror or War on Liberties?" *Jurist* (March 17). Available at: http://www.commondreams.org/views04/0317-12.htm (accessed September 15, 2009).

Donohue, Laura K. 2000. "Civil Liberties, Terrorism, and Liberal Democracy: Lessons from the United Kingdom." BDP 2000-05 and EDP ESPD-2000-01. Cambridge, Mass.: Harvard University, John F. Kennedy School of Government.

———. 2005. "Terrorism and the Counter-Terrorist Discourse." In *Global Anti-Terrorism Law and Policy,* edited by Victor V. Ramraj, Michael Hor, and Kent Roach. Cambridge: Cambridge University Press.

Duffy, Helen. 2005. *The War on Terror and the Framework of International Law.* New York: Cambridge University Press.

Dworkin, Ronald. 1986. *A Matter of Principle.* Cambridge, Mass.: Harvard University Press.

———. 2008. "Why It Was a Great Victory." *New York Review of Books* 55 (August 14).

European Digital Rights. 2008. "Germany: New Basic Right to Privacy of Computer Systems." *EDRI-gram* (February 27). Available at: http://www.edri.org/edrigram/number6.4/germany-constitutionalcourt (accessed September 15, 2009).

Fenwick, Mary. 2005. "Japan's Response to Terrorism Post-9/11." In *Global Anti-Terrorism Law and Policy,* edited by Victor V. Ramraj, Michael Hor, and Kent Roach. Cambridge: Cambridge University Press.

Fenwick, Helen, and Gavin Phillipson. 2005. "Legislative Over-Breadth, Democratic Failure, and the Judicial Response: Fundamental Rights and the U.K.'s Anti-Terrorist Legal Policy." In *Global Anti-Terrorism Law and Policy,* edited by Victor V. Ramraj, Michael Hor, and Kent Roach. Cambridge: Cambridge University Press.

Finn, John E. 1991. *Constitutions in Crisis: Political Violence and the Rule of Law.* New York: Oxford University Press.

———. 2001. "Electoral Regimes and the Proscription of Anti-Democratic Parties." In *The Democratic Experience and Political Violence,* edited by David C. Rapoport and Leonard Weinberg. London: Routledge.

———. Forthcoming. "Sunset Clauses and Democratic Deliberation: Assessing the Significance of Sunset Provisions in Antiterrorism Legislation." *Columbia Journal of Transnational Law* (forthcoming 2010).

Foreign and Commonwealth Office (FCO). 2005. *Counter-Terrorism Legislation and Practice: A Survey of Selected Countries.* FCO Research Paper (Straw Review). London: FCO (December 10). Available at: http://www.fco.gov.uk/en/newsroom/latest-news/?view=PressR&id=4186457 (accessed September 15, 2009).

Grebinar, Jonathan. 2003. "Responding to Terrorism: How Must a Democracy Do It? A Comparison of Israeli and American Law." *Fordham Urban Law Journal* 31(1): 261–84.

Gross, Emanuel. 2002. "Terrorism and the Law: Democracy in the War Against Terrorism—the Israeli Experience." *Loyola L.A. Law Review* 35(3): 1161–1216.

Gross, Oren. 2006. "What Emergency Regime?" *Constellations* 13(1): 74–88.

Hajjar, Lisa. 2005. *Courting Conflict: The Israeli Military Court in the West Bank and Gaza.* Berkeley: University of California Press.

Harvey, Colin. 2005. "And Fairness for All? Asylum, National Security, and the Rule of Law." In *Global Anti-Terrorism Law and Policy,* edited by Victor V. Ramraj, Michael Hor, and Kent Roach. Cambridge: Cambridge University Press.

Haubrich, Dirk. 2003. "September 11, Anti-Terror Laws, and Civil Liberties: Britain, France, and Germany Compared." *Government and Opposition* 38(3): 3–28.

Hocking, Jenny. 2003. "Counter-Terrorism and the Criminalization of Politics: Australia's New Security Powers of Detention, Proscription, and Control." *Australian Journal of Politics and History* 49: 355–71.

Human Rights Watch. 2004. "Neither Just nor Effective: Indefinite Detention Without Trial in the United Kingdom Under Part 4 of the Anti-Terrorism, Crime, and Security Act 2001." Briefing paper (June 24). Available at: http://hrw.org/backgrounder/eca/uk/7.htm#_ftn77 (accessed September 15, 2009).

Israel Ministry of Foreign Affairs. 2005. *Judgments of the Israel Supreme Court: Fighting Terrorism Within the Law* (January 2). Available at: http://www.mfa.gov.il/MFA/Government/Law/Legal+Issues+and+Rulings/Fighting+Terrorism+within+the+Law+2-Jan-2005.htm (accessed September 15, 2009).

James, Matthew H. 1997. "Keeping the Peace—British, Israeli, and Japanese Legislative Responses to Terrorism." *Dickinson International Journal of Law* 15(2): 405–50.

Kallergi, Oleg. 2005. "Exporting U.S. Anti-Terrorism Legislation and Policies to the International Law Arena: A Comparative Study: The Effect on Other Countries' Legal Systems." Cornell Law School Inter-University Graduate Student Conference Papers. Ithaca, N.Y.: Cornell Law School. Available at: http://lsr.nellco.org/cornell/lps/clacp/4 (accessed September 15, 2009).

Kelly, James. 2006. "Canada's Anti-Terrorism Act: Securing Balance Through Parliamentary Scrutiny." Paper presented to the International Political Science Association (IPSA) conference. Fukuoka, Japan (February 17).

Krishnan, Jayanth K. 2004. "India's Patriot Act: POTA and the Impact on Civil Liberties in the World's Largest Democracy." *Law and Inequality Law Journal* 22(265): 265–300.

Lal, Vinay. 1994. "Normalization of Anti-Terrorism Legislation in Democracies: Comparative Notes on India, Northern Ireland, and Sri Lanka." *Lokayan Bulletin* 11(1): 5–24. Available at: http://www.sscnet.ucla.edu/southasia/History/Independent/anti_terr.html (accessed September 15, 2009).

Lepsius, Oliver. 2004. "Liberty, Security, and Terrorism: The Legal Position in Germany." *German Law Journal* 5(5): 435–60.

———. 2006. "Human Dignity and the Downing of Aircraft: The German Federal Constitutional Court Strikes Down a Prominent Anti-Terrorism Provision in the New Air-Transport Security Act." *German Law Journal* 7: 761–777.

Locke, John. 1960. *Two Treatises of Government*, edited by Peter Laslett. Cambridge: Cambridge University Press. (Orig. pub. in 1690.)

Mazer, Alex. 2002. "Debating the Anti-Terrorism Legislation: Lessons Learned." *Canadian Parliamentary Review* 26(2): 1–26. Available at: http://www.iog.ca/publications/alfhales2002.pdf (accessed September 17, 2009)

Mersel, Yigal. 2006. "Judicial Review of Counter-Terrorism Measures: The Israeli Model for the Role of the Judiciary During the Terror Era." *New York University Journal of International Law and Politics* 12(38): 67–120.

Midford, Paul. 2003. "Japan's Response to Terror: Dispatching the SDF to the Arabian Sea." *Asian Survey* 43(2): 329–51.

O'Connor, Michael P., and Celia M. Rumann. 2003. "Into the Fire: How to Avoid Getting Burned by the Same Mistakes Made Fighting Terrorism in Northern Ireland." *Cardozo Law Review* 24: 1657–1751.

Parachini, John V., and Katsuhisa Furukawa. 2007. "Japan and Aum Shinrikyo." In *Democracy and Counterterrorism: Lessons from the Past*, edited by Robert J. Art and Louise Richardson. Washington, D.C.: United States Institute of Peace Press.

Ramraj, Victor V. 2005a. "Introduction." In *Global Anti-Terrorism Law and Policy*, edited by Victor V. Ramraj, Michael Hor, and Kent Roach. Cambridge: Cambridge University Press.

———. 2005b. "Terrorism, Risk Perception, and Judicial Review." In *Global Anti-Terrorism Law and Policy*, edited by Victor V. Ramraj, Michael Hor, and Kent Roach. Cambridge: Cambridge University Press.

Ramraj, Victor V., Michael Hor, and Kent Roach. 2005. "Postscript: Some Recent Developments." In *Global Anti-Terrorism Law and Policy*, edited by Victor V. Ramraj, Michael Hor, and Kent Roach. Cambridge: Cambridge University Press.

Reinares, Fernando. 1998. "Democratic Regimes, Internal Security Policy, and the Threat of Terrorism." *Australian Journal of Politics and History* 44(3): 351–71.

Reinares, Fernando, and Rogelio Alonso. 2007. "Spain and the ETA." In *Democracy and Counterterrorism: Lessons from the Past*, edited by Robert J. Art and Louise Richardson. Washington, D.C.: United States Institute of Peace Press.

Richardson, Louise. 2007. "Britain and the IRA." In *Democracy and Counterterrorism: Lessons from the Past,* edited by Robert J. Art and Louise Richardson. Washington, D.C.: United States Institute of Peace Press.

Roach, Kent. 2005a. "Canada's Response to Terrorism." In *Global Anti-Terrorism Law and Policy,* edited by Victor V. Ramraj, Michael Hor, and Kent Roach. Cambridge: Cambridge University Press.

———. 2005b. "The Criminal Law and Terrorism." In *Global Anti-Terrorism Law and Policy,* edited by Victor V. Ramraj, Michael Hor, and Kent Roach. Cambridge: Cambridge University Press.

———. 2006. "Must We Trade Rights for Security? The Choice Between Smart, Harsh, or Proportionate Security Strategies in Canada and Britain." *Cardozo Law Review* 27: 2151–2221.

Rosenfeld, Michel. 2006. "Judicial Balancing in Times of Stress: Comparing the American, British, and Israeli Approaches to the War on Terror." *Cardozo Law Review* 27(5): 2079–2150.

Rossiter, Clinton. 1948. *Constitutional Dictatorship.* Princeton, N.J.: Princeton University Press.

Scheppele, Kim Lane. 2004. "Other People's Patriot Acts: Europe's Response to September 11." *Loyola Law Review* 50: 89–148.

———. 2006. "The International Emergency After 9/11." *Insights on Law and Society* 6(2): 7–10; 30.

Shapiro, Jeremy. 2007. "France and the GIA." In *Democracy and Counterterrorism: Lessons from the Past,* edited by Robert J. Art and Louise Richardson. Washington, D.C.: United States Institute of Peace Press.

Shinoda, Tomohito. 2003. "Koizumi's Top-Down Leadership in the Anti-Terrorism Legislation: The Impact of Political Institutional Changes." *SAIS Review* 23(1): 19–34.

Sim, Joe, and Philip A. Thomas. 1983. "The Prevention of Terrorism Act: Normalizing the Politics of Repression." *Law and Society* 10(1): 71–84.

Sunstein, Cass. 2002. "The Laws of Fear." *Harvard Law Review* 115: 1119.

———. 2003. "Terrorism and Probability Neglect," *Journal of Risk and Uncertainty* 26: 121–36.

Tushnet, Mark. 2005. "Controlling Executive Power in the War on Terrorism." *Harvard Law Review* 118(8): 2673–82.

Vijayakumar, V. 2005. "Legal and Institutional Responses to Terrorism in India." In *Global Anti-Terrorism Law and Policy,* edited by Victor V. Ramraj, Michael Hor, and Kent Roach. Cambridge: Cambridge University Press.

Wallace, Paul. 2007. "India: Kashmir and Khalistan." In *Democracy and Counterterrorism: Lessons from the Past,* edited by Robert J. Art and Louise Richardson. Washington, D.C.: United States Institute of Peace Press.

Williams, George. 2002. "New Anti-Terrorist Laws for Australia? Balancing Democratic Rights Against National Security." Paper presented to the Asia-Pacific Cross-Border Online Rights Network (ACORN) "Workshop: National

Security Laws and Constitutional Rights in the Asia Pacific Region." Canberra, Australia (October). Available at: http://dspace.anu.edu.au/bitstream/1885/42067/1/George.pdf (accessed September 15, 2009).

Wong, Mary S. 2005. "Terrorism and Technology: Policy Challenges and Current Responses." In *Global Anti-Terrorism Law and Policy*, edited by Victor V. Ramraj, Michael Hor, and Kent Roach. Cambridge: Cambridge University Press.

Yoo, John. 2005. *The Powers of War and Peace: The Constitution and Foreign Affairs After 9/11*. Chicago: University of Chicago Press.

Zedner, Lucia. 2005. "Securing Liberty in the Face of Terror: Reflections from Criminal Justice." *Journal of Law and Society* 32(4): 507–33.

Zoller, Verena. 2004. "Liberty Dies by Inches: German Counter-Terrorism Measures and Human Rights." *German Law Review* 5(5): 464–94.

Chapter 3

The Uses and Abuses of Terrorist Designation Lists

Chantal de Jonge Oudraat and Jean-Luc Marret

Terrorist designation lists are policy instruments that identify people and organizations believed to be responsible for or supportive of terrorist acts. People and entities listed become subject to sanctions and judicial prosecution. Although terrorist designation lists predate the terrorist attacks in the United States on September 11, 2001, their use has greatly expanded since 9/11. In a short period of time, terrorist designation lists have become the hallmark of "serious" national and international counterterrorist policies.

There are three main problems with terrorist designation lists. First, there is no internationally accepted definition of terrorism. The proliferation of terrorist designation lists has not led to a greater consensus on who should be considered a terrorist. On the contrary, one could argue that the greater number of lists has vindicated the slogan that "one's man's terrorist is another one's freedom fighter." Terrorist designation lists have the potential of increasing international tensions. Second, the criteria for designation vary greatly from one country to another, and from one international institution to another. Decisions to list are often highly political, and the decisionmaking process leading to listings is often obscured by national security concerns. In some cases, listing occurs without sufficient political supervision and people are put on the lists for no apparent reason. Third, the procedures to challenge designations are often unclear. This impedes the ability of those being listed to present an effective defense and goes against the fundamental principles of a rule-based society, such as the right to a fair hearing. Such listings can also contradict the fundamental right of effective judicial protection.

In sum, terrorist designation lists are powerful international and national policy instruments. However, without safeguards in place to appeal listing decisions, these lists may easily become a source of discord abroad and undermine civil liberties at home. The fight against terrorism requires international cooperation and international consensus on how to deal with this threat. It also requires a delicate balancing act between preventing harm to innocent civilians and respecting fundamental human rights and civil liberties.

In the first section of this chapter, we review the practice of terrorist designation lists. We identify the competent listing authorities and examine the criteria, legal basis, and review mechanisms for listings. We do this for the United Nations (UN), the European Union (EU), the United States, the United Kingdom, Russia, and China.[1] In the second section, we provide an overall assessment of terrorist designation lists. We examine the reasons why states establish terrorist designations lists, review the functions of these lists—in terms of target audiences and objectives—and consider the drawbacks of terrorist designation lists. We conclude with general thoughts regarding the effectiveness and utility of terrorist designation lists.

Terrorist Designations Lists: The Practice

Terrorism is difficult to define. The issue has bedeviled the United Nations for over forty years. One of the main issues that have divided the international community concerns the boundaries and differences between terrorism and other forms of political violence. Although most experts and policymakers condemn the deliberate killing and maiming of civilian populations, many also insist that people under foreign occupation have a right to violent resistance and argue that a definition of terrorism should not override such a right.

The absence of a commonly accepted definition has not prevented UN member states from outlawing certain terrorist acts, such as the hijacking of aircraft, the kidnapping of diplomats, the taking of hostages, and the killing of innocent civilians.[2] That being said, it was only in the late 1990s that the international conventions specified that no political, ethnic, racial, or religious motivations could ever justify a prohibited act (see Dumitriu 2004, 586). The absence of a definition did not prevent the UN General Assembly from adopting a "Global Counter-Terrorism Strategy" on September 8, 2006 (see UN 2006). What has been made difficult in the absence of a definition is the elaboration of an internationally uniform set of legal rules and responses to acts of international terrorism.

Countries around the world all have their own sets of definitions. Even within a country there are often many different definitions of terrorism.[3] Some national agencies and regulations take concrete acts—such as hijacking and kidnapping—as points of departure, while others take a more subjective approach and emphasize intent, political motivation, the targeting of noncombatants, or the subnational and clandestine nature of terrorist groups.[4] The European Union in its definition of terrorism combines objective elements (specific acts of terrorism) and subjective elements—that is, the intent of the act.[5] Finally, the EU definition introduces the notion of proportionality: it stipulates that the consequences of the act have to be serious.[6] The EU definition is the first international attempt to define terrorism in a comprehensive manner.[7]

Terrorist designation lists are another way of defining terrorism. They focus on the authors, or potential authors, of terrorist acts, including supporters of such acts. Terrorist designation lists identify people and organizations believed to be responsible for or supportive of terrorist acts. Now a key element in both international and national counterterrorist policies, terrorist designation lists open up the way for judicial prosecution and the application of financial and travel sanctions. More generally, they are foreign policy instruments that allow states to signal to other states their concern about certain people and organizations. Publication of a list is frequently accompanied by requests for international assistance in combating these groups.

A review of the UN, EU, U.S., U.K., Russian, and Chinese terrorist designation lists shows that international organizations and states have very different notions about who should be designated a terrorist. It also explains some of the underlying tensions among these international actors regarding counterterrorist policy responses.

The United Nations

The UN Security Council maintains one terrorist designation list. It is a continuously updated list of individuals and entities associated with the Taliban or Al Qaeda. Individuals and organizations on the list are subject to UN sanctions, including financial and travel sanctions, as well as arms embargoes. All UN member states are obliged to comply with this sanctions regime.[8]

The UN Security Council imposed sanctions against the Taliban in 1999 after the Taliban refused to extradite Osama bin Laden to the United States.[9] Bin Laden was accused of involvement in the 1998 bombings of the U.S. embassies in Nairobi, Kenya, and Dar-es-Salaam, Tanzania, and had been indicted for these acts by the United States. The Security Council also established a committee—known as the 1267 Committee—to monitor overall implementation of its sanctions regime and to maintain and update a list of names of individuals and organizations to be sanctioned.[10]

All UN member states are allowed to submit names to the 1267 Committee for inclusion on the list. States that submit names must provide a statement supporting the inclusion of a person or organization on the list. States must also indicate which portions of their statements can be made public. Much of the supporting evidence comes from intelligence sources—sources that states rarely reveal. It is not necessary that individuals or organizations be the subject of prior criminal charges or convictions, "as sanctions are intended to be preventive in nature."[11] The 1267 Committee decides on listings by consensus. Members have five working days to object to a listing; if no such objections are tabled, the listing moves forward.[12]

After September 11, 2001, the list expanded significantly and became the subject of much political bargaining among UN member states.[13] Some Security Council members were keen on having their "freedom fighters" branded as "Al Qaeda–affiliated" terrorist groups and included on the list. For example, when in September 2002 the East Turkistan Islamic Movement (ETIM) was included on the list, many observers believed that this was a reward for Chinese support of UN counterterrorist resolutions and more generally as a reward for its support of the U.S. war against terrorism. Indeed, terrorism experts generally consider ETIM a local rather than a global Al Qaeda–affiliated terrorist group. Similarly, in 2003, Chechen rebel groups appeared on the UN list.[14]

Many states and nongovernmental organizations (NGOs) have pointed to the deficiencies of the list maintained by the 1267 Committee. Problems have ranged from uncertain spellings of names due to different foreign-language transliterations to lack of details with regard to birth dates, addresses, or other identifying information. Insufficient data are an impediment to the actual implementation of the UN sanctions regime. Think tanks and human rights organizations have also criticized the criteria and procedures of listing and delisting and noted the lack of legal remedies for individuals and entities listed.[15] For example, individuals and organizations are not informed prior to listing. In addition, legal challenges against listing can proceed only insofar as domestic legal orders allow an individual to challenge UNSC resolutions; that is an unlikely scenario, since action by the Security Council under chapter VII cannot be challenged domestically (for more, see Fassbender 2006). When, in 2005, two individuals questioned their inclusion on the list through the EU Court of First Instance, they challenged the EU, not the UN (for more, see Fassbender 2006).[16] That being said, the court rejected their challenge. Indeed, the court ruled that decisions by the UN Security Council fall outside the scope of judicial review.[17]

Until March 2007, the 1267 Committee had no formal review mechanism.[18] This deficiency was partly rectified in March 2007, when the Security Council established within the UN Secretariat a focal point for delisting and humanitarian exemptions. Individuals and entities listed may now directly petition the focal point for review. The focal point then transmits this information to the 1267 Committee, which ultimately decides on delisting and exemptions.[19] Such decisions are based on political considerations—that is, the perceived threat to international peace and security—not legal considerations.

In October 2006, the UN list contained the names of 142 individuals and one financial institution (the Afghanistan Momtaz Bank) associated with the Taliban.[20] It also contained the names of 217 individuals and 123 entities that were affiliated with Al Qaeda. The Al Qaeda–affiliated organizations included mostly financial institutions and charitable organizations with locations in places as diverse as the Bahamas, Dubai, Kenya, the Netherlands, Somalia, Sweden, the United States, and Yemen. The list also included a number of rebel groups and local "freedom fighters" active in the Caucasus, China, and the Philippines. Finally, the list contained the names of 19 delisted individuals and entities.

Assessments of the effectiveness of the list are mixed. First, the 1267 Committee and the Analytical Support and Sanctions Monitoring Team have repeatedly deplored the small number of states that have contributed names to the list. Second, the monitoring team has deplored the absence of certain well-known names from the list. Third, the presence of names of people generally believed to be dead undercuts the credibility of the list. Fourth, listing does not ensure that the individuals and organizations listed are subject to sanctions. For a variety of reasons, many states often do not implement UN Security Council resolutions.[21] The monitoring team, which assists the 1267 Committee by monitoring the implementation of sanctions, pointed out in its 2007 report that of the 217 individuals listed as associated with Al Qaeda, only seventy-nine were detained; twelve were believed to be dead, and 126 were believed to be alive and free.[22] In addition, the team noted that between January and September 2006, ten new individuals and four entities were added to the list, but only one state was reported to have frozen assets—of one individual covering a mere US$620.[23] Last but not least, and relatedly, the amounts of the financial assets that are frozen under the UNSC Resolution 1267 sanction regime are small. The great majority of assets were frozen in the immediate aftermath of the September 11, 2001, attacks. Since then, the amounts have changed little, despite changes in the list (see de Jonge Oudraat 2003).[24]

That being said, the UN list remains the only truly international list and is an essential element in rallying international support against the Taliban and Al Qaeda. It stigmatizes those associated with the group and strengthens international opprobrium with regard to jihadist terrorism. As such, it is a powerful symbolic instrument.

The European Union

The European Union maintains two lists of terrorist organizations. The first replicates the UN list of Al Qaeda and Taliban individuals and entities.[25] The second (hereafter called "the EU list") was established to comply with UNSC resolution 1373 (2001), the resolution adopted after the September 11, 2001, terrorist attacks in the United States that called on all UN member states to take measures to suppress and prevent future terrorist activities.[26] The EU list makes a distinction between "domestic" terrorist groups and individuals, such as the Real Irish Republican Army (Real IRA) and the Basque Freedom and Homeland Organization (ETA), and foreign groups or groups that have broader (non-European) aims and connections, such as the Dutch-based extremist Islamic Hofstad group.[27] The so-called domestic groups and individuals are subject only to strengthened police and judicial cooperation measures, while the others are also subject to the freezing of their financial assets.[28]

Terrorist designation lists fall within the purview of the EU's Common and Foreign Security Policy (CFSP) and are the responsibility of the Council of the European Union.[29] The latter has adopted several "common positions" that member states are required to implement, as well as regulations (so-called European Community [EC] regulations) that deal with asset freezes. Regulations are also binding and subject to judicial review by the Court of Justice and the Court of First Instance of the European Communities in Luxembourg. The EU Commission is responsible for monitoring the implementation of Council decisions and regulations. It is also responsible for the publication of the terrorist designation lists.[30]

Any EU member state and even third-party countries may propose names for the EU list. That being said, only individuals and entities that are under official investigation or are being prosecuted in connection with terrorist acts can be added to the list.[31] Proposals for listing are examined by the relevant national authorities of the EU member states before the Council endorses them.[32] Listing and delisting discussions are secret, and decisions are adopted by consensus. Lists are reviewed every six months.[33] In 2007 the EU list included the names of fifty-four individuals, of whom thirty-five were considered "nondomestic" and subject to financial asset freezes, and forty-eight organizations, of which thirty-one were considered "nondomestic" and subject to financial asset freezes.[34]

The EU list includes a high number of local—that is, European-based—and extreme left-wing groups and regional independence movements. This is not surprising given the history of European countries with extreme leftist groups and autonomous movements, notably in the 1970s and 1980s. Italy in particular has been keen to make sure that its extreme leftist and anarchist groups are included on the EU list.

Non-European independence groups have generally been included at the request of the governments of third-party countries. Inclusion of these movements is intended to prevent the diasporas living in Europe from fomenting trouble at home or to provide allied or friendly governments with added legitimacy in combating those groups. For example, the Revolutionary Armed Forces of Colombia (FARC) was initially not on the EU list. The Colombian government, however, outraged by this omission, went on an intense and ultimately successful diplomatic campaign to have the FARC included on the list.

That being said, close allies do not always get heard, and inclusion or exclusion on the list is a political decision. For example, despite frequent and insistent demands by the United States and Israel, the EU list does not include Hezbollah as a terrorist group. This omission reflects the political consensus among European governments that Hezbollah is part of the political landscape in Lebanon and should not be confronted head on. France in particular has strong historical and cultural ties with Lebanon and has been successful in keeping Hezbollah off the EU list.[35] The fact that Hezbollah has scaled down its violent activities considerably since September 11, 2001, may have also helped keep the organization off the list.

Hamas, on the contrary, was added to the list in September 2003 after claiming responsibility for a bloody suicide attack in Israel; hopes in Europe for a constructive role by Hamas in the peace process had already collapsed by then.

The EU list does not feature any Iraqi insurgent groups. Again, this reflects the prevalent notion in Europe that the violence in Iraq is part of the civil war in that country. Neither does the EU list mention the two most active Algerian Islamist groups in Europe—the Islamic Armed Group (GIA) and the Salafist Group for Preaching and Combat (GSPC), now merged with Al Qaeda as Al Qaeda in the Islamic Maghreb.[36]

More generally, the EU tends to maintain a restrictive definition of the jihadist terrorist threat. Again, this represents realities on the ground. For most European countries, the jihadist terrorist threat comes not from foreign organizations but from within.

Identification of these homegrown jihadist elements has become increasingly difficult. Cells are small and no longer ethnically homogenous. In the 1990s, jihadist cells were primarily Arab, but by 2006 such cells had become increasingly multiethnic, including converted Europeans, West Indians, Africans, and Arabs. Multiethnicity has also led to a more approximate jihadist vision. For example, many of the jihadists arrested in the Netherlands, Italy, and France do not have Arabic-language skills. Unable to consume jihadist ideology firsthand, they are dependent on secondhand translations provided over the Internet, or they construct their own doctrines of radical Islam. In addition, jihadist elements in Europe have fewer and fewer connections to transnational jihadist networks. Instead, there has been a steady increase in the number of self-trained and self-radicalized, European-born individuals (for more, see Marret 2006).

The EU list has been the subject of criticism by human rights organizations. The problem is that those on the list are not privy to the evidence presented against them, nor do they know who put them on the list. This makes it difficult to present a defense. In December 2006, the European Court of First Instance annulled the decision by the EU Council in 2002 to list the People's Mujahidin of Iran (OMPI), arguing that "fundamental rights [such as] the right to a fair hearing, the obligation to state reasons and the right to effective judicial protection" were violated.[37] Similarly, in July 2007 the Court of First Instance annulled the Council decision to freeze the funds of Jose Maria Sison and the Dutch-based foundation Al-Aqsa.[38] It considered that the EU decisions infringed on the rights of defense and fair hearing, the obligation to state reasons for the listing, and the right to effective judicial protection.

In its rulings, the court emphasized that a distinction needed to be made between the UN Al Qaeda/Taliban list maintained by the 1267 Committee—the UN Security Council list of names that is simply transposed by the EU (the Council and the Commission) without the EU having any influence on decisions about who is put on the list—and the EU list established to comply with UN Resolution 1373, for which the EU has the power to decide who is listed and hence who has assets frozen.

In the first case, the court cannot review the lawfulness of the decisions given the fact that UN law and decisions by the UN Security Council prevail over EU Community law. At most, the court can check the lawfulness of an EU regulation that gives effect to a Security Council decision by examining the regulation "in the light of higher rules of general international law falling within the scope of *jus cogens*."[39] In cases where the EU has discretionary power over who gets listed, the court can review the lawfulness of such EU decisions against the fundamental rights guaranteed by EU law.[40] Because the OMPI, Sison, and Al-Aqsa cases all fell under the 1373 regime, the court could test the respect of certain fundamental rights against EU law.

In response to the Court of First Instance cases, the EU Council has started to improve procedures for the listing and delisting of individuals and entities. As of 2007, the Council provides a statement of reasons for each individual or organization subject to the asset freeze and informs them individually if possible. The Council has also pledged to establish clearer procedures for review (for a critical analysis, see Hayes 2007).[41]

Several problems with the EU list remain. First, the EU is not in a position to freeze the assets of many "internal" or "domestic" terrorists—that is, terrorist groups that have their roots, main activities, and objectives within the EU.[42] Second, many terrorist organizations have no legal personality and hence do not own financial assets. Listing thus is more of a symbolic gesture. Third, the amounts of money frozen are limited (see Europol 2007, 21).[43] In addition, as controls over money movements are tightened, terrorists find new ways of moving assets around (Europol 2007, 22).[44] Finally, the list is far from comprehensive. Many individuals suspected of terrorist offenses are not on the list. For example, of the 550 people arrested in 2006 because of suspected terrorist offenses, only 41 percent were suspected of being members of a terrorist organization. Half of them were linked to a terrorist organization that could be specified, and only five of these organizations were on the EU list (Europol 2007, 14).

The United States

The United States maintains several terrorist designation lists. The two main lists are the specially designated global terrorists (SDGT) list and the foreign terrorist organizations (FTO) list. The SDGT list was created by presidential executive order 13224 following the attacks of September 2001 and is maintained by the secretary of the treasury. It includes those on the UN list as well as a great number of other individuals and organizations. Those on the list are targeted with financial sanctions. By 2006 the list was over nine hundred pages long (for more, see Cronin 2003).[45]

The FTO list is a smaller list maintained by the State Department. It imposes travel and financial sanctions and makes it a crime to support those organizations.[46] Foreign terrorist organizations are designated by the secretary of state, in consultation with the secretary of the treasury and the attorney general and after review by Congress. Congress has seven days to review the designations (see U.S. Department of State 2008). After two years, the designations expire unless they are redesignated. The Office of the Coordinator for Counter-Terrorism in the State Department (S/CT) continually monitors the activities of terrorist groups that are active across the world to identify potential candidates for designation. Organizations may appeal their listing in the U.S. Court of Appeals in the District of Columbia within thirty days of the publication of the designation in the *Federal Register*.

A key criterion for designation is that the organization must threaten the security of U.S. nationals or the national security of the United States—that is, its national defense, foreign relations, or economic interests. Two other criteria must also be fulfilled: the organization must be foreign, and it must be engaged in terrorist activities or terrorism or retain the capability and intent to engage in terrorist activity or terrorism. Country of origin is only one factor that the secretary of state takes into consideration in determining whether an organization is "foreign." Other considerations include the location of the group's activities, its leadership, and sources of its support. The United States also designates organizations that threaten allies.[47]

Over time the number of organizations on the FTO list has steadily increased—from thirty in 1997 to forty-two in 2005 and forty-four in 2008. It has also become more focused on jihadist groups.[48] Al Qaeda and Osama bin Laden appeared on the list in 1999, after the latter was indicted for the 1998 bombings of the U.S. embassies in Dar-es-Salaam and Nairobi.[49] That same year the United States dropped three organizations from the list because their involvement in terrorist activity had ceased (see U.S. Department of State 2001). The Islamic Movement of Uzbekistan was included in 2000. Two new FTOs were added prior to September 2001—the Real Irish Republican Army and United Self-Defense Forces of Columbia (AUC).[50] The United States redesignated twenty-six of the twenty-eight organizations on the list after the terrorist attacks of September 2001 and combined two previously designated groups, Kahane Chai and Kach, into one.[51] Since October 2001, the list has steadily grown. The United States has no formal report mechanisms.[52]

Thus, by 2008 the U.S. State Department had designated forty-four foreign organizations as terrorist organizations—of which seven were Palestinian Islamic organizations and seventeen were jihadist groups (U.S. Department of State 2008; see also U.S. Department of State 2006).[53] The U.S. list is notable in that it excludes many left-wing European terrorist organizations. Those who are on the list are included upon the express request of allies, and their inclusion can be seen as incentives or rewards for support of certain U.S. policies. For example, the Basque Freedom and Homeland Organization (ETA) is included, and so is the Kurdistan Workers Party (PKK). The Revolutionary Armed Forces of Colombia (FARC) is listed, but not all of the violent paramilitary organizations in Colombia that fight the FARC are included. Given U.S.-Russian relations, it should come as no surprise that despite insistent Russian requests, separatist groups from Chechnya are not included on the list.

Domestic factors also play a role in designations. For example, despite repeated requests by the United Kingdom—one of the closest allies of the United States —the United States has never included the Irish Republican Army (IRA) on the list. A strong Irish lobby in the United States has dissuaded successive U.S. administrations from designating the IRA as a terrorist organization.

The United Kingdom

The United Kingdom maintains one list of prohibited terrorist organizations. The list is based on the Terrorism Act 2000, which introduced permanent antiterrorism legislation and a broad definition of terrorism that extended legislation to all forms of terrorism—domestic and international (see chapter 5). The act allows the home secretary to outlaw organizations that are "concerned with terrorism."[54] Until now, only nationalist/separatist Irish groups involved in the conflict in Northern Ireland were outlawed.[55] The list of proscribed organizations has to be approved by the British Parliament. Once an organization is put on the proscription list, the police are allowed to seize all property of the organization. Criteria for proscription include the nature and scale of the organization's activities, including its activities in the United Kingdom; the threat that the organization poses to the United Kingdom and to British nationals overseas; and the extent to which British international commitments to fight terrorism are involved.

The adoption of the Terrorism Act 2000 was an expression of the belief that terrorism was no longer just an Irish problem. British intelligence had become increasingly concerned about jihadist elements inside the United Kingdom. The discourse in the London mosques had become very radical by the end of the 1990s. In addition, one of the main propaganda materials ("Al-Ansar") of the Algerian Islamic Armed Group (GIA) was published in London.[56] British intelligence also discovered that a large number of Algerian asylum-seekers were Salafists—believers in a pure Islamic religious community—and were linked to the Islamic Armed Group (see Marret 2005).

The Terrorism Act 2006 broadened the basis for proscribing organizations to include those that promote or encourage terrorism. The 2006 act made it a criminal offense to engage in such activities. A working group within the government reviews the list every three months—it includes individuals from the Home Office, the Foreign and Commonwealth Office, and the appropriate security agencies. In addition, the Terrorism Act 2006 provides for a review of the act by an independent reviewer. Over the course of the year, that individual presents several reports on the different counterterrorist acts to Parliament (see, for example, Lord Carlile of Berriew QC 2007).

Organizations can write to the home secretary to have their name removed from the list. If the request is refused, the organization may appeal to the Proscribed Organizations Appeal Commission (POAC). The lord chancellor appoints the members of the POAC.[57] Most procedures of the POAC follow the secrecy rules of security tribunals. For example, the commission can hear evidence behind closed doors, with the applicants and their representatives excluded from the proceedings. As a last resort, organizations may go to the Court of Appeal, which considers only applications that raise points of law and does not challenge the principle of proscription and POAC procedures. The Iranian Islamic group the Mujahedin-e Khalq (MEK) was removed from the list in June 2008 as a result of a POAC and Court of Appeal decision.

The list of proscribed organizations published in 2000 and 2001 contained twenty-one foreign organizations and fourteen Irish groups. The 2006 list of proscribed organizations contained the names of forty-six foreign organizations and was heavily focused on Iraqi and transnational jihadist networks, as well as Pakistani and Kashmiri groups. The 2006 list also included the names of fourteen Irish groups.[58] By 2008, the list contained forty-five foreign groups, since the MEK was no longer proscribed. Two of those were proscribed for glorifying terrorism under the powers introduced in the Terrorism Act 2006.

As in other cases, review procedures have been criticized by human rights organizations. They argue that international and European human rights law requires that individuals or organizations be told about evidence deployed against them. The independent reviewer Lord Carlile of Berriew has also been critical of the slowness of the proceedings of the POAC.

Russia

Russia published a list of organizations it considered terrorist organizations in 2006.[59] The list was approved by the National Supreme Court and included seventeen organizations. A key criterion for inclusion on the list was the extent to which the organization threatened the security of the Russian state and was "trying to change Russia's constitutional order."[60]

The Russian list included global jihadist groups such as the Taliban, Al Qaeda, and Al Qaeda–affiliated jihadist, as well as a number of charities, such as Al Haramein, which is active in the Caucasus. All these groups were also on the UN list. In addition, the Russian list included a number of Egyptian organizations—notably the Muslim Brotherhood, a radical Egyptian organization that is very actively proselytizing in the Caucasus.[61] Finally, the Russian list included the Islamic Movement of Uzbekistan and the Islamic Party of Turkmenistan. Both are alleged to have ties to insurgents in Chechnya. That being said, many other groups active in Central Asia were not included. The purely local character of these groups explains their omission from the Russian list.

According to Yury Sapunov, head of antiterrorism at the Federal Security Service (FSB), the list did not include Hamas or Hezbollah because neither organization was a threat to Russia and neither was linked to terrorist groups operating in the North Caucasus or Central Asia.[62] In addition, Aleksei Malashenko of the Carnegie Moscow Center has argued that the omission of Hamas and Hezbollah was motivated by Moscow's desire "to strengthen its role as a mediator in the Middle East."[63]

For Russia, the publication of its terrorist designation list seems primarily a way to legitimize its fight against domestic separatist groups—that is, its fight against the rebels in the Caucasus.[64]

China

China has long been battling separatist groups in northwest China. Before 9/11, China sought to downplay links between Xinjiang separatist groups that sought to establish an independent Islamic state in the northwestern part of China and foreign movements such as Al Qaeda. In the aftermath of the 9/11 attacks, however, China actively lobbied to have these groups added to the UN list of Al Qaeda–affiliated organizations. By linking these groups to Al Qaeda, China hoped to internationalize and legitimize its struggle with these groups. In 2002 it was successful in convincing the United States and other Central Asian states to have the East Turkistan Islamic Movement (ETIM) added to the UN list.[65]

In April 2004, the Chinese government reported to the UN Counter-Terrorism Committee that it had designated four organizations as terrorist organizations. In addition to ETIM, it also listed the Eastern Turkistan Liberation Organization (ETLO), the World Uyghur Youth Congress (WUYC), and the Eastern Turkistan Information Center (ETIC).[66]

Terrorist Designation Lists: An Assessment

States have different reasons for creating and maintaining terrorist designation lists. Their history of terrorist attacks, national interests, foreign policy considerations, domestic political considerations—all play a role. In this section, we review the main motivations of states to create terrorist designation lists. We also examine the target audiences for these lists, as well as their objectives. Finally, we examine the drawbacks of terrorist designation lists.

Driving Forces

Historical experiences as well as national interests are primary drivers of national terrorist designations. A key criterion in designating an individual, group, or state as terrorist is the extent to which the group or state is seen as threatening national interests and territorial security. The history of terrorist attacks is crucial. For the United States, Al Qaeda became an issue in the 1990s when it started to attack U.S. nationals and U.S. interests abroad. After the terrorist attacks of September 11, 2001, Al Qaeda and affiliated jihadist terrorist groups became a key concern for the United States. For many states, autonomists or other regional groups fighting for independence are a key concern and are often branded as terrorists. For example, Russia sees Chechen rebels as terrorists who directly threaten the security and stability of Russia. Similarly, the Chinese government labels most opposition groups in Xinjiang as terrorists.[67] Europeans have also generally been preoccupied with secessionist movements and leftist groups that question the authority of the state (see Europol 2007).

Terrorist designations—or the lack thereof—are also determined by foreign policy commitments and objectives. International obligations, including Security Council resolutions and regional arrangements, may require a country to create a terrorist designation list. States may also publish lists for reputational purposes—that is, to show their good faith in combating international terrorists. Support for allies or friends may inspire the inclusion of certain individuals or groups on a state's list. Terrorist designations may result from international quid pro quos. For example, when the United States announced in 2002 that it would freeze the assets of the Eastern Turkistan Islamic Movement (ETIM), most observers saw this as a payoff for Chinese support of the U.S. war against terrorism.[68] Foreign policy objectives may also inspire governments not to list certain groups or individuals. For example, Norway, although not a member of the EU, had been following the EU on terrorist designations. On January 4, 2006, however, Norway announced that it would no longer follow the EU lead concerning the designation of terrorist organizations not included in the UN-designated terrorist list. Norway argued that "continued alignment with the EU list could cause difficulties for Norway in its role as neutral facilitator in certain peace processes."[69] Norway has traditionally played a role in the Middle East and has been hesitant to apply sanctions to certain Palestinian groups, including Hamas. It has also been argued that Norway hopes to play a role in the conflict ravaging the Philippines. The 2005 EU listing of some Philippine groups as terrorist groups would have foreclosed such a role for Norway.[70] Similarly, because Norway no longer follows the EU rulings, it was able to retain its monitors in Sri Lanka to try to help save what was left of the crumbling ceasefire it helped negotiate in February 2002.[71] Similarly, the omission of Hamas and Hezbollah on the Russian list has been explained in terms of a possible diplomatic mediator role for Russia in the Middle East.

Finally, terrorist designations—or the lack thereof—may be the result of domestic political considerations. The absence of the IRA on the American list and Hezbollah on the European lists are two well-publicized examples. Some observers have also argued that the restrictive definition of the jihadist threat by Europeans is dictated by the domestic political situation in many European countries—that is, by the presence of large Muslim populations.[72]

In sum, lists are political constructs and the result of both domestic and international political calculations.

Target Audiences and Objectives

Insofar as terrorist designation lists target the activities and behavior of terrorists groups or supporters of such groups, they have two main objectives: first, to complicate terrorist operations, and second, to prevent and deter people and states from engaging in and supporting terrorist activities. Although designation and the imposition of sanctions following listing may complicate the activities of terrorist groups, such activities are rarely inhibited by these moves.[73] That being said, listings and the accompanying threat of sanctions have been shown to have a certain deterrent effect. At a minimum, these actions have changed the declaratory attitudes of people and states toward terrorist groups (see de Jonge Oudraat 2007, 335–52). Terrorist designation lists alert and inform international and local authorities as well as the general public about who is considered an enemy of the state, and they warn of the consequences of supporting listed groups or individuals. At the national and international level, lists can be deterrents, and there is some evidence that lists and the threat of sanctions may discourage the support of listed individuals and organizations because of fear of the consequences.

Terrorist designation lists also affect law enforcement officials and have an operational objective. Lists allow judicial and executive officials to take actions against the individuals and groups listed—such as prosecution, deportation, the freezing of financial assets, and the prohibition of entry into a country.[74] In addition, lists provide a concrete framework for national and international coordination and cooperation in combating terrorists. At the national level, lists help local authorities coordinate policies. At the international level, lists allow states and their executive agents to cooperate on specific cases.

Finally, terrorist designation lists target a diplomatic audience and the general public and have a political agenda–setting role. The publication of a list allows a government to orient and frame the counterterrorism debate at both the national and international levels. Lists may help internationalize a problem and legitimize combat against internal enemies. This has been one of the main rationales for the Russian and Chinese terrorist designation lists. Finally, lists may help in defining a common enemy—this is particularly true for the UN list, which has become a powerful instrument in building and maintaining an international coalition against Al Qaeda and the Taliban.

Drawbacks of Terrorist Designation Lists

Despite their increased popularity, terrorist designation lists are no panacea. There are three main types of problems associated with terrorist designation lists: operational problems, political problems, and legal problems (see Pillar 2001, 152–56).

First, publishing the names of individuals and groups may tip them off and push these individuals and groups further underground. This might make surveillance—and thus the prevention of terrorist acts—more difficult.

Second, lists often lump together all terrorists and supporters of terrorist groups. Groups on these lists are very different, however, in terms of size, goals, ideology, tactics, geographical reach, and the extent to which they are incorporated into a nonviolent political process.

Third, the publication of names stigmatizes groups and shuts off negotiating tracks. The publication of names also freezes policy positions—once a group is branded a terrorist group, it becomes harder for a state to engage with it. The delisting of groups is possible, but if done too frequently or without broad international support, delisting undercuts the legitimacy and credibility of such lists. It also leaves states open to accusations of double standards.[75]

Fourth, the publication of a list leaves a state open to pressure by other states, which will want to have their own enemies listed. Ultimately, inclusion on a list may have less to do with national security threats than with other political bargains. This in turn weakens the list and invites justifiable criticisms of double standards, if not hypocrisy.

Fifth, the criteria and procedures for terrorist designations differ widely. They are often vague and unclear. In addition, a lot of the material used as evidence for inclusion comes from intelligence agencies and is secret—even for those designated. This makes recourse extremely difficult—and the possibilities for abuse are obvious. Designated individuals and groups increasingly turn to national and international courts. Even so, and even in well-established democracies, an appeal for reconsideration of the listing through the judicial system is an expensive and slow-moving proposition. Meanwhile, great damage may have been done to innocent groups and individuals. In addition, the right to challenge a designation may be curtailed by the state's responsibility to safeguard national security. For example, under article 15 of the European Convention on Human Rights, states can derogate from the right to a fair trial in a "public emergency threatening the life of the nation" (see Bowring 2006, 54). Many states have similar language in their constitutions. The decision as to whether the life of the nation is at risk is ultimately a political decision, not a legal decision. It is in this context that debates about the definition of terrorism become important. Whether terrorism is seen as a form of war or as a criminal activity changes the balance between national security and civil liberties. It also activates different sets of legal rules.

The European Court of First Instance has recognized that there is a conflict between the "power to intern for imperative reasons of security during the course of an emergency, and a right to due process by a court in more settled times." The court has ruled that times of emergency trump procedural rights but not rights that fall under jus cogens: rights that have become part of customary international law and from which no derogation is permitted—for example, the right not to be tortured or subjected to inhumane or degrading treatment, the right to life, the protection of personal freedom, and the prohibition of discrimination on racial grounds (see Bowring 2006, 29–30).[76]

The ruling of the European Court of First Instance is particularly important with respect to possible challenges to the UN Security Council terrorist designation list.[77] Bardo Fassbender (2006, 19), who conducted a study for the UN Legal Office on "fair trial rights" when faced with UN Security Council resolutions, concluded, "At present, customary international law does not provide for sufficiently clear rules which would oblige international (intergovernmental) organizations to observe standards of due process vis-à-vis individuals." International human rights law—most of which has crystallized as customary law—includes the right of due process, yet this body of law was developed to protect individuals from their own state, not from an international organization.

International law is not a static set of rules. Instead, it is constantly evolving under pressures of practice, case law, and legal discourse. In this regard, Fassbender recognizes the pioneering role of EU law and its influence on customary international law. He points to the trend to widen the scope of customary international law in regard to due process to include the "direct 'governmental' action of international organizations vis-à-vis individuals" (see Fassbender 2006, 20). Indeed, UN sanctions under chapter VII of the Charter that target individuals and entities have a direct impact on the rights and freedoms of these individuals and groups and are a direct expression of UN "governmental" action. UN member states are responsible for implementation and enforcement, but they have no right to question the decision of the UN Security Council to sanction certain individuals or groups. Fassbender concludes that UN governmental action—that is, UN Security Council resolutions that involve terrorist designations and sanctions—should at a minimum include the following procedures: the right to be informed about being listed, the right to be heard, the right to be advised or represented, and the right to an effective remedy (see Fassbender 2006, 28).

The last right is essential. Sanctions within the context of the Security Council are not intended to punish targets. Sanctions imposed by the Security Council are political, not legal, instruments. They are discretionary measures decided upon by the Council outside any legal or disciplinary context (see de Jonge Oudraat 2001, 345, n. 8). Security Council members invoke legal rules and international agreements to support their decisions, but ultimately their decisions are based on political considerations, not legal reviews. It is thus important that individuals and entities be able to show that their actions do not—or no longer—threaten international peace and security (see also Fassbender 2006, 28–32).

Conclusion

There is broad international consensus on the necessity of fighting terrorism. There is no international agreement, however, on how to define terrorism. The proliferation of terrorist designation lists attests to their popularity but not to any greater consensus on the nature of the terrorist threat. To the contrary, our review of terrorist designation lists shows that there are many different definitions of the "terrorist" threat. These definitions change over time and are determined by many factors, such as a country's experience with actual terrorist attacks, its position in the international system, and its political alliances, as well as its domestic political conditions.

The absence of a common definition of terrorism allows states to translate generic antiterrorist rhetoric into very different policy responses and to combat a diversity of groups. The international and national counterterrorist policies put into place by countries around the world are rarely in tune with each other and may even work at cross purposes. The proliferation of national terrorist designation lists increases the potential of policies to undercut each other. Efforts by one country to combat group *X* may be undone by another country's effort to negate the terrorist nature of that group and concentrate instead on group *Y*. The tug of war between Europe and the United States over the Hezbollah designation is a case in point. Even within the UN context, one could argue that the 1267 regime (the Al Qaeda/Taliban designation list) is in competition with the 1373 regime—the regime that led many states to draw up their own terrorist designation lists. Countries quite naturally want to concentrate their efforts on those groups from which they have the most to fear, and those are the groups they put on their national lists.

Some states make a distinction between domestic and transnational terrorism, but states also increasingly recognize that many terrorist groups are transnational and hence that combating these groups requires international cooperation. International cooperation in the fight against terrorism is a necessity, yet such cooperation often falls prey to coordination problems (for more on these coordination problems, see Enders and Sandler 2006). Coordination is hard in the absence of a common foe. Similarly, cooperation is difficult if states are unable to define a common interest. Our examination of terrorist designation lists suggests that states have trouble coordinating counterterrorist policies because there is no common foe. Nevertheless, they may from time to time cooperate with each other on specific cases. Terrorist designation lists may help identify such cases.

Above and beyond the identification of individuals and groups accused of terrorism, terrorist designation lists also pose operational, legal, and political problems. We believe that the operational problems of designations (notably, pushing groups underground) are offset by the potential gains of listings. Lists are a great way to focus national and international cooperative efforts. The legal problems involved in terrorist designations are serious, and nongovernmental watchdogs do well to draw attention to the necessity of having safeguards in place that respect fundamental human rights and principles of due process. Some progress with regard to transparency and accountability has been made, but more needs to be done in this respect. All groups and individuals have a right to be informed about being listed, a right to be heard, a right to be represented, and a right to an effective remedy. These are essential rights that should be respected by all states and international organizations. Legal scholars should be encouraged to make the legal case for these rights. Ultimately, however, terrorist designation lists raise political dilemmas and require that a balance be struck between national and international security, on the one hand, and the protection of and respect for individual human rights and civil liberties, on the other. Increasingly, this must be an internationally agreed-upon balance.

As such, counterterrorist policies are no different from other policies that try to combat "global public bads." Effective international counterterrorism efforts will require unity of effort and some common understanding of the nature of the threat. We believe that with the right safeguards in place, terrorist designation lists can contribute to this effort.

Appendix

Table 3A.1 Lists of Terrorist Organizations

Terrorist Organizations	Number of Organizations
EU list[a]	
Palestinian organizations: Abu Nidal Organization; Al-Aqsa Martyrs' Brigade; Al-Aqsa e.V. Hamas, including Hamas-Izz ad-Din al-Qassam; Palestine Liberation Front; Palestinian Islamic Jihad; Popular Front for the Liberation of Palestine (PFLP); PFLP-GC (General-Command)	6
Jihadist groups: Al-Takir wal-Hijrah[b]; Gama'a al-Islamiyya; Islamic Great Eastern Raiders Front (IBDA-C)[c]; Hizb-ul-Mujahideen (HM)[d]; Hofstadgroep; Holy Land Foundation for Relief and Development; Al-Aqsa Nederland, aka Stichting Al-Aqsa Nederland	7
Anarchists/far leftist groups: Nuclei Territoriali Anti-imperialisti (Italy); Cooperativa Artigiana Fuoco e Affini, Occasionalmente Spettacolare (Italy)*; Nuclei Armati per il Comunismo (Italy)*; Cellula Contro Capitale, Carcere i suci Carcerieri e le sue Celle (CCCCC: Italy)*; Grupos Armados Antifascistas Primero de Octubre (GRAPO; Spain)*; Brigate Rosse per la Costruzione Partito Comunista Combattente (Italy)*; Epanastatiki Pirines (Greece)*; Epanastatikos Agonas*; 17 November (Greece)*; Revolutionary People's Liberation Party Front (DHKP-C; Kurdistan); Epanastatikos Laigos Agonas (ELA; Greece); Sendero Luminoso (Peru); Solidarietà Internazionale*; Brigata XX Luglio (Italy)*; Nucleo di Iniziativa Proletaria Rivoluzionaria (Italy); Nuclei di Iniziativa Proletaria (Italy); Federazione Anarchica Informale (Italy)*	17
Far rightist groups: Kahane Chai (Kach)	1
Regionalists/Autonomists/Independentists: Babbar Khalsa[e]; Communist Party of the Philippines, including New People's Army (NPA), linked to Jose Maria Sison; Continuity Irish Republican Army*; Basque Freedom and Homeland Organization (ETA; Basque Country, Spain, France)* (the following organizations are part of the ETA: KAS, XAKI, Ekin, Jarrai-Haika-Segi, Gestoras Pro-Amnistia, Askatasuna, Batasuna); International Sikh Youth Federation (ISYF)[f]; Khalistan Zindabad Force	18

TABLE 3A.1 (*Continued*)

Terrorist Organizations	Number of Organizations
(ZF); Kongra Gel[g] (Kurdistan); Liberation Tigers of Talim Eelam (LTTE); Loyalist Volunteer Force (Ireland)*; Ejercito de Liberacion Nacional; Orange Volunteers (Ireland)*; National Liberation Army (Ejército de Liberación Nacional); Real IRA (Ireland)*; Red Hand Defenders (Ireland)*; Revolutionary Armed Forces of Colombia (FARC; Colombia); Teyrbazen Azadiya Kurdistan (TAK), aka Kurdistan Freedom Falcons, aka Kurdistan Freedom Hawks; Ulster Defense Association (Ireland)*; United Self-Defense of Colombia (AUC; Colombia)	
Other/sects: Aum Shinrikyo (Japan); Mujahedin-e Khalq Organization (MKO, or MEK)*	2
U.S. list[h]	
Palestinian organizations: Abu Nidal Organization; Al-Aqsa Martyrs' Brigade; Hamas; Palestinian Liberation Front; Palestinian Islamic Jihad (PIJ); PFLP; PFLP-GC	7
Jihadist groups: Abu Sayyaf (Philippines); Al Qaeda; Islamic Armed Group (GIA; Algeria); Asbat al-Ansar (Lebanon); Gama'a al-Islamiyya (Egypt); Harakat al-Mujahidin (HUM[i]; Pakistan); Islamic Jihad Group (Egypt); Islamic Movement of Uzbekistan (IMU; Uzbekistan)[j]; Jaish e Mohammed (JEM)[k]; Jamaa Islamiyya (Indonesia); Lashkar e Tayyiba (LT)[l]; Lashkar i Jhangvi (LIJ)[m]; Lybian Islamic Fighting Group; Moroccan Islamic Combatant Group (GICM); Al Qaeda; Salafist Group for Preaching and Combat (GSPC; Algeria); Tanzim Qaidat al-Jihad fi Bilad al-Rafidayn[n] (Iraq)	17
Anarchists/far leftist groups (mainly European): Revolutionary Nuclei (Italy); 17 November (Greece); DHKP-C; Sendero Luminoso (Peru)	4
Far rightist groups	None
Regionalists/Autonomists/Independentists: ETA; Communist Party of the Philippines; Continuity Irish Republican Army; Hezbollah; Kongra-Gel (former PKK); LTTE; National Liberation Army; FARC; AUC; Real IRA	10
Other/sects: Aum Shinrikyo; Kahane Chai; MEK	3[o]

(*Table continues on p. 116.*)

TABLE 3A.1 (*Continued*)

Terrorist Organizations	Number of Organizations
U.K. list[p]	
Jihadist organizations: Abu Sayyaf Group; Gama'a al-Islamiya; Al Ghurabaa[q] (U.K.); Al Ittihad al Islamia; Al Qaeda; Ansar al Islam; Ansar al Sunna; Groupe Islamique Armée; Asbat al-Ansar; Egyptian Islamic Jihad; GICM; Harakat-ul-Jihad-al-Islami; Harakat-ul-Jihad-al-Islami (Bangladesh); Harakat al-Mujahidin/Alami (HUM/A) and Jundallah; Harakat Mujahideen; Hezb-e Islami Gulbuddin; Islamic Army of Aden; Islamic Jihad Union (IJU; Uzbekistan); IMU; JEM (Kashmir); Jemaah Islamiyah (Southeast Asia); Khuddam ul-Islam (KUI; Kashmir); Lashkar e Tayyaba; GSPC; Saved Sect (U.K.); Sipah-e Sahaba Pakistan; Libyan Islamic Fighting Group; Jammat-ul Mujahideen Bangladesh (JMB); Tehrik Nefaz-e Shari'at Muhammadi (TNSM; Afghanistan)	30
Irish proscribed groups: Continuity Army Council; Cumann na mBan; Fianna na hEireann; Irish National Liberation Army; Irish People's Liberation Organization; Irish Republican Army; Loyalist Volunteer Force; Orange Volunteers; Red Hand Commando; Red Hand Defenders; Saor Éire; Ulster Defense Association; Ulster Freedom Fighters; Ulster Volunteer Force	13
Separatist/regionalist/nationalist organizations: Babbar Khalsa (Sikh); ETA; Baluchistan Liberation Army; ISYF; Kongra Gel Kurdistan (former PKK); LTTE; Teyre Azadiye Kurdistan	7
Palestinian groups: Abu Nidal Organization; Hamas-Izz al-Din al-Qassam Brigades; Palestinian Islamic Jihad—Shaqaqi	3
Other: Hezbollah External Security Organization	1
Far leftist groups: 17 November Revolutionary; DHKP-C	2
Sect: MEK	1
Russian list[r]	
Palestinian organizations	None
Jihadist groups: Shura of the United Forces of the Mujahedeen of the Caucasus; People's Congress of Ichkeria and Dagestan (Caucasus); Al Qaeda (transnational); Asbat al-Ansar[s] (Lebanon); Al-Jihad (Egypt);	17

TABLE 3A.1 (*Continued*)

Terrorist Organizations	Number of Organizations
Al-Gama'a al-Islamiya (Egypt); Hizb ut-Tahrir (Central Asia and international)[t]; Laskar-e-Taiba (Pakistan); Jamaat-e-Islami[u]; Taliban (Afghanistan); Islamic Party of Turkistan (Central Asia)[v]; Jamaat Ihia al-Turaz al-Islami (Caucasus, Kuwait)[w]; Al-Haramein[x]; Islamic Jihad (Egypt); Jund ash-Sham (Lebanon); Jamiat al-Islah a-Ijtima; Al-Ikwan al-Muslimeen (Muslim Brothers; Egypt and international)	
Sects	None
Chinese list[y]	
Regionalists/Autonomists/Independentists: East Turkistan Islamic Movement (ETIM); Eastern Turkistan Liberation Organization (ETLO); World Uyghur Youth Congress (WUYC); East Turkistan Information Center (ETIC)	

Source: Authors' compilation.

a. See Council common position 2007/931/CFSP (June 28, 2007). Groups or entities marked with an * are subject to financial sanctions.

b. Al-Takir wal-Hijrah (aka Anathema and Hegire) is not an organization but a movement with an eschatological worldview. It first appeared in Egypt in the 1970s.

c. The IBDA-C is a Salafist group that advocates Islamic rule in Turkey and considers Turkey's present secular leadership to be "illegal." In February 2000, the group claimed responsibility for four bomb attacks in Istanbul.

d. HM, formed in 1989, is one of the largest terrorist groups operating in Jammu and Kashmir.

e. The Babbar Khalsa is a militant group considered to be among the oldest and most prominent of Sikh organizations calling for the formation of an independent Sikh state. It is largely sponsored by the Sikh diaspora.

f. Organization founded in the United Kingdom in 1984 after Operation Blue Star, conducted on June 5, 1984, to flush out Sikh terrorists from the Golden Temple complex in Amritsar in the Indian Punjab.

g. Former PKK.

h. Foreign terrorist organizations (FTO); see http://www.state.gov/documents/organization/10300.pdf (accessed September 9, 2007).

i. HUM is an Islamic militant group based in Pakistan that operates primarily in Kashmir. It is politically aligned with the radical political party Jamiat Ulema-i-Islam's Fazlur Rehman faction (JUI-F). In 2003, HUM began using the name Jamiat ul-Ansar (JUA). Pakistan banned JUA in November 2003.

j. The IMU is a group of Islamic militants from Uzbekistan and other Central Asian states. IMU militants are scattered throughout South Asia, Tajikistan, and Iran. The area of operations includes Afghanistan (against the Coalition), Iran, Kyrgyzstan, Pakistan, Tajikistan, Kazakhstan, and Uzbekistan.

(*Table continues on p. 118.*)

TABLE 3A.1 (*Continued*)

k. The Jaish e Mohammed (JEM the Army of Muhammad) is an Islamic extremist group based in Pakistan that was created in 2000 by Masood Azhar upon his release from prison in India. The group's aim is to unite Kashmir with Pakistan. It is politically aligned with the radical political party Jamiat Ulema-i-Islam's Fazlur Rehman faction. By 2003, JEM had splintered into Khuddam ul-Islam (KUI), headed by Azhar, and Jamaat ul-Furqan (JUF), led by Abdul Jabbar, who was released in August 2004 from Pakistani custody after being detained for suspected involvement in the December 2003 assassination attempts against President Musharraf. Pakistan banned KUI and JUF in November 2003.
l. LT is the armed wing of the Pakistan-based religious organization Markaz-ud-Dawa-wal-Irshad (MDI), an anti-U.S. organization created in 1989 and based in Muridke (near Lahore) and Muzaffarabad.
m. Lashkar i Jhangvi (LIJ), formed in 1996, is a Sunni-Deobandi Muslim radical group that began in the Punjab region of Pakistan and the port of Karachi. It has confirmed links with Al Qaeda and has assisted in several attacks on westerners in Pakistan, including (probably) the January 2002 kidnapping and murder of *Wall Street Journal* reporter Daniel Pearl.
n. Al Qaeda in Iraq.
o. See www.state.gov/s/ct/rls/fs.
p. See 2006, no. 2016, "Prevention and Suppression of Terrorism" (the Terrorism Act 2000), proscribed organizations amendment order 2006, Home Office, July 25, 2006, available at: http://www.homeoffice.gov.uk/security/terrorism-and-the-law/terrorism-act/proscribed-groups (updated September 6, 2007).
q. Al Gurabaa, a splinter group of Al-Muhajirun, disseminates materials that glorify acts of terrorism.
r. Radio Free Europe, "Russian Supreme Court Approves List of 17 'Terrorist' Groups," July 28, 2007, available at: http://www.rferl.org/featuresarticle/2006/07/398cc38f-b2bd-49cc-9071-7500302be628.html.
s. Asbat al-Ansar—the League of the Followers—is a Lebanon-based, Sunni extremist group linked to transnational jihadist networks.
t. The Hizb ut-Tahrir is a radical Muslim organization that aims for a caliphate across Central Asia. It is especially targeted by the Uzbek authorities. On July 28, 2006, the Russian authorities updated their official list of proscribed entities and added the Hizb ut-Tahrir. On August 3, 2006, Russia extradited twelve Uzbek nationals involved in local disturbances.
u. Jamaat-e-Islami is Pakistan's oldest religious party. The Jamaat-e-Islami ranks among the leading and most influential Islamic revivalist movements.
v. See note j.
w. The Society for the Revival of the Islamic Heritage is a charity in Kuwait.
x. An international NGO connected to transnational jihadist networks.
y. See GlobalSecurity.org, "China Identifies Eastern Turkistan Terrorist Organizations, Terrorists," December 15, 2003, available at: http://www.globalsecurity.org/wmd/library/news/china/2003/china-031216-pla-daily01.htm; see also UN document S/2004/342, April 30, 2004.

TABLE 3A.2 UN List of Entities Belonging to or Associated with the Taliban and Al Qaeda (by Country)

Country	Number of Entities
Afghanistan	11
Albania	1
Algeria	4
Austria	1
Bahamas	4
Bangladesh	1
Bosnia and Herzegovina	6
Canada	1
Comoros	1
Egypt	1
Ethiopia	1
Germany	1
India	2
Indonesia	3
Iraq	3
Italy	7
Kenya	1
Lebanon	1
Libya	1
Liechtenstein	6
Morocco	2
Netherlands	2
Pakistan	11
Philippines	2
Russia	2
Saudi Arabia	1
Somalia	22
Sweden	2
Tanzania	1
Turkey	1
Turkistan	1
United Arab Emirates	9
United States	8
United Kingdom	6
Uzbekistan	1
Yemen	4
Transnational (Al Qaeda, Global Relief Foundation, Benevolence International Foundation)	3

Source: Authors' compilation.

Notes

1. France, Germany, and most other European states follow EU directives.
2. Since 1963, thirteen major multilateral conventions and protocols combating terrorist acts have been adopted, including the Convention on Offenses and Certain Other Acts Committed On Board Aircraft (1963); the Convention for the Suppression of Unlawful Seizure of Aircraft (1970); the Convention on the Prevention and Punishment of Crimes Against Internationally Protected Persons, Including Diplomatic Agents (1973); the International Convention Against the Taking of Hostages (1979); the Convention on the Physical Protection of Nuclear Material (1980); the Convention for the Suppression of Unlawful Acts Against the Safety of Maritime Navigation (1988); the Protocol for the Suppression of Unlawful Acts Against the Safety of Fixed Platforms Located on the Continental Shelf (1988); the Convention on the Marking of Plastic Explosives for the Purpose of Detection (1991); the International Convention for the Suppression of Terrorist Bombings (1997); the International Convention for the Suppression of Financing of Terrorism (1999); and the Convention for the Suppression of Acts of Nuclear Terrorism (2005).
3. Definitions are often the result of delicate negotiations between different government agencies. Each agency has different functions, capabilities, and bureaucratic interests—and not surprisingly, they have different ways of looking at the problem. In the analytical literature, terrorism has similarly defied a common definition or approach. Some analysts have focused on terrorist tactics, and others are more concerned with the conditions conducive to the spread of terrorism, the effects of terrorism, or the national and international policy responses.
4. For example, one of the definitions of terrorism used by the U.S. State Department is "premeditated politically motivated violence perpetrated against noncombatant targets by sub-national groups or clandestine agents"; see "Fact Sheet of the Office of Counterterrorism on Foreign Terrorist Organizations," available at: www.state.gov/s/ct/rls/rpt/fto (accessed September 12, 2009).
5. Terrorist intent is defined as "seriously intimidating a population, or unduly compelling a Government or international organization to perform or abstain from performing any act, or seriously destabilizing or destroying the fundamental political, constitutional, economic or social structures of a country or an international organization." The EU Council adopted the EU definition on June 13, 2002.
6. The framework decision talks about offenses with the aim of "*seriously* intimidating a population . . . *unduly* compelling a Government . . . and *seriously* destabilizing or destroying the fundamental political, constitutional, economic or social structures of a country or an international organization" (emphasis in the original). For a discussion of the EU definition, see Dumitriu (2004).

7. The 1977 European Convention on the Suppression of Terrorism did not define terrorism. It referred either to specific activities or to existing international agreements. Similarly, the 2002 Inter-American Convention against terrorism does not define terrorism but refers to offenses listed in existing conventions.
8. The UN Security Council (UNSC) Resolution 1267 (1999) setting up sanctions against the Taliban and Al Qaeda does so under chapter VII of the UN Charter—that is, under the council's responsibilities to restore and maintain international peace and security. All resolutions adopted under chapter VII are mandatory resolutions; see also article 25 of the UN Charter.
9. See UNSC Resolution 1267 (1999); see also UNSC Resolution 1333 (2000), which strengthened the sanction package and required all UN member states to close all Taliban offices in their countries and to freeze the financial assets of Osama bin Laden and his associates. It also imposed an arms embargo on the Taliban. See also UNSC Resolutions 1388 (2002), 1390 (2002), and 1455 (2003). The UN Counter-Terrorism Committee (CTC), established by UNSC Resolution 1373 (2001), a resolution adopted shortly after the terrorist attacks in the United States on September 11, 2001, does not maintain a list of individuals or organizations believed to be associated with terrorist organizations. Such designations remain the prerogative of each individual state. The CTC only monitors implementation of Resolution 1373 (2001)—that is, whether states have put into place counterterrorist legislation. Similarly, the Non-Proliferation Committee created by UNSC resolution 1540 (2004) to monitor states' adoptions of legislative measures to prevent terrorists from obtaining weapons of mass destruction (WMD) does not maintain a list. Nor does the working group established by UNSC Resolution 1566 (2004) after the terrorist attacks in Beslan (Russia); that group was tasked with examining measures that could be imposed on individuals or organizations other than those on the Al Qaeda list.
10. The 1267 Committee is a subsidiary committee of the UN Security Council and consists of all members of the UNSC. For the complete "Consolidated List Established and Maintained by the 1267 Committee with Respect to Al-Qaida, Osama bin Laden, and the Taliban and Other Individuals, Groups, Undertakings, and Entities Associated with Them," see http://www.un.org/sc/committees/1267/consolist.shtml (accessed September 12, 2009).
11. See UNSC 1267 Committee, "Fact Sheet on Listing," available at: http://www.un.org/sc/committees/1267/index.shtml (accessed September 12, 2009).
12. See UNSC 1267 Committee, "Guidelines of the Committee for the Conduct of Its Work," February 12, 2007, available at: http://www.un.org/sc/committees/1267/consolist.shtml (accessed September 12, 2009). States may also request more time for consideration of the listing. On average, listings take a few weeks. See also UNSC, "Sixth Report of the Analytical

Support and Sanctions Monitoring Team," S/2007/132 (March 8, 2007), para. 43 and 44, available at: http://daccessdds.un.org/doc/UNDOC/GEN/N06/622/70/PDF/N0662270.pdf?OpenElement (accessed September 12, 2009).

13. In January 2001, the list contained the names of seventy-five individuals and five entities associated with the Taliban and ten individuals associated with Al Qaeda; see SC/6844 (April 13, 2000) and AFG/124, SC/6998 (January 25, 2001). In November 2001, the list contained the names of 152 individuals and nine entities associated with the Taliban and fifty-four individuals and sixty-six entities associated with Al Qaeda; see AFG/169, SC/7222 (November 26, 2001).

14. See, for example, the Russian report to the 1267 Committee, S/AC.37/2003/(1455)/28, and the Algerian report, S/AC.37/2003/(1455)/14.

15. See, for example, Watson Institute (2006, para. 43 and 44); see also the reports of the Analytical Support and Sanctions Monitoring Team of the 1267 Committee and the report of the special rapporteur on "The Promotion and Protection of Human Rights While Countering Terrorism," A/61/267, August 16, 2006.

16. The individuals challenged the EU list, which was based on the UN list. For other litigation cases related to the UN list, see UNSC, "Fifth Report of the Analytical Support and Sanctions Monitoring Team," S/2006/750 (September 20, 2006), available at: http://daccessdds.un.org/doc/UNDOC/GEN/N06/529/76/PDF/N0652976.pdf?OpenElement (accessed May 23, 2009).

17. That is, the court could not judge the lawfulness of UNSC decisions. The court did feel empowered to check the lawfulness of the European Commission (EC) regulation against "jus cogens, understood as a *peremptory norm of public international law* from which neither the Member States nor the bodies of the United Nations may derogate. It includes, in particular, the mandatory provisions intended to secure universal protection of human rights" (emphasis in original). But even on this basis, the court rejected the challenge. It found that the European Commission regulation (and hence indirectly the UN committee decision to list the applicants) did not infringe on fundamental rights—in this case the right to property, the rights of defense, and the right to effective judicial review. See EU, "Judgments of the Court of First Instance," press release 79/05, September 21, 2005; see also EU press release 57/06, July 12, 2006.

18. Committee members could request at any time a review of a listing, and the UN Secretariat circulated every year a list of names that had not seen any updating activities in four or more years.

19. See UNSC Resolution 1730 (2006), December 19, 2006, and UNSC document S/2007/178, March 30, 2007.

20. The Analytical Support and Sanctions Monitoring Team, which assists the 1267 Committee, has commented that despite the revival of the Taliban and the emergence of new leaders, no new names have been added to the list since

February 2001; see UNSC, "Sixth Report of the Analytical Support and Sanctions Monitoring Team," S/2007/132 (March 8, 2007), para. 8 (see n. 12).

21. See ibid., para. 14–23.
22. Ibid., para. 32.
23. See UNSC, "Fifth Report of the Analytical Support and Sanctions Monitoring Team," S/2006/750 (September 20, 2006), para. 61–63 (see n. 16).
24. In the first three months after the September 2001 attacks, US$112 million was frozen, but only US$10 million was blocked in the following eight months.
25. See EU common position 2002/402/CFSP (May 27, 2002), amended by CP2003/140/CFS, and EC regulation 881/2002 (May 27, 2002), amended by several EU Commission regulations, available at: http://ec.europa.eu/external_relations/cfsp/sanctions/measures.htm (accessed September 2009).
26. See EU common positions 2001/930 and 2001/931/CFSP (December 27, 2001). The latter was amended by common position 2007/448/CFSP (June 28, 2007). In conjunction with common positions 2001/931/CFSP and 2007/448/CFSP, see also EC regulation 2580 (2001) (December 27, 2001), amended by several EU Commission regulations, and Council decision 2005/671/JHA. For full references, see: http://ec.europa.eu/external_relations/cfsp/sanctions/measures.htm (accessed September 2009).
27. On the list, an asterisk indicates the domestic groups and individuals. For the 2007 list, see EU common position 2007/448/CFSP (June 28, 2007). A member of the Hofstad group murdered the Dutch filmmaker Theo van Gogh in Amsterdam in 2004. The Hofstad group falls under "nondomestic" groups because of its foreign connections with Moroccan jihadist networks and the Groupe Islamique Combattant Marocain (GICM).
28. The EU cannot impose autonomous sanctions against individuals and entities where there is no foreign policy dimension. That being said, national sanctions, including financial sanctions, may be applicable.
29. The Council of the European Union is an intergovernmental body and the EU's main decisionmaking body; together with the European Parliament (EP), it has legislative power. The Council of the EU meets monthly at the ministerial level and defines and implements the EU's Common Foreign and Security Policy (CFSP), based on guidelines set by the European Council. The latter meets four times a year at the level of heads of state or government and with the president of the EU Commission.
30. The EU Commission is a supranational body that upholds collective European interests and implements decisions by the Council of the EU. For more on the legal basis of EU decisions and implementation, see Council of the EU, "Guidelines on Implementation and Evaluation of Restrictive Measures (Sanctions) in the Framework of the EU Common Foreign and Security Policy," document 15114/05 (December 2005); and "Restrictive Measures: EU Best Practices for the Effective Implementation of Restrictive Measures," document 10533/06 (June 2006). In 2004 a special Council body—

Relex/Sanctions—was created to exchange experiences and best practices in the implementation and application of sanctions, including sanctions to combat terrorism. The Commission also participates in meetings of Relex/Sanctions. In 2007 the Council established a special committee—called the Working Party on Implementation of Common Position 2001/931/CFSP on the Application of Specific Measures to Combat Terrorism (CP931 WP)—to evaluate and examine listing and delisting issues. For details on the working methods of CP931WP, see Council of EU, document 10826/1/07 Rev.1 (June 28, 2007).

31. The criteria that have to be met are spelled out in article 1(4) of common position 2001/931/CFSP: "The list in the Annex shall be drawn up on the basis of precise information or material in the relevant file which indicates that a decision has been taken by a competent authority in respect of the persons, groups and entities concerned, irrespective of whether it concerns the instigation of investigations or prosecution for a terrorist act, an attempt to perpetrate, participate in or facilitate such an act based on serious and credible evidence or clues, or condemnation of such deeds. . . . 'Competent authority' shall mean a judicial authority, or, where judicial authorities have no competence in the area covered . . . an equivalent competent authority in that area."
32. National authorities have a minimum of two weeks for vetting and consideration.
33. See note 31.
34. See EU common position 2007/488/CFSP (June 28, 2007).
35. This is not to say that there is no debate in France about putting Hezbollah on the list. For example, during the French presidential campaign Nicolas Sarkozy publicly described Hezbollah as a terrorist group and advocated for its inclusion on the EU list.
36. Both groups are on the UN list and thus are covered by the EU list.
37. See Court of First Instance, "Judgment of the Court of First Instance in Case T-228/02," press release 97/06 (December 12, 2006). The Palestinian group Al-Aqsa was expected to make similar arguments in a hearing on January 16, 2007; see Andrew Rettman, "Mujahidin Case Could Reshape EU Anti-Terror Work," *EU Observer*, December 12, 2006; see also Graig S. Smith, "European Court Says Exiled Iranian Group Was Unfairly Labeled," *New York Times*, December 13, 2006. More generally, for an analysis of the legal remedies open to organizations that are designated terrorist organizations, see Bowring and Korff (2004).
38. See Court of First Instance, "Judgment of the Court of First Instance in Cases T-47/03 and T-327/03," press release 47/07 (July 11, 2007).
39. In the case of *Ahmed Ali Yusuf and Yassin Abdullah Kadi v. the EU*, the court rejected the challenges of Yusuf and Kadi. With respect to the "right of defense," the court found that no rule of jus cogens required a personal hearing of individuals listed by the 1267 Committee. It believed that the possi-

bility to address a request to the UN committee to be removed from the list, through their national authorities, was sufficient. Similarly, with respect to the "right of effective judicial review," the court pointed out that the right of access to the courts is not absolute and that the lacuna in the judicial protection available to those listed is not in itself contrary to jus cogens; see EU Court of First Instance, press release number 79/05 (September 21, 2005).

40. EU law comprises the European Community and European Union treaties as well as case law.
41. See Council of the EU, "Fight Against the Financing of Terrorism," document 10826/1/07 (June 28, 2007).
42. See Gijs de Vries, EU counterterrorism coordinator, speech in Brussels, September 24, 2004 (personal source). The new EU treaty proposed by the German presidency in 2007 would allow for autonomous EU sanctions against "domestic" groups.
43. Relatively small sums of money are necessary to carry out a terrorist attack. The estimates for the 2004 Madrid bombings range from €8,000 to €15,000.
44. National and international authorities have little knowledge about how much money is involved to keep terrorist networks going. Europol (2007, 22) noted that "no estimates are available about the amount of money collected legally or illegally within the EU that could be misused for terrorism funding."
45. The Treasury Department also maintains a specially designated terrorists (SDT) list. Created in January 1995, it is specifically oriented toward people and organizations trying to disrupt the Middle East peace process. Under presidential executive order 12947 (January 25, 1995), the United States designated Hamas a terrorist organization.
46. This list was first put into effect in October 1997. The State Department also maintains the terrorist exclusion list (TEL), which designates terrorist organizations for immigration purposes only.
47. For more, see the fourth report of the United States to the UN Counter-Terrorism Committee, UN document S/2006/69 (February 3, 2006).
48. The 2006 "U.S. National Strategy for Combating Terrorism" defined the terrorist enemy as a nonmonolithic "transnational movement of extremist organizations, networks and individuals" not controlled by any single individual, group, or state, but united by a common vision that exploits Islam and uses terrorism for ideological ends. See "2006 U.S. National Strategy for Combating Terrorism" (September), 5, available at: http://www.cfr.org/publication/11389/www.cfr.org/content/publications/attachments/NSCT0906.pdf (accessed September 20, 2009). The "2003 US National Strategy for Combating Terrorism" had a more unidimensional vision of the threat. It argued that the terrorist threat was exemplified by Al Qaeda, which was defined as a "multinational enterprise with operations in more than 60 countries" See "2003 US National Strategy for Combating Terrorism," 3, available at: http://fas.org/irp/threat/nsct2006.pdf (accessed September 21, 2009).

49. It may be noted that in 1999 the UN started a sanction regime against the Taliban and Al Qaeda.
50. The Real Irish Republican Army (IRA) is a paramilitary group that has been declared illegal in the Republic of Ireland. It is branded a terrorist group by the United States and the United Kingdom. The Real IRA has been responsible for a number of bombings, including a bombing in 1998 that killed twenty-nine people. The AUC (United Self-Defense Forces of Colombia) is a Colombian group that comprises several right-wing paramilitary groups.
51. Kahane Chai and Kach are two extremist Israeli groups. Israel outlawed Kach and its offshoot Kahane Chai in 1994.
52. In February 2009, the U.S. House of Representatives passed legislation establishing a process for Americans to challenge their placement on governmental watch lists.
53. The United States also has a state sponsors of terrorism (SST) list. It is the only country that officially designates other countries as state sponsors of terrorism. In 2006 it listed five countries as state sponsors of terrorism: Cuba, Iran, North Korea, Syria, and Sudan.
54. The home secretary can also remove organizations from the proscription list.
55. The United Kingdom first started to proscribe organizations in Northern Ireland in 1974, under "emergency" antiterrorism legislation.
56. The GIA is a radical offshoot of Algeria's main Islamist opposition and has been responsible for many terrorist attacks in Europe.
57. The lord chancellor, a member of the U.K. cabinet, is responsible for the effective functioning and independence of the courts.
58. See U.K. Home Office, Office for Security and Counter Terrorism, "Proscribed Terrorist Groups," available at: http://security.homeoffice.gov.uk/legislation/current-legislation/terrorism-act-2000/proscribed-groups (accessed May 16, 2009).
59. Russia also has a federal financial monitoring service (Rosfinmonitoring) that monitors the financial transactions of organizations and individuals associated with terrorist and extremist activities. It includes individuals and entities on the UN list, individuals who are under criminal investigations, and organizations that have been suspended by order of the Supreme Court. See the fourth report of the Russian Federation to the UN Counter-Terrorism Committee, UN document S/2006/98 (February 2006).
60. See Robert Parsons, "Russia Supreme Court Approves List of 17 Terrorist Groups," *Radio Free Europe/Radio Liberty*, July 28, 2006.
61. See "The Moslim Brothers Group Accuses the Egyptian Government of Depriving It from the Coming Parliamentary Elections," ArabicNews.com (September 19, 2000), available at: http://www.arabicnews.com/ansub/Daily/Day/000919/2000091926.html (accessed May 16, 2009).
62. See Parsons, "Russia Supreme Court Approves List of 17 Terrorist Groups"; Henry Meyer, "Hezbollah Not on Russia's Terrorist List," *The Guardian*,

July 29, 2006; *BBC News*, "Russia Names Terrorist Groups," *BBC News*, July 28, 2006; Simon Saradzhyan, "The Shortsightedness of Russia's Terror Blacklist," *ISN*, December 14, 2006.

63. Cited in Saradzhyan, "The Shortsightedness of Russia's Terror Blacklist."
64. Moscow has often accused the United States and the EU of double standards and has been particularly irritated by the rejection of extradition requests for former Chechen rebels. Yet its own list is very unidimensional and focuses only on its immediate enemies.
65. Beijing sees cooperation with the United States against terrorist groups as a means of gaining international support for its own counterterrorism effort; see Roy (2006).
66. See the fourth report of China to the UN Counter-Terrorism Committee, UN document S/2004/342 (April 30, 2004), p. 20.
67. See Cindy Sui, "China Issues First Ever List of Terrorist Groups," *World Tibet Network News* (Canada Tibet Committee), December 16, 2003.
68. The fact that the UN shortly thereafter added ETIM to the list of organizations associated with the Taliban and Al Qaeda was also seen as a reward for China.
69. Quoted in Victor Comras, "Norway Drops Implementation of EU Terrorist List" (January 16, 2006), available at: http://counterterrorismblog.org/2006/01/norway_drops_implementation_of.php (accessed May 17, 2009).
70. Ibid.
71. In 2006 the EU decided to list the Tamil Tigers as a terrorist organization. The Swedish head of the Sri Lanka Monitoring Mission (SLMM) considered that EU decision a grave mistake and argued that it would lead to a rise in violence—which it did. It also led to the expulsion of thirty-nine Swedish, Danish, and Finnish members of the SLMM, leaving only eighteen Norwegian and Icelandic monitors in the country and spelling the virtual doom of that mission. See Lisbeth Kirk, "Swedish General Slams EU for Terror Listing Tamil Tigers," EUObserver.com, July 25, 2006.
72. Europeans have also adopted a restrictive definition of the jihadist threat to avoid being dragged into military operations in countries around the world.
73. See also n. 44.
74. Paul Pillar (2001, 151–52) has pointed out that in the United States, terrorists or terrorist supporters can easily be apprehended with other existing legal instruments.
75. Designation as terrorist would not necessarily foreclose discussions with such a group. As a matter of fact, such discussions often take place at an operational (intelligence) and unofficial level, but official discussions will be opened only when the group formally renounces terrorism.
76. Certain due process rights, such as the right to be heard, may belong to jus cogens; see Fassbender (2006, 20).

77. That is, challenges to resolutions adopted by the Security Council under chapter VII of the UN Charter—in other words, when the Security Council carries out its responsibility to restore and maintain international peace and security. See also our previous discussion of the court rulings in the section dealing with the EU.

References

Bowring, Bill. 2006. "The Human Rights Implications of International Listing Mechanisms for Terrorist Organizations." Background paper for Office of Democratic Institutions and Human Rights/General (ODIHR/GAL) 14/07. Presented to the Organization for Security and Cooperation in Europe–Office of Democratic Institutions and Human Rights (OSCE-ODIHR) and United Nations Office of the High Commissioner for Human Rights (UN OHCHR) "Expert Workshop on Human Rights and International Cooperation in Counterterrorism" for ODIHR/GAL final report. Triesenberg, Lichtenstein (November 15–17).

Bowring, Bill, and Douwe Korff. 2004. "Terrorist Designation with Regard to European and International Law: The Case of the PMOI." Paper presented to the International Conference of Jurists. Paris (November 10). Available at: www.statewatch.org.

Carlile of Berriew QC, Lord. 2007. "Report on the Operation in 2006 of the Terrorism Act 2000." Paper presented to Parliament pursuant to section 126 of the Terrorism Act 2000. London: House of Lords (June). Available at: http://security.homeoffice.gov.uk/news-publications/publication-search/terrorism-act-2000/lord-carlile-report-07 (accessed September 2009).

Cronin, Audrey Kurth. 2003. "The 'FTO List' and Congress: Sanctioning Designated Foreign Terrorist Organizations." CRS Report for Congress RL32120. Washington: Library of Congress.

De Jonge Oudraat, Chantal. 2001. "UN Sanction Regimes and Violent Conflict." In *Turbulent Peace: The Challenges of Managing International Conflict*, edited by Chester A. Crocker, Fen Osler Hampson, and Pamela Aall. Washington, D.C.: United States Institute of Peace Press.

———. 2003. "The Role of the Security Council." In *Terrorism and the UN: Before and After September 11*, edited by Jane Boulden and Thomas Weiss. Bloomington: Indiana University Press.

———. 2007. "Economic Sanctions and International Peace and Security." In *Leashing the Dogs of War: Conflict Management in a Divided World*, edited by Chester A. Crocker, Fen Osler Hampson, and Pamela Aall. Washington, D.C.: United States Institute of Peace Press.

Dumitriu, Eugenia. 2004. "The EU's Definition of Terrorism: The Council Framework Decision on Combating Terrorism." *German Law Journal* 5(5 May): 585–602.

Enders, Walter, and Todd Sandler. 2006. *The Political Economy of Terrorism*. Cambridge: Cambridge University Press.

Europol. 2007. *EU Terrorism Situation and Trend Report 2007*. The Hague: Europol (March).

Fassbender, Bardo. 2006. "Targeted Sanctions and Due Process" (the "Fassbender Report"). Discussion paper on supplementary guidelines for the Review of Sanctions Committee's listing decisions. A study commissioned by the UN Office of Legal Affairs (March 20). Available at: http://www.un.org/law/counsel/Fassbender_study.pdf (accessed May 21, 2009).

Hayes, Ben. 2007. "Terrorist Lists: Still Above the Law." *Statewatch Analysis* (August). Available at: www.statewatch.org.

Marret, Jean-Luc. 2005. *Les fabriques du jihad*. Paris: Presses Universitaires de France.

——. 2006. "Evolution of Jihadi Profiles." Working paper. Washington, D.C.: Center for Transatlantic Relations.

Pillar, Paul. 2001. *Terrorism and U.S. Foreign Policy*. Washington, D.C.: Brookings Institute Press.

Roy, Denny. 2006. "Lukewarm Partners: Chinese Support for U.S. Counterterrorism in Southeast Asia." Honolulu: Asia-Pacific Center for Security Studies (March). Available at: http://handle.dtic.mil/100.2/ADA445080 (accessed May 21, 2009).

United Nations (UN). 2006. *Uniting Against Terrorism: Recommendations for a Global Counter-Terrorism Strategy*. Report of the UN Secretary-General. UN document A/60/825. New York: UN (April 26).

U.S. Department of State. Office of Counterterrorism. 2005. *Fact Sheet: Foreign Terrorist Organizations*. Washington: U.S. Government Printing Office (October).

———. 2006. *Patterns of Global Terrorism*. Washington: National Security Archives.

———. 2008. *Fact Sheet: Foreign Terrorist Organizations*. Washington: U.S. Government Printing Office (April).

U.S. Department of State. Office of the Spokesman. 2001. *Fact Sheet: Secretary of State Designates Foreign Terrorist Organizations*. Washington: U.S. Government Printing Office (October 5).

Watson Institute. Targeted Sanctions Project. 2006. *Strengthening Targeted Sanctions Through Fair and Clear Procedures*. White paper. Providence: Brown University (March 30).

Chapter 4

Immigration Policy as Counterterrorism: The Effects of Security on Migration and Border Control in the European Union

Gallya Lahav

Although the political aims of terrorism are government concessions that will further a cause (Friedland and Merari 1985; Long 1990), its psychological effects of fear and anxiety (Crenshaw 1986) often produce unintended consequences. Ironically, the jihadist terrorist charges against Western liberal societies provoked those societies to adopt counterterrorist policy responses that undermined some of their own most fundamental democratic norms. Nowhere is this more evident than with regard to the politics of immigration and immigrant control in Europe. Reverberating well beyond the borders of the United States, sweeping counterterrorist responses have extended to the politics of migration. The broad spectrum of policies that have emerged on national defense and homeland security in response to the horrific events of September 11 focuses not only on efforts to develop sensors to detect explosives and biological weapons of mass destruction (WMD) but also on policies toward foreigners, domestic insurgents, and travelers.

The role of foreigners and foreign networks in the 9/11 terror plots and, particularly, in those carried out in Madrid and London later stoked national security debates and sanctioned the use of immigration policy as a tool in counterterrorism. Acting with unprecedented speed, the European Council met in an extraordinary session on September 20–21, 2001, and adopted a detailed and ambitious plan of action to combat terrorism, based on a "coordinated and comprehensive approach."[1] The following day, the presidency convened a meeting with the ambassadors of the then-candidate countries. They agreed unanimously to align themselves with the action plan, adopting law enforcement and judicial measures for cooperation against terrorism (see alignment of candidate-countries with conclusions, European Council).[2]

Their American counterparts gave more teeth to the new strategy of comprehensiveness when top foreign officials outlined their visions for migration and border control. At a closed meeting of the European Union (EU) Strategic Committee on Immigration, Frontiers, and Asylum on October 26, 2001, the head of the American delegation told EU member-state representatives that, "since the events of 11 September 2001, the whole system of visas, border control, management of legal migration, *etc*, had come under close scrutiny." He expressed "a need for a more effective system across the board, not targeted specifically at terrorism but taking the events of 11 September as the trigger for developing a new approach." The U.S. official also enumerated a set of demands that the U.S. administration intended to impose on European governments and companies.[3]

The calls for international cooperation and coordination of police, law enforcement, and border controls underscored the ascendancy of migration regulation in the development of "a new and comprehensive" security framework. As demands for transatlantic cooperation in the "war on terror" and in law enforcement became paramount, the link between migration and counterterrorism gathered steam in a formal way. Against the backdrop of a growing intersection of migration and security, a key question emerged: how far could liberal states go in pursuing a comprehensive approach to migration that balanced national security and societal interests with individual protections of justice, freedom, civil liberties, and immigrant integration? This paradox has been most evident at the EU level, where member states are forced to balance national impulses of protectionism with communitarian demands for more cooperation.

The employment of migration policy as a tool in counterterrorism has brought many competing pressures and political conflicts to the surface, and it raises several practical questions. What are the effects of counterterrorism on immigration, border control, and policies of exclusion in a Europe of changing boundaries? Has the security-migration link fostered closer cooperation or nationalist protectionism among EU member states? To what degree has the framing of the migration issue as a security issue and migration policy as an instrument in counterterrorism opened up new opportunities for managing migration and overcoming constitutional guarantees and normative constraints (for example, civil liberties and democratic norms)? On balance, what can the comprehensive counterterrorism approach to migration tell us about European norms regarding the migration-security-rights trilemma?

This chapter examines the emerging role and implications of immigration policy as a tool of counterterrorism in the European Union. In exploring historical and empirical developments in the EU, the analysis identifies three broad trends related to the emergence and consolidation of a security-driven migration agenda in a Europe of changing borders. Broadly speaking, the "securitization" of migration, as it is often called, has had the effects of (1) Europeanizing migration policy (institutionalizing, formalizing, and accelerating policy links at the EU level); (2) shifting migration to the foreign policy arena and bolstering the EU as a foreign policy and security actor; and (3) politicizing migration-related issues. In challenging some core democratic values, the security-driven migration agenda has generated a politicization that might otherwise have been absent. To the degree that some cross-national and transatlantic convergence around these practices has emerged, the agenda masks important differences among national political actors. In the final section, I reflect on some cross-national trends in counterterrorism and migration in Europe and the United States to show that despite similar impulses to use migration as a tool in counterterrorism, there are important variations in the constraints and opportunities posed by counterterrorism approaches to migration.

Migration and Security in Europe

Theoretical Overview

The link between migration and security is not new. Security in its various forms has assumed various meanings across cultures and time. The traditional security agenda has been embedded in the notion of protection from external aggression, or national interests in foreign policy, and has thus been linked to state sovereignty and identity. The term, however, has been broadly attached to societal, personal, national, or more basic human security, including economic, physical, health, environmental, cultural, and political dimensions (see United Nations Development Programme 1994). A few scholars developed the link between international migration and security as early as the 1980s. Although Myron Weiner (1992, 1993) was the first political scientist to address the relationship between immigration and security issues, several scholars indirectly captured this linkage in their work on immigration and refugees in U.S. foreign policy (for example, Teitelbaum 1984; Zolberg 1995). Scholars of European politics broadened their security-migration focus to include demographics (Koslowski 2000, 2001; Weiner and Teitelbaum 2001), societal and cultural conflicts (Huysmans 1994; Heisler and Layton-Henry 1993; Lavenex 1999), and identity politics (Waever et al. 1993). Although the security ramifications of immigration have thus been evident for a long time, the broad counterterrorism agenda that has emerged more recently underscores the need to find consensus regarding the scope and definition of security as it relates to international migration.

As immigration-related issues have increasingly been linked to national security (Bigo 2001; Huysmans 2002; Rudolph 2006) and physical threat, the issue's salience on the international agenda has grown considerably. A marked increase in bilateral and multilateral activity on international migration, including two UN experts' coordination meetings, the launching of the independent Global Commission on International Migration, and a plethora of EU venues, have underscored the changing nature of migration. In the language of international relations, migration issues have shifted from the technical domain of "low politics" (for example, economic and social questions) to those related to security or "high politics" (for example, issues pertaining to political and national integrity and security).

The central role of foreign networks in terrorist attacks has not only catapulted migration to the foreign policy agenda but also notably politicized the issue in a new light. The consolidation of migration on the international agenda has shifted the predominant focus from "development" to "security."[4] The growing tendency to view international migration-related questions through a national security lens has not only found support in nationalist political circles but also generated political debates about democratic practices and norms.

How can democratic policymakers reconcile their liberal global market and rights-based norms with their political and security interests to protect their borders? This is the "migration-security-rights trilemma" (Lahav 2005). On the one hand, the realist pursuit of state sovereignty to protect citizens and national territory demands more protectionist approaches to border control and international mobility. On the other hand, the global economic imperatives of open markets for trade and tourism, coupled with societal interests in civil liberties, social cohesion, democratic values, and constitutional guarantees, promote liberal norms and practices. This chapter provides a perspective from which to examine EU policy responses to these cross-pressures as they relate to counterterrorism and migration.

Historical Overview

Ironically, in the contemporary era the "securitization of migration," as it is often called, emerged earlier in Europe than in the United States, and well before September 11, 2001. Immigration politics had already become politicized and "securitized" in the 1980s (and even earlier, in the 1960s, in some European countries) when it was linked to law-and-order concerns. European scholars (Pastore 1991; Bunyan 1991; Van Outrive 1990), like American scholars today, began to worry about evolving images of police states and the extent to which free societies were essentially turning into garrison states in order to survive terrorism (Etzioni 2004; Rosen 2001). Indeed, popular anxieties about immigration as a risk to physical safety and designs for more draconian border controls predated September 11 (Faist 2002, 7), and they coincided with the reemergence of anti-immigrant politics on the extreme right.

In Europe, this securitization process was rooted in the permanent settlement of large ethnically and culturally distinct ethnic minority populations within the major immigration-receiving countries (Alexseev 2005; Bigo 2001; Huysmans 1994, 2000; Weiner 1995). Although posing a minor threat before the 1980s, mass immigrant settlement had been mired in economic and cultural fears and seen as an "internal" danger to public order, cultural identity, societal security, and labor market stability (Huysmans 2000; Waever 1998; Heisler and Layton-Henry 1993). The two distinct, but inextricably linked, immigration policy frameworks—those related to immigration and admissions and those related to immigrant policies and integration (see Hammar 1985)—began to intersect in the 1980s.

The notion that immigration control includes both internal and external mechanisms was aggravated by the construction of the European Union, when the boundaries between internal and external threats fused (Bigo 2001, 121–22; Geddes 2001, 29–30). European integration compounded the challenges that immigration issues had long posed to states' exercise of sovereignty in terms of control over territory, identity, and citizenship. Coinciding with the construction and widening of the European Union and globalization, the reinvention of borders compelled Europeans to rethink questions of "us" versus "them" (Lahav 2004a).

The political situation with migration changed dramatically by the end of the century and reached a definitive turning point in the post–Cold War era. On the global agenda, the shift from socioeconomic or development concerns to "new security" issues such as terrorism, ethnic conflict, and migration occurred at about the same time that the Iron Curtain fell and the Cold War ended. The earth-shattering terrorist infiltration of September 11, reinforced by the Madrid and London bombings, gave further prominence to the linkages between immigration, crime, and security that had previously been only implicit in European societies (see Bigo 2001). The linkage between organized crime, terrorism, and Islamic fundamentalism obscured the distinction between internal and external security (Lavenex 2005; on the externalization of migration, see Boswell 2003). Notably, since then, the talk of "invasion, insecurity, and foreign terrorists" has begun to reflect an electorate that identifies immigration as a threat, not just a serious problem (Marie 2004; Council of the European Union 2004).

The growing tendency toward restrictive and protectionist migration policies across Europe stems less from demographic changes than from the reactions of policymakers and populaces to migration in the context of changing borders (Lahav 2004a). Indeed, in the absence of a great influx of new migration, the rush to control migration seemed initially puzzling in a Europe that was built on the principle of free movement, depended on global mobility (Marie 2004, 11), and faced the demographic crisis of an aging population and falling birth rates (see Fargues 2005). Although the proportion between EU and non-EU (that is, Third World, nonwhite, non-Christian) foreigners has been skewed toward the latter group, this "problem area" has barely changed over the last twenty years (see table 4.1).[5] The data reveal relatively minor new migration flows, an indication of a very low level of mobility within the EU (in high contrast to the United States, where 6 percent of the population is reported to move out of the country every year). In fact, it is estimated that only 2 percent of EU citizens live and work in an EU country outside their country of origin—a situation of great concern to European policymakers. This limited mobility and failure to promote a real European labor market even prompted the European Commission to dedicate 2006 to the "Year of Workers' Mobility" and to initiate the European Mobility Bus tour. The policy goals of promoting the free movement of peoples conflict, however, with an interest in limiting the mobility of select foreigners, terrorists, drug smugglers, and so forth. Clearly, the framing of migration in a security context skews these priorities and reorganizes the migration-security-rights equation.

TABLE 4.1 Foreign Populations in EU Countries, 1996 to 2002

Country	Total Population (in thousands)	Number of Foreigners (in thousands)	Percentage of Foreigners/ Total Population	Percentage of EU Foreigners/ Total Population	Percentage of Non-EU Foreigners/ Total Population	Number of Muslims (in thousands)[a]
Austria	8,040	728.2	9.0%	—	—	300
Belgium	10,143	910	9.0	5.5%	3.6%	370
Denmark	5,251	223	4.3	.9	3.3	150
Finland	5,117	69	1.4	.4	1.0	20
France[b]	56,577	3,597	6.4	2.4	4.0	4,000–5,000
Germany	81,817	7,173	8.8	2.2	6.6	3,040
Greece	10,465	155	1.5	.4	1.0	370
Ireland	3,626	117	3.2	2.0[e]	1.2[e]	n.a.
Italy[c]	54,780	1,095.6	2.0	.2[e]	1.8[e]	700
Luxembourg[d]	419	142.8	34.1	27.3[e]	6.8[e]	38
Netherlands	15,494	726	4.7	1.2	3.5	696
Portugal	9,921	169	1.7	.4	1.3	15
Spain	39,742	499	1.3	.6	.7	300–400
Sweden	8,837	531	6.0	2.0	4.0	250–300
United Kingdom	56,652	1,992	3.4	1.4	2.0	1,406

Source: Eurostat 1999 (reporting on 1997 figures, unless noted otherwise); Systeme d'Observation Permanente sur les Migrations (SOPEMI; Organisation for Economic Co-operation and Development [OECD] 1992, 1999).

Note: OECD and Eurostat data are derived from population registers of foreigners, except for France (census), Portugal and Spain (residence permits), and Ireland and the United Kingdom (Labor Force Survey). Figures do not equal 100 percent total owing to the differences in reports.

a. Marechal (2002), cited in Buijs and Rath (2002).

b. OECD 1992 (reporting 1990 figures).

c. OECD 1999 (reporting 1996 figures).

d. Eurostat 1999 (reporting 1996 figures).

e. Eurostat 1994 (reporting 1992 figures).

The buildup of migration controls despite the liberalization of borders with respect to other global economic factors (see Lahav 2004a) underscores not only "the unintended effects of incomplete integration" (Geddes 2002, 196) but also the "externalities of EU migration policy"(Lavenex and Uçarer 2002, 4). That is, the growing interdependence between migration and other policy domains, from foreign affairs to welfare policy, means that migration outcomes are mediated by developments in other policy areas. As this study suggests, the impact of "new security" threats and counterterrorism on migration control in Europe is formidable. It is mediated by other constraints such as human rights, market interests, and welfare concerns. The following section examines the longitudinal policy and institutional developments that are related to migration in context of counterterrorism.

An Empirical Analysis of Counterterrorism and Migration Policy Cooperation in the EU

Although to many observers the post-9/11 initiatives appeared to be knee-jerk reactions to American pressures, the counterterrorism policy reactions of EU member states were already well developed and part and parcel of the European integration process. Security questions, which have loomed large in European politics in response to the changing borders of the European Union, have been caught in the institutional conflicts between proponents of intergovernmental (state-centric) versus supranational decisionmaking. Although many such policies have been particularly sensitive to national impulses, the momentum toward European integration has increased the demand for EU competence in areas such as migration (Geddes 2000; Lahav 2004a).

The September 11 watershed events provided international legitimacy for the institutionalization of measures that were already on the EU agenda but had not yielded to shared competence. As this section reveals, three of the most notable changes in migration control stemming from its linkage to security and counterterrorism in Europe have been the rapid acceleration of cooperative initiatives at the EU level, the strengthening of proponents of regional integration, and a rapid institutionalization and Europeanization of migration. These trends are manifest in policy and institutional developments at the EU level.

Policy Developments

The political polarization surrounding the securitization of migration issues was already evident prior to 9/11. It needs to be understood in terms of broader domestic and EU security concerns about the changing geopolitical landscape, concerns that were spurred by European integration. Issues of immigration and immigrant integration were directly linked to debates over the proposed EU Constitutional Treaty, the EU's recent and future enlargement, and the "war on terror." Many of those who voted "no" in the French referendum on the Constitutional Treaty, for example, were reportedly motivated by fears that the constitution and EU enlargement threatened to allow in new immigrants. Although many were fearful that immigrants would steal native jobs or undermine the welfare system, others feared that immigration could provide an entry route for terrorists. These types of concerns coincided with the rise of populism. Although not limited to extreme right parties, the threats were politically manipulated by extreme right anti-immigration parties, which in some European countries reemerged with considerable success (see table 4.2).

Domestic concerns about European integration were clearly responsible for the acceleration of migration initiatives at the EU level. Before the 2001 terrorist attacks—at the Tampere European Council of 1999, for example—EU leaders agreed to develop balanced common policies, but the 2002 Seville summit focused almost exclusively on fighting illegal migration. This change was due as much to the rise of xenophobic populist parties in Europe as to concerns about the "war on terror." As a result, immigration and asylum became high priorities for member-state governments, which entrusted the European Commission with launching a large number of initiatives in the area.[6]

Enlargement negotiations were also tied to migration concerns, and heightened security on external EU borders had a significant impact on the ten applicant states (now member states). However, this change was in the direction that the EU was already going (see Koslowski 2005; Migration News Sheet [MNS] 2001). Thus, before 9/11 candidate states were given a grace period after access to comply with current member states' internal security and border control capacities, whereas after September 11 the grace period was terminated.

To a large degree, the September 11 attacks merely provided the necessary political impetus for European policymakers to address some of these long-standing concerns (Gilmore 2003, 11). Central to the European response to the catastrophic events of 9/11 was the seemingly hasty decision of the EU ministers of interior and justice, set in motion by the September meetings, to adopt a series of law enforcement and judicial measures designed to facilitate cooperation against terrorism, both within Europe and with the United States. Many of these proposals were under

TABLE 4.2 The Extreme Right in Select European and EU Countries, 1998 to 2003

Country/Extreme Right Electoral Organization	Electoral Results and Year	Number of Seats	Prominent Leader
Austria			
Freedom Party (FPO)	27.7% of 1999 general election vote; 10.2% of 2002 vote	52 seats in the 183-seat parliament; junior partner in government coalition	Jörg Haider
Belgium			
Flemish Vlaams Bloc (VB)	11.6% of 2003 general election vote	18 seats in the Chamber of Representatives (total: 150)	Frank Vanhecke
Front National (FN)	2% of 2003 general election vote	1 seat in the Senate (total: 40)	Daniel Feret
Denmark			
Danish People's Party (DPP)	12% of 2001 general election vote	22 seats in the parliament	Pia Kjaersgaard
France[a]			
Front National (FN)	12.45% of 2002 vote in legislative election; 19.2% of 2002 vote in presidential election	No national seats	Jean Marie Le Pen
Germany			
Republikaner (REP)	Less than 2% of 2002 federal election vote	No national seats	Rolf Schlierer

(*Table continues on p. 140.*)

TABLE 4.2 *(Continued)*

Country/Extreme Right Electoral Organization	Electoral Results and Year	Number of Seats	Prominent Leader
Italy			
National Alliance (AN)	12.0% of 2001 general election vote	No national seats	Gianfranco Fini
Northern League (NL)	3.9% of 2001 general election vote	31 seats in 630-member Chamber of Deputies and 16 senators in 315-seat upper house	Umberto Bossi
Netherlands			
Centrumdemocraten (CD)	1% of 1998 general election vote	No national seats	Mat Herben Hans Janmaat
List Pim Fortuyn (LPF)	17% of 2002 general election vote; 5.7% of 2003 general election vote	26 seats in the 150 seat parliament; 8 seats in 2003	Harry Wijnschenk
Norway			
Progress Party (FRP)	14.6% of 2001 general election vote	26 seats in 165-seat national parliament	Carl Hagen
Portugal			
Popular Party (PP)	8.75% of 2002 general election vote	14 seats in 230-seat parliament	Paulo Portas

Spain			
Independent Liberal Group (GIL)	No national representation	No national seats	Jesus Gil
Sweden			
Sweden Democrats (SD)	1.43% of 2002 general election vote	No national seats; 50 municipal councillors	Mikael Jansson
Switzerland			
Swiss People's Party (SVP)	26.6% of 2003 general election vote	63 seats in 200-member House of Representatives; 2 seats in Senate; 2 members of 7-seat cabinet	Ueli Maurer, Christopher Blocher, leading spokesmen
United Kingdom			
British National Party (BNP)	11.4% of May 2002 *local* election vote	21 councillors	Nick Griffin

Source: Institute of Race Relations (IRR), "The Extreme Right in Local and Central Government," available at: www.irr.org.uk/Europe (last updated October 2004); data provided by the IRR unless otherwise noted.

a. Extreme Right Electorates and Party Success (EREPS) Research Group, "Electoral Results of Extreme Right Parties in Western Europe," available at: http://www.politk.uni-mainz.de/ereps.

consideration well before the so-called turning point, however, as part of the border transformations prompted by European integration. The EU had long been seriously debating measures to streamline law enforcement and judicial cooperation among the member states, with the aim of fighting terrorism, human trafficking, and the smuggling of illegal drugs and humans. As discussed later in the chapter, these measures became more politically palatable in the aftermath of 9/11. Thus, as explicitly stated, the strategy formulated by the Justice and Home Affairs (JHA) Council on September 20–21 was "to harness all the measures already adopted at the EU level" and "to speed up the process of creating an area of freedom, security and justice."[7]

Despite the proliferation of initiatives after September 2001, it is important to underscore that when the extraordinary meeting of the European Council convened that September, it was *not* addressing a new issue. Rather, its discussions took place in the context of more than a quarter century of engagement with the complex and multidimensional problems of terrorism. Already in the 1970s, the issues of terrorism and migration were institutionally linked. European Communities (EC) ministers of the JHA Council came together in Rome in 1975 and created TREVI "in the wake of continued indigenous and Middle Eastern terrorism" as an intergovernmental network of national justice and interior ministers. Under the auspices of European political cooperation (EPC; the name of EU foreign policy coordination), TREVI was established as an intergovernmental committee outside the EC framework and was intended as a forum to coordinate an effective response to international terrorism (Anderson et al. 1995). With the enactment of the Maastricht Treaty, the subject was subsumed within the Third Pillar (intergovernmental branch) of the EU.

One of the newer and most controversial projects launched by the Amsterdam Treaty in 1997 was the creation of an area of freedom, security, and justice (AFSJ).[8] The institutional aim was to disperse these issues across the EU's supranational First Pillar (concerned with visa and asylum policy and related matters pertaining to the movement of persons) and intergovernmental Third Pillar (covering police and judicial cooperation) in order to provide a coherent program for EU action on asylum, immigration, and police and judicial cooperation in civil, family, and criminal matters. The Treaty of Amsterdam also formally incorporated the Schengen Convention into acquis communitaire (community law), paving the way for the extension of EU membership and the fortification of implementation strategies (for example, shared national data banks, fingerprinting, joint deportation agreements, and so forth).[9] Although not prominent on the JHA agenda, terrorism continued to be an active subject of policy debate—a fact well illustrated by the adoption in the European Parliament (EP) on September 5, 2001, of a resolution on the role of the EU in combating terrorism—six days *prior* to the catastrophic events of the time.

The new atmosphere of urgency following 9/11 prompted the physical and operational implementation of measures that until then had remained controversial and slow. The quick introduction of the much-debated and long-stalled European arrest warrant to replace extradition between member states (an initiative with roots in the Tampere European Council of October 1999) and the adoption of a common definition of terrorism—both controversial issues that had been under examination for approximately two years—were vivid examples.

In the rush, the September meetings of European heads of state and government led to the uneasy approval of a series of these long-contested measures, such as a common definition of terrorism, a common arrest warrant, the strengthening of police cooperation (including the creation of an antiterrorist unit at Europol), guidelines for common sentencing of terrorists, enhancement of air-transport security, measures to address financial fraud and money laundering as sources of terrorist financing, and the further development of the EU's "Common Foreign and Security Policy" and "European Security and Defense Policy."

Amid much political wrangling and criticism during 2002 and 2003, the EU worked to adopt many of these measures. These included judicial procedures and sentencing guidelines for terrorist cases; the creation of a new institution, Eurojust, to help coordinate judicial cooperation in the area; mutual recognition of procedures for freezing assets in criminal cases; the establishment of joint investigation teams; and inclusions of antiterrorism provisions in agreements with third countries. In December 2003, the EU approved its first "Security Strategy," with terrorism identified as the first of several "key threats" to Europe that required a serious foreign policy response.[10]

These intensive cooperative initiatives had long been stalled because of diverse objections regarding human rights; dispersed resources; misleading links between terrorism, organized crime, and illegal migration; risks of scapegoating; loss of social cohesion; and the risk of perversely promoting clandestine organizations (Bigo and Guild 2005). Special concerns in terms of migrants and asylum-seekers were human rights and the principle of non-refoulement (the nonreturn of refugees to places where their lives would be in danger), as well as arbitrary detention.

Human rights groups were concerned that the European Commission "Proposal for a Council Framework Decision to Combat Terrorism of

September 19, 2001," provided a definition of terrorism that could be used against legal dissent. The concerns raised about the proposed European arrest warrant were its nonconformity with international fair-trial standards and apparent promotion of arbitrary action or abuse.[11] Arbitrary detention proposals also raised the hackles of human rights advocates. Some EU member states proposed that persons suspected of acts of terrorism who could not be returned to their own countries or to a different country, owing to article 3 concerns of the European Convention on Human Rights, should be indefinitely detained as national security threats and released only when they no longer posed such a risk or at such time when a third country agreed to accept them and protect them from article 3 violations. Human Rights Watch protested that this would contravene article 5 of the European Convention on Human Rights, which guarantees liberty and security of persons and enshrines the prohibition against arbitrary detention.

The terrorist attacks in Madrid on March 11, 2004, and in London on July 7, 2005, added fuel to the level of urgency in the EU's counterterrorism agenda for migration and further bolstered proponents of supranational cooperation. Capitalizing on the momentum toward European cooperation, the EU adopted a contentious package of restrictive proposals in the "Official Declaration on Combating Terrorism" on March 25, 2004. European leaders also identified new areas for further development of EU counterterrorism efforts, including foreign policy actions, border controls, facilities and transport protection, and cooperation with third countries and multilateral institutions (see Aaron et al. 2004, 6). The most visible innovation of the updated antiterrorism package was the appointment in March 2004 of a counterterrorism coordinator in charge of coordinating all relevant activities within the Council of the EU, monitoring their implementation (under the authority of the secretary general of the Council, Javier Solana), and maintaining "an overview of all the instruments at the Union's disposal in the fight against terrorism."[12]

The adoption of the Hague Program in November 2004, following the completion of the five-year Tampere Program, went further to produce the first set of legally binding, EU-level agreements on asylum, immigration, and terrorism.[13] Setting a new five-year course to strengthen the area of freedom, security, and justice within the EU member states, the Hague Program effectively represents the EU's agenda for the development of migration and asylum policies. Notably, the program also delegates more policymaking authority to European institutions. While previously only the JHA Council had the power to decide, the bodies now responsible for these issue areas include the European Commission, the JHA Council—

including twenty-seven ministers responsible for immigration in each member state—and the European Parliament.[14]

Since migration is more closely tied to security, institutional momentum clearly leans toward cooperation and shared EU competence. Activities related to freedom, security, and justice are increasingly shared by national and EU jurisdictions. With the creation of an AFSJ in the 1997 Amsterdam Treaty, these issues were carefully distributed across the First and Third Pillars of the EU. Thus, the relationship between national sovereignty and EU competence entered a new phase as sensitive questions, such as asylum and policing, shifted from exclusively national competence to common legally binding EU law and policy.

Institutional Developments

Institutionally, the proliferation of cooperative policy initiatives launched after the introduction of the Third Pillar with the Maastricht Treaty of 1992 and its development in the Amsterdam Treaty of 1997 are testament to the soaring weight of the "freedom, security, and justice" area (see Walker 2004). Since 1999, justice and home affairs (JHA) has been the fastest-growing policy area in the EU. This remarkable expansion includes the adoption of well over two hundred legislative measures, involving nearly forty bodies, and the proliferation of meetings from four times per year to every month. The secretariat of the European Council itself reportedly dedicates roughly 40 percent of its meetings and workload directly or indirectly to matters related to AFSJ (Monar 2005).

JHA has come to constitute one of the largest areas of attention on the EU agenda (Uçarer 2003). Freedom, security, and justice policies have witnessed an almost threefold increase in spending earmarked for them—from around 0.5 percent in 2006 to around 1.3 percent in 2013, as foreseen in the 2007–2013 "Financial Framework for the EU" adopted in April 2005 by the College of Commissioners.[15] Although the JHA remains the smallest budget compared to those areas that still dominate the traditional European Communities policies, such as sustainable development, economic competitiveness, and social cohesion (Liberatore 2005, 21), its relative growth and substantive impact are considerable.

According to legal experts in the field, these developments represent some of the most revolutionary changes since the launching of the single-market program (Monar 2005; Walker 2001–2002). Although this claim may seem exaggerated to some, there is no doubt that these developments are dramatic in the sense that the JHA Council has moved the EU on a massive scale into areas that had for decades remained an exclusive preserve of national sovereignty. In addition, as the 2004 Hague Program embarked on its five-year mission, the JHA Council was increasingly sharing competence with the other European institutions, such as the European Commission and the European Parliament.

As an in-depth analysis of causal antecedence reveals, many of these controversial proposals were already on the table, but they were fast-tracked and institutionalized at the EU level after 2001. This trend was especially apparent in the cooperation between security and intelligence agencies and police services (including the reactivation of Europol's counterterrorism task force, which had become largely obsolete as a result of limited input by national authorities). From September 29 to October 8, 2001, the EU quickly unleashed "Operation High Impact": more than 10,000 police officers from fifteen member states and the ten candidate countries apprehended 1,350 illegal migrants and thirty-four migrant smugglers over the ten days (see Koslowski 2005, 5).

The search for counterterrorist solutions to migration has prompted a flurry of cooperative activity on police and security matters and a proliferation of new actors at the national, regional, and transatlantic levels. This expanding migration playing field includes a complex web of actors and institutions, such as the police, intelligence services, military professionals, private security agencies, airline and travel agents, diplomats, bureaucrats, and policymakers at the local and international levels. Several regional, bilateral, and multilateral arrangements between member states for information-sharing and operational cooperation have also emerged (for example, cooperation at the French-German border zone and Anglo-French police cooperation around the Channel Tunnel). In an attempt to control illegal migration across Europe's southern borders following the 2002 Seville meeting, for example, "Operation Ulysses" was deployed among five EU countries (Spain, Britain, France, Italy, and Portugal) to coordinate police, customs, and navy ships. This represented the first time EU members formally coordinated their efforts in this way; according to Spain's interior minister, Ángel Acebes, the operation was envisioned as a precursor to a common European border police force (see Emma Daly, "Anti-Migration Patrols Start in Mediterranean," *New York Times*, January 29, 2003).

From 2001 to 2004, cooperation between the United States and the European Union also grew as U.S. and European agencies and institutions that had never worked together before—and in some cases had not even existed—began to coordinate their efforts. For example, in September 2002, Attorney General John Ashcroft became the first U.S. attorney general to meet formally with his EU counterparts, the ministers of interior and justice (the JHA Council). Another notable development was the establishment of the "Policy Dialogue on Border and Transport Security" in April 2004, which brought together relevant officials from the U.S. Department of Homeland Security, Department of State, and Department of Justice and representatives from the European Commission, the Council of Ministers, and the EU presidency to discuss ways of improving security. In September 2004, U.S. Secretary of Homeland Security Tom Ridge met with European Commissioner António Vitorino and representatives of the EU presidency and continued the dialogues.

Under the Third Pillar, professional policy and criminal justice networks across and beyond Europe have flourished. The extension and thickening of these networks has included the advent of the Operational Task Force of European Chief Police Officers, a body that since September 11, 2001, has been accorded responsibility for the coordination of counterterrorist efforts within the EU; twinning arrangements between member-state police forces and those in accession states; and the launch of the European Police College (Statewatch 2001). In addition, as part of the Second Pillar, the "European Defense and Security Policy for Crisis Management and Intervention" was adopted at the European level to include a rapid reaction force encompassing a combination of military and police personnel for peacekeeping and other functions. Other initiatives have been taken to facilitate the building of an effective network of national judicial authorities and procedures and the harmonization of judicial policy and practice across a wide range of cross-border crimes, including terrorism.

The EU has made great efforts to revitalize institutions, such as the Police Chiefs Task Force and Europol, that build on the momentum toward further integration in the area of law enforcement (Aaron et al. 2004, 17). Eurojust was institutionalized after Tampere, and since 2000 the European Public Prosecutors' Office was set up. Europol (created under the terms of the 1992 Maastricht Treaty, it had an early life as a drugs unit) had become fully operational in 1999. Europol was entrusted with developing more comprehensive information-sharing among member-state police departments, including a database of criminal investigations. Its field of formal legal competence now reaches beyond drugs to encompass illegal immigration, trafficking in humans, stolen vehicle trafficking, money laundering, currency forgery (with special reference to the euro), terrorism, and the smuggling of nuclear materials. In this way, the practice of policing, long considered a constitutive element of the legal and political sovereignty of modern states, has been unhitched from the nation-state and resituated within networks of actors operating across national frontiers. Not surprisingly, the ratification of Europol's capacity to coordinate the "exchange of information and intelligence" through EU-wide networks of liaison officers was met with enormous resistance by the national law enforcement agencies of some member states (European Drug Unit [EDU]/Europol 1997; Bigo 2000).

This expansion of the EU migration regulatory field has given rise not only to international but also to national conflicts between government departments (Bigo and Guild 2005). In some cases, an "escape to Europe" approach has served to strengthen particular government actors who aim for better leverage in domestic politics (also known as the "autonomy-seeking behavior of JHA officials"; see Guiraudon 2003). In general, European ministers of justice and interior have tried to impose security imperatives while foreign affairs and finance ministers, as well as judges, support the primacy of global diplomacy and respect for rights. As the focus on EU border control shifted from systematically checking documents at borders to profiling and identifying threats emanating from foreign countries, the role of national ministries for foreign affairs and diplomatic and consular authorities has become more central (see Bigo and Guild 2005, 213, 240).[16] Although these institutions are often divided within their own countries, where they vie for legitimacy and resources, the pressure is to have more collaboration (Bigo 2001), often as leverage for more national control (Guiraudon 2000; Guiraudon and Lahav 2000).

The Europeanization of migration reflects the expansion and complexity of the migratory regulatory playing field. The counterterrorism agenda has strengthened security actors and promoted the role of supranational actors, such as the EU, foreign states, and nonstate, private actors, in the regulation of migration. It has also generated some new political conflicts and reinvented political alignments (see Lahav 2000, 2004b).

Migration as a Foreign Policy Issue

The use of migration as a tool in counterterrorism has not only strengthened the forces seeking to communitarize more policy areas and deepen European integration but also raised the profile of the EU as a foreign policy and security actor. The framing of migration as counterterrorist strategy has coincided with the strengthening of EU institutions and the formal involvement of the EU in foreign policy.

Interestingly, in the immediate aftermath of 9/11, the EU appeared relatively slow to act as a security actor. In the days after the horrific attacks, the EU took a back seat to NATO and the national capitals in orchestrating a foreign policy position. The tremendous transatlantic embrace in the aftermath of 9/11 seemed to attenuate foreign policy tensions that had been brewing between Europe and the United States (over issues such as the Kyoto Protocol on global warming, the International Criminal Court, and a comprehensive nuclear test ban treaty; see Walker 2001–2002). On September 12, NATO invoked article 5 (the common defense clause) for the first time in its history (Aaron et al. 2004, 1), and Europeans scheduled the urgent intra-EU meeting in September (described earlier) to renew discussions. Deferring counterterrorism initiatives to national actors, the EU was preoccupied with the institutional issues surrounding the introduction of the single euro currency by January 1, 2002, and with its new round of enlargements (Walker 2001–2002).

Although terrorism was a salient issue in European public opinion, it competed with other important issues, such as enlargement of the EU, the euro, and the constitution (Commission of the European Communities 2001–2005). Moreover, while Europeans were most preoccupied with the issues of enlargement and constitution-building, their focus on terrorism was mired in concerns over immigration.[17] The sense of European involvement in counterterrorism was heightened after 9/11 investigators learned that many of the hijackers had spent considerable time in Europe, especially in Germany and Britain (see Commission on Terrorist Attacks upon the United States 2004). The unprecedented terrorist events of September 11 on American soil, plotted among global Islamic cells largely operating in Europe, gave credence to the global links between security and human mobility. By November 2001, European public opinion polls revealed overwhelming support—an EU member-state average of 88 percent—for delegating the fight against terrorism to EU authorities in some form or other (either exclusively or with national authority).[18] In the context of shifting geopolitics and political alignments, member states slowly delegated more power to the EU to act as a foreign policy actor in coordinating "secure" and comprehensive migration and border policies that would meet counterterrorist goals. The growth of the EU as a foreign policy and security actor, sanctioned by counterterrorism, legitimized the EU's security role in migration regulation.

Two of the most substantial changes in migration control stemming from these security and counterterrorism concerns were the increasing shift of migration to the foreign policy arena and the incorporation of third states and foreign actors into processes of externalization (Boswell 2003; Lavenex 2005), delegation (Guiraudon and Lahav 2000, 2006), and devolution

(Lahav 1998). These developments represented efforts to push migration and border controls out (for example, to third states and nonstate actors) in an expanding migration playing field. They mirrored developments in the United States, where the Department of Homeland Security espoused the principle that the security of American citizens could only be assured by taking measures well outside its frontiers, not simply at border crossings (Bigo and Guild 2005, 221). These initiatives have created new institutional conflicts and political turf wars. To this end, DHS has tried to challenge the monopoly over foreign relations exercised by the Departments of State and Defense (Bigo and Guild 2005).

The reframing of the European security agenda in an altered geopolitical context of enlargement revived a foreign policy frame that put a premium on third-state cooperation. Specifically, the geopolitics of enlargement in Europe (linked to concerns about constitution-building, terrorism, and migration) revived foreign policy frames and approaches toward former non-EU eastern countries. The enlistment of these states in the externalization of migration control was strongly motivated by the fall of the Iron Curtain to the east. According to Sandra Lavenex (2005), the end of the Cold War and the relationship of the Central Eastern European Countries (CEEC) to the EU were major motors behind the securitized migration policy agenda. These countries' geographic positions on major transit routes for migrants and asylum-seekers heading toward Europe prompted member states to include them in an emerging system of migration control.

Although these processes were inspired by the fall of the Iron Curtain, they have since been propelled by the interdependence within and vulnerability toward the EU's new neighborhood. With the changing external borders of the European Union after enlargement, cooperation with Mediterranean third countries was revisited (Cassarino 2005). The new European neighborhood policy (ENP), created by the Wider European Initiative launched in 2003, widened the number of actors, especially third countries, in border and migration management.[19] The June 2003 Thessaloniki European Council fully reflected these priorities when it emphasized "the importance of developing an evaluation mechanism to monitor relations with third countries who do not cooperate with the EU in combating illegal migration."[20] The negotiations aimed to further implement economic and political reforms and to promote cooperation in the fields of justice and home affairs—particularly on border controls, legal and illegal migration, police cooperation, and the fight against human trafficking. They facilitated the conclusion of readmission agreements, the coordination of the external borders of EU member states, the formal establishment of immigration liaison officers' networks in third countries, and the implementation of effective return policies with third countries.

The "new" neighborhood policies illustrate the desire to reframe the patterns of partnerships already existing in the Euro-Mediterranean partnerships (EMPs), a concern already raised by the end of the Cold War. For example, the Barcelona Declaration of 1995 for European-Mediterranean cooperation and the ensuing process (which came after the fall of the Berlin Wall) were explicitly designed to tackle security issues at a time when Europeans were starting to worry about emerging Mediterranean threats. Such concern for "soft and hard" security (economic and social development; and political unrest and military proliferation) prompted cooperation in order to stem future security threats. The ENP attempted to go further in institutionalizing these efforts by offering credible incentives.[21] According to Jean-Pierre Cassarino (2005, 3), this growing externalization of EU migration and asylum policy has been conducive to the emergence of unprecedented forms of interconnectedness between the EU and Mediterranean non-EU countries, even turning some of them into strategic partners (especially Morocco and Tunisia). Similarly, the Neptune Project in January 2004 aimed to strengthen controls at the maritime borders of the EU in the Mediterranean through joint border patrols and operations against illegal migration and human trafficking.[22] But such cooperation had in fact existed before: in the 1990s, most of the signatory states had participated in consultative meetings on migration management, organized on an intergovernmental basis.

These types of policy initiatives reflect the implementation of previous blueprints in a new public climate of "high politics" and counterterrorism. They captured not only the prominence of asylum and migration issues in the EU's external relations with third countries but also the EU's desire to broaden the comprehensiveness of its approach to migration and asylum by extending its borders outward and shifting responsibilities onto third parties. To reinforce the monitoring of migration flows in third countries and facilitate cooperation between member states, the February 19 European Council adopted regulation 377/2004 on the creation of a network of immigration liaison officers (ILOs). The regulation defines the tasks of immigration liaison officers abroad in terms of the collection of both operational and strategic information to be used either in the fight against illegal immigration or in the management of legal immigration. It also enables liaison officers to build local or regional cooperation networks with each other, with the aim of information exchange. The ILOs, who are normally posted to national consular authorities, may also share tasks and guard the interests of other member states that are not represented in the respective host country. The provisions of this regulation were based on the previous experience of member states in fostering cooperation between ILOs posted in third countries (for example, the Belgian-led ILO network in the Balkans). The creation of the ILO network can be regarded as a small step toward a common external security arm of the EU's immigration policy.

The management of EU external borders has been high on the Council's agenda, and the EU has institutionalized such cooperation over time. On October 26, 2004, member states reached final agreement on Council regulation (EC) 2007/2004 establishing the European Agency for the Management of Operational Cooperation at the External Borders (FRONTEX). The agency, which came into operation in October 2005, is mainly funded from the EC budget. It has been vested with considerable operational powers that go distinctly beyond those of other agencies in the JHA (for example, Europol and Eurojust). Given the substantial functions and powers of such an agency, member states have retained tight control over its activities through a management board, which consists of one representative from each member state (and two representatives from the European Commission). Although the agency does not constitute a "European border guard" as such, it does represent a coordinating command structure. Through its specialized branches, the agency has a direct reach into national border guard forces that could at a later stage considerably facilitate the buildup of European border guard structures.[23] According to experts, this new border management agency is an important step toward a more integrated and institutionalized management of external borders (Monar 2005, 137).

The EU Constitutional Treaty, if ultimately adopted, envisions the foreign policy and security dimension of external relations as more visible and central. This is reflected in the double-hat figure of a Union minister of foreign affairs and external relations commissioner, and the expected reform of the EU external service to be comparable with other giants of EU external relations, namely trade (Liberatore 2005).

Clearly, the role of foreign policy actors in migration regulation has been incrementally bolstered by counterterrorism objectives in a changing European landscape. As some migration observers note, compared to the tedious decisionmaking processes in areas of internal policy harmonization (for example, on the admission of third-country nationals), the evolution of cooperation on immigration control and the greater involvement of sending and transit countries have been remarkable (Lavenex

1999, 8). By identifying the inherent role of asylum and migration in international relations, the EU acknowledged that the credibility and effectiveness of its common asylum and migration policy was dependent on the participation of origin and transit countries in the joint management of migration flows. The EU was also boosting the profile of the "security" dimension of JHA and AFSJ over the "freedom" and "justice" areas related to rights. Given the centrality of JHA issues, this framework of third-country cooperation (for example, ENP) in migration management could not but be predominantly security-oriented, at least in the short term.

Indeed, the growing inability of states to manage immigration unilaterally and effectively—while responding adequately to growing public insecurity—has led to greater bilateral and multilateral efforts to restrict the flow of persons across national borders (Levy 2005; Messina and Thouez 2002). To consider counterterrorism an opportunity rather than a constraint on EU regulatory power corroborates the rare but practical view that states may act more effectively by delegating authority to supranational actors such as the EU (Lahav 1998, 2004a; Guiraudon and Lahav 2000) or by externalizing migration to foreign actors in order to negotiate the migration-security-rights trilemma (and more protectionist migration norms).

Given the expansion of the EU apparatus, such as the JHA, and the growing perception by domestic constituencies of immigration as a threat emanating from the international environment, what is interesting is not that immigration issues have yielded to cooperation, but that they have converged around protectionist norms (Lahav 2004a). Paradoxically, the increasing push for border cooperation came less from counterterrorist pressures after 9/11 than from national fears of relinquishing internal borders. Some observers even argue that the widening or externalization of the EU migration regime has been tied to its internal deepening and may even stem from integration "spillover" dynamics (Lavenex 2005, 6). The development of the SIS (Schengen Information System), SIRENE (Supplementary Information Request at the National Entries), EURODAC (an electronic database), and VIS (Visa Information System) points to the coincidence of increasing securitization of external borders with the abolition of internal borders. The development of the relationship between the EU and third-state actors in meeting counterterrorism national goals thus captures a global era that is marked by intense pressures for collaboration and cooperation and offers new possibilities for migration regulation.

The proliferation and diversification of counterterrorist instruments used to control migration involves tighter border controls, increased visa requirements, readmission agreements, carrier sanctions, buffer zones, EURODAC fingerprinting and SIS databases, "safe third countries," and accelerated return procedures and coordination (see Lahav 2004a). All of these initiatives fundamentally rely on EU cooperation as well as coordination with and incorporation of third states, nonstates, and private actors who provide services, resources, technology, and nonpublic practices that have otherwise been unavailable to central government officials (Gilboy 1997, 1998; Lahav 2000, 2003). The logic often involves a political desire to control movement *and* actors willing and able to play on the links between migration, crime, and security (see Guiraudon and Lahav 2000). Since these actors have the economic, social, technological, and political resources to facilitate or curtail immigration and return, they provide states with different sites and tools to fight terrorism and control migration at the source. They also provide liberal states with the political means to circumvent intense political debate and the most-liberal rights constraints.

In pressing neighboring or transit countries, like Ukraine or Libya (which were already challenged in this area), to take responsibility for migration, for example, the EU could be seen as compromising certain democratic norms. The case of Ukraine reveals the ways in which many neighboring countries are limited in their ability to fulfill basic obligations, such as proper access to asylum, adequate conditions of detention, and protection from return to torture or persecution. As long as neighboring countries like Ukraine pursue close ties with the EU, the latter can put pressure on them to detain, host, and accept the return of ever-greater numbers of migrants.

The EU has also proposed to offer development aid and humanitarian assistance to increase the ability of such countries outside the EU to host refugees from the region through the European Commission's Regional Protection Program. Opponents have criticized this initiative as merely another way to deny access to asylum in the EU. Another controversial proposal made by Germany and Italy during the October 2004 G-5 meeting in Florence was to create centers in North Africa to process asylum-seekers' claims en route to the EU. Unsurprisingly, this proposal was vehemently rejected by human rights groups and governments in North Africa.

Although the most controversial dimension of the EU externalization agenda—processing asylum-seekers outside the EU—has been shelved, the EU remains committed to "outsourcing" both control of migration and determination of asylum. New components now include: the refusal of entry into EU territory of asylum-seekers who come from countries designated as "safe countries of origin" and the refusal of transit through such countries; the interdiction at sea of persons attempting to reach EU territory; the conclusion of readmission agreements with countries outside the EU; and extended support to border enforcement and detention capacity in neighboring transit countries.

As these policy developments indicate, the EU is paradigmatic of how a counterterrorism framework can broadly reframe the migration equation—namely, away from rights and liberties. The increasing momentum toward externalization by engaging countries of migrant origin and transit reflects a foreign policy frame that emphasizes the control and security aspects of migration over open borders for markets and liberal rights (Lavenex 2005, 1). As this institutional analysis suggests, these trends reflect the fact that the impulse to shift responsibility and incorporate new actors in border and migration control is oriented toward the compromise of liberal rights norms.

The Politicization of Migration: The Politics of the Migration-Security-Rights Trilemma

The incorporation of migration as a tool in counterterrorism not only reframed the migration-security-rights equation but also politicized previously technical issues. One of the broad effects of counterterrorism was to place migration-related issues on the EU public and political agendas in a way that inflamed ideological and national sensibilities about liberal norms, civil liberties, human rights, international mobility, and democratic practices more broadly. What were predominantly bureaucratic and technocratic issues became subject to normative debates seen in electoral campaigns and party contestation, emerging international conflicts, growing judicial and constitutional activity, and increasing public support for protectionist political forces and actors.

The case of biometrics identification is a notable example of the impact of counterterrorism on the politicization of migration. Biometrics was first applied in the Schengen Agreement of 1985, when the issue of border control became a European issue rather than an exclusively national one. The idea reemerged following the Dublin Convention on Asylum of June 1990, when the ministers responsible for immigration agreed on a European Community-wide system to compare the fingerprints of asylum-seekers (in 1991) in efforts to avoid asylum-shopping. Following the entry into force of the Amsterdam Treaty, the idea of the EURODAC system was expanded, and biometrics was applied not only to asylum-seekers but also to persons who crossed an external frontier of the EU in an irregular manner. The European Council in Laeken (December 2001) and Seville (June 2002), in adopting the common Visa Information System (VIS), further agreed to include biometric identifiers to prevent "visa-shopping" and improve the administration of the common visa policy in order to contribute to internal security and to fight terrorism.[24] In September 2003, the Commission proposed to put biometrics in the visas and residence permits of third-country nationals.[25] These proposals reversed the previous order by putting biometric identifiers of facial images first and fingerprints second.

The story behind the evolution of biometrics reveals that these tools of law enforcement were used in specific national contexts well before 9/11, but were universally incorporated afterward by EU legislation. Prior to September 2001, for example, biometrics was used for access to education and commercial buildings and in the health sector with electronic patient records, but not with passports or national identity cards. After 9/11, biometrics in the travel documents of EU citizens was introduced as a result of some external pressures by the United States, but mostly by internal pressures in the EU.[26] That is, the consistency argument made at the Council in Thessaloniki in 2003—that similar requirements should apply to all travel documents issued by EU member states—exposed the pressures of counterterrorism on European integration and national cooperation. Moreover, with the new emphasis on security in the EU, issues as traditionally technocratic and depoliticized as biometrics entered the public debate as parliaments, advocacy organizations, the media, and authoritative experts (not only in biometrics but also in the legal, social, and constitutional aspects of its implementation and its implications) participated in the discourse (Liberatore 2005, 17). Biometrics not only became politicized but also emerged as a subpolicy in itself with its own policy community—consisting of objectives and applications that cut across various policy issues (from migration to terrorism) and fields (for example, justice and home affairs, internal markets, and external relations).

The salience of biometrics in the media and on the political agenda after September 11 reflected concerns about the character of surveillance systems and their impact on civil liberties. The issues under debate included: the purpose and actual use of the data stored, as well as their amount, type, and quality; the range of reporting authorities and of authorities that have access to data, with related accountability aspects; the right to information of the individuals whose information is stored; and possible impacts on fundamental rights. These concerns were heightened after the attacks in Madrid on March 11, 2004, when intense debate took place over VIS—specifically, the storage of biometric data and the necessity of having the same data stored in two systems, SIS Accord II and VIS, plus EURODAC.[27]

The prevalence of a security-driven migration agenda on the EU level has created some notable political conflicts and national divergences regarding the order of migration-security-rights priorities. The use of migration policy to combat terrorism has generated political discourse over issues such as civil rights, human mobility, privacy, human rights, and open borders. The proliferation of the new actors and instruments used for migration and border control in the context of counterterrorism also triggered market fears and EU concerns about uneven practices for mobility and citizenship.

For example, it is telling that one of the most notable sources of tension in transatlantic cooperation against terrorism was the introduction of biometric passports, visa requirements, and the passenger name record (PNR) requirement. In addition to the polarization over biometrics, compliance with the US-VISIT program (that is, the U.S. requirement that all visa entrants have a biometric passport) proved highly problematic when the United States extended its requirements to include those previously on the visa waiver program, thus creating disparate rights for EU citizens.[28] Applied to airline passengers, the PNR requirement represented the desire to enhance screening and make transport more secure, but it triggered fundamental sensibilities regarding competence, privacy, and law enforcement procedures. By meeting demands to supply passenger information to the United States, European carriers allegedly put themselves in violation of the EU's privacy directive, which maintains strict controls over how private companies may store and share information on individual customers. European companies thus faced either fines in the United States (and possible prohibition of entry) or fines in European courts of law. Furthermore, it was argued that these types of counterterrorist measures could affect the competitiveness of the businesses and commercial facilities that used them.[29]

These conflicts reflect the cross-pressures between rights, markets, and security. In exposing substantial ideological and national variations, the disputes have politicized and polarized actors, both in the EU and outside it. These issues, like other counterterrorism-related issues, have drawn criticism from those concerned with the human rights dimension of the migration-security-rights trilemma (see Lahav 2005). Lack of policy transparency, restricted information flows, accountability, and migrant protection are examples of such concerns. The outsourcing of important regulatory functions was contested, for example, because it could compromise the human rights of migrants, asylum-seekers, and refugees.[30] These efforts to shift responsibility for migration to countries beyond the EU and to other non-democratically accountable actors were predictably criticized by those fearful of intrusions on rights.

Democratic shortcomings also include the marginal role of national legislatures and the European Parliament, the non-accountability of Eurojust to the European Court of Justice (ECJ), and the concealment of police cooperation from the public. The suspension of legal norms in light of the war against terrorism incrementally reverses the institutional hierarchies of democratic political systems in favor of executive branches (Liberatore 2005, 2). Clearly, the promotion of the EU as a foreign policy actor in migration has coincided with the institutional dominance of the security-oriented JHA. Within the EU, the intergovernmental JHA ministries (strong actors in any national executive) play the most visible role (Liberatore 2005, 17). The Council and the Commission are also the external relations ministers responsible for economic competition. To foster the competitiveness of the information technology (IT) sector in the context of EU-U.S. relations, for example, these institutions have played an important role in pushing for issues such as biometrics. Despite the expansion of the regulatory playing field, an institutional security network has gained the upper hand over the due process of law and powerful bureaucracies have emerged with their own corporate agendas. Often shielded from scrutiny for operational reasons, these agendas elude parliamentary oversight. To a large degree, the activity of the migration security regime is driven by bargaining among networks of bureaucrats and professional elites seemingly disconnected from publics.

Ironically, the retreat from liberal norms in these modes of regulatory practices is sanctioned by diffuse public opinion, and it reflects converging public and elite attitudes (Lahav 2004a, 2004b). As public opinion in the EU corroborates, under conditions of threat the movement of people takes second place to border security. This is not surprising. Social psychologists and behavioral political scientists have provided ample evidence that threat increases in-group solidarity, ethnocentrism, and xenophobia (LeVine and Campbell 1971; Seago 1947; Huddy et al. 2002; Tajfel and Turner 1979; Brown 1995). Threat promotes intolerance and willingness to forgo basic civil liberties, personal freedoms, and minority rights in exchange for a greater sense of security from immigration, terrorism, and globalization (Huddy et al. 2003, 2005; Davis and Silver 2004; Gibson 1996, 1998; Sniderman et al. 1996). Threat leads to closed-mindedness (Rokeach 1960). Policy developments across the board confirm the psychological effects triggered by the link between migration and security. For example, countries that have experienced attacks by foreign terrorists are those most likely to impose new border restrictions (see the case of Israel in Bartram 1998, 303–25).

Notably, the European public became increasingly ready to grant greater powers to law enforcement when deadly attacks killed more than three hundred people after November 2003 in Turkey, Spain, and Britain (*Concord Online Monitor,* January 23, 2005). More surprisingly, these rights trade-offs did not produce a noticeable surge in populist movements. In fact, in some of the European countries where the anti-immigrant extreme right movements were most prevalent in the aftermath of 9/11—the Netherlands, Spain, and Austria—extreme right party support has dropped precipitously. It is possible that the horrific terrorist attacks moderated reactionary sentiments by introducing them to the mainstream political agenda. Mainstream parties—many of which stole the thunder away from radical groups after the initial peak of the latter in 2001—also embraced these issues. The counterterrorist offensive after September 11 not only triggered xenophobia and "Islamophobia" but also had a contagion effect on public anxieties more generally. It spawned anti-Semitism (among Europeans and immigrant populations) and violence against Muslims and people who appeared to belong to Muslim groups, such as Sikhs.[31] Diffuse anti-immigrant sentiment was provoked against ethnic minorities, asylum-seekers, and unskilled labor (both legal and illegal) from eastern Europe.[32] Reframing the discourse from "immigrants" to "threats" seemed to broaden and widen xenophobic attitudes (Chebel d'Appollonia 2008, 220).

The proliferation of new actors and the rapid institutionalization of counterterrorist policy responses into a more restrictive migration regime may have thereby displaced the marginal fringe groups that long fought the immigrant menace. As migration experts have noted, if security is linked to migration, we may expect more limited debate on democratic values or civil liberties and ultimately depoliticization (Liberatore 2005, 2). By incorporating migration into the counterterrorism agenda, liberal states may be able to skew and defuse political debate, mobilize hostile anti-immigrant public opinion, diffuse the costs of security, and overcome liberal constitutional constraints. More importantly, these regulatory strategies enable the EU to neutralize the contradictions between open borders for goods, capital, and services and limited borders for the movement of people. Liberal democracies have been able to deploy draconian policy instruments that are legitimized by widespread public opinion, thereby reconciling the migration trilemma.

The emphasis on the surveillance of movement since 9/11 has substantially reversed the order of priorities of free movement and travel over security within the context of the area of freedom, security, and justice. The Amsterdam Treaty's creation of an AFSJ under a loose singular body reflected serious efforts to institutionalize a comprehensive approach to migration cooperation by including all aspects of immigration and integration policies. These efforts had some success in shifting migrant integration from national to EU jurisdiction (Geddes and Guiraudon 2004), which ultimately produced the Racial Equality Directive and the Employment Equality Directive.[33] However, the consolidation of the three principles (security, justice, freedom) into a comprehensive approach to security, in terms of both border control and human security (see footnote 7), has resulted in downplaying the importance of protecting vulnerable members of the community. Effective implementation of the equality directives has been difficult owing to exceptions for public safety and order, burden-of-proof provisions, and discrimination against ethnic minorities not listed in the directives (Chebel d'Appollonia 2008, 218–19).

Traditionally in liberal democracies, the right of free movement and travel takes priority and security concerns are the exception. Recently, in many but not all European countries, these priorities have been reversed, which partially accounts for the growing politicization of the issue. As Didier Bigo and Elspeth Guild (2005, 223) conclude, the EU has opened opportunities for more controls in the name of freedom. The EU level has moved to incorporate measures to fight terrorism (such as defining it) into Union law, but has simultaneously deferred to the national level on questions of civil liberties in the form of rights. These areas are subject to differing legal regimes governing privacy and personal data protection. Moreover, procedural rules relating to criminals have shifted into immigration policies.

One irony of the migration-security link is that many control and surveillance techniques, such as the census and civil registration developed to grant civil rights, have become means for states to gain more information about and control over their citizens. Whereas the abolition of borders has been the mantra of "frontier-free Europe," today's EU has witnessed the reappearance of passports or national identification cards as prerequisites for air travel and in many cases for internal travel. There are also proposals to introduce a new medical history record on chips for EU health cards and to integrate national identification cards, driver's licenses, and health cards into one single biometric identifier (*Eurozine*, November 23, 2005). As the recent debate over national identity cards in the United States and over driver's licenses in New York State illustrate, these issues may become politicized precisely because they trigger concerns over civil liberties and freedoms, such as racial and ethnic profiling. The security-driven migration agenda thus introduces to the public discourse issues traditionally relegated to the technical and administrative domains.

Immigration Policy as Counterterrorism in Comparative Perspective

It is important that any effort to build theoretical models to explain the effects of counterterrorism on broad policy areas, such as immigration, consider the enormous heterogeneity in counterterrorist responses that stem from diverse political contexts and cultures, national exigencies, and issue framing. The tendency to downplay differences with regard to security threats overlooks the different policy contexts, actors, and goals involved in counterterrorism. Differences in geopolitical positions and domestic contexts are extremely important to understanding the politicization of migration and the contentious foreign policy issues that remain between diverse actors and transatlantic allies.

Despite the salience of terrorism on the world stage, its link to migration policies varies dramatically. For example, in the United States counterterrorism and migration controls have radically changed, but in Europe ongoing legislative and policy trends have been enhanced so as to establish more activist integration policies. These differences reflect divergent formulations and conceptualizations of the migration-security-rights equation. Considerable convergence exists among liberal democracies around the migration-security-rights trilemma, but the order of priorities reveals slight but critical differences. Even when policy responses are similar, underlying motives, priorities, and objectives may diverge. A comparative analysis of U.S. and EU counterterrorist reactions helps explicate nuances of the migration-counterterrorism link.

First and most broadly, substantial differences derive from historical experiences with terrorism on European soil. On the one hand, intimate familiarity with terrorism has made European leaders particularly sensitive and vigilant about the fight against terrorism. On the other hand, European solutions have been based on more long-term considerations and have thus appeared to treat terrorism more moderately and "softly" compared to the "hard" military responses embraced by the United States. Tempered by their own national experiences with terrorism, Europeans identify terrorism as first and foremost a crime. Thus, counterterrorist responses related to migration control focus on a combination of law enforcement techniques, crime-fighting procedures, judicial instruments, political negotiations, and fairly limited military action. European long-term strategies to balance strict protective measures with efforts to address the socioeconomic roots of such violence reflect a fundamental conviction that terrorist eradication is unlikely (Aaron et al.

2004, vii). These approaches have been criticized as insensitive to the new urgency.

Second, these divergent approaches have strengthened different policy actors. Indeed, one of the most substantial differences between the policy environment in the United States and that in the EU is in orientation toward building cooperation in law enforcement and judicial matters. Within this context, illegal immigration is perhaps as much a law enforcement priority as it is part of the counterterrorism trajectory. The move to consolidate Europol and Eurojust as key institutions in the construction of pan-European law and judicial communities epitomizes this strategy. Nonetheless, in contrast to the United States, EU efforts have been less about giving law enforcement and judicial authorities *new* powers than about enhancing cooperation across EU member-state boundaries. Of course, this effort has been complicated by the accession of the twelve new members, all of which were obligated to adopt new counterterrorism legislation and many of which have had to construct new border controls (Aaron et al. 2004, 7).

Third, these divergent counterterrorist approaches and issue framings (that is, war versus crime) inherently reflect positions on civil liberties and privacy. The military logic of the "war on terror" has led to a greater propensity to suspend normal rules in the name of national security. Thus, while the detentions of foreign combatants and others at Guantánamo Bay are justified as a wartime necessity by the United States, Europeans broadly interpret the practice as a symbol of the U.S. sense of urgency generating extreme results (Aaron et al. 2004, 12). Furthermore, distinctions between intelligence material and information admissible in a criminal court are different in military tribunals and civil courts. Broad differences in civil liberties perspectives and political culture have also sanctioned diverse policing and surveillance practices concerning individual privacy. These differences are significant obstacles to cooperation.

Fourth, while migration policy was linked to security in the United States as a secondary tool in counterterrorism (outranked by the "war on terror"), its salience in European counterterrorist strategy reflects critical differences in migration concerns and management. Reinforcing their law enforcement proclivities, European countries adopted "a strategy of policing foreigners rather than an immigration policy" (Council of the European Union 2004, 41). In contrast to the American emphasis on strict control of entries, Europeans adopted counterterrorism policing strategies that focus on internal control (Marie 2004, 26). These strategies include increased identity checks, more stringent conditions for issuing residence and work permits, new automated systems for registration of foreigners, closer monitoring of foreigner accommodations, limited rights of appeal, the broadening of categories of potential deportees, and tougher penalties for assisting illegal migration and employing foreigners.

Thus, despite the appearance of migration in the foreign policy arena, immigration control in Europe has focused more on internal control of migrants than protecting external borders.[34] As one member of European Parliament (MEP) interviewed in 2004 emphatically explained, "The issue of immigration is really an issue of integration" (author interviews cited in Lahav and Messina 2005, 870). EU cooperation and the securitization of migration have focused more on issues of controlling and incorporating Muslims inside the territory than border control per se. Over time, the linkage between organized crime, terrorism, and Islamic fundamentalism has made the ongoing flow of migrants, not territorial borders, the object of control (Gammeltoft-Hansen 2006).

These differences stem from different migration histories and nation-state identities. Cultural homogeneity has been a prominent feature of European nations over the centuries, but Americans have been keenly wedded to the historical myth of the melting pot and religious pluralism (van Selm 2005). Europeans are late to acknowledge the unintended consequences of labor migration—the emergence of multicultural societies and religious pluralism (Klausen 2005; Lahav 2009). Leaving aside the indigenous Muslim communities in the Balkans and other eastern and southeastern European countries, the bulk of Muslims arrived in Europe for labor beginning in the 1950s (Buijs and Rath 2002). While many national governments have been forced to deal with the socioeconomic issues of integration, others are sensitive to the tensions that antiterrorism measures may create among large Muslim communities (see table 4.1) and also to the effects of growing support for extreme right parties (see table 4.2).

The role of religion in state politics illuminates further differences. Active participation in organized religion among Americans is strong, and in the United States there is acceptance of expressions of faith, including the expectation that the roughly 1 percent of Americans who are Muslims will practice their religion in various ways. Although Europe has remained culturally attached to its Christian roots, it has generally become more secular in recent decades; in this context the head scarf issue, for example, recently became a political crisis of integration in France. Although participation in religious services is slowly rising again in many European countries, it remains low. Many Europeans equate Islam with Muslim fundamentalists (Lahav 2009), and "the simple fact of practicing a religion at all puts a person outside the mainstream" (van Selm 2005, 2). Roughly 4.5 percent of the

EU population is Muslim, with France having the largest Muslim minority at nearly 5 million (8.5 percent of the population). The practice of religion is higher in this group than among Europeans more broadly (van Selm 2005).

These preoccupations with immigrant policies and minority integration may explain why EU policymaking related to migration and security accelerated after 2004 rather than after September 11, 2001. The murder of Dutch filmmaker Theo van Gogh by an Islamic extremist on November 2, 2004, shocked everyone who subsequently learned that his murderer was actually born and raised in the Netherlands (despite holding dual Dutch and Moroccan nationality). The Madrid train bombings on March 11, 2004, and the July 7, 2005, bombings of the London Underground and a London bus also encouraged the perception that Islam was a threat to the European social and political system. At the same time, these attacks induced governments and politicians to search for integration solutions by reconsidering how Islam might become a "European religion" (see Klausen 2006, 2). In this vein, though French president Jacques Chirac enjoyed overwhelming political victory in the National Assembly for his proposed law prohibiting Muslim head scarves in schools, ironically one of his sole opponents was the National Front's anti-immigrant leader Jean-Marie Le Pen, who feared parallel restrictions on Christians (Klausen 2006, 1).

Given the diverse preoccupations with different dimensions of the immigration equation (that is, immigration in the United States versus immigrant integration in Europe), it is logical that Muslims have been perceived as internal risks in Europe rather than, as in the United States, external risks linked to international relations. In the post-9/11 order, these different risk perceptions led the United States to emphasize border control, while Europe focused on integration and internal control. This orientation in Europe was abetted by the "zero migration" rhetoric already in place in most European countries. The fear of an "internal threat" was fed by migration trends that suggested that the social integration of migrants would soon become a top domestic priority for European states—a fear that reemerged as a burning topic with the 2005 riots in France. The fear of further alienating and radicalizing the ethnic minorities and immigrant communities in their midst prompted the EU to seek partnerships across Euromed, the western Balkans, and the Asia-Europe Meeting (ASEM) and to seek cooperation with Algeria and Morocco as well (Cassarino 2005, 5).[35] The proliferation of initiatives (including a plethora of expert groups under the Sixth and Seventh EU Research Frameworks in 2006 and 2007, respectively) studying radicalization in the Mediterranean region highlights the geographic vulnerabilities of European countries and blurs the lines between internal and external security.

Comparative analysis of European and American approaches to migration-security linkages underscores the diverse motivations, constraints, and opportunities posed by a counterterrorism approach to migration. The comparison also reminds us that the transferability of policy tools is conditioned by national contexts. Even when states are on parallel tracks and adopt similar instruments, important differences remain.

CONCLUSION

The framing of migration as a security issue and migration policy as an instrument in counterterrorism has opened up new opportunities for managing migration in Europe. Although the migration issue had been securitized in Europe since the 1980s (and in some cases since the 1960s), when immigration became linked to law-and-order concerns, the migration-security link gathered steam in a formal way on the foreign policy agenda as EU institutions became more involved with counterterrorism.

Concerns about counterterrorism gave traction to the preexisting but glacially slow-moving Europeanization of migration policies. Since 9/11, and particularly after the terrorist attacks in Europe in 2004 and 2005, momentum toward European policymaking accelerated. The migration-security link was institutionalized, implemented, and politicized. As this analysis reveals, the incorporation of immigration policy as part of a broad counterterrorist strategy has had the political effect of strengthening intra-EU cooperation on security and migration matters.

The growth of EU institutions (for example, JHA), linked to a diverse web of nonstate actors and foreign states in an expanding migration regulatory field, has coincided with a notable retreat from core liberal values, such as democratic accountability, transparency, due process of law, privacy, and international mobility. As EU policy developments and public opinion norms confirm, under conditions of threat the movement of people and the protection of other civil liberties take second place to border security. The prevalence of a security-driven migration agenda has reframed the debate over civil liberties, international human rights, and democratic governance.

Indeed, the expansion and diversity of stakeholders in migration control (in some cases agencies that never worked together before) have created political tensions with implications for liberal and democratic norms. The circumvention of democratic values and liberal norms has generated a politicization that might otherwise have been absent. Infringements on these norms has politicized previously technical issues and reframed broad political alignments. Transatlantic conflicts over issues of PNR and biometric passports, for example, illustrate the cross-pressures between rights, markets, and security and reveal different national priorities when security logic is pitted against market or rights interests.

Despite their parallel tracks, European responses to counterterrorism and European interest alignments have been fairly distinct from those of their American counterparts. In the United States, the migration-security link has predominantly focused on border control and external relations, while in Europe the use of migration as counterterrorism has been tied to concerns about migration as an internal security issue. Policy is bound to domestic issues involving anti-immigration parties, the place in society of ethnic communities, and migrant integration. The American preoccupation with external threats has been more likely to produce suspensions of rights and norms. The distinction between the two broad categories of migration policy may also explain why the EU has succeeded in cooperation related to law and antiterrorism initiatives of border control, while simultaneously deferring to national competences on questions of civil liberties, human rights, and integration policies.

The prevailing preoccupation with integration-related security concerns is reflected in institutional and attitudinal norms. For example, the U.S. model lacks a federal integration policy other than for resettled refugees, but in Europe, with its strongly entrenched welfare states, legal or even in some cases illegal residents are never excluded from the full range of nationally available welfare benefits such as schooling, health care, and income support (see van Selm 2005). This constraint reinforces the importance and the challenge of migrant integration for European policymakers.

Across the board, liberal democracies have responded to the new security world by pursuing a balanced and comprehensive approach to migration control, but their solutions for the migration-security-rights equation reveal important cross-national variations. Although to a large degree policy tools seem to be converging, important differences stem from diverse migration histories and orientations toward that equation. The impact of counterterrorism is most pronounced in domestic political contexts and thus merits consideration in the analysis of divergent counterterrorist responses.

This chapter thus urges both a broad view of counterterrorism efforts and a nuanced view of security as applied to migration and border control practices and norms. The distinctive European approach to counterterrorism, especially as it relates to migration policy, has two important implications. First, the European approach is indicative of long-term ideological and national limitations to cooperation on counterterrorism in relation to migration. Second, differences between Europe and the United States reveal important variations in the conceptualization of the migration-security-rights equation and approaches to migration as a tool of counterterrorism.

Notes

1. This coordinated and interdisciplinary approach emphasized the following themes: "enhancing police and judicial cooperation, developing international legal instruments, ending the funding of terrorism, strengthening air security, prioritizing cooperation with the U.S., and coordinating EU's global action"; see Council of the European Union, "Conclusion and Plan of Action of the Extraordinary European Council Meeting on September 21, 2001," Council of the European Union document (GMT 2001, 33, p. 1).
2. See the Extraordinary Brussels European Council external (September 23, 2001), "Belgian Presidency, Alignment of the Candidate counters with the Conclusions of the European Council." On October 4, the European Parliament adopted a highly supportive resolution; see ibid. See also Belgian EU presidency, "Conclusions and Plan of Action of the Extraordinary European Council Meeting on September 21, 2001," press release (September 22, 2001).
3. See Council of the European Union, "Outcome of Proceedings of the Strategic Committee on Immigration, Frontiers, and Asylum Meeting with the United States Dated October 26, 2001," Council of the European Union document 13803/01 ASIM 21 USA 24 (Brussels, November 12, 2001).
4. The genesis of international initiatives prior to the "High-Level Dialogue on International Migration and Development," held in September 2006 and sponsored by the UN system, may be traced to the 1994 International Conference on Population and Development (ICPD) in Cairo, where migration emerged at the forefront of international policy circles as a demographic and socioeconomic concern (Thouez and Rosengärtner 2007).
5. The available official data prior to the addition of the ten new countries indicated that out of a population of roughly 330 million, approximately 19 million non-nationals lived legally in one of fifteen EU member states (Council of the European Union 2004). Fewer than one-third (30 percent, or 6 million) were citizens of EU member states, meaning that the majority of foreigners were third-country nationals (TCNs), mostly comprising Third World, nonwhite, non-Christian populations considered the "problem area."
6. For example, following the 2002 Seville meeting, "Operation Ulysses" was deployed among five EU countries (Spain, Britain, France, Italy, and Portugal) to coordinate police, customs, and navy ships in an attempt to control illegal migration across Europe's southern borders.
7. See Council of the European Union, "Conclusions Adopted by the Council (JHA)," Council of the European Union document 12156/01 (2001, 1).

8. According to Amsterdam Treaty provisions, "the Union's objective is to provide citizens with a high level of safety within an area of freedom, security and justice by developing common action among the member-states in the field of police, judicial cooperation and criminal matters and by preventing and combating racism and xenophobia."
9. By May 2005, some Schengen countries (for example, Belgium, Germany, Spain, France, Luxembourg, the Netherlands, and Austria) had signed the Schengen III agreement for closer cooperation in fighting terrorism and crime. This convention called for shared national data banks to store DNA information, fingerprints, and vehicle identification; armed security escorts on planes; measures to fight illegal migration; the establishment of immigration liaison officers to advise countries on new information in the fields of migration and fraud documents; and joint expulsions and actions on the repatriation of illegal migrants.
10. See Council of the European Union, "A Secure Europe in a Better World" (December 12, 2003).
11. The former was a particular concern after a survey of cases brought before the European Court of Human Rights (ECtHR) from the last decade indicated that fair-trial standards were often violated in a number of EU member states and in most of the forty-three Council of the EU member states governed by the ECtHR, including many EU accession countries; see Statewatch (2001).
12. The first counterterrorism coordinator was Gijs de Vries, former president of the Liberal Group in the European Parliament and former Dutch deputy minister of interior.
13. See Council of the European Union, "Declaration on Combating Terrorism" (March 25, 2004). The Hague Program prescribes for the freedom, security, and justice area on the following issues: immigration, terrorism, fundamental rights, access to justice, accordance with the Geneva Convention on Refugees, regulation of migration flows, control of the external borders of the EU, the fight against organized cross-border crime, the threat of terrorism, Europol, and Eurojust.
14. The European Commission drafts and issues proposals and submits them to the JHA Council and European Parliament, which together have decision-making power.
15. See European Commission, "Financial Framework for the EU" (2005); see also Vandermosten (2006) and European Commission (2004a).
16. This is also evident in the United States, as exemplified by Department of Homeland Security (DHS) encroachment on foreign relations.
17. Notably, fighting terrorism and illegal migration have ranked neck and neck among public preoccupations (see Commission of the European Communities 2001–2005).

18. This figure derives from a short flash survey on the "International Crisis," conducted by the European Commission, November 13–23, 2001 (*Eurobarometer*, 114).
19. These came out of the June 2002 Seville European Council, presented in May 2003 as the "road-map"; see Council of the European Union, "Road-Map for the Follow-up to the Conclusions of the European Council in Seville," 6023/04/0 (Brussels, May 5, 2003).
20. See European Commission to the Council and the European Parliament, "Wider Europe—Neighborhood: A New Framework for Relations with Our Eastern and Southern Neighbors," (COM 2004) 104 Final (Brussels, March 11, 2003).
21. See Euro-Mediterranean Conference of Ministers of Foreign Affairs, "Presidency Conclusions" (December 2–3, 2003).
22. Introduced by the Italian interior minister Giuseppe Pisanu during the 2003 Italian presidency of the EU, the Neptune Project has been backed by Cyprus, France, Germany, Greece, Malta, the United Kingdom, the Netherlands, Spain, and Europol. A joint center of surveillance was established in Palermo with a view to preventing and acting quickly against illegal migration and human trafficking in the Mediterranean.
23. This may be one reason why the United Kingdom and Ireland do not participate in the agency.
24. In a European Commission feasibility study on VIS presented to the Council in May 2003, VIS was expected to connect at least twenty-seven member states, twelve thousand VIS users, and thirty-five hundred consular posts worldwide (European Commission 2004b; see Council of the EU, "Decision Establishing the Visa Information," 9559104 (May 25).
25. See European Commission, "Biometric Identifiers for Visa and Residence Permits for Third-Country Nationals" (2003, 8).
26. Prior to 9/11, visitors from countries listed in the U.S. Visa Waiver Program (including most EU countries) did not need a visa to enter the United States. In 2002 the U.S. Congress passed the Enhanced Border Security and Visa Entry Reform Act, according to which such visitors need a visa unless they have biometric passports.
27. See European Commission (2004b).
28. Of the fifteen EU member states (prior to May 2004), all but Greece are in the visa waiver program; among the new countries, only Slovenia is a participant.
29. The Container Security Initiative (CSI), like the PNR system, which focuses on human mobility, raised concerns about the international mobility of goods. The CSI announced by the U.S. Customs Service in January 2002 (which later became part of the DHS) authorized containers that had been prescreened at foreign ports to have priority in unloading at U.S. ports. The objection voiced by the European Commission was that ports participating in CSI would have an unfair competitive advantage over other ports, thereby distorting trade and running counter to the EU single-market rationale. The

Commission further reproached the United States for its intergovernmental maneuvering, arguing that since customs was a long-established area of EU competence, the member states had no authority to negotiate such deals individually (Aaron et al. 2004, 9).

30. See Human Rights Education Associates, "EU: Outsourcing Migration Control Puts Human Rights at Risk" (October 17, 2006), available at: http://www.hrea.org (accessed November 12, 2007).
31. See European Union Monitoring Centre on Racism and Xenophobia (EUMC), "Manifestations of Anti-Semitism in the EU" (2002–2003); see also Pastore (2005, 12) and van Selm (2005).
32. See EUMC, "Attitudes Towards Minority Groups in the European Union Member States" (2003); see also EUMC, *Annual Report on Racism and Xenophobia in the EU Member States* (2005).
33. Article 13 of the 1997 Amsterdam Treaty granted the European Community new powers to combat discrimination on the grounds of sex, racial or ethnic origin, religion or belief, disability, age, and sexual orientation. The Racial Equality Directive (2000/43/EC) implements the principle of equal treatment between individuals irrespective of racial or ethnic origin, and the Employment Equality Directive (2000/78/EC) establishes a general framework for equal treatment in employment and occupation.
34. It is noteworthy that despite the post-9/11 climate and conventional wisdom about the securitization of migration, immigration issues have not seemed to be more linked to security and foreign policy in the minds of European parliamentarians over time (see Lahav and Messina 2005). Longitudinal surveys of members of the European Parliament (MEPs) attitudes toward immigration (conducted 1994 to 2004) revealed that even when MEPs were concerned about security, there were significant and consistent variations in the cultural meaning it held for them. In the 1993–94 study, for example, French MEPs tended to link immigration to insecurity and crime, while Greek MEPs associated immigration with security in terms of Turkey (Lahav 1995, 107).
35. The Euro-Mediterranean Partnership, also known as Euromed, was relaunched in 2008 as the Union for the Mediterranean. It includes all of the EU states, and sixteen countries of the Mediterranean and the Middle East.

References

Aaron, David, Ann Beauchesne, Frances Burwell, C. Richard Nelson, K. Jack Riley, and Brian Zimmer, eds. 2004. "The Post-9/11 Partnership: Transatlantic Cooperation Against Terrorism." Policy paper. Zurich: Atlantic Council (December).

Alexseev, Mikhail. 2005. *Immigration Phobia and the Security Dilemma: Russia, Europe, and the United States.* New York: Cambridge University Press.

Anderson, Malcolm, Monica den Boer, Peter Cullen, William Gilmore, Charles Raab, and Neil Walker. 1995. *Policing the EU.* Oxford: Clarendon Press.

Bartram, David. 1998. "Foreign Workers in Israel: History and Theory." *International Migration Review* 32(2): 304–25.

Bigo, Didier. 2000. "When Two Become One: Internal and External Securitizations in Europe." In *International Relations Theory and the Politics of European Integration*, edited by Morten Kelstrup and Michael Williams. London: Routledge.

———. 2001. "Migration and Security." In *Controlling a New Migration World*, edited by Virginie Guiraudon and Christian Joppke. London: Routledge.

Bigo, Didier, and Elspeth Guild. 2005. "Policing at a Distance: Schengen Visa Policies." In *Controlling Frontiers: Free Movement into and Within Europe*, edited by Didier Bigo and Elspeth Build. London: Ashgate.

Boswell, Christina. 2003. "The 'External Dimension' of the EU Immigration and Asylum Policy." *International Affairs* 79(3): 619–38.

Brown, Rupert. 1995. *Prejudice: Its Social Psychology*. Oxford: Blackwell.

Buijs, Frank, and Jan Rath. 2002. "Muslims in Europe: The State of Research." Paper prepared for the Russell Sage Foundation. New York (October).

Bunyan, Tony. 1991. "Towards an Authoritarian European State." *Race and Class* 32(3): 179–88.

Cassarino, Jean-Pierre. 2005. "Migration and Border Management in the Euro-Mediterranean Area: Heading Towards New Forms of Interconnectedness." In *Mediterranean Yearbook 2005*. Barcelona: European Institute of the Mediterranean (IEMed) and Fundació CIDOB.

Chebel d'Appollonia, Ariane. 2008. "Immigration, Security, and Integration in the European Union." In *Immigration, Integration, and Security: America and Europe in Comparative Perspective*, edited by Ariane Chebel d'Appollonia and Simon Reich. Pittsburgh: Pittsburgh University Press.

Commission of the European Communities. 2001–2005. *Eurobarometer: Public Opinion in the European Community*, nos. 45–50. Brussels: Commission of the European Communities.

Commission on Terrorist Attacks upon the United States. 2004. *The 9/11 Commission Report: Final Report of the National Commission on Terrorist Attacks upon the United States*. New York: W. W. Norton.

Council of the European Union. 2004. *Preventing Illegal Immigration: Juggling Economic Imperatives, Political Risks, and Individual Rights*, edited by Claude-Valentin Marie. Brussels: Council of the European Union.

Crenshaw, Martha. 1986. "The Psychology of Political Terrorism." In *Political Psychology*, edited by Margaret Harmann. New York: Jossey-Bass.

Davis, Darren, and Brian Silver. 2004. "Civil Liberties vs. Security: Public Opinion in the Context of the Terrorist Attacks on America." *American Journal of Political Science* 48(January): 28–46.

Etzioni, Amitai. 2004. *How Patriotic Is the Patriot Act? Freedom Versus Security in the Age of Terrorism*. New York: Routledge.

European Commission. 2004a. "Building Our Common Future: Policy Challenges and Budgetary Means of the Enlarged European Union, 2007–2013." European Commission Communication (2004) 101 Final (February 10).

———. 2004b. Justice and Home Affairs, Data Protection Working Party. "Opinion 9/2004 on a Draft Framework Decision on the Storage of Data, Data Processed and Retained for Prevention, Investigation, Detection, and Prosecution of Criminal Acts, Including Terrorism." Working paper 99 (November 11, 2004).

European Drug Unit (EDU)/Europol. 1997. *Annual Report: European Law Enforcement Cooperation.* The Hague, Netherlands: Europol.

Eurostat (Statistical Office of the European Commission). 1999. *Yearbook 1998–1999: A Statistical Eye on Europe, Data 1987–1997.* Luxembourg: Office for Official Publications of the European Communities.

———. 1994. *Yearbook: A Statistical Eye on Europe, 1992–1993.* Luxembourg: Office for Official Publications of the European Communities.

Faist, Thomas. 2002. "Extension du Domaine de la Lutte: International Migration and Security Before and After September 11, 2001." *International Migration Review* 36(1): 7–14.

Fargues, Philippe. 2005. "Migration and Mobility in the Euro-Mediterranean Area: A Problem for Governments, a Solution for Populations?" Paper presented to the New York University/European University Institute (NYU/EUI) conference "An Immigration Policy for Europe?" Florence, Italy (March 13–15).

Friedland, Nehemia, and Ariel Merari. 1985. "The Psychological Impact of Terrorism: A Double-Edged Sword." *Political Psychology* 6(4): 591–604.

Gammeltoft-Hansen, Thomas. 2006. "Filtering Out the Risky Migrant: Migration Control, Risk Theory, and the EU." Working paper 52/2006. Aalborg: Academy for Migration Studies in Denmark (AMID).

Geddes, Andrew. 2000. *Immigration and European Integration: Towards a Fortress Europe?* Manchester, U.K.: Manchester University Press.

———. 2001. "Migration Policy in an Integrating Europe." Paper presented to the European Studies Association Conference. Madison, Wisc. (May 31).

———. 2002. "The EU Migration Regime's Effects on European Welfare States." In *Migration and the Externalities of European Integration,* edited by Sandra Lavenex and Emek Uçarer. Lanham, Md.: Lexington Books.

Geddes, Andrew, and Virginie Guiraudon. 2004. "The Emergence of a European Union Policy Paradigm Amidst Contrasting National Models: Britain, France, and EU Anti-Discrimination Policy." *West European Politics* 27(2): 334–53.

Gibson, James. 1996. "A Mile Wide but an Inch Deep? The Structure of Democratic Commitments in the Former USSR." *American Journal of Political Science* 40(2, May): 396–420.

———. 1998. "Sober Second Thought: An Experiment in Persuading Russians to Tolerate." *American Journal of Political Science* 42(July): 819–50.

Gilboy, Janet. 1997. "Implications of 'Third-Party' Involvement in Enforcement: The INS, Illegal Travelers, and International Airlines." *Law and Society Review* 31(3): 505–29.

———. 1998. "Compelled 'Third-Party' Regulatory Process: Legal Duties, Culture, and Noncompliance." *Law and Policy* 20(2): 135–55.

Gilmore, Bill. 2003. "The Twin Towers and the Third Pillar: Some Security Agenda Developments." EU working paper LAW no. 2003/7. San Domenico, Italy: European University Institute (EUI), Badia Fiesolana.

Guiraudon, Virginie. 2000. "European Integration and Migration Policy: Vertical Policy-Making as Venue-Shopping." *Journal of Common Market Studies* 38(2): 249–69.

———. 2003. "The Constitution of a European Immigration Policy Domain: A Political Sociology Approach." *Journal of European Policy* 10(2): 263–82.

Guiraudon, Virginie, and Gallya Lahav. 2000. "A Reappraisal of the State Sovereignty Debate: The Case of Migration Control." *Comparative Political Studies* 33(2, March): 163–95.

———. 2006. "Immigration Policy in Europe: The Politics of Control." *West European Politics* 29(2, March): 287–303.

Hammar, Tomas. 1985. *European Immigration Policy: A Comparative Study.* Cambridge: Cambridge University Press.

Heisler, Martin O., and Zig Layton-Henry. 1993. "Migration and the Links Between Social and Societal Security." In *Identity, Migration, and the New Security Agenda in Europe,* edited by Ole Waever, Barry Buzan, Morten Kelstrup, and Pierre Lemaitre. London: Pinter.

Huddy, Leonie, Nadia, Khatib, Nadia, and Theresa Capelos. 2002. "The Polls-Trends: Reactions to the Terrorist Attacks of September 11, 2001." *Public Opinion Quarterly* 64: 309–350.

Huddy, Leonie, Stanley Feldman, Gallya Lahav, and Chuck Taber. 2003. "Fear and Terrorism: Psychological Reactions to 9/11." In *Framing Terrorism: The News Media, the Government, and the Public,* edited by Pippa Norris, Montague Kern, and Marion Just. New York: Routledge.

Huddy, Leonie, Stanley Feldman, Charles Taber, and Gallya Lahav. 2005. "Threat, Anxiety, and Support of Antiterrorism Policies." *American Journal of Political Science* 49(3, July): 593–608.

Huysmans, Jef. 1994. "The Migrant as a Security Problem." In *Migration and European Integration: The Dynamics of Inclusion and Exclusion,* edited by Robert Miles and Dietrich Thranhardt. London: Pinter.

———. 2000. "The European Union and the Securitization of Migration." *Journal of Common Market Studies* 38(5): 751–77.

———. 2002. "Defining Social Constructivism in Security Studies: The Normative Dilemma of Writing Security." *Alternatives* 27: 41–62.

Klausen, Jytte. 2005. *The Islamic Challenge: Politics and Religion in Western Europe.* Oxford: Oxford University Press.

———. 2006. "Counterterrorism and the Integration of Islam in Europe." *Watch on the West* (Foreign Policy Research Institute, FPRI) 7(7, July).

Koslowski, Rey. 2000. *Migrants and Citizens: Demographic Change in a European State System.* Ithaca, N.Y.: Cornell University Press.

———. 2001. "Personal Security and State Sovereignty in a Uniting Europe." In *Controlling a New Migration World,* edited by Veronica Guiraudon and Christian Joppke. London: Routledge.

———. 2005. "Toward Virtual Borders: Expanding European Border Control Policy Initiatives and Technology Implementations." Paper presented to the New York University/European University Institute (NYU/EUI) conference "An Immigration Policy for Europe?" Florence, Italy (March 13–15).

Lahav, Gallya. 1995. "Old Values and Changing Frontiers in the European Union: A Study of Attitudes of Members of the European Parliament Towards Immigration." Ph.D. dissertation, City University of New York.

———. 1998. "Immigration and the State: The Devolution and Privatization of Immigration Control in the EU." *Journal of Ethnic and Migration Studies* 24(4): 675–94.

———. 2000. "The Rise of Non-State Actors in Migration Regulation in the United States and Europe: Changing the Gatekeepers or Bringing Back the State?" In *Immigration Research for a New Century: Multidisciplinary Perspectives*, edited by Nancy Foner, Rubén Rumbaut, and Steven Gold. New York: Russell Sage Foundation.

———. 2003. "Migration and Security: The Role of Non-State Actors and Civil Liberties." UN/POP/MIG/2003. New York: United Nations, Population Division. Available at: http://www.un.org/esa/population/publications/secoord2003/secoord.htm

———. 2004a. *Immigration and Politics in the New Europe: Reinventing Borders*. Cambridge: Cambridge University Press.

———. 2004b. "Public Opinion Toward Immigration in the European Union: Does It Matter?" *Comparative Political Studies* 37(10): 1151–83.

———. 2005. "The Migration, Security and Civil Rights Trilemma in the United States and Europe." Paper presented to the Robert Schuman Center for Advanced Studies, European University Institute. Florence, Italy (November 15, 2005).

———. 2009. "Organizing Immigration Interests in the European Union: Constraints and Opportunities for Supranational Migration Regulation and Integration." In *Bringing Outsiders In: Transatlantic Perspectives on Immigrant Political Incorporation*, edited by Jennifer Hochschild and John Mollenkopf. Ithaca, N.Y.: Cornell University Press.

Lahav, Gallya, and Virginie Guiraudon. 2000. "Comparative Perspectives on Border Control: Away from the Border and Outside the State." In *The Wall Around the West: State Borders and Immigration Controls in North America and Europe*, edited by Peter Andreas and Timothy Snyder. Lanham, Md.: Rowman and Littlefield.

———. 2005. "The Limits of a European Immigration Policy: Elite Opinion and Agendas Within the European Parliament." *Journal of Common Market Studies* 43(4): 851–75.

Lavenex, Sandra. 1999. *Safe Third Countries: Extending the EU Asylum and Immigration Policies to East and Central Europe*. Budapest: Central European University Press.

———. 2005. "Internationalization as Externalization: The Foreign Policy of European Immigration Control." Paper presented to the New York University/European University Institute (NYU/EUI) conference "An Immigration Policy for Europe?" Florence, Italy (March 13–15).

Lavenex, Sandra, and Emek Uçarer, eds. 2002. *Migration and the Externalities of European Integration.* Lanham, Md.: Lexington Books.

LeVine, Robert A., and Donald T. Campbell. 1971. *Ethnocentrism: Theories of Conflict, Ethnic Attitudes and Behavior.* New York: John Wiley.

Levy, Carl. 2005. "The European Union After 9/11: The Demise of a Liberal Democratic Asylum Regime?" *Government and Opposition* 40(1): 26–59.

Liberatore, Angela. 2005. "Balancing Security and Democracy: The Politics of Biometric Identification in the European Union." Robert Schuman Centre for Advanced Studies (RSCAS) working paper 2005/30. San Domenico, Italy: European University Institute (EUI), Badia Fiesolana.

Long, David. 1990. *The Anatomy of Terrorism.* New York: Free Press.

Marechal, Brigitte. 2002. *A Guidebook on Islam and Muslims in the Wide Contemporary Europe.* Louvain-a-la-Neuve, Belgium: Academica Bruylant.

Marie, Claude-Valentin. 2004. *Preventing Illegal Immigration: Juggling Economic Imperatives, Political Risks, and Individual Rights.* Brussels: Council of the European Union Publishing.

Messina, Anthony, and Colleen Thouez. 2002. "The Logics and Politics of a European Immigration Regime." In *West European Immigration an Immigrant Policy in the New Century,* edited by Anthony Messina. Westport, Conn.: Praeger Press.

Migration News Sheet (MNS). 2001. *Migration NewsSheet.* Brussels: Migration Policy Group (MPG).

Monar, Jörg. 2005. "Justice and Home Affairs." *Journal of Common Market Studies* 43: 131–46.

Organisation for Economic Co-operation and Development (OECD). 1992. *Trends in International Migration: SOPEMI report for 1991.* Paris: OECD.

———. 1999. *Trends in International Migration: SOPEMI report for 1998.* Paris: OECD.

Pastore, Ferrucio. 2005. "The European Union and the Fight Against Terrorism." In *Is There a European Strategy Against Terrorism?* edited by Ferrucio Pastore, Jorg Friedrichs, and Alessandra Politi. Working paper 12/2005. Rome: Centro Studidi Politica Internazionale (CeSPI).

Pastore, Massimo. 1991. "A Historical Critical Overview of European Intergovernmental Cooperation on Matters of Immigration, Asylum, and Internal Security." Paper presented to the nineteenth annual conference of the European Group for the Study of Deviance and Social Control. Potsdam (September 4–8).

Rokeach, Milton. 1960. *The Open and Closed Mind: Investigations into the Nature of Belief Systems and Personality Systems.* New York: Basic Books.

Rosen, Jeffrey. 2001. "A Watchful State." *New York Times Magazine* (October 7, p. 38).

Rudolph, Christopher. 2006. *National Security and Immigration: Policy Development in the United States and Western Europe Since 1945.* Stanford, Calif.: Stanford University Press.

Seago, D.W. 1947. "Stereotypes: Before Pearl Harbor and After." *Journal of Social Psychology* 23: 55–63.

Sniderman, Paul, Joseph Fletcher, Peter Russell, and Philip Tetlock. 1996. *The Clash of Rights: Liberty, Equality, and Legitimacy in Pluralist Democracy*. New Haven, Conn.: Yale University Press.

Statewatch. 2001. "EU Links Protests and Terrorism in Action Plan." *Statewatch Bulletin* 11(5, August–October): 19–23.

Tajfel, Henri, and John C. Turner. 1979. "An Integrative Theory of Intergroup Conflict." In *The Social Psychology of Intergroup Relations*, edited by William G. Austin and Stephen Worchel. Monterey, Calif.: Brooks/Cole.

Teitelbaum, Michael. 1984. "Immigration, Refugees, and Foreign Policy." *International Organization* 38(3): 429–50.

Thouez, Colleen, and Sarah Rosengärtner. 2007. "Discussing Migration in Global Policy Circles." Paper presented to the conference "Migration, International Relations, and the Evolution of World Politics" at Princeton University, Woodrow Wilson School of Public and International Affairs. Princeton, N. J. (March 16–17).

Uçarer, Emek. 2003. "Justice and Home Affairs." In *European Union Politics*, edited by Michelle Cini. Oxford: Oxford University Press.

United Nations Development Programme (UNDP). 1994. *Human Development Report 1994: New Dimensions of Human Security*. New York: UNDP.

Vandermosten, René. 2006. "Migration as a Multi-Pillar Issue: An Insider's View." Paper presented to the Robert Schuman Centre for Advanced Studies (RSCAS), European University Institute. Florence, Italy (March 1).

Van Outrive, Lode. 1990. "Migration and Penal Reform: One European Policy?" Paper presented to the annual conference of the European Group for the Study of Deviance and Social Control. Haarlem, Netherlands (September 4–7).

Van Selm, Joanne. 2005. "Immigration Is Becoming a Key Issue for Europe's Future." *European Affairs* (Washington) (Summer): x1.

Waever, Ole. 1998. "Identity, Integration, and Security: Solving the Sovereignty Puzzle in EU Studies." *Journal of International Affairs* 48(2): 389–431.

Waever, Ole, Barry Buzan, Morten Kelstrup, and Pierre Lemaitre. 1993. *Identity, Migration, and the New Security Agenda in Europe*. London: Pinter.

Walker, Martin. 2001–2002. "Post-9/11: The European Dimension." *World Policy Journal* (Winter): 1–10.

Walker, Neill. 2004. *Europe's Area of Freedom, Security, and Justice*. Oxford: Oxford University Press.

Weiner, Myron. 1992. "Security, Stability, and International Migration." *International Security* 17(3): 91–126.

———. 1993. *International Migration and Security*. Boulder, Colo.: Westview Press.

———. 1995. *The Global Migration Crisis: Challenge to States and to Human Rights*. New York: HarperCollins.

Weiner, Myron, and Michael S. Teitelbaum. 2001. *Political Demography, Demographic Engineering*. Oxford: Begham Books.

Zolberg, Aristide. 1995. "From Invitation to Interdiction: U.S. Foreign Policy and Immigration Since 1945." In *Threatened Peoples, Threatened Borders*, edited by Michael S. Teitelbaum and Myron Weiner. New York: W. W. Norton.

Part II

National Counterterrorism Responses

CHAPTER 5

THE SOCIAL CONTRACT AND THE THREE TYPES OF TERRORISM: DEMOCRATIC SOCIETY IN THE UNITED KINGDOM AFTER 9/11 AND 7/7

DIRK HAUBRICH

The United Kingdom has a long history of fighting terrorism. This chapter analyzes the threat that terrorism has posed to the country, the evolution of the country's policy to counter it, and the effectiveness of that policy in bringing terrorist suspects to justice, as well as the unforeseen effects that policy has had on British society. The terrorist attacks on September 11, 2001, in the United States and July 7, 2005, in London offer two dates appropriate to demarcate three distinct types of terrorism to which the United Kingdom—and arguably other Western democracies as well—have been exposed over time: *domestic* terrorism, followed by *transnational* terrorism, and, most recently, *compounded* terrorism.

The first three sections explicate the distinct dynamics at work between the ruler and the ruled for each of the three types with regard to the ferocity of the terrorist attacks, the scope of the governmental measures taken to counter them, and the ramifications for the democratic fabric of society. Social contract theory is proposed as a theoretical framework to explain the differences unearthed, because it stipulates the limitations on terrorist perpetrators and governments alike in pursuing their objectives. Democratic principles—with regard to individual rights and liberties, civil-military relationships, the strengthening of executive power, government concealment, and so on—have been compromised to a different degree as the country has had to deal with these phenomena. This conclusion elicits, in the fourth section, an analysis of the extent to which the United Kingdom has gained, in exchange for these principles, a greater capacity to bring terrorist suspects to justice.

Type 1: Domestic Terrorism

The origins of the first type of terrorism can be traced back to the various Irish Republican paramilitary organizations that emerged after the Easter Rising in 1916, although for reasons of scope it is useful to limit the analysis to 1969, when the Provisional Irish Republican Army (later referred to simply as the IRA) broke away from the (soon-to-be-defunct) Official IRA.[1] In the 1970s, 1980s, and 1990s, the type of terrorism that the IRA and related organizations inflicted on the country was what I refer to as *domestic*, defined as terror where the aggressors' and victims' homelands overlap. To draw out the differences compared to the country's policy in the post-9/11 and post-7/7 eras, a brief synopsis is in order.

Akin to the situation with the Basque Freedom and Homeland Organization (ETA) in Spain—but slightly less so compared to Italy's Brigate Rosse (Red Brigades) and Germany's Rote Armee Fraktion (RAF, Red Army Faction), groups whose domestic terrorism was driven primarily by "revolutionary" political ideology—domestic terrorism in the United Kingdom was motivated by the goals of secession and national self-determination. Terrorist acts were predominantly perpetrated over the question of whether Northern Ireland should remain part of the United Kingdom, in a context where religious affiliation (Catholics versus Protestants) and political loyalties (Republicans versus Unionists) happened to coincide.

The strategy and tactics that the British government has employed to neutralize its different terrorist threats have varied widely. Some have been reactive, and others proactive or preventive. Some have been short-term responses, while others are long-term. Yet only a very few approaches have been as overtly coercive as the U.K. government's policy in Northern Ireland during the 1970s. In August 1971, in an effort to curtail the increasing statistics of terrorist violence, the British authorities launched "Operation Demetrius" and authorized the British army and the Royal Ulster Constabulary to arrest and intern without charge or trial anyone accused of being a member of an illegal paramilitary group. The policy lasted until December 1975 and led to a total of 1,981 such detentions; 95 percent of the detainees were Catholic-Republican.[2] Allegations of abuse and torture of the detainees were also made and brought before the European Court of Human Rights (ECtHR).

During the trial, the British government argued that the interrogation techniques—which involved hooding, wall-standing, subjection to noise, relative deprivation of food and water, and sleep deprivation—had been necessary to combat a rise in terrorist violence. The court found the techniques to be "cruel, inhuman and degrading" and in breach of the European Convention on Human Rights (ECHR), but it stopped short of describing them as torture.

Britain's international image was greatly tainted by the ruling. In fact, the British government was ultimately obliged to give "a solemn undertaking" to the court that the techniques would never again be employed on British territory.[3] More important, the four-year internment period significantly inflamed sectarian tensions in Northern Ireland. The strategy failed in its stated aim of arresting IRA members and resulted in the arrest of hundreds of people who were completely unconnected to the organization. Further tensions and killings ensued after the British army shot fourteen unarmed protesters at an anti-internment march in Derry in January 1972, an incident that later became known as "Bloody Sunday."

In terms of loss of life, 1972 was the most violent of the entire Irish conflict: of the 3,560 individuals who were killed during the four decades, 495 died in that year alone, among them 259 civilians, 151 police and army forces, 11 Loyalist paramilitaries, and 74 Republican paramilitaries (Esther Addley, "British Troops Leave After 38 Years," *The Guardian*, August 1, 2007). As acknowledged by Patrick Mercer, an officer with the British army in Northern Ireland between 1975 and 1992 and now a Conservative member of Parliament (MP), the policy and military operations carried out in the region were a very serious mistake that yielded little intelligence but fiercely radicalized a generation (Addley, *The Guardian*, August 1, 2007).

The use of internment provided a powerful recruiting tool: it convinced many Catholics that repression and discrimination against the minority had to be resisted. Political and funding support for the IRA in the United States increased greatly, and a fresh cohort of bitter and determined people were injected into the organization (Richardson 2007). The antagonism between British authorities and large sections of the Irish population could not have been greater.

The period of internment ended in 1975, followed by a significant reform of the police force in Northern Ireland. In parallel, the more pragmatic and politically astute political leaders of the IRA, and of Sinn Féin (as the political wing of the IRA), recognized that they had to enter the political arena if they were to have any chance of securing the changes they desired (Wilkinson 2006, 32). The parties involved in the conflict embarked on a remarkable process of change, the major milestones of which can be only mentioned here. Interparty talk on the future of Northern Ireland commenced in September 1977. Following the Good Friday Agreement of 1998, the IRA refrained from attacks on British security forces (but continued to murder Roman Catholics). In 2000 international arms inspectors were allowed to visit the arms dumps of the IRA, which in 2005 reported that it had indeed decommissioned all its weapons. At the very end of the road emerged the unprecedented situation—in western Europe anyway—of a terrorist movement succeeding in transforming itself into a peaceful political party.

The parties seemed to have learned from their past mistakes, and Northern Ireland was given a chance to change for the better as a result. Back in the 1970s, however, the situation was bad not only in Northern Ireland but also on the British mainland, where anti-Irish sentiment was being whipped up, primarily through the Prevention of Terrorism (Temporary Provisions) Act (PTA) 1974, which put the entire Irish community under suspicion. The government also used exclusion orders to ban prominent Sinn Féin members of Parliament, like Gerry Adams and Martin McGuinness, from entering Great Britain. The public regarded the policy as a means of social control in order to repress the political activity of an entire community. Tony Bunyan (1977) reported that in the first six months after the act came into being, 489 people were detained under its provisions, of whom only sixteen were later charged with an offense; all others were released, often many months or years later, without charge. The cases of a few individuals who were convicted and imprisoned at the time represented some of the most outrageous injustices in U.K. history. Some of them, such as the imprisonment for sixteen years of the "Birmingham Six"—a group of six men found guilty of committing the Birmingham pub bombings in November 1974—were not rectified until the 1990s.[4]

The failure of the coercive measures taken by the U.K. government contributed to the premature end of the initiative. The measures had alienated the public from the authorities, severely compromised intelligence gathering in the region, and further polarized an already fractured political environment. As D. P. J. Walsh remarked (1982, 37–38), the adverse publicity and the obviously counterproductive effects of using such heavy-handed methods persuaded the British government that it would be more sensible to appear to be using the ordinary legal process to deal with suspected terrorists. A more conciliatory approach was developed, and the first experiments with power sharing were introduced and later expanded.

Political theory provides a useful explanation for the abandonment of the United Kingdom's internment policy. When governments introduce exaggerated emergency measures, they court the danger of undermining the state's legitimacy to rule. According to the orthodox and common interpretation, state legitimacy is based on the idea of the "social contract," as first developed by scholars such as Immanuel Kant, Thomas Hobbes, John Locke, and Jean-Jacques Rousseau. The ideas of these thinkers had a significant impact beyond the contemporary scholarly discourse in political philosophy: they influenced the actual formation, in the seventeenth and eighteenth centuries, of liberal democracies such as Britain, France, and the United States.

These thinkers challenged their contemporaries to imagine a hypothetical "state of nature" before there was any political authority. All individuals were on their own, and there was no higher authority that commanded their obedience or protected their interests and possessions. Since their self-interested behavior could lead to situations of conflict between them, individuals agreed to establish institutions that would define and impartially enforce binding decisions on individuals so that their lives would be preserved in a physically and economically more secure environment. They entered a voluntary agreement, the social contract, to create a state to which they would hand over their power and whose laws and actions they pledged to abide by. In return, the state guaranteed the protection of individuals' rights at home and against aggression from abroad.

The crucial relationship between state legitimacy, on the one hand, and state coercion (to deal with aggression), on the other, is that the latter can be either a response to or a provoker of a breakdown in the former. If legitimacy appears to be eroding because society, or a section of it, no longer grants the state the exclusive authority to use force, then the state may try to restore obedience by increasing coercive pressures. Such force, however, may cause further violence, brought about by a populace that deems the oppression unjustified and excessive.

The large-scale detention policy in the United Kingdom in the 1970s brought these hypothetical mechanisms into play and proved that "winning the hearts and minds" of the people can be an essential component of an effective strategy against domestic terrorism. When the government is not responsive to the economic and political needs of the population and the conflicting interests between the executive and the population are allowed to widen, then terrorists are more likely to find active and tacit antigovernment support among the population.

Hence, employing overly coercive measures in order to identify, detain, and punish a few transgressors is not usually a recommended policy option for democratic governments, which must forgo ostensibly more effective (but also more draconian) measures as a result. Thus, respect for the social contract as well as strategic reasons constrain democratically elected governments in their fight against domestic terrorism.

Conversely, "domestic terrorists" are equally eager to secure support from the domestic population. Although they belong to conspiratorial organizations, their use of violence is nonetheless aimed at political change. They depend on popular support to attain their political goals of national self-determination (or ideological supremacy in countries such as Germany and Italy) and tend to portray themselves as the "real defenders of the people." The need to acquire public support thus also constrains the potential ferocity of terrorists' activities: in domestic scenarios, terrorists tend to refrain from *explicitly* targeting civilians. They tend to limit their choice of targets to members of the police force, the military apparatus, or the ruling economic or political regime that they intend to overthrow or whose authority they are eager to undermine. Of the 3,560 fatalities during the IRA conflict after 1969, only sixty-four were civilians on British territory.[5]

Therefore, in the case of domestic terrorism in a liberal democracy such as the United Kingdom, there is a mutual check at work that limits domestic terrorist actions and governmental reactions alike. The need of both opponents to woo support from the same domestic public limits the scope, intensity, and ferocity of the conflict, as well as the knock-on effects on the democratic fabric of society.

Type 2: Transnational Terrorism

The danger of losing public support is imminent, however, only if the threat is posed by an enemy who comes from within. A different assessment has to be made when the terrorist incident involves perpetrators from outside the society under attack (Haubrich 2005). The first incident of this kind in a liberal democracy occurred on September 11, 2001. Of course, terrorist attacks with an "international" or "foreign" element existed long before the 9/11 attacks. Yet most of these prior attacks fall outside the explanatory remit of this study because they were targeted not at Western democracies but at nondemocratic or transitional regimes; they would contribute little to a study that aims to develop an explanatory framework for the impact of counterterrorism policy on democratic societies, with the United Kingdom as a case study. Other such prior attacks did target Western democracies, but the impact was confined to their assets and security interests abroad—

that is, the attacks did not occur in their domestic territories. Such was the case with the attack on U.S. soldiers in the Berlin nightclub La Belle in the 1980s; the bombings of the U.S. embassies in Nairobi, Kenya, and Dar-es-Salaam, Tanzania, in the late 1990s; and the bombing of the U.K. consulate in Istanbul in the autumn of 2003, to mention but a few. Finally, when Western democracies *were* targeted in previous attacks, it was not the domestic society itself that was targeted, but a foreign and thus ostensibly discernible subgroup temporarily residing in the territory of that society. Such was the case when eleven Israeli athletes were killed by the Palestinian terrorist group Black September during the 1972 Olympic Games in Munich, and when Palestinian terrorists from the Abu Nidal Organization murdered eighteen passengers and staff of the Israeli airline El Al at the airports of Vienna and Rome in December 1985.

Inevitably, any categorization does some violation to historic events, and the chronological differentiation into domestic, transnational, and compounded terrorism proposed here is no exception. One Western democracy—France—did indeed experience a foreign terrorist threat on its soil prior to 9/11. Ever since decolonialization in the 1950s, the country had pursued an active policy to protect its interests in the Middle East and North Africa. By the early 1980s, this policy had begun to conflict directly with the policies of Syria, Iran, and Libya, the principal state sponsors of terrorism in the Middle East. The conflict culminated in a series of attacks on French soil in 1986, during which eleven individuals died and over 220 were injured. The apparent objective of the attacks was to force the French government to alter its policies in the Middle East. Yet, while the alleged political motivation was aimed at France's postcolonial policies abroad, the attacks were actually planned and executed by existing Palestinian and Lebanese networks in France. Although a less clear-cut case, France's history with terrorism is conceptually distinct and can therefore be considered as falling outside the transnational category used in this study.

The more clear-cut cases mentioned earlier, in turn, constituted attacks that had an international dimension but posed only a limited, if not nonexistent, threat to the national security of the territory of the affected society, and thus its democratic fabric. The impact on the domestic societies involved was negligible, as were the counterterrorism measures taken by the affected governments to reduce the threat domestically.

The 9/11 attacks, by contrast, constituted the first case of transnational terrorism proper, and thus the use of the term here is distinct from earlier usages (for example, Sandler, Tschirhart, and Cauley 1983), which define a transnational terrorist act as an attack on the territory of a liberal democracy by foreign substate actors. What separates this type of terrorism from domestic terrorism is the perpetrators' lack of interest in securing support among the domestic population. Their intention is to create a particular psychological effect, terror, among the targeted victims directly—and indirectly among third parties who are put in a state of constant fear of becoming victims of future attacks. To achieve their political objective, if identifiable at all, transnational terrorists need not gain the backing of the population among whom their attacks occur.

Conversely, the affected government, fearing no potential alliance between the population and the perpetrators, is less at risk of seeing terrorists exploit societal grievances: unlike domestic terrorists, external aggressors lend themselves less convincingly to the role of defenders of the people if the people are actual or potential victims of their aggression. And where the probability of an alliance between the terrorists and the public is low or nonexistent, governmental reactions to terrorism are much less constrained.

Contrary to domestic scenarios, then, there is no mutual check in place that limits the intensity of transnational terrorist actions and governmental reactions, and as a result, the countermeasures taken by governments may have much more severe implications for domestic society.

Preliminary analyses at the time suggested that the attacks were planned by Al Qaeda, a movement based on loose networks across national borders. The immediate reaction by the states in the "coalition of the willing" (initially numbering fifteen) was therefore to attack and neutralize the perceived threat abroad. The plot appeared to have been hatched from the territory of another democracy, in this case Germany, against which a military retaliation by the United States would have been unimaginable. Military interventions in Afghanistan and Iraq ensued instead (Haubrich 2006).

Yet, given the potential threat from collaborators at home, or "sleeper cells," counterterrorism policy was seen as requiring a domestic component even in cases of terrorism with foreign perpetrators. As a result, extensive new legislation was implemented in the United States after September 11. And although the attacks occurred on American territory, the U.K. government soon followed suit. Given Britain's close cultural, economic, and military ties to the United States and its similar stance in foreign policy matters, the country considered itself a likely target for future attacks. Added impetus was provided by the fact that eleven of the nineteen attackers suspected of carrying out the attacks had flown to their temporary American destinations in the months leading up to the attacks from the British airports of Heathrow and Gatwick. For most of these individuals, it could not be established at the time whether they had done so merely as transit passengers or whether they had actually stayed on British territory.

The government submitted comprehensive antiterrorism legislation to the legislature. Usually, in cases where civil liberties are about to be restricted, legislative procedures involve years of negotiations between the various interest groups, political parties, and expert committees before new laws are created. Yet the U.K. Parliament, warned of the possibility of immediate follow-up attacks on its own territory and pushed by an impatient government, wasted no time in bringing about far-reaching changes to the country's laws in the form of the Anti-Terrorism, Crime, and Security Act (ATCSA) 2001: after scheduling just sixteen hours over a three-day period for MPs to debate the emergency measure, the government rushed through the legislative process so as to give the bill royal assent on December 13, 2001. At that point, barely a month had passed since the bill was submitted to the legislature. Even the House of Lords was given only nine days to reflect on it (Haubrich 2003, 8).

The act brought about a multitude of changes. Internet and phone providers were required to keep communications data for two years. Freight forwarders and carriers were required to retain information on freight and passengers and to furnish them to the enforcement agencies. Governmental authorities, including the Inland Revenue, obtained the power to disclose any information required by the secret services or the police. Financial institutions were ordered to provide information on bank accounts for up to ninety days, and institutions would commit an offense if they failed to report knowledge or suspicion of transactions for terrorist purposes.

The jurisdiction of the British Transport Police (BTP) was extended to allow it the same privileges as constables of the police force. The use of threatening, abusive, or insulting words or behavior in a religious context was put under greater legal punishment. The government's ability to forfeit and freeze property, including assets or cash, "intended to be used for the purposes of terrorism" became legal. The Ministry of Defense Police became entitled to operate beyond its usual geographical jurisdiction (within defense sites) and was allowed to operate in cooperation with, and indeed with the same powers as, the national police force. Even so, the Defense Police remained accountable only to the executive and thus fell outside the jurisdiction of the police complaints authority.

Police powers were expanded to include the British secret services. Judgment on what constituted subversive action that would require the involvement of these services therefore became no longer subject to the scrutiny typically associated with British democracy, for example, through select committees. What was needed in the interests of national security became a matter for the judgment of those within the services (Haubrich 2003).

Not all of these measures were entirely new. Some of them had been contemplated in the Home Office for a long time, had repeatedly been rejected in parliamentary hearings as too far-reaching, and had been waiting for several years for a suitable legislative opportunity to arise.

The single most controversial provision of the act was to allow the detention without trial of suspected terrorists who were of foreign nationality and could not be deported to their home country because they might be tortured there. The government had to proclaim (and, for years to come, continued to operate under) a case of public emergency in order for this particular stipulation of the ATCSA to meet the country's international treaty obligations on human rights.

It was the only way for the country to be able to derogate from article 5 of the European Convention on Human Rights, which prohibits imprisonment without a fair trial. Article 15 allows for derogation "at times of war or other public emergencies," a public emergency being defined as a situation that threatens the life of a nation. It is, as such, just one notch down from a full-scale war, a revolution, or a civil war. In derogating from the European Convention on Human Rights, the U.K. government announced such an emergency, despite repeatedly reassuring the public of the contrary. Out of forty-one signatories that ratified the Convention, the United Kingdom was the only country after 9/11 to deem it necessary to take such a comprehensive step.

Under this provision, dozens of men were detained and held in London's Belmarsh Prison, often for many years, without charges being specified or access to legal counsel granted. It took the Law Lords until December 2004 to rule, with a majority of eight votes to one, that detention without trial was in breach of human rights. Although this ruling should have prompted either the release of the Belmarsh detainees or the bringing of charges against them, the Home Office refused to do so and indicated that it would change existing law to accommodate the Law Lords' ruling.

In March 2005, the government enacted the Prevention of Terrorism Act (PTA) 2005, which repealed part 4 powers under the ATCSA 2001 and replaced them with a system of "control orders" (in public commonly referred to as "house arrest"). The act's sixteen sections allow the home secretary to implement control orders for people he suspects of involvement in terrorism; these orders can prohibit or restrict the following: prohibiting the use of Internet or phones; restricting work or business activities; prohibiting association or communication with certain individuals; restricting the suspect's place of residence or who is allowed into the premises; restricting the suspect's movement and travel; requiring the suspect to be at specified places or in a particular area at certain times or days; allowing officials to search the suspect's home; and monitoring the suspect by electronic tagging or other means.

Control orders were imposed on all of the Belmarsh detainees on the very day they were released. The U.K. Parliament renewed the legislation on control orders twice, on February 21, 2008 and on March 3, 2009, by which time fourteen control orders remained imposed. Nine of them were foreigners, six were British nationals, and all of them were Muslims (*The Guardian*, "Control Orders Failure as Terror Suspects Flee," October 17, 2006). The legal criticism aside, control orders were questioned for their effectiveness as well. By July 2007, the number of individuals had increased to eighteen, but seven of them had absconded, and some of those remaining had launched an appeal in the House of Lords (*The Times*, "The Battle for Hearts and Minds," July 8, 2007).

Of course, Guantánamo Bay—the American variant of Belmarsh—appears to be a much more worthy case for analysis. After all, addressing U.S. security issues by relocating the legal assessment of hundreds of suspects outside domestic democratic jurisdiction appears to violate the fundamental principle of the rule of law on which modern societies have been built. Yet Belmarsh is just as striking an example in that the U.S. administration decided to ship the detainees to an offshore naval base and, in so doing, thought to have left the democratic jurisdiction of the home territory intact. By contrast, the emergency laws that allowed detention without trial in the United Kingdom actually applied to the British homeland; such powers were unprecedented in peacetime Britain.

U.K. domestic laws were being stretched by this antiterrorism legislation in two directions: an upstream dissolution of the line between crimes and acts of war, and a downstream dissolution of the line between crimes and minor public order disturbances (Hörnqvist 2004).

An upstream conflation occurred because crimes are usually dealt with by civil agencies, whereas acts of war are countered by military agencies. Once the events of September 11 were no longer described as "terrorist attacks" but as "acts of war" and stateless terrorists were equated with "terrorist states," the so-called war on terrorism became a matter for both police and the military. Once such a shift occurred, previously distinct areas of responsibility for internal and external security became blurred, with the latter commanding much less rigid levels of democratic scrutiny and investigative constraints. Procedural safeguards, too, were often suspended, such as the principle of "innocent until proven guilty."

The downstream conflation occurred between crimes and public order disturbances. Traditionally, a public order disturbance is deviant behavior that is not a criminal offense, such as those caused by graffiti writers, beggars, troublesome tenants, or protesters. What constitutes deviant behavior, however, is contingent upon a society's perception of public order and security. Security is compromised by fear, which is a product of an individual's subjective interpretation of an objective situation. And fear is more readily fueled by a (real or perceived) threat that is unidentifiable, foreign, and ostensibly not containable by domestic law enforcement.

When searching for domestic collaborators in such conditions of uncertainty, the focus of state coercion then shifts from what a suspect has done to what he might do—that is, the threat he *could* pose to security and the government's ability to rule. As is well known from conventional crime prevention scenarios, countermeasures are then deployed on the basis of probabilities and risk assessments rather than actual events, and suspects are identified not on the basis of an actual crime but because they correspond to a certain surveillance profile, move in certain circles, or hold certain opinions.

The result is a significant increase in surveillance of the lawful conduct of citizens. Any law-abiding citizen wishing, for example, to send money to relatives in a state where terrorist groups are active could be accused of sponsoring terrorism. The same applies to activists who chain themselves in front of trains transporting nuclear waste, farmers who protest against agricultural policies by blocking roads with tractors, or (as we shall see in the discussion here on the third type of terrorism) protesters who rally against the country's policy in Iraq. Any form of political pressure exerted on the government that is not channeled through conventional political and parliamentary processes may be regarded as unduly compelling the government into a course of action that it would not have taken otherwise.

The price in terms of civil liberties may be worth paying if the anti-terrorism laws show demonstrable success in detecting terrorists, a subject to which we return later in the chapter. First, however, we assess the third type of U.K. counterterrorism policy.

Type 3: Compounded Terrorism

The attack on the London transport system on July 7, 2005, constitutes the second event relevant to this analysis. That morning, suicide bombers detonated three explosives in the London Underground and a fourth on the upper deck of a bus. The bombings killed fifty-two innocent people and caused a severe, daylong disruption of the city's transport and mobile telecommunications infrastructure. Post-incident forensic analysis showed that the explosions were caused by homemade organic peroxide–based devices that were packed into backpacks. Such bombs are dangerous to manufacture but do not require much expertise and can be made using readily available materials and domestic equipment.

One aspect of this event in particular brings about an analytical relocation: although the London suicide bombers were apparently of African or Asian descent and were probably inspired by the same explosive cocktail of militant anti-Western religious beliefs as the perpetrators of the September 11 attacks, they held U.K. passports and were born and brought up in Britain. They were not foreign nationals, but legal citizens of the same democratic state that they decided to attack.

July 7, 2005, then, marks the advent of a third type of terrorism: compounded terrorism, an amalgamation of the attackers' (foreign) ethnicity, culture, and extreme religious beliefs with their (domestic) citizenship. These terrorists are willing to use an utmost of destruction indiscriminately against their co-citizens, whose support they do not require to further their cause. With regard to actors, compounded terrorism is domestic—in that it emerges from within society—but its motivation is transnational and inspired by adversarial foreign (mis)representations of that society.

The validity of the analytical distinction between domestic terrorism, transnational terrorism, and amalgamated terrorism, and the different degree of ferociousness ascribed to them, is confirmed by the fact that the number of fatalities incurred by the July 7 attacks by far exceeded the total of thirty-four Londoners killed by the IRA in the 1970s, 1980s, and 1990s combined.[6] As it happened, three weeks after the London bombings the IRA announced the end of its armed struggle against British rule in Northern Ireland. Given the rationale presented here, this may not have been an unexpected development: the unquestionable success of the peace process in Northern Ireland aside, in the post-7/7 era the IRA would have found it difficult to continue attracting the public's attention for its cause by displaying a ferocity that matched or superseded the 7/7 atrocities. It may well turn out that, as compounded terrorism emerges in the United Kingdom, domestic terrorism will vanish for good.

Of greater relevance for this analysis, however, is an examination of the countermeasures that the U.K. government has taken, and is planning to take, in order to contain the threat of compounded terrorism, and a comparison of these efforts with the reactions to the 9/11 attacks.

To recall, after 9/11 many Western governments embarked on an ill-conceived journey misleadingly labeled the "war on terrorism" in an attempt to respond to a threat that was much more subtle and tactical in nature than so extensive a label suggests (Freedman 2001). They were too quick to equate stateless terrorists with terrorist states in order to justify the intuitive reaction of states when attacked from abroad: mounting a military intervention against a foreign country. As is well known now, the military campaign turned out to have been based on wrong (if not nonexistent) intelligence about Iraq's alleged link to the 9/11 attacks and its alleged possession of weapons of mass destruction (WMD). What is more, the military coalition had no sustainable plan to restore peace in the territories to which it brought war and chaos: six years after the official end of the war, Iraq continues to suffer from suicide attacks on a near-daily basis and has become home to terrorist organizations.

The challenge after 7/7 was different. Liberal democracies such as the United Kingdom would face near-certain strategic exhaustion if they were to embark on a strategy similar to the strategy pursued after 9/11. As of the autumn of 2007, the military operations in Iraq and Afghanistan had cost the lives of more than 3,760 U.S. service men and women, as well as 168 soldiers from the United Kingdom. The war had cost $310 billion, and another $9 billion were being added to the bill for every month the coalition forces decided to keep their soldiers in Iraq. By 2010, the war is expected to have cost $1 trillion. Another engagement of this sort, or an intensification of existing campaigns in Iraq or Afghanistan, would be infeasible.

The threat of strategic exhaustion aside, there is of course no logical rationale for a foreign engagement either. In the months following the 9/11 attacks, Western governments had at least a limited rationale for falling back on their conventional synchronous foreign military response. After all, the perpetrators were of foreign origin. In the post-7/7 era of compounded terrorism, by contrast, even that meager rationale for a military campaign abroad disappeared: the perpetrators were all homegrown.

In reacting to the 7/7 attacks, the U.K. government had to take several factors into account: the attacks were not directed by a terrorist mastermind (either at home or abroad); they did not require any sophisticated technical equipment, knowledge, or support network; and they could easily spawn "copycat" operations, as became evident with the attempted, but unsuccessful, attempts two weeks later. What is more, the domestic population could not be easily separated into some discernible minority of potential perpetrators requiring observation, on the one hand, and a majority of citizens going about their lives in a lawful manner, on the other. As a result, the number of potential perpetrators became vast, as did the number of potential terrorist targets, both subjects and objects.

The social contract thesis developed here suggests that the ferocity of the government's reactions to the third type of terrorism, compounded terrorism, may exceed its reactions to the other two types: the lack of a viable option for a foreign military engagement leaves the domestic population as the only policy target remaining. Within only a few months of the London attacks, the government introduced additional legal measures and policies to help control, track, and monitor the domestic population. These and other incidences are indicative of how the response to compounded terrorism has altered the balance of power—between the government and individuals, between the government and bureaucratic agencies, and between the government and the legislature. Six of those incidences are worth revisiting here.

The first occurred on July 22, 2005, when the most fundamental civil right there is, the right to life, was wiped out for Jean Charles de Menezes, an innocent civilian who was shot in a London Tube station by an armed police officer who thought he was a suicide bomber. In the days and weeks following the event, various sources disseminated speculations and incorrect information about its unfolding, including the claim that de Menezes was wearing a suspicious-looking padded jacket, that he was running away from police officers, and that he was vaulting the ticket barriers inside the Underground station. The police soon knew that none of these claims was true: confiscated CCTV (closed-circuit television) camera tapes had recorded de Menezes calmly picking up a newspaper in the station concourse and walking down the escalators. Even so, police statements would fail to produce a correct account of how the shooting actually happened. The reaction by the public, used to a police force with only a very limited number of officers authorized to carry weapons, was generally negative, although an extended BBC Radio phone-in and debate showed that a sizable minority saw the unintended shooting of innocent people as a price the population would have to pay if the fight against the terrorist threat was to be won.[7]

An investigation into the shooting by the Independent Police Complaints Commission (IPCC) one year later confirmed that there had been no grounds to suggest that de Menezes was involved in terrorist activities.[8] Based on this report, however, the Crown Prosecution Service (CPS) concluded that no police officers were to be prosecuted over the fatal shooting, because the two marksmen who fired the fatal shots (and were subsequently suspended from firearms duties) had "genuinely believed" that de Menezes was a suicide bomber. The Office of the Commissioner, the body that formally and legally oversaw the operation, faced only a single charge over the affair—for a relatively minor breach of the Health and Safety at Work Act 1974.

As such, no individual officers were held to account, nor were police strategies as a whole scrutinized. Instead, health and safety legislation that had been enacted three decades before in order to "secure the health, safety and welfare of persons at work" was invoked to deal with the actions of trained marksmen unloading seven rounds into the head of a civilian who was lawfully minding his own business. Moreover, the police commander in charge of the operation was not reprimanded or charged. On the contrary, a year later she was one of only four police officers to be recommended for promotion to the office of deputy assistant commissioner; in this position, which she took, she is responsible for the protection of the royal family (*The Times*, "Yard Promotion," September 13, 2006).

It was only after de Menezes's family challenged this decision—a ten-week trial was held in the U.K. High Court in the summer of 2008—that the public would finally learn what had happened that day. The evidence presented by civilian and police witnesses—and reported to the public on a day-by-day basis—suggested a litany of serious errors by the Metropolitan Police, including firearms officers colluding in insisting that they had shouted warnings prior to the shooting, despite universal denial from every civilian in the Tube train at the time; the failure by all of the officers involved to conclusively identify de Menezes as a terrorist suspect; the radio communications being almost inaudible; and surveillance and firearms officers not carrying a picture of de Menezes to help in the identification process.

Although this evidence led many to believe that the police would eventually be held responsible for the events of that day, the investigation ended as controversially as it had begun two years earlier: after the last witness was heard, Coroner Sir Michael Wright instructed the jury *not* to consider a verdict of "unlawful killing" against the police. Defending his decision by stating that "the facts did not justify allowing the jury to consider an unlawful killing," he gave the jury the choice between "lawful killing" and an "open verdict" only. As a result, further anger and resentment erupted among the public, who saw the doubtful openness and impartiality of the proceedings and the interference by the coroner as yet another example of the bias of the British legal system in favor of the state. The jury eventually passed an "open verdict," thus rejecting the police account that de Menezes was killed lawfully (BBC News, "Open Verdict in de Menezes Inquest," December 12, 2008). But since unlawful killing was ruled out as a verdict, no further legal recriminations are expected for either the police officers or the institutions involved.

The trust in the professionalism of law enforcement agencies in general and the reliability of police intelligence in particular was further undermined in June 2006 when details emerged about yet another bungled police operation. During the early morning raid of a house in Forest Gate, London, the Metropolitan Police executed a search warrant issued under the Terrorism Act 2000. In the course of the operation, one of the two residents of the two-bedroom terraced house was shot in the shoulder by one of the 250 police officers invading the premises and subsequently detained. On the front pages the next day, the press reported the "Hunt for the 'Poison Bomb'" (*Daily Telegraph*), the "Police Hunt for Lethal Chemical Suicide Vest" (*The Times*), and the "Fears of Chemical or Biological Attack [that] Triggered Terror Raid" (*The Guardian*).[9]

The dramatic headlines notwithstanding, the two individuals had to be released without charge only a few days later. After a week's intensive search of the premises, no evidence, hazardous or otherwise, had been secured. Once again, an innocent man had been shot, although this time not fatally. As in the de Menezes case, it emerged that the operation had been based on questionable intelligence—in this case said to have been drawn from a single source. Yet, in a further resemblance to the de Menezes case, the resultant IPCC investigation concluded that the incident was an "accident" and that the police involved "committed no criminal or disciplinary offence."[10]

A second illustrative example, albeit less detrimental to human life and safety, emerged two months later in the form of the forcible removal of Walter Wolfgang, an eighty-two-year-old conference delegate and veteran activist of fifty-seven years for the governing Labor Party, from the party's conference venue in Brighton. His crime was the shouting of "Nonsense—you know that's a lie," as Foreign Secretary Jack Straw was giving a speech about the motives for, and success of, Britain's military campaign in Iraq, including the statement that Britain was in Iraq to help bring democracy to the country.

The same night, the BBC News broadcast to the nation how Wolfgang was forcibly removed from the conference venue, subsequently held under section 44 of the Terrorism Act (TA) 2000, and refused permission to reenter the hall.[11] The story was picked up the next morning by the four major broadsheet newspapers, as well as by some of the tabloids, all of which made it their front-page headline.[12] The images were further disseminated through other TV channels; the prime minister and the deputy chairman of the Labor Party had to apologize publicly, and the story continued to feature prominently for another ten days or so.

I review the TA 2000 and its effectiveness in more detail later in the chapter, but section 44 of the TA merits a brief excursion here because it removed the requirement that the police have "reasonable suspicion" that a crime has been, or is about to be, committed before they stop and search suspects. The police force also became empowered to search for articles that might be used in connection with terrorism in a particular area, as long as a police officer of the rank of assistant chief constable or higher has authorized the use of these powers, which must later be approved by the home secretary. The order is made in secret with no court review.

The TA 2000 had been enacted prior to 7/7, and even before 9/11, but the stipulations of section 44 were first applied in the aftermath of 7/7. The area where the powers under section 44 can be imposed may be as large as a city. In London, for instance, there were rolling twenty-eight-day authorizations for the whole of the area policed by the Metropolitan Police and the City of London Police. London is the only U.K. city to have had continuous section 44 authorizations. Following a review of the use of section 44 powers at the end of 2004, the Metropolitan Police refrained from authorizing the powers in eight of the London boroughs, although areas within them may be covered by other authorities, such as the British Transport Police.[13] The most recent figures available demonstrate that section 44 is still widely in use: in 2006 the Metropolitan Police carried out 22,700 stop-and-searches, only 0.1 percent of which led to terrorism-related arrests (*The Times*, "Thousands More Stop and Searches Follow Failed Car Bomb Attacks," August 7, 2007).

Walter Wolfgang's frailty and his escape from Nazi Germany in 1937 to live in a free society such as Britain have probably been particular causes for embarrassment for the Labor government. Given that at the time the government was drafting another antiterrorism bill, the media attention that ensued was also inconvenient. The party leadership therefore felt compelled to offer Wolfgang an apology, but no such treatment was afforded to the other six hundred anti–Iraq War activists who had protested against the G-8 summit at Gleneagles, Scotland. They were held by police under the same section 44 provision, although none of them was suspected of terrorist links (*The Scotsman*, "Over 600 Held Under Terror Act at Labor Conference," October 3, 2005). In all these cases, the downstream conflation between terrorist offenses, on the one hand, and civil dissent or lawful behavior, on the other, resulted in innocent and lawful civilians being tainted by the same brush as suspected terrorists.

In the weeks after July 7, political leaders on both sides of Parliament made their opinions known via statements and commentaries fed to the media. These utterances serve as the third illustrative example, because they hinted at the additional legal proposals that would materialize many months later. In the *Daily Telegraph* ("Judges Must Bow to the Will of Parliament," August 10, 2005), Michael Howard, the Conservative opposition leader at the time, accused judges of "aggressive judicial activism" and of blocking the will of MPs over the fight against terrorism. He suggested that politicians and judges should form a team and pull together for the common cause. The prime minister, in turn, warned judges that he would repeal parts of the Human Rights Act (HRA) 1998 if the courts blocked the deportation of extremists to countries where they were likely to face torture.[14]

In this instance, the judiciary, or the rule of law more generally, was an easy target for politicians and media across the political spectrum. The HRA had implemented into British law the European Convention of Human Rights. Although neither the HRA nor the British judiciary had anything to do with the European Union institutions (much derided among the British public), the public perception that "some European law" would interfere with British life and trump British law to the detriment of the country's security was a fertile and promising soil on which to base a public demand for judicial cooperation.

Although the well-known principle of parliamentary sovereignty grants the U.K. government considerably greater power than the U.K. judiciary compared to most democracies with written constitutions (including the United States), the proposed intrusion was absolutely unprecedented. Such attempts to undermine the independence of the judiciary, as well as the jurisdiction of international legal treaties, ran counter to one of the most important democratic norms developed in the past three centuries: the separation of powers between the executive, the legislature, and the judiciary. After all, it is the function of the judiciary to uphold the constitution (written or not), and its duty to raise objections if existing legislation poses a threat to the rule of law. Especially in periods of vast parliamentary majorities, which the country has seen for both the Labor and Conservative Parties over the last twenty-five years, an independent judiciary is one of the few remaining safeguards in a democracy. The reaction of the judiciary bench was expectedly direct: when judges in office were barred from making political statements in public, the country's previous chief justice, Lord Harry Woolf, warned of a looming constitutional crisis and called on politicians to stop "knocking judges" (*The Times*, "Stop Knocking Judges, Former Chief Justice Tells Ministers," May 31, 2007).

The dissolution of previously sacrosanct democratic boundaries continued in November 2005 with a fourth development: Sir Ian Blair—the newly appointed commissioner of the Metropolitan Police and as such the highest-ranking police officer in the country—used a televised lecture to call for a fresh national debate on policing in the United Kingdom and lobbied, together with colleagues from other branches of law enforcement, for a new piece of antiterrorism legislation proposed by the government.[15]

Democratic principles do not allow for politicians to wear uniforms, and it is similarly unprecedented and controversial for unelected police officers to campaign overtly, politically, and in quite a partisan way for a particular piece of legislation.

A fifth example is provided by the great success of the police in tracing the identity of the London bombers after the 7/7 attacks. Within a week of the attacks, the detailed accounts and CCTV camera footage published by the police, and distributed by the media, tracked the whereabouts of the suicide bombers on the day of the attacks. Identifying the bombers was to become a key success story in an otherwise rather bleak police investigation, and the success of the effort reinforced the government's case for additional camera installations to "safeguard" public and private spaces.

Today the average inhabitant of London is filmed approximately 300 times a day; fellow citizens in Liverpool and Edinburgh are exposed to 100 to 150 video shots daily. Estimates published in the autumn of 2005 were that the number of CCTV cameras in the United Kingdom—which are not counted or registered officially—would rise from 4 million to 7 million at that time to more than 25 million by 2009. The United Kingdom is the country with the highest CCTV penetration per square foot in the world: its inhabitants represent less than 1 percent of the world population, but they are monitored by what is estimated to be more than 20 percent of the world's CCTV cameras. Given the widespread support for the measure among a population keen on a safe living environment, the country is unlikely to relinquish this position anytime soon (Webster 2003, 236).[16] The ostensible benefits of CCTV cameras in reconstructing the events that led to the 7/7 attacks are likely to sway the public even further. That CCTV cameras have been unable to prevent terrorist attacks, and are no deterrent to suicide bombers in particular, is a fact that does not feature prominently in public debates. As a report commissioned by the U.K. information commissioner states, high-tech measures, such as CCTV, create the appearance of definite action and give the impression that the exits are sealed, but they also support a business-as-usual attitude that fails to engage with more conventional means (Surveillance Study Network 2006, 87).

The sixth and final observation relates to the additional legislation introduced by the government after the 7/7 attacks, most prominently in the form of the Terrorism Act 2006, the fourth act concerned with terrorism within five years. Although not a direct response to the July attacks on

London, the Home Office ensured that any lessons learned from the attacks would enhance the writing-up of the legislation. The act created a number of new offenses (acts preparatory to terrorism, encouragement of terrorism, dissemination of terrorist publications, and giving or receiving terrorist training) and extended existing provisions (warrants to enable the police to search any property owned or controlled by a terrorist suspect, extending terrorism stop-and-search powers to cover bays and estuaries, extending police powers to detain suspects after arrest for up to twenty-eight days, improved search powers at ports, and the power to proscribe groups that glorify terrorism).

Unlike the ATCSA 2001, the passing through Parliament of the Terrorism Act 2006 was a rough ride for the government. On November 9, 2005, Prime Minister Blair suffered his first parliamentary defeat as prime minister when MPs voted against the proposed bill in the report stage—by 322 votes to 291, with forty-nine Labor MPs rebelling against their own government. The main cause of the resistance was the government's proposal to extend from fourteen to ninety days the time that police can hold (domestic or foreign) terror suspects without charge. The rebellion forced the government to withdraw the proposal and settle for a compromise of twenty-eight days. The government had another go only two years later, when it tried to extend the period from twenty-eight days to forty-two. This time the government won in the House of Commons with a majority of 315 to 306 votes, but was defeated three months later in the House of Lords, who ruled against the extension with a majority of 309 to 118 votes (BBC News, "Brown Wins Crunch Vote on 42 Days," June 11, 2008; BBC News, "Peers Throw Out 42-Day Detention," October 13, 2008).

The legal concession in 2006 resembled a Pyrrhic victory, however, for when asked in Parliament, the prime minister (and on a separate occasion the commissioner of the Metropolitan Police) was unable to cite any existing case in which, had a ninety-day period been in place, law enforcement agencies would have been able to charge individuals they had to release because of the shorter fourteen-day rule. Unnoticed by Parliament and the media went the additional fact that the detention period had only very recently (and quietly) been extended, from forty-eight hours to seven days, through the Terrorism Act 2000, and then from seven days to fourteen by an act unrelated to terrorism, the Criminal Justice Act 2003.

One of the new offenses created by the Terrorism Act 2006 was the glorification or praise of terrorism, a stipulation that sounds ostensibly valid but has a grave impact on the freedom of speech. Given the vague definition of terrorism, praising rebellious groups in a foreign war of liberation is now potentially an offense. Celebration of the Easter Rising in Northern Ireland, for example, or support for Nelson Mandela's fight against apartheid in South Africa would (and could) now lead to arrest and prosecution, as the renitent groups involved may be freedom fighters to some, but terrorists to others.

The TA 2006 is not the only law that comes to mind in this context: additional (and separate) laws not primarily concerned with terrorism have undermined democracy even further. The hardly noticed Inquiries Act 2005 is one such example: it was designed to provide a framework under which future inquiries could operate effectively, in reasonable time, and at a reasonable cost. In so doing, however, the act gives ministers unprecedented control over parliamentary inquiries into governmental business. As the actions of their ministry are being reviewed by a public inquiry, ministers would have the authority to thwart the efforts of the inquiry at every step. They are able to appoint the members of the inquiry, set its terms, restrict public access, suppress evidence, and shut down the inquiry without having to explain their decision. Also, the resultant inquiry reports are now presented to the ministers whose departments have been scrutinized and not, as they once were, to Parliament.

The British Parliament's Joint Committee on Human Rights (JCHR) voiced serious concerns about these aspects of the act, as did the Law Society of England and Wales and Amnesty International, the latter of which even asked members of the British judiciary not to serve on any inquiry held under the act.[17]

With the scrutiny from inside Parliament restricted in this way, hope rests with the scrutiny exercised from the outside by academics, journalists, and other members of the public. The prospects are ostensibly promising, because one of the legal pledges made by the Labor government when it came to power in 1997 was to establish a legal right for any member of the public to request and be given any information held by a public authority. Since such a right would facilitate external scrutiny, the government decided to delay its implementation for eight years, until January 2005.

Yet it took barely two years for the resultant (albeit much watered-down) Freedom of Information Act 2005 to show its limits: the government had identified too many "very high cost cases" brought by "serial requesters," such as the BBC, *The Guardian*, the *Evening Standard*, and *The Sunday Times*, as expensive and time-consuming obstacles (incurring total costs of £24 million, or US$45 million). A leaked report in the summer of 2006 revealed that Lord Falconer, the constitutional affairs secretary, had called for requests to be rejected in the future if they were too expensive to answer.

A cost-benefit analysis attached to his proposal was later criticized for making dubious assumptions with regard to, first, the number of hours it took civil servants and ministers to respond to requests and, second, the cost of the time involved (*The Guardian*, "Cabinet Confidential," October 30, 2006).

The analysis failed to mention that the stated cost of £24 million paled when compared to the staffing costs for the 3,200 people employed in the government's press and public relations function to tell the public about the government's good work, or the benefits of exposing bureaucratic waste. By the autumn of 2007, Lord Falconer's plan had resulted in a bill being submitted to and discussed by Parliament, whose Constitutional Affairs Committee (CAC) concluded "that there is no objective evidence that any change is necessary."[18] As such, no decision has been reached as of yet, but if the caps are introduced, the most skilled researchers (who are likely to submit the most controversial requests that require particularly lengthy assessments by ministers as to what information should be released) are expected to be barred from scrutinizing the executive.

In 2006 the government also tried to get the Legislative and Regulatory Reform Bill through Parliament; this bill was designed (and presented) as one that would allow ministers to lighten the load of parliamentary business regulations and to relieve some of the pressure on the limited time available for readings in the legislature. During the debates in Parliament, it became clear that, if implemented as introduced by the executive, the bill would give ministers the constitutional power to introduce, amend, and ax legislation with only very limited parliamentary scrutiny. It was also revealed that the law could be used to abolish jury trials, increase control orders of terrorist suspects under the PTA 2005, and even rewrite immigration laws. On this occasion, MPs maintained their resistance: the government eventually backed down in the fall of 2006 and had to withdraw the bill.

These six legal measures aside, the U.K. government also employed some "soft" means to combat Islamic extremism and radicalization. In 2005 the prime minister, Tony Blair, set up a "Muslim Task Force" in cooperation with (often self-appointed) representatives of the Muslim community, such as the Muslim Council of Britain, in an attempt to win hearts and minds. Two years later, surveys indicated that the strategy had not helped to win hearts and minds or change attitudes. A poll commissioned in June 2007 by TV station Channel 4 revealed that almost one-quarter of Britain's 2 million Muslims still did not believe that the July 2005 attacks were carried out by the four named suicide bombers—even though two of them had left videotaped testimony. More than half of those polled also felt that the security services had made up evidence to convict terror suspects (GfK NOP 2007). A separate survey a year earlier, in July 2006, found that 13 percent of Muslims in Britain viewed the 7/7 bombers as heroic, and 16 percent said that, while the attacks were wrong, their cause was right (*The Times*, "The Battle for Hearts and Minds," July 8, 2007).

The Impact of the Laws

This chapter has explicated the extent to which the democratic fabric of society is curtailed by the counterterrorism measures and legislation: given that the perpetrators of the 7/7 attacks were domestic, military operations abroad—the dominant measure taken after the "transnational" attacks on 9/11—were no longer an alternative. Government policy has therefore been directed primarily at the domestic population.

Democratic principles and liberal norms may have been worth surrendering if they had been traded for increased success in prosecuting terrorist suspects and preventing attacks. The extent to which it is feasible to assess the issue of prevention is, of course, limited, since assessment faces both methodological and practical obstacles: an independent academic analysis is not privy to confidential intelligence information about foiled terrorist plots, and even if it was, such an analysis would have to tackle the difficult task of bringing clarity to the obscurity of the unactualized possibilities of counterfactuals (that is to say, assessing whether the terrorist plots would have been foiled if the laws had not been introduced). The level of threat to which the nation is exposed, and the extent to which law enforcement agencies are able to obstruct terrorist attacks, must therefore rely on observation, intelligence leaks, and (potentially biased) governmental statements.

By contrast, an assessment of the objective of legal prosecution is more feasible, because some data—both qualitative (legal texts) and quantitative (figures on charges and arrests on terrorism offenses)—are available for inspection. Such an assessment is the concern of this section.

The Anti-Terrorism, Crime, and Security Act 2001 discussed earlier was not the first law of its kind, of course. The United Kingdom has a long history of, and experience with, legislative measures against political terrorism, predominantly in relation to the territorial dispute over Northern Ireland (for a detailed discussion, see Rogelio Alonso, this volume). Accumulating since the early 1800s has been a long list of acts that established special powers in relation to the life of Ireland, including the creation of a special antiterrorist unit, the suspension of habeas corpus, special arrest powers, search and detention powers, and the limitation of the right to silence in relation to terrorism. The Prevention of Terrorism (Temporary Provisions) Act 1974 then consolidated the various stipulations and concentrated special police powers in relation to terrorist suspects. Although intended to be only temporary measures, most provisions in the 1974 act are still binding law, albeit ones that were subsequently amended in 1976, 1984, 1989, and 1996 (Haubrich 2003).

Antiterrorism legislation in the United Kingdom did not, however, become enshrined in permanent form until the coming into effect of the Terrorism Act 2000. The government at the time took the position that "there will be a continuing need for counter-terrorist legislation for the foreseeable future," regardless of the threat of terrorism related to Northern Ireland, and that the time had come for such legislation to be put on a permanent footing (quoted in Bailey, Harris, and Ormerod 2001, 567). This was achieved by repealing the previous emergency legislation related to Northern Ireland and reenacting the bulk of it with substantial amendments. The more significant sections of the act are:

Section 11: Membership in a proscribed organization[19]

Section 12: Support for a proscribed organization

Section 15: Fund-raising for a proscribed organization

Section 16: Use and possession of property for terrorist purposes

Section 17: Funding arrangements for terrorist purposes

Section 18: Money laundering in relation to terrorist property

Section 44: Stop and search powers

Section 54: Weapons training—offering training or instruction

Section 57: Possession of articles for terrorist purposes

Section 58: Collection of information for terrorist purposes

The act extended to any terrorism—domestic, Irish, or international—thereby creating a definition of terrorism with a uniform framework of regulation. The term "terrorism" itself was extended to include serious violence with religious or ideological purposes, a stipulation that exacerbated the contentious and politically charged character of any definition of terrorism (as it could potentially apply to industrial disputes). The executive justified this initiative on the grounds that the methods employed by terrorists and the effects of their actions were common whatever cause they espoused (Bailey, Harris, and Ormerod 2001, 570). With the introduction of such permanent legislation, terrorism was for the first time acknowledged as a constant part of the social and political landscape in the United Kingdom—an eternal problem that can only ever be dealt with through the use of specialist laws, agencies, and expertise.

Seen in this legal-historical context, the provisions of the ATCSA 2001 emerge as a continuation of a string of antiterrorism measures legislated previously. Those acts were initially targeted at the territorial dispute over Northern Ireland but were soon broadened to include other forms of terrorism. As Parliament's Joint Committee on Human Rights puts it, even prior to the enactment of the ATCSA 2001, "the U.K.'s armory of anti-terrorism measures [was] already widely regarded as among the most rigorous in Europe."[20]

Given the apparent absence of a central data source in the United Kingdom that would track terrorist trials, I had to compile my own data set so as to be able to assess the government's effectiveness in bringing suspects to justice. I used a variety of different sources in the process, including the Crown Prosecution Service (CPS); the Home Office Research Development and Statistics (RDS) directorate; proceedings in the House of Commons and the House of Lords, as published in *Hansard;* press releases of the London Metropolitan Police; articles from the BBC Online News Services, the *Daily Telegraph, The Times, The Guardian,* and *The Scotsman;* NGOs such as Liberty and Amnesty International; online updates of academic textbooks, such as Clive Walker (2002); and personal communications with various human rights lawyers, academic lawyers, journalists, and others.

These efforts have brought to light a total of 130 terrorism-related trials that were conducted in the United Kingdom between September 2001 and September 2005.[21] The data gathered for each trial include the name and nationality of the suspect; the date of arrest; the charges for which the suspect was arrested; the laws invoked; the date of the verdict (if applicable); the sentence (if applicable); offenses for which the suspect was convicted (if applicable); the names of the judge, prosecutor, and attorney; the court of law where the trial was held; and some contextual information about the case.

The most striking result of the research is that, compared to the TA 2000, the ATCSA 2001 pales as a means to prosecute terrorist suspects. The ATCSA 2001 has been the basis of not a single charge, let alone conviction, during the period. The majority of recent trials have invoked the Terrorism Act 2000—legislation that had already come into effect *prior* to the 9/11 attacks—and from that act, sections 11 (membership in a proscribed organization), 57 (possession of articles for terrorist purposes), and 58 (collection of information for terrorist purposes) have accounted for the bulk of the charges (U.K. Secretary of State for the Home Department 2004, 59). Other legislation unrelated to terrorism has also been invoked, most notably the Offenses Against the Person Act 1861, the Explosive Substances Act 1883, the Criminal Law Act 1977, the Criminal Attempts Act 1981, the Forgery and Counterfeiting Act 1981, and the Chemical Weapons Act 1996.

This is a rather uncomplimentary verdict on the ATCSA 2001, which was introduced by the government as an essential requirement for combating terrorism. Constituting the largest single piece of legislation passed by Parliament since the end of World War II, it was rushed, despite its far-reaching implications for civil liberties, through the legislative process in a matter of days.

Only one power created by the ATCSA 2001 has been used extensively, but by its very nature it has had no impact on terrorist trial statistics: the power to detain individuals without trial, as stipulated in part 4, section 23, of the act. Section 23 provides an immigration power for the secretary of state for home affairs, who is now entitled to detain foreign nationals suspected of involvement in terrorism, who pose a threat to national security, and who would otherwise be removed but for the fact that they may face torture or the death penalty. Suspects are detained by immigration officers, usually supported by police officers, and held in secure prison accommodations, usually the high-security prison at Belmarsh.

Several dozens of foreign nationals have been detained in this way (many of them until the spring of 2005, when part 4 was replaced by control orders). As explained in the earlier discussion on transnational terrorism, unlike people detained for "ordinary" crimes, these detainees were not charged with an offense, did not have the right to know the evidence against them, did not have the right to deny or explain that evidence, and did not have the right to a public jury trial. In all these cases, the effectiveness of the laws in bringing terrorist suspects to justice is difficult to assess. What is certain, however, is that none of the suspects has ever been convicted of a crime.

A further conclusion that can be drawn from the research is that more than half of the 130 trials never led to any convictions: the charges were either dropped or thrown out by the judges, or the defendants were released without charge. Most of the cases attracted a great fanfare by the media, the police, and politicians at the time of the initial arrests, only to be dropped quietly weeks or months later. Arguably the most striking case was the alleged "U.K. Ricin Cell": ten individuals arrested in 2003 and 2004 with great national and international publicity and fanfare. Within days of the arrests, the events were referred to by the British prime minister, before the U.K. Parliament, as evidence of the danger from weapons of mass destruction and by then–U.S. Secretary of State Colin Powell, before the UN Security Council, as proof that Iraq was aiding Al Qaeda terrorism against the West.

Yet the government had to admit (and did so very quietly) that no ricin was ever found and that the evidence consisted of twenty castor beans, some cherry stones, apple pips, botched "nicotine poison" in a Nivea jar, a pestle, a mortar, and documents downloaded from the Internet. This evidence was sufficient to convict one suspect, Kamel Bourgas, to seventeen years of imprisonment for "conspiracy to commit a public nuisance by the use of poisons and explosives to cause disruption, fear or injury." The other nine members of the "cell" were either acquitted or not even tried.

Another trial, which was heralded with a similar fanfare, ended significantly short of expectations, too, although for slightly different reasons. During the trial, eight men were accused of conspiracy to commit murder by setting up a "bomb factory" in a flat in East London and using "liquid explosives" to blow up planes traveling from the United Kingdom to North America in midflight. The arrests in 2006 sparked a huge airport security alert, the consequences of which passengers can feel until the present day: the tough airport baggage restrictions and body searches introduced overnight have resulted in years of delays, cancellations, and inconvenience. The rules were designed to stop terrorists from smuggling on board separate and seemingly innocuous household and personal objects that, when put together, are said to create a homemade bomb.

By September 2008, only three of the eight men had been convicted for conspiracy to murder, but the jury failed to reach a verdict on whether they intended to blow up transatlantic jets. Five others were released without charge. By then, it had emerged that the accused had to be arrested much earlier than was desired, partly owing to U.S. authorities ignoring a U.K. request to delay the arrest of Rashid Rauf, the group's contact man in Pakistan. The quality of the evidence that U.K. authorities were able to gather by the time of the premature arrests of the eight men was insufficient to secure more comprehensive convictions.

Quantitative data can be added to inform the discussion of these two case studies: while the 130 terrorism-related court *trials* were collected through my own research, the U.K. Home Office has collected more comprehensive figures on terrorism-related *arrests*.[22] For the period of September 2001 to September 2005, the Home Office reported a total of 895 arrests (see table 5.1). While 496 were later released without charge, only twenty-three

TABLE 5.1 Charges and Convictions Under the Terrorism Act (TA) 2000, September 11, 2001, to September 30, 2005

Number of people arrested	895
Of which convicted of offenses under the TA 2000	23
Of which charged under the TA 2000 (of which also charged with offenses under other legislation)	138 (62)
Of which charged under other laws, including criminal offenses, such as murder and grievous bodily harm	156
Of which transferred to immigration authorities	63
Of which on bail to return	20
Of which cautioned	11
Of which received a final warning for non–TA 2000 offenses	1
Of which dealt with under mental health legislation	8
Of which dealt with under extradition legislation	1
Of which returned to Prison Service custody	1
Of which transferred to Police Service of Northern Ireland custody	1
Of which released without charge	496

Source: Authors' compilation.

suspects were eventually convicted. The remaining 376 were charged with offenses under non-terrorism-related legislation; transferred to immigration authorities; set on bail to return; or processed in other ways.[23]

The figures in table 5.1 are incomplete, however, because they capture only arrests made under the TA 2000; data on arrests under other terrorism-related legislation are not available. The lack of comprehensive data is a concern that has been echoed in the proceedings of the House of Commons Select Committee on Home Affairs, which recommended in the summer of 2005 that in order "to maintain public trust, it is vital that statistics about arrests, charges and convictions under the counter-terrorism legislation be as detailed and reliable as possible" and that the recording procedures need to be improved.[24]

It appears, then, that the antiterrorism legislation introduced since 9/11 has added little value to the country's ability to prosecute suspected terrorists. The ATCSA 2001 and the PTA 2005 are ineffective in bringing terrorist suspects to justice, while the effects of the TA 2006 cannot yet be assessed. This is not to say that law enforcement agencies do not have sufficient legal means to do their work. Dozens of terrorism trials have succeeded in bringing suspects to justice, but they have done so by reverting either to terrorism laws that were already in force prior to 9/11 or to laws that are not related to terrorism. The crimes most likely committed (conspiracy to murder, murder, weapons possession, illegal passports, and so forth) are already offenses under existing legislation (on terrorism or otherwise), have been so for decades, but may require more vigorous enforcement.

Conclusion

Despite its long history with terrorism, Britain has no ready-made answers at its disposal to counter the threat posed to the country after the attacks on 9/11 and 7/7. The terrorism inflicted on the country by the IRA in the 1960s, 1970s, and 1980s had only limited implications for the democratic structure and constitution of the country. In this first type of terrorism—domestic terrorism—there is a mutual check at work that limits domestic terrorist actions and governmental reactions alike. Because both opponents must woo support from the same domestic public, the scope, the intensity, and the ferocity of the conflict are limited, as are the knock-on effects for the democratic fabric of society.

The danger of losing public support is only imminent, however, if the threat is posed by an enemy who comes from within. A different assessment has to be made when the terrorist incident involves perpetrators from outside the society under attack. The demarcating characteristic of this second type of terrorism—transnational terrorism—is that the perpetrators have no interest in securing support among the domestic population. Achieving their political objective, if identifiable at all, does not require the backing of the population where the attacks occur. Similarly, without the threat of a potential alliance between the population and the perpetrators, the government is less at risk of terrorists exploiting societal grievances; unlike domestic terrorists, external aggressors lend themselves less convincingly to the role of defenders of the people if the people are actual or potential victims of that aggression. And where the probability of an alliance between the terrorists and the public is low or nonexistent, governmental reactions to terrorism are much less constrained.

In discussing type 2 terrorism here, I explicated the implications of this dynamic for the democratic fabric of British society. An upstream conflation has occurred between crimes, which are usually dealt with by civil agencies, and acts of war, which are countered by military agencies that face much less rigid levels of democratic scrutiny and investigative constraints. At the same time, a downstream conflation has occurred between crimes, on the one hand, and public order disturbances or civil dissent, on the other, a development that has resulted in innocent and lawful civilians being tainted by the same brush as suspected terrorists. Examples have been given to illustrate that any form of political pressure exerted on the government but not channeled through conventional political and parliamentary processes is now seen as unduly compelling the government into a course of action that it would not have taken otherwise, and thus as pressure that merits restrictive countermeasures by law enforcement agencies.

This dynamic was exacerbated after the terrorist attacks on the London transport system on July 7, 2005. Those attacks constituted the third type of terrorism—compounded terrorism. As argued earlier, in the absence of a clearly identifiable enemy abroad, counterterrorism legislation—policy as well as operations—is directed exclusively at the domestic society, with severe implications for the democratic fabric of society. Operations by British law enforcement agencies were found to be ineffective, based on wrong intelligence, and posing a threat to (or even extinguishing) the lives of innocent members of the public. The right to criticize the government (whether over its policy in Iraq or other matters) became curtailed by antiterrorism legislation. The political leaders of the governing Labour Party as well as the Conservative opposition called for changes to the constitutional order of the country that would effectively undermine the separation of powers between the judiciary and the executive. The chief of the Metropolitan Police, by publicly advocating a particular piece of legislation, crossed yet another democratic boundary. Finally, additional legislation was introduced that tipped the balance between the state and the individual even further.

A loss of liberty on such a scale is worth incurring if the legislative and operational measures causing this loss succeed in bringing terrorist suspects to justice. To the extent that it is possible, the final section has shown that the effectiveness of the antiterrorist laws introduced after 9/11 has been limited: the terrorist trials (and the small number of convictions) identified in my research did not invoke those laws but rather legislation enacted prior to the 9/11 attacks.

The U.K. government has successfully taken advantage of the dynamics of transnational and compounded terrorism that have emerged since 9/11 and 7/7 by imposing unprecedented legislative countermeasures, thereby suffocating criticism of, dissent from, and resistance to its policies. In exchange, the country has improved little in terms of its capacity to prosecute and bring to justice terrorist suspects. Quite clearly, then, other paths need to be pursued (or reemphasized) if the level of threat is to decrease, including better counterintelligence, a reevaluation of the country's foreign policy priorities, and consideration of what is commonly (and often condescendingly) referred to as the "root causes" of terrorism.

Notes

1. See Global Terrorism Database entry on "Irish Republican Army," available at: http://www.start.umd.edu/gtd/search/Results.aspx?perpetrator=417 (accessed August 2009).
2. See Conflict Archive on the Internet (CAIN), University of Ulster, "Internment: Summary of Main Events," available at: http://cain.ulst.ac.uk/events/intern/sum.htm (accessed September 2007).
3. See European Court of Human Rights (ECtHR), *Ireland v. United Kingdom*, 5310/71 (1978) ECtHR 1 (January 18, 1978), available at: http://www.worldlii.org/eu/cases/ECHR/1978/1.html (accessed September 2007).
4. See CAIN, University of Ulster, "A Chronology of the Conflict: 1991," available at: http://cain.ulst.ac.uk/othelem/chron/ch91.htm#14391 (accessed September 2007).
5. Author's calculations, using "location" as first variable and "status" as second variable, based on CAIN, University of Ulster, "Malcolm Sutton: An Index of Deaths from the Conflict in Ireland: Crosstabulations," available at: http://cain.ulst.ac.uk/sutton/crosstabs.html (accessed August 2009).
6. Author's calculations, based on the Memorial Institute for the Prevention of Terrorism (MIPT) Terrorism Knowledge Base, available at the Global Terrorism Database (GTD): http://www.start.umd.edu/gtd/search/Results.aspx?expanded=no&casualties_type=&casualties_max=&perpetrator=417&ob=CountryText&od=asc&page=1&count=100#results-table (accessed August 2009).
7. For a selection of comments made to BBC Radio, see BBC News, "Is Police Anti-Terror Policy Justified?" (August 3, 2005), available at: http://news.bbc.co.uk/1/hi/talking_point/4711189.stm (accessed September 2007).
8. See Independent Police Complaints Commission (IPCC), "An Investigation into Complaints About the Metropolitan Police Services Handling of Public Statements Following the Shooting of Jean Charles de Menezes on 22 July" (2006), available at: http://www.ipcc.gov.uk/index/resources/evidence_reports/investigation_reports/stockwell_two.htm (accessed September 2007).
9. For an overview of the headlines that day, see BBC News, "Papers Focus on Aftermath of Raid" (June 3, 2006), available at: http://news.bbc.co.uk/1/hi/uk/5043438.stm (accessed September 2007).
10. See IPCC, "Independent Investigations into Complaints Made Following the Forest Gate Counter-Terrorist Operation on 2 June 2006" (2006), available at: http://www.ipcc.gov.uk/forest_gate_2_3report.pdf (accessed September 2007).
11. For the video clip, see Nick Assinder, "Wolfgang Highlights Deeper Disquiet," BBC News (September 29, 2005), available at: http://news.bbc.co.uk/1/hi/uk_politics/4293502.stm (accessed September 2007).

12. See "Obsessed with Rights, Blind to Liberty," *Daily Telegraph*, September 30, 2005; "Blair Leads Party Apologies to Activist," *The Independent*, September 30, 2005; "Delegate, 82, Is Thrown Out After Heckling Straw," *The Times*, September 29, 2005.
13. See U.K. Home Affairs Committee, "Terrorism and Community Relations," sixth report of session 2004–2005, vol. 1, together with formal minutes and appendix (2005), para. 47.
14. For Tony Blair's answers in the transcripts of his July and August 2005 press conferences, see U.K. Prime Minister's Office, "PM's Press Conference—26 July 2005," available at: http://www.number-10.gov.uk/output/Page7999.asp; and "PM's Press Conference—5 August 2005" available at: http://www.number-10.gov.uk/output/Page8041.asp (both accessed September 2007).
15. See BBC News, "Transcript of Sir Ian Blair's Speech" (November 16, 2005), available at: http://news.bbc.co.uk/1/hi/uk/4443386.stm (accessed September 2007).
16. A 2001 Market and Opinion Research International (MORI) poll suggested that 90 percent of Londoners are in favor of installing more CCTV cameras on pubic transport; available at: http://mayor.london.gov.uk/mayor/ppp/mori_poll/mori_poll.pdf, p. 12 (accessed September 2007).
17. See Joint Committee on Human Rights (JCHR), "Inquiries Bill," fourth report of the 2004–2005 session, House of Lords (November 24, 2004), p. 7. For Amnesty International's statement, see http://www.amnesty.org/en/library/asset/EUR45/010/2005/en/dom-EUR450102005en.html (accessed August 2009).
18. See Constitutional Affairs Committee (CAC), "Freedom of Information: Government's Proposals for Reform," fourth report of the 2006–2007 session, House of Commons 415 (June 24, 2007).
19. The list of (presently fifty-four) proscribed organizations can be found at: http://www.homeoffice.gov.uk/security/terrorism-and-the-law/terrorism-act/proscribed-groups (accessed July 2006).
20. See JCHR, "Anti-Terrorism, Crime, and Security Bill: Further Report," fifth report of the 2001–2002 session, House of Lords 37, House of Commons 372 (2002), para. 30.
21. Detailed publication of the research is forthcoming as "Terrorist Trial Report Card U.K." on the website of the New York University Center on Law and Security, available at: http://www.lawandsecurity.org/index.cfm (accessed September 2007).
22. U.K. Home Office, "Carlisle Report" (2009), available at: http://security.homeoffice.gov.uk/news-publications/publication-search/general/Lord-Carlile-report-2009/Lord-Carlile-report.pdf?view=Binary (accessed August 2009).
23. These numbers may change over time as individuals move through the immigration process. Also, figures on TA 2000 arrests in Northern Ireland are handled by the Northern Ireland Office (NIO) and are not included here.

24. See House of Commons Select Committee on Home Affairs, "Terrorism and Community Relations," sixth report of session 2004–2005, vol. 1, together with formal minutes and appendix (2005), para. 58, 161.

References

Bailey, S. H., D. J. Harris, and D. C. Ormerod. 2001. *Civil Liberties: Cases and Materials.* London: Butterworth.

Bunyan, Tony. 1977. *The History and Practice of the Political Police in Britain.* London: Quartet Books.

Freedman, Lawrence. 2001. "The Third World War?" *Survival* 43(4): 61–88.

GfK NOP Social Research. 2007. *Attitudes to Living in Britain: A Survey of Muslim Opinion—For Channel 4 Dispatches.* London: GfK NOP.

Haubrich, Dirk. 2003. "September 11, Anti-Terror Laws, and Civil Liberties: Britain, France, and Germany Compared." *Government and Opposition* 38(1): 3–28.

———. 2005. "Civil Liberties in Emergencies." In *Governments of the World: A Global Guide to Citizens' Rights and Responsibilities,* vol. 1, edited by C. Neal Tate. Detroit: Macmillan Reference.

———. 2006. "Modern Politics in an Age of Global Terrorism: New Challenges for Domestic Public Policy." *Political Studies* 54(2): 399–423.

Hörnqvist, Magnus. 2004. "The Birth of Public Order Policy." *Race and Class* 46(1): 30–52.

Richardson, Louise. 2007. "Britain and the IRA." In *Democracy and Counterterrorism: Lessons from the Past,* edited by Robert J. Art and Louise Richardson. Washington, D.C.: United States Institute of Peace Press.

Sandler, Todd, John T. Tschirhart, and Jon Cauley. 1983. "A Theoretical Analysis of Transnational Terrorism." *American Political Science Review* 77: 36–54.

Surveillance Study Network. 2006. *A Report on the Surveillance Society.* London: U.K. Information Commissioner's Office.

U.K. Secretary of State for the Home Department. 2004. "Counter-Terrorism Powers: Reconciling Security and Liberty in an Open Society." Discussion paper Cm 6147. London: Her Majesty's Stationery Office (HMSO).

Walker, Clive. 2002. *Blackstone's Guide to the Anti-Terrorism Legislation.* London: Blackstone.

Walsh, D. P. J. 1982. "Arrest and Interrogation." *Journal of Law and Society* 9(1): 37–62.

Webster, William R. 2003. "The Diffusion, Regulation, and Governance of Closed-Circuit Television in the U.K." *Surveillance and Society* 2: 230–50.

Wilkinson, Paul. 2006. *Terrorism Versus Democracy: The Liberal State Response,* 2nd ed. London: Routledge.

Chapter 6

Confronting Terrorism in Northern Ireland and the Basque Country: Challenges for Democracy and Legitimacy

Rogelio Alonso

This chapter analyzes the effects of specific counterterrorist policies aimed at the Basque Freedom and Homeland Organization (Euskadi ta Askatasuna, ETA) and the Irish Republican Army (IRA) on the societies in which they were implemented. Since a comprehensive examination of the consequences of all the measures introduced against these types of terrorism would exceed the limitations of this chapter, special attention is paid to two policies that have often been defined as undemocratic: the banning of political parties and media censorship. The chapter argues that such a view is superficial when causes and effects of those policies are assessed in terms of the Spanish and Irish examples.

These initiatives did not fundamentally damage democratic freedoms because they were aimed precisely at terrorist activities that deprived citizens of their rights. A serious challenge to democracy like the one posed by terrorism sometimes requires drastic but lawful responses in order to confront efficiently those who are defying basic democratic values. My approach widens the focus of this volume's analysis of the consequences for democracy of counterterrorist policies because it takes into consideration the effects of failing to apply policy instruments that are less conventional but nonetheless legal.

As the Northern Ireland and Basque cases reveal, terrorists articulate their challenges to the state on several different fronts, and their fight for legitimacy represents an important dimension of this multifaceted approach. This acknowledgment is of great relevance for counterterrorist strategies, since the effectiveness of terrorist groups like ETA and the IRA has relied on the legitimization and endorsement that they receive. Thus, before examining specific policies, the chapter outlines the democratization processes that have considerably weakened support for violence in both regions. This outline reveals the evolution of counterterrorism measures that facilitated the decline of the IRA and ETA by forcing them to search for alternative paths to terrorism.

Nonetheless, the decrease in violence perpetrated by terrorist groups occurred in parallel with their tactical decision to remain in existence in order to exert considerable pressure on society and political players. This scenario has posed important challenges for democracy, demanding appropriate responses from governments that have been tempted to increase the legitimacy of terrorist movements that for years have been constantly delegitimized. This change has been a key component of recent counterterrorist strategy in Spain and the United Kingdom.

As the chapter demonstrates when looking at the consequences of controversial initiatives such as the proscription of ETA's political wing and the media ban applied to Sinn Féin, these organizations largely failed in their attempts to undermine the legitimacy of the democratic states in which they perpetrated their violence. Nonetheless, certain governmental responses in both areas, once violence decreased and gave way to what has been termed a "peace process," encouraged the legitimization of those who threatened democracy. This chapter argues that political pragmatism and leniency toward separatist movements that allegedly set out on a transition from terrorism to peaceful politics after protracted violence can be more counterproductive than beneficial to the strengthening of democracy.

Despite the decrease in violence, the refusal of both terrorist organizations to disband and the coercion they both tried to exert on the political process in Northern Ireland and in the Basque Country following their formal declarations of ceasefire demonstrate that states still had to respond to the challenges posed to governance by these terrorist groups and the parties closely linked to them. The absence of systematic terrorist attacks and the two governments' engagement with political parties linked to terrorist groups during the "peace processes" did alter the stage of what is always, in Brian Jenkins's (1975, 4) graphic description, the "theater" of terrorism.

It is true that, to a great extent, "the terrorism that plays itself out in newspapers and on television screens to rapt audiences around the world, is to be understood as activity that is primarily expressive in character rather than outcome-oriented," since it mainly expresses "virulent and unregulated opposition to the preconditions of successful civility" (Lomasky 1991, 105–6). Nonetheless, terrorist groups aim at subverting public order and democracy, and these are goals that can be pursued in the absence of systematic terrorist attacks. In fact, during the "peace processes," systematic terrorist violence was replaced in Northern Ireland and the Basque Country by a new strategy whereby a reduced level of terrorist activity complemented other criminal activities as a means of exerting pressure on legitimate democratic parties.

Terrorism and the Legitimacy of Democracy: A Comparative Perspective

Violence and the Battle for Hearts and Minds

Since the late 1960s, the Spanish and British states have faced serious terrorist campaigns by ETA and the IRA. These organizations—which are both part of what has been referred to as the third wave of modern terrorism (Rapoport 2004)—have espoused an ethno-nationalist ideology on the basis of which they have legitimized their campaigns for over thirty years. The political, social, and cultural contexts in which these terrorists groups emerged provide some explanation for the origins of their violent campaigns.

However, despite the changes in these contexts during the last three decades, the actuality of or the threat of terrorism persists. Therefore, in order to explain why terrorism happens, it is also useful to understand why terrorism continues over time, as well as the reasons behind its decline (Crenshaw 1981, 2003). A key variable in understanding both the continuation and the progressive decline of ETA and the IRA is the degree of legitimacy achieved by each terrorist organization, as well as that of the state.

In this respect, the roles of society in general and the communities from which the terrorists and their political representatives seek support are relevant when confronting terrorism. Experience demonstrates the importance of policies that delegitimize terrorist groups in the communities in whose interests they claim to be fighting. Delegitimization and condemnation of violence by the majority prevents terrorists from increasing their social support and is a necessary, but not sufficient, precondition for terrorism to remain a minority phenomenon (Crenshaw 1983; Schmid 1993, 2000).

Therefore, counterterrorism in Northern Ireland and the Basque Country has also required the encouragement of such delegitimization and isolation, which have been particularly efficient coming from political or religious leaders who are respected in the communities from which these groups drew their support. Certain policies have allowed these leaders to exert a positive influence on other members of that section of the population as part of the "battle for hearts and minds."[1]

The evolution of the IRA and ETA during the last four decades—since the outbreak of terrorism in Northern Ireland and the Basque Country—shows that violence has gradually decreased in both areas. More than 3,600 people have died since the outbreak of violence in Northern Ireland, with the IRA being responsible for most of these killings, including a considerable number of Catholic civilians. Statistics attribute to the IRA and other splinter groups almost 60 percent of all the killings caused during the conflict. Loyalist terrorists were responsible for 28 percent of all deaths, and security forces, including the army and the police, for 10 percent (McKittrick et al. 1999, 1473–93; Fay, Morrissey, and Smyth 1997; Fay, Morrissey, and Smyth 1999, 168–71). In 1972, the year with the highest number of casualties, 496 people were killed, whereas the deaths between 1980 and 1990 amounted to a total of 972. During the following decade, violence kept diminishing, to the level of 468 killings between 1991 and 1999.

In the Basque Country, ETA has been responsible for the deaths of almost one thousand people since the beginning of its campaign. Furthermore, during the transition from authoritarian rule in the second half of the 1970s after the death of General Francisco Franco, right-wing extremists, including those of Basque origins, and a number of Italian neofascists related to reactionary members of the state security agencies killed ten people in France and twenty-three others inside Spain. The victims were presumably chosen because of their suspected relationship with ETA (Alonso 2005). Also, between 1983 and 1987, a similar campaign of terrorist activity against suspected members and supporters of ETA was carried out by a shadowy organization known as GAL (Grupos Antiterroristas de Liberación, or Liberation Antiterrorist Groups), resulting in the killing of twenty-seven individuals (Woodworth 2001). ETA's violence peaked in 1981, then gradually decreased until, from 2004 to December 2006, the terrorist group failed to commit any murders. Two people were killed on December 30, 2006, when a bomb planted by ETA went off at Madrid's airport. Between then and the end of 2008, six other people were killed by the terrorist group.

Like the IRA, ETA's decreasing level of violence confirms the declining cycle of the group: 1968 to 1975, 45 deaths; 1976 to 1980, 280 deaths; 1981 to 1987, 277 deaths; 1988 to 1995, 178 deaths; 1996 to 2003, 70 deaths (Alonso 2005, 132). These decreases occurred in parallel with the successful political and coercive measures adopted over time by successive governments in the United Kingdom and Spain (Neumann 2003; Reinares and Alonso 2007).

In this context, the political and social weakness of the IRA and ETA, as well as that of the parties that traditionally represented their views, Sinn Féin and Batasuna, created a scenario in which the end of terrorism seemed a real possibility. In August 1994, the IRA declared a ceasefire; it broke down in February 1996, but was reinstated in July 1997. In September 1998, ETA called a truce that broke down in 1999 but was followed by a new ceasefire in March 2006. Once again, ETA returned to killing on December 30, 2006, when two men were murdered in a terrorist attack at Madrid's airport. In June 2007, ETA formally declared the reopening of "all fronts against the State."

Democratization and the Reform of the State

When both groups became active in the late 1960s, the political arenas in which they emerged were clearly characterized by an important democratic deficit (Elorza 2000; Whyte 1994; Tonge 2006). General Franco's dictatorship in Spain represented for Basque nationalists a serious grievance that, in the view of some of them, demanded a violent response. In Northern Ireland, the Unionist-controlled government that had excluded the nationalist minority in the region since the creation of the state in 1922 had long ignored the need for reforms that would address the just grievances of a significant section of the population in the region.[2] Although reforms were implemented in the late 1960s and most of the demands by the civil rights movement had by then already been satisfied, the outbreak of intercommunal violence in that period facilitated the emergence of the IRA.

Once violence erupted, the Spanish and British states engaged in serious processes of democratization and reform that evolved in tandem with their security policies. To some extent, the decrease in both terrorist campaigns can be seen as a result of these processes, which delegitimized terrorism.

In Spain, new political institutions and a legal framework replaced Franco's regime. In 1978 a new Spanish constitution opened the door for the decentralization of the state, and the 1979 "Statute of Autonomy of the Basque Country" was approved by popular referendum. The statute, which provides for Basque institutions of territorial self-government, has the status of constitutional law and provides autonomous authorities with extensive powers, including a separate fiscal system, a regional police force under the command of the Basque executive, and complete responsibility for education and health, as well as a long list of matters with respect to which the regional authorities enjoy sole jurisdiction. The process of administrative decentralization undergone by Spain in the last decades has been described as "unparalleled in the rest of Western Europe" and "tantamount to a revolution" (Conversi 1993, 264).

This significant decentralization eroded support for violence in the Basque Country and contributed to the consolidation of democracy in the region (Tejerina 2001; Mees 2001). Aiding the consolidation was the gradual professionalization and modernization of the security agencies, which had been distrusted by society because of their previous association with an authoritarian regime (Jaime 2002). Moreover, between 1975 and 1977, nearly nine hundred ETA members and collaborators who had been exiled or imprisoned under the dictatorship were freed. After the Spanish National Court was set up in 1977, terrorist crimes were dealt with by judges instead of military courts. Finally, after 1982, social reinsertion measures based on individual pardons were applied to individuals who were prepared to distance themselves from the terrorist organization.

In Northern Ireland, the reform process aimed at improving living conditions and equality for all sections of the population. As it gathered force during the first half of the 1970s, it was complemented by a greater involvement of the British government through different political initiatives aimed at pacifying the region, a process in which the Irish government was also involved (Alonso 2001a, 131–236). In 1972 the British government suspended the autonomous Stormont administration, which had been established in 1922 and was exclusively controlled by Unionists throughout its existence. Its suspension was followed by the introduction of direct rule from London: the administration of Northern Ireland became the exclusive responsibility of the British government. Coinciding with the outbreak of violence between 1969 and 1973, the British government established the three main principles on which its policy would be based for the following decades.[3]

First, the so-called principle of consent established that the British government accepted as legitimate the possibility of the unification of the North and the South of Ireland as long as the majority of Northern Irish people consented. Second, what was known as the "Irish dimension" recognized Northern Ireland's position within Ireland as a whole and considered it "desirable" that, as far as possible, the provisions for governing Northern Ireland would also be accepted by the Irish state. This would require some institutional expression of the Irish dimension. Third, decentralization would lead to the devolution of powers to an autonomous government that would be based on greater consensus than the Stormont regime. The executive would not be controlled by a party representing only one of the communities in the divided Northern Irish society.

Overall, this approach heightened the IRA's crisis of legitimacy to the point that, even in supportive communities, criticism of IRA violence became not uncommon (Burton 1978). In fact, the high level of IRA intimidation in the ghettos of Northern Ireland reveals that, rather than "admired," the group was merely "tolerated" (Mallie and Bishop 1987, 288). As two former IRA members put it, the organization "went into a serious decline" between 1972 and 1974, so that, "apart from the British occupation, there is very little injustice there that's worth an armed struggle, and an armed struggle can't win on that basis" (Alonso 2007a, 96).

Attitudes Toward Terrorism

Following some early abuses and miscarriages of justice by authorities in both countries, the British and Spanish states adopted a more selective and successful security and judicial approach. However, the early counterproductive measures against terrorism contributed to the sustaining of significant and lasting popular support for the terrorists and their political wings. Those measures went from the introduction of internment and the excessive use of force by the army and the police in Northern Ireland to the extension of normal detention periods and the lack of judicial control over home searches in Spain, as well as the maltreatment of prisoners in both areas. Nonetheless, the initial pattern of massive raids and convictions was replaced by a higher degree of efficiency with fewer detentions but higher percentages of convictions. The result was a decrease in alienation among those sections of the population who were most likely to become radicalized or sympathetic to the terrorist point of view.[4]

The combination of all these factors guaranteed that terrorism would remain, in both Northern Ireland and the Basque Country, a minority phenomenon that was never widely supported despite the existence of a significant minority who still empathized with terrorist groups or those who represented them politically. Public opinion studies conducted from 2003 to 2008 found that, compared to earlier surveys, the rejection of ETA among Basque citizens was year after year stronger than ever before and remained, interestingly enough, the majority's attitude even among Batasuna's constituency—that is, those who voted for the terrorist group's political wing.[5] This pattern marked an important shift from previous positions. In 1978 nearly half of the Basque adults perceived ETA members as either patriots or idealists, and only 7 percent of those interviewed in public opinion surveys called them plain criminals. In 1989, however, fewer than one-quarter of Basque citizens referred to them in more or less favorable terms, those who portrayed members of ETA simply as criminals having more than doubled in comparison with figures from the previous decade (Llera 1993, 97–117; Linz 1986, 617–65).

The poor performance of ETA's political wing in general elections over the years confirms the decreasing support that violent nationalism has found among the Basque people: in 1979, it garnered a 15 percent vote; in 1982, 14.8 percent; in 1986, 17.8 percent; in 1989, 16.8 percent; in 1993, 14.6 percent; and in 1996, 12.3 percent.[6] Another indicator of the decreasing support for ETA and the growing dissociation of important sections of Basque society from the terrorist group is evidenced in an increasing mobilization of citizens against violence, a phenomenon articulated in a number of associations that have regularly held public demonstrations, with strong turnouts, demanding the end of terrorism (Funes 1998; Uriarte 2003).

On the other hand, terrorist violence seems to be more highly condoned in Northern Ireland than in the Basque Country, although such approval is still restricted to a significant minority of the population, as the surveys conducted in the region would indicate (Hayes and McAllister 1996). In 1968, 51 percent of Protestants and 13 percent of Catholics believed that it was right to use violence. In 1973, 16 percent of Protestants and 25 percent of Catholics saw violence as a legitimate way to achieve goals. In 1978, 35 percent of Protestants and 46 percent of Catholics regarded IRA members as patriots and idealists. Twenty years later, in 1998, 69 percent of Protestants expressed no sympathy toward Loyalist terrorist groups, whereas 24 percent of Protestants indicated some sympathy, and 7 percent a lot of sympathy, for them. At the same time, 72 percent of Catholics showed no sympathy toward Republican terrorism, whereas 21 percent of Catholics had some sympathy for Republican violence, and 7 percent of Catholics a lot of sympathy. Surprisingly, one in five Catholics had "some sympathy" for Loyalist terrorists, and one in ten Protestants shared "some sympathy" for Republicans (Hayes and McAllister 2001, 913–14). Successive results at general elections contested by Sinn Féin are also indicative of the limited endorsement received by violent republicanism: in 1983, Sinn Féin received

13.4 percent of the vote; in 1987, 11.4 percent; in 1992, 10 percent; and in 1997, 16.1 percent.[7]

These patterns indicate that as the IRA and ETA declined in terms of mobilization potential and frequency of attacks, a core element remained supportive of the aims and means employed by the terrorist organizations. It was in these contexts that two particular measures were implemented in order to further diminish the legitimacy of both organizations. Given the repressive nature of these controversial initiatives, they could have undermined the legitimacy of the states rather than that of the terrorist groups. Nonetheless, the effects for society were quite positive, the timing of the introduction of these measures being decisive in such an outcome. At a time when terrorists in both areas persisted in their attempts at undermining the resilience of the state and society, these policies sought to wear out those who defied the system, deepening their political and social isolation. Thus, more common coercive measures were complemented with extraordinary tools that managed to further delegitimize the means used by the terrorist movements, which became increasingly demoralized.

Marginalizing the Terrorists: The Banning of ETA's Political Wing

The Consequences of Outlawing Batasuna

One of the most controversial measures implemented by the Spanish state was the banning of ETA's political wing, formerly known as Batasuna. In 2002 the Spanish Parliament approved new legislation that allowed the executive, upon the request of the legislature, to demand judicial procedures to outlaw political groups that were unwilling to condemn terrorism or that maintained links with a terrorist organization.

Even before this law was passed, Judge Baltasar Garzón, a magistrate from the National Court who had been investigating Batasuna's links with ETA, had already suspended the party's activities as a result of the close relationship between the two wings of the movement. The basis for the banning of Batasuna rested in the belief that the party was part of the network of organizations ultimately led by ETA. The movement shared objectives as well as membership with the party.[8] Following the September 2002 suspension of Batasuna's activities through the penal code, the government also asked the Supreme Court to outlaw the party, which took effect in March 2003.

This initiative was widely criticized by nationalist politicians in the Basque Country, who claimed that it would trigger more violence and deepen the delegitimization of the state (Alonso and Reinares 2005). The outcome has been positive, however, in democratic terms. First, lethal terrorist action, as well as urban terrorism, has decreased, since ETA has been unable to regain the popular support it lost over the years. Second, the banning of Batasuna has had significant material consequences because the measure deprived the political party of generous public funding from different institutions at both the national and European levels, amounts that represented a valuable source of income for ETA (Buesa 2006). Since the proscription of Batasuna resulted in the expulsion of the party from the institutions of municipal and local government throughout the Basque Country, the organization's ability to exert social and political control over the population has eroded.

Another positive outcome has been that the state was seen as confronting terrorism with determination but through legal means, rather than the illegal means adopted in the early 1980s when members of the Spanish Ministry of Interior were linked to the terrorist actions of GAL. The democratic credentials of the state were seriously damaged by GAL's crimes, since the group benefited from the passivity and allegiance of some prominent figures. Fortunately, Spain proved to be a functioning democratic regime, and the rule of law was finally applied: the police officers, gangsters, and Socialist Party politicians involved all received severe court sentences.

The state's reaction of banning Batasuna came at a time when ETA's intimidation had reached extraordinary levels. In 1995 ETA introduced a campaign of "socializing the suffering": representatives of non-nationalist parties were targeted in an attempt to push them to the margins of the political system. The group pursued a systematic campaign of violence and intimidation against Basque citizens who did not share a nationalist ideology. The extent of the threats and abuses of human rights led Judge Baltasar Garzón to accuse ETA and Batasuna of pursuing a campaign of "ethnic cleansing."[9] Garzón's report argued that both organizations had promoted the "depuration of the census" in the Basque Country through the elimination of those citizens who would block a nationalist hegemony. This strategy coincided with ETA's concerns (as expressed in an internal document dated July 1999) about the need to establish a "national census" as well as a "definition of who is a citizen of Euskal Herria" and who is entitled to vote (Domínguez 2003, 260–61).[10] The ideological hunt that followed resulted in the premeditated harassment and intimidation of more than forty-two thousand people, as estimated by the nongovernmental organization (NGO) Gesto por la Paz (Gesture for Peace) ("Gesto por la Paz estima que 42,000 personas sufren la amenaza directa de los etarras," *El País*, November 9, 2002). Under these circumstances, the state had to act in order to protect a section of society that felt vulnerable and defenseless.

Despite the fears of some politicians and observers at the time, the ban is now regarded as a useful measure. That ETA feared such a measure would be taken can be inferred from an internal document dated March 2002 in which ETA, referring to moderate nationalists in the PNV (Partido Nacionalista Vasco, or Basque Nationalist Party), wrote: "The PNV argues that the banning will strengthen Batasuna at a time of weakness. However, if that repressive attack was really beneficial, why is it that the PNV doesn't ask to be banned too accepting the subsequent police surveillance, listening devices, raids, [and] canceling of demonstrations."[11]

Other internal ETA documents confirm how damaging the ban was for ETA as it deepened the isolation of the movement by depriving it of valuable resources.[12] Furthermore, in the aftermath of the proscription, the number of lethal terrorist actions decreased and ETA was incapable of regaining more popular support. The dismantling of the satellite structures that had supported ETA, together with increased formal sanctions on violent activism, accelerated the group's decline and reduced the levels of social control imposed by ETA's supporters. These harsh measures had positive consequences for threatened citizens, since they were relieved of the pressure exerted by the terrorist network.

The banning of Batasuna was strongly criticized by all of the nationalist parties in the Basque Country, which saw the proscription as a serious violation of fundamental rights and liberties.[13] Subsequently, the nationalist parties joined forces in the Basque Parliament and voted against the ban. ETA sympathizers considered the fact that the majority of Basque political representatives disagreed with the proscription as evidence of a lack of freedom and democracy for Basque citizens.[14]

This was a view that many nationalists from the main party in the region, the PNV, also endorsed. The Basque government decided in September 2003 to formally accuse the Spanish state of violating articles 6, 7, and 11 of the European Convention on Human Rights (ECHR). On February 2004, however, the European Court of Human Rights (ECtHR) unanimously agreed to reject the Basque government's claim, on the grounds that an autonomous government within a state is unable to sue its own state.

The highest judicial bodies in Spain, the Constitutional Court and the Supreme Court, had already rejected the Basque government's claim. The Supreme Court declared in March 2003 that the benefit derived from banning ETA's political wing was the protection of democracy and the rights of society. In a very relevant endorsement, in June 2009 the European Court of Human Rights confirmed the ruling by the Spanish Supreme and Constitutional Courts that had banned Batasuna. The ECtHR argued that banning "corresponded to a pressing social need."

Defending Democracy from Violence

At the core of these opposing arguments is an important debate about democracy and terrorism. The majority of nationalist politicians portrayed the measure as a denial of the human rights of a section of Basque society. ETA's sympathizers used the term "apartheid."[15] Moreover, the representatives of the main nationalist parties in the region lent credibility to charges of discrimination and repression by the Spanish state, expressed by constant demonstrations of public support for critics of the ban.

In contrast, supporters of the proscription argued that its critics failed to face up to the fundamentally antidemocratic values of ETA's political apologists. They argued that Spanish democracy is an achievement that must be defended against projects that violate fundamental democratic principles. Regarding democracy as a vulnerable system that needs to be defended, these supporters argued that political projects that violate the principles on which democratic political institutions are built are unacceptable. As Katherine Sawyer (2003, 1580–81) concluded, "Political parties are obliged to operate within the bounds of the Constitution and of established notions of democracy. If a given party, in aligning itself with a terrorist organization, chooses not to do so, it may not, then, invoke those same constitutional principles as shield nor seek legal refuge in the very provisions that it has chosen to violate."

When discussing human rights in the context of intrastate violent conflicts, it is not uncommon to assume that violations of rights and liberties originate mainly with the state. The fact that terrorist organizations violate human rights and that states must deploy measures that prohibit such infringements is often ignored. Democracies are vulnerable, and they should have mechanisms to prevent the electoral expression of groups that advocate violent, racist, genocidal, or discriminatory ideas (Casadevante 2006, 163–94).

For this reason, the Spanish state opted to ban a political party, a measure that had previously been implemented by different European states and contemplated by the legislation of others (Casadevante 2006). Therefore, contrary to what the main Basque nationalist parties have argued, this initiative should be seen as a protection of rights that were being abused rather than as an unjust and illegal restriction of those rights. It aimed at denying terrorists the possibility of exploiting the advantages offered by democracy.

SILENCING TERRORISTS: THE BROADCASTING BAN IN IRELAND AND THE UNITED KINGDOM

An Unlimited Freedom of Expression?

A similar argument can be made with regard to another antiterrorist measure adopted by liberal democracies, specifically the United Kingdom and the Republic of Ireland in the late 1980s and early 1970s, respectively. Both states introduced legislation that forbade the broadcasting of interviews with representatives of terrorist organizations on television and radio (Hogan and Walker 1989, 267–69; Donohue 2008, 293–94). At the beginning of the 1970s, the Irish government took preexisting legislation that prohibited the broadcasting of material that could promote or incite crime or that tended to undermine the authority of the state, and it added a prohibition on the transmission of interviews with Sinn Féin representatives or any other illegal organizations in Northern Ireland—in other words, Unionist and Republican terrorist groups. In October 1988, the British authorities followed this model and imposed similar prohibitions in the United Kingdom. Nevertheless, the restrictions in Ireland were more severe than in the United Kingdom, where the words of the silenced voices were read by actors.[16]

Many commentators criticized the ban on the same grounds used to oppose the Batasuna banning. Nonetheless, Paul Wilkinson's (1990, 33) coherent defense of the media restrictions is relevant to both cases: "No freedom of expression is totally unlimited. Most of us believe for example that pornography should be banned from TV and radio. Inviting terrorists on TV to crow about their latest atrocity is the ultimate pornography of violence."

Views on the relationship between the effects these prohibitions had on society in general and on terrorist circles conflict. On the one hand, some claim that even if such measures served to limit the publicity that Sinn Féin obtained, the costs outweighed the benefits because the limitations on the freedom of speech were so serious (Ewing and Gearty 1990, 248). Similarly, critics of the ban argued that it prevented those who "communicated through the use of violence" from expressing their arguments on radio and television (Article 19, 1989). Alan Protheroe, the BBC's assistant director general at the time the legislation was applied, argued that maintaining democracy entailed listening to "unpopular" and "even dangerous views" (Murdock 1991, 110).

On the other hand, supporters of the legislation considered it necessary to pay a price to protect democracy, and some argued that "experience in the Republic of Ireland certainly shows that such a ban can be operated smoothly and efficiently for many years without in any way threatening parliamentary democracy" (Wilkinson 1990, 33). The former Irish prime minister Garret FitzGerald supported the broadcasting ban. Commenting in the *Irish Times* on December 20, 2008 ("Distinguished Writer and Political Meteor Who Illuminated Our Lives") on the death of Conor Cruise O'Brien, who as minister of posts and telegraphs introduced the ban, FitzGerald explained:

> First, it is a patent liberal fallacy that free speech and debate will demolish the stance of extremists. I do not recall any journalist succeeding in down-facing Ian Paisley or, after they were released on to the airwaves some 15 years later, either Gerry Adams or Martin McGuinness. . . . In second place RTÉ [Radio Telefís Éireann] is this state's public broadcasting system, and if it had been permitted to broadcast interviews with IRA leaders during their campaign of violence, this could have dangerously confirmed unionist delusions that our State was in league with those running the murder campaign, thus increasing the risk to nationalists from loyalist paramilitary gangs. . . . Finally, but far less important, the ban provided a huge incentive to the publicity-hungry IRA to abandon violence and thus secure coveted access to the airwaves.

The Consequences of the Broadcasting Ban

Despite the claims of the policy's detractors, the restrictions had negative consequences for Sinn Féin. Its head of publicity, Danny Morrison, explained:

> We monitored the media and discovered that in the three or four month period before the ban there were something like 500 phone calls, ranging from requests for interviews through to asking for information. That dropped to about 100 in the four months afterwards. It's an occasion for opening a bottle of champagne when we get a request for an interview from the broadcasting media at the moment. Broadcasting journalists don't even bother phoning us up because of the internal fights in their organisations, having to go and get clearance and such like. Anybody who goes out of their way to fight for objectivity in the broadcasting media now is considered to be a Provo, there's no question of that. (Moloney 1991, 47)

Other prominent members of the IRA and Sinn Féin agreed that media restrictions had an "enormous" effect on the republican movement, since "republicans weren't able to get their voice across" (Alonso 2007a, 175–78). Contrary to the argument of those who thought that the imposition of such significant restrictions would strengthen the more militaristic elements within the republican movement (Pollak 1993, 114; Ewing and Gearty 1990, 250), the IRA ceasefire in 1994 and the testimony of some of its members demonstrate not only that this was not the case, but also that the ban encouraged the IRA to give up terrorism. As former IRA members acknowledged, the media proscription was "very detrimental" for the republican movement, since it constantly emphasized the association between Sinn Féin and IRA terrorism. It constrained their competitiveness in the political system and blocked the achievement of power by the combination of terrorism and politics (Alonso 2007a, 178–79). The well-known republican strategist Jim Gibney admitted that, from the perspective of the British and Irish governments, the media ban was a success. In an interview with *An Phoblacht* published on April 16, 1992 ("Lessons to Be Learned"), he described the effect on Sinn Féin after the party's disastrous electoral results:

> Sinn Féin faces obstacles on a daily basis which no other party has to confront. Among these is censorship, which, although it has always been applied in relation to the South, this was our first election to be contested in the conditions of institutionalised censorship North and South. For us therefore, the ability to communicate directly through the media to the electorate was severely limited. . . . The SDLP [Social Democratic and Labor Party] entered this election with the dissenting nationalist voices—Sinn Féin—censored off the media for the previous four years, what party wouldn't like that advantage?

One veteran analyst of the Northern Ireland conflict also thinks that the ban "removed the organisation from television screens and by so doing isolated it from its voters and potential electorate," inflicting "a damaging blow to a party whose political/military strategy depended for success on winning a steadily growing share of Northern Ireland's nationalist vote" (Moloney 1991, 27). The ban contributed to the failure of the republican strategy, which assumed that mixing violence with a greater politicization of the movement through Sinn Féin would lead to a loss of electoral hegemony for John Hume's Social Democratic and Labor Party (SDLP), the voice of moderate nationalism. The combination of violence and politics had been the basic pillar of the "Armalite and ballot box" strategy, a phrase coined by Danny Morrison in 1981. However, the contradictions inherent in this dual strategy, which aimed to "take power in Ireland with the ballot paper in one hand and the Armalite in the other," prevented it from succeeding. The IRA leadership decided not to carry on with an activity that resulted in considerable losses rather than gains.

Therefore, the broadcasting ban was an effective tool of the "battle for hearts and minds" that affected the nationalist opinions of those who supported violence. The impact of such a measure in the Republic of Ireland is revealing. It became an important instrument in shaping public opinion, thus limiting the effectiveness of IRA propaganda. In 1983 the Irish television and radio corporation RTÉ (Radio Telefís Éireann) was prevented from broadcasting supporters' shouts in favor of Gerry Adams when he won the seat for West Belfast in the British Parliament. Years earlier, in 1972, the government had sacked the RTÉ management team after the broadcast of an interview with IRA leader Sean MacStiofain. In short, the Irish authorities took strong action to delegitimize the political discourse of Sinn Féin and the IRA, aware that the integrity of the state could not tolerate the slightest challenge from republicans.

Thus, the IRA and Sinn Féin lost the battle for respectability in the South of Ireland, where the public was prepared to accept limitations on freedom of expression. This attitude reinforced the irrelevance of republicans as a political force south of the border throughout the conflict. Before 1997, Sinn Féin had not won a single seat in the Irish Parliament since "the Troubles" began in the 1970s. In the 1997 elections, Sinn Féin obtained a 2.6 percent share of the vote, which rose to 6.5 percent in 2002. This clearly contradicted the republican analysis of the conflict, as Albert Reynolds, Irish prime minister from 1992 to 1994, pointed out when he told *The Economist* on March 19, 1994 ("The Provocations of the IRA") that the IRA was not in conflict with the British government but rather with the Irish people—both north and south of the border—an Irish people who longed for peace and were prepared to accept the existence of Northern Ireland.

Political Vetting in the United Kingdom

The delegitimization of support for violence achieved by the broadcasting ban was deepened by another initiative also deemed repressive. It was known as "political vetting": canceling public funding for social and cultural associations from which terrorist organizations could benefit. Between the late 1980s and early 1990s, around twenty associations saw their funding cut off. The main legal basis was the following statement made in Parliament by then–Secretary of State for Northern Ireland Douglas Hurd: "I am satisfied, from information available to me, that there are cases in which some community groups, or persons prominent in the direction or management of some community groups, have sufficiently close links with paramilitary organisations to give rise to a grave risk that to give support to those groups would have the effect of improving the standing and furthering the aims of a paramilitary organisation, whether directly or indirectly."[17] Such a generic statement was used shortly afterward to cancel the funding of a number of community groups.[18]

This drastic measure was supported by the main nationalist party in Northern Ireland, the SDLP.[19] Brian Feeney, a leader at the time, argued that some government-aided community centers were "IRA fronts," and he demanded that the authorities cut off all grants to these groups. He also suggested seizing property that belonged to individuals and companies involved in racketeering.[20] Moderate nationalists supported the measure because it "tainted" Sinn Féin and the IRA and made it hard for them to attract individuals and organizations that were afraid of the "vetting" (Political Vetting of Community Work Working Group 1990, 27). This was another means of strengthening the influence of moderates within the communities where radicals strove to exert their influence. Their support was reduced only after Glór na nGael, an association devoted to the promotion of the Irish language, was affected by the measure, which was then widely criticized in nationalist circles.

Ending the Violence and the Transition from Terrorism to Democracy

Pragmatic Counterterrorism?

Although less attention is usually paid to conflicts once violence decreases, the reaction of democratic players at this stage is still important. Democracy can be seriously damaged if terrorist groups remain in existence under a publicly declared ceasefire and groups linked to terrorism manage to achieve a certain degree of legitimacy because of governmental policies. Although pragmatism and leniency toward those who have allegedly set out on a transition from terrorism to peaceful politics seems reasonable at first glance, such an approach can be counterproductive.

The IRA's prolonged campaign of violence in Northern Ireland was ended in two stages. In the first stage, the main democratic parties in the region and the British and Irish governments unanimously refused to allow the IRA to entertain any hopes of victory, thus confirming the ineffectiveness of its use of violence and providing the group with an incentive to abandon terrorism. The 1994 ceasefire was a direct consequence of this approach (Patterson 1997).

During the second stage, this strategy alternated with one of concessions to the IRA and its political wing, Sinn Féin, on the basis that this was what the transition from terrorism to democracy required (Bew, Frampton, and Gurruchaga 2009). In practice, however, this policy led to indulging the needs of Sinn Féin to such an extent that the democratic framework was undermined. Political normalization of the region was slowed while the IRA continued to exist. The Northern Ireland experience suggests that similar policies would have similar effects with respect to ETA.

It is valuable to compare the two groups because, since the 1990s, some political and social actors in Spain have insisted on replicating the peace process in Northern Ireland. ETA's ceasefire in 1998 was a result of a pact reached between the terrorist group and the main nationalist political parties, which was based on a deliberate misrepresentation of the events that led to the IRA ceasefire (Alonso 2004). The parties to the agreement argued that it would facilitate the disappearance of ETA by creating a united nationalist front representing a more radical constitutional nationalism that ETA would interpret as being in its interests.

This approach conveniently ignored the fact that the IRA's attempt to establish a similar coalition was rejected by nationalist representatives, both in the North and the South of Ireland, on the grounds that it would effectively legitimate terrorism. Not only would such an alliance have been counterproductive, but it would also have made reaching an agreement with the Unionist community impossible. By rejecting this proposal, the Nationalists deepened the IRA's isolation. Because the effectiveness of the antiterrorist measures adopted by the British and Irish governments had also weakened its position, the IRA decided to call a ceasefire in August 1994 (Smith 1995).

Certain factors were decisive in the process by which IRA terrorism was brought to an end. On the one hand, IRA internal dynamics allowed the views of those critical of continuing violence to finally hold sway. At the same time, attempts by Sinn Féin and the IRA to blackmail other political actors into concessions in exchange for a promised cessation of violence were met by an appropriately firm response from democratic parties and states. This rejection was particularly important in leading the IRA to judge that its violence was not effective.

It is important to remember that the leaders of these groups had freely chosen to engage in terrorist activities after ruling out other possible forms of action. Terrorism is not a simple expression of spontaneous protest beyond the control of the individuals who perpetrate it, nor is it an inevitable reaction to material and historical conditions. It is one possible strategy that is preferred to others. When the political and human costs are high and the expectations of success disappear, terrorism is usually abandoned (Crenshaw 1991; Alonso 2007a, 102–90). These dilemmas led the IRA to question its use of violence and subsequently to end its terrorist campaign by accepting principles that the group had previously considered to be anathema, as set out in the Good Friday Agreement of April 1998. Ultimately, Sinn Féin participated in the very system it had previously tried to destroy (Horowitz 2002; Alonso 2001b).

The weakening of the IRA through effective government coercion was therefore the main reason behind the cessation of violence. A similar line of reasoning was apparent in some ranks of ETA. In the summer of 2004, six well-known ETA prisoners recognized that the organization had clearly failed to achieve its objectives, an admission that led them to advocate the end of terrorist activities despite the absence of political concessions. As they themselves admitted, ETA's "politico-military strategy has been defeated by the enemy's repression" (quoted in *El Correo*, November 3, 2004).

Experience indicates that during the transitional period, which is necessary to ensure that declining terrorist groups definitively disappear, there is a dangerous temptation to make concessions in order to consolidate the peace. This is clear if we examine the situation in Northern Ireland from the time of the ceasefire called by the IRA in the 1990s to the present.

From Terrorism to Something More Suited for the Times

Although the IRA called a ceasefire despite having obtained little in return, in the political process that followed the political wing of the movement benefited considerably from concessions made by both the British and Irish governments. Such gestures had negative consequences for the political normalization of the region. The Northern Ireland Assembly, which gave the region limited political autonomy, remained suspended from October 2002 to May 2007 because of the IRA's reluctance to give up training, recruitment, intelligence-gathering, and criminality.[21] The IRA abandoned its traditional campaign of terror but did not stop recruiting members, stocking arms, or engaging in other criminal activities that guaranteed the group financing and power. As Ian Pearson, one of the ministers in the Northern Ireland Office (NIO), noted to a *Sunday Times* reporter on March 20, 2005 (Dean Godson, "Look Around You, Tony, No One Else

Is Still Wooing Sinn Féin"), the republican movement became one of the largest and most sophisticated criminal gangs in the world. The IRA was "being deliberately restructured to something more suited for the times" (Independent Monitoring Commission 2006a, 17).

In February 2006, the Independent Monitoring Commission (IMC), a body set up to supervise the status of the ceasefire, corroborated that the IRA continued to be involved in illegal activities (Independent Monitoring Commission 2006a, 18). The commission argued that "intelligence gathering" was "predominantly directed towards supporting the political strategy" of Sinn Féin, involving "among other things the continuation of efforts to penetrate public and other institutions with the intention of illegally obtaining or handling sensitive information." As the IMC observed, this raised "the question of whether the commitment to exclusively democratic means is full and thoroughgoing, or whether there remain elements of a continuing subversive intent going beyond the boundaries of democratic politics." The IMC acknowledged that intelligence gathering was "authorised by the leadership," including "some very senior members." They engaged in the accumulation of information about individuals and groups, including members of the security forces. Although the commission added that they did not think "there is any intent to mount attacks," such activities were in clear breach of the IMC's guiding principles, among them the principles that "the rule of law is fundamental in a democratic society" and that "violence and the threat of violence can have no part in democratic politics. A society in which they play some role in political or governmental affairs cannot be considered either peaceful or stable" (Independent Monitoring Commission 2004, 6).

Nevertheless, some observers played down the fact that the organization remained active and engaged in illegal activities, among them "intelligence gathering directed towards supporting the political strategy" of Sinn Féin (Independent Monitoring Commission 2006a, 18). The British government was inclined to underestimate the seriousness of such a level of criminality, in part because of the absence of fatalities. This dynamic led to incoherent behavior, such as the positive assessment of the IRA's activities in the October 2006 Independent Monitoring Commission report. The main Northern Ireland parties were under considerable pressure to reach an agreement that would permit autonomous institutions to be put in place after four years of suspension when the commission produced a very upbeat report. Its purpose was to facilitate this political step. The contradictions contained in the report, however, reveal the dangers for democracy that stem from accepting inconsistencies in the rule of law in the name of political expediency.

The IMC stated: "What might be described as *military* or *terrorist* intelligence gathering has ended. We do not think that PIRA [Provisional Irish Republican Army] is gathering intelligence on members of the security forces for the purpose of attacking them or that illegal action is being planned or undertaken on the basis of intelligence." The commission also asserted, however, that

> we believe that PIRA remains interested in information which supports its political strategy and maintains cohesion of the movement. . . . We believe that what we say above, taken together, presents convincing evidence of PIRA's continuing commitment to the political path. It is implementing the policy, sometimes vigorously (though legally) so far as individual members are concerned. We refer above to the disbanding of those departments which were directly involved in the campaign of terrorism; such structures as remain are largely concerned with preserving the cohesion of the organisation and serving the wider purpose of the republican movement as a whole in a period of major change of strategy and direction.

Therefore, the report concluded, "we believe there has been further evidence of the implementation of the strategy whereby PIRA is following a political path and differences of view within the organisation will not divert the leadership from implementing it" (Independent Monitoring Commission 2006b, 15–16).

As these quotes demonstrate, the existence of an illegal organization linked to a political party and engaged in obviously illegal activities such as the gathering of "information which supports its political strategy" was not judged unacceptable and clearly unfair to democratic parties. The consequence of the pragmatism justifying this attitude is that a party linked to a terrorist organization is treated favorably, thus undermining the democratic principle that terrorism should not result in any political advantage or gain whatsoever. Dialogue in a democratic society must take place between the citizens' legitimate representatives in the context of and according to the rule of law.

Weakening the Moderates While Strengthening the Extremists

Several statements of the Irish and British prime ministers are also particularly revealing. In January 2005, Bertie Ahern, the Irish prime minister, admitted in the Irish Parliament that in his attempt to bring

Sinn Féin within the party system he had ignored the IRA's criminal activities. A year before, Tony Blair stated that the representatives of the people's will should not be obliged to share the government of Northern Ireland with a party like Sinn Féin, which was associated with a still-active terrorist group, the IRA.[22] Unionist politicians had criticized these concessions for years, although their criticism had been systematically ignored by the British and Irish governments, who took the view that a politically strengthened Sinn Féin would ensure that the IRA's ceasefire would hold.

The dangers of such a policy were clearly exposed in a speech delivered by Prime Minister Tony Blair in November 2002 in which he acknowledged that the continuing existence of the IRA as an active paramilitary organization justified the Unionists' refusal to share power in Northern Ireland. He added: "To this blunt question: how come the Irish Government won't allow Sinn Féin to be in Government in the South until the IRA ceases its activity, but Unionists must have them in Government in the North?, there are many sophisticated answers. But no answer as simple, telling and direct as the question."[23]

The approach of the British and Irish governments ignored fundamental democratic principles. Instead, they accepted Sinn Féin's blackmailing tactics, so adroitly used by its president and one of the main leaders of the IRA, Gerry Adams. By way of example, in May 2005 Adams called for northern nationalists to vote for Sinn Féin on the grounds that this would ensure the disappearance of the IRA, while also warning that without such votes the political vacuum would be filled by violence. One month earlier, Adams's call to the IRA to consider giving up the armed struggle had a similar objective, as observed by Michael McDowell, the Irish minister of justice, who saw this public statement as an election stunt designed to attract nationalist votes (Mary Dundon, "IRA Told Disband Before May Election," *Irish Examiner*, April 11, 2005).

Faced with the failure of thirty years of violence, Adams used the IRA as his trump card to rehabilitate his image as president of Sinn Féin, a party that, until the ceasefire declaration, had failed to overtake the democratic nationalists of the SDLP in the North and whose support in the Republic was electorally insignificant. By presenting himself as the key player, the one whose position needed to be strengthened through concessions because this was the only way in which he would be able to convince the IRA of the need to give up the armed struggle, Adams deliberately perpetuated the terrorist group's existence while reinforcing his political power. He used coercion by promising the disappearance of the IRA while it continued to break the law through extortion, contraband, and other criminal activities, including murder (Richards 2007). The implied threat of a return to increased levels of violence if concessions were not made placed a great strain on both politicians and society as a whole, transforming the peace process into an instrument of coercion (Alonso 2008a).

The SDLP and the UUP (Ulster Unionist Party), which until recently had represented most of the Nationalist and Unionist electorate, experienced the counterproductive effects of this policy directly. The two parties lost much ground in the 2005 British general election to Sinn Féin and the DUP (Democratic Unionist Party), led by the Reverend Ian Paisley. Northern Ireland's Unionists, led until May 2005 by the UUP's David Trimble, clearly resented the inconsistent approach of the British government and punished Trimble, who in 1998 had accepted Tony Blair's promise of support in the event that Adams reneged on his pledge to deliver on the decommissioning and disbanding of the IRA. Blair's support often arrived too late to help Trimble.

Various observers have accused the Unionists of obstructing the move toward peace by refusing to cooperate with Sinn Féin. Yet Sinn Féin, which had the same leadership as the IRA, including Adams and Martin McGuinness (Moloney 2002; Clarke and Johnston 2001), took no steps to disband the terrorist group. Trimble repeatedly gave Adams and McGuinness the benefit of the doubt when they promised that they were working toward this end, but his failure to obtain cooperation undermined his credibility.

In addition, the pressure brought to bear on Adams and the IRA by the British, Irish, and American governments after the 2004 Northern Bank robbery in Belfast confirmed what Unionists had been arguing for years: the IRA and Sinn Féin gave ground only when they were put under pressure. This being the case, Unionists decided that Ian Paisley was the best means of putting pressure on the IRA, a strategy that appeared to have worked in the past.

Therefore, British policy during the peace process considerably undermined political leaders such as John Hume and David Trimble, both recipients of the Nobel Peace Prize in 1998, and seriously weakened their influence in society and politics while strengthening less moderate parties (Bloomfield 2007). Former secretary of state Peter Mandelson criticized Blair's "unreasonable" and "irresponsible" behavior for giving too much credence to "excessive" IRA demands. As reported in *The Guardian* (March 13, 2007) and the *Belfast Telegraph* (March 14, 2007), Blair's policy of "conceding and capitulating" to republican demands ended up "alienating unionists and upsetting nationalists because on that side of the community they are in competition for the same votes."

Seamus Mallon, former deputy leader of the SDLP and former deputy first minister of the Northern Ireland executive, shared this view. Mallon argued that "peace" could and should have been delivered without the counterproductive effects of the government's approach: "Anyone who knows the north of Ireland would not have contemplated actions which sold middle unionism to Paisley, just as the same way in which our party [the SDLP] was treated" (*The Guardian*, March 14, 2007).

The Political Legitimization of Violence

Disarmament

Experience has shown that failing to require Sinn Féin to abide by the democratic rules of society was a major mistake.[24] Fred Halliday, in *El País Domingo*, summed up the prejudicial consequences of treating Sinn Féin with kid gloves:

> Adams himself has presented himself as a man of peace, even, God help us, as a statesman, offering advice to the Basques about the prospects for peace in Spain and producing mawkish autobiographies that make him out to be some sort of neo-Celtic gentleman. His policy of weakening and overtaking the more moderate, anti-violence, SDLP, has been greatly helped by the passage of time: a younger generation in north and south forgets the killings, disappearances and tortures and admires him for getting the kind of TV coverage that the more staid, and responsible, SDLP leaders John Hume and Seamus Mallon never got. Yet the IRA has not changed, and the pretence of a difference between IRA and Sinn Féin, whereby Adams issues "appeals" to the IRA is no more than that between a ventriloquist and his dummy.[25]

The disarmament of the IRA proved to be a particularly important prerequisite for peace and for the political normalization of the region. In the *Sunday Times* in 1999, Michael Oatley, a member of the British secret service MI6, criticized Unionist demands for IRA decommissioning as an "excuse to avoid the pursuit of peace" ("Forget the Weapons and Learn to Trust Sinn Féin," October 31). Similarly, important figures in the Northern Ireland Office (NIO) argued that the release of prisoners should not be made a concession in return for the IRA's disarmament. However, this viewpoint, which came to be accepted by leading civil servants and politicians, overestimated the alleged good faith of Sinn Féin's leaders. It ignored the fact that supporting the Adams approach undermined the confidence of the democratic parties because his strategy created a system that protected those threatening to destroy it—namely, the IRA and its political wing.

The underlying logic of not insisting on disarmament was that the transition to democracy required concessions to those who, theoretically, were going to make the transition possible. It now appears that the best policy would have been to require Sinn Féin to adhere to exactly the same democratic rules as any other political party. It should not have been given any favorable treatment simply because of the intimidating and coercive presence of a terrorist group waiting in the wings.

Such an approach would have exposed the IRA's manipulation of the situation. As Ed Moloney, the veteran journalist and expert on the IRA, put it in the *Sunday Tribune* ("Adams Conned Governments," October 7, 2001): "Gerry Adams has cleverly played on the belief that the hard men of the IRA will not allow him the room to manoeuvre. The record of this post Good Friday Agreement period will, when it appears, show to the contrary that this was a man who was utterly in control of the military and political wings of his organisations and who could have, had he wished, moved much sooner and more substantially on IRA weapons. The two governments were brilliantly conned and Adams exploited their doubts masterfully."

The British and Irish strategy ignored the nature of the relationship between the two wings of the terrorist movement and the pursuit of a common objective through alternative means such as elections and terrorism.[25] Thus, the complacency of both governments facilitated Sinn Féin's increasing legitimization and access to power. Political concessions to those who challenge the rule of law have negative consequences for democracy.

Dialogue Under the Pressure of Violence

Such a response is clearly at odds with the main principles of Spanish antiterrorist policy since 2000, as reflected in the "Pact in Favor of Freedom and Against Terrorism" (Pacto por las Libertades y contra al Terrorismo), which was agreed to by the Spanish Socialist Party (Partido Socialista Obrero Español, PSOE) and the Popular Party (Partido Popular, PP) that year. Both parties agreed to "work towards the disappearance of any attempt at direct or indirect political legitimization of violence," thus ensuring that "under no circumstances should terrorist violence result in any political advantage or gain whatsoever." The pact also stated that "the dialogue typical of a democratic society must take place between the citizens' legitimate representatives, in the context of and according to the rules contained in our Constitution and State and, of course, without the pressure of violence."

The case of Northern Ireland shows that entering into dialogue with political representatives of terrorist groups while the threat of violence remains risks marginalizing moderates and increasing the appeal of those who continue to legitimize violence. The contradictory nature of some British policies was also reflected in the speech given by Blair on November 18, 2002, in which he demanded "an end to tolerance of paramilitary activity in any form," as well as "one law for all applied equally to all," and promised that "a criminal act is a criminal act."[26]

The political, legal, and even moral impunity resulting from policy in Northern Ireland damaged its fledgling democratic structures (Bloomfield 2007). It allowed the republican movement to obtain a propaganda victory since it provided legitimacy to those who had vetoed progress in the democratic process, thus weakening constitutional authority and democracy. The political and social polarization demonstrated in an institutional blockage that lasted from 2002 to 2007 was another consequence of this type of management.[27]

Such a precarious scenario emerged as a result of a policy whose ambiguity some leaders described as constructive, despite having created a destructive dynamic (Aughey 2005) that could be repeated in another country like Spain, where Northern Ireland is often cited as a model. The decrease in ETA's violence after 2003 raised speculation about possible pathways out of terrorism. Many voices demanded governmental responses like the ones adopted in Northern Ireland. It was in this context that in May 2005 the Spanish Parliament approved entering into dialogue with ETA should it end its terrorist campaign. The proposal made negotiations with ETA conditional on its demonstrating "a clear willingness to end the violence" through "unequivocal attitudes that may show such a conviction."[28] This formula thus established limits that allowed the proposal to obtain widespread support, although without the much-needed endorsement of the main opposition party, the PP.

ETA's Tactical Truce and the State's Response

ETA's ceasefire declaration in March 2006 prompted hopes that the terrorist group was willing to end its violent campaign. Skeptics proved, however, to be right: ETA was still reluctant to disappear, and it understood the truce as a means of reorganizing itself (Europol 2007, 4, 13, 27–31). ETA was following a strategy similar to the one outlined in documents seized in France following the arrest of ETA leader Mikel Albizu, alias Mikel Antza, in October 2004 (*El País*, July 18, 2005). ETA's plans contemplated the possibility of temporary, incomplete, and tactical cessations of violence in return for important political concessions to be extracted gradually. ETA did not envisage disappearing but instead wanted to retain a coercive capacity that would achieve its objectives by affecting political negotiations.

ETA was probably relieved by the significant policy shift adopted by the Spanish government after the Socialist Party won the country's general election on March 14, 2004 (Alonso 2006b, 2007c). In contravention of the antiterrorist pact signed by the two main political parties, representatives of the Socialist Party had maintained contacts with ETA at least since 2002. After 2004, the government negotiated a truce with ETA in exchange for political concessions, which indicated to the terrorist group that the threat of violence could pay off. The extraordinary importance of the issues negotiated between ETA representatives and the Spanish government, which culminated in a preliminary agreement accepted by both sides, demonstrated how the terrorist group had managed to bring the state closer to its demands.[29]

This response weakened those within the terrorist organization who were abandoning violence given its high cost. At a time when dissenting voices within ETA were questioning the usefulness of continuing terrorism, the Spanish government encouraged those opposed to the interruption of violence by offering negotiations.

Furthermore, negotiations with ETA took place as the state considerably reduced pressure on the terrorist group, despite criticism from Spanish and French counterterrorist officials. As senior counterterrorist experts put it, the policy implemented by the Socialist government provided ETA with oxygen for more years at a time when the group had been on the brink of defeat.[30]

In June 2007, ETA issued a public statement ending its "cessation" of violence and declaring that it had again opened "all fronts" against the Spanish state. ETA's terrorist activities had not ceased during the truce.[31] In fact, public statements during the truce made it quite clear that the ceasefire "was not irreversible."[32] Nonetheless, the Spanish government authorized negotiations, thus contravening Parliament's resolution in May 2005 that "dialogue with those willing to put an end to violence" could begin only if ETA demonstrated "clearly" and "unequivocally" its willingness to abandon terrorism. The fact that ETA did not show any signs of willingness to put an end to violence did not deter Prime Minister José Luis Rodríguez Zapatero from authorizing negotiations. The shift in the government's policy strengthened ETA, which could argue that the Spanish government had violated Parliament's mandate even though violence had continued.

The Spanish government underestimated ETA in part because of the emergence of a new terrorist threat in Madrid on March 11, 2004. The high lethality and indiscriminate nature of the terrorism perpetrated by Muslim extremists led to a certain undervaluation of the threat still posed by ETA. In fact, ETA benefited from the comparison. In reality, ETA could damage the political and social system without engaging in the same kind of violence practiced by Muslim extremists.

Those who believed that the lack of deaths since May 2003 revealed a radical change in the Basque situation, which justified negotiating with ETA, were engaging in wishful thinking.[33] The offer of talks in return for promises rather than actions confused antiterrorist policy and divided the democratic parties. The government's insistence on entering into dialogue with ETA despite the fact that the conditions established by Parliament were not met further polarized society, as evidenced by massive public demonstrations in 2005 and 2006 in opposition to the government's shift.

Terrorists Dividing the Enemy

The Spanish minister of interior highlighted the dangers of eroding a strong consensus among democratic parties in the fight against terrorism. In September 2005, he claimed that ETA was an organization that remained "alive, active, operational and with the capacity to commit murder," adding that "hypothesizing and prospecting about the future with no basis in reality weaken democracy and raise obstacles in the combat against terrorism"—the reality being that ETA had no intention of disappearing from the political scene (*El País*, September 21, 2005).

Causing division among democratic parties was also the IRA's objective when the organization was put under pressure. In 1992, Danny Morrison, a prominent IRA and Sinn Féin leader at the time, made this clear in a letter written from prison to Gerry Adams. He recognized that violence succeeded only in uniting the IRA's enemies and that therefore the best course of action was to stop terrorist activities and exploit the doubts that would arise in the subsequent political process, thus dividing the democratic parties (Morrison 1999, 242). This strategy is seen in the IRA's refusal to disarm completely and its failure to disband, despite Sinn Féin's repeated promises that it would do so.

Since 2004, ETA's political wing has deliberately raised hopes of a ceasefire, using a type of language that has seduced many even as the group has not provided any proof of a real willingness to end terrorism. When the ceasefire was called in March 2006, ETA did not abandon terrorism, but sections of Spanish public opinion and some politicians still argued that the terrorist group had given up its campaign. The breakdown of the truce on December 30, 2006, exposed the mistake made by those who had trusted ETA's propaganda.

The Northern Ireland experience shows the negative consequences of favoring concessions in the absence of the effective and total dissolution of the organization. As the process in Northern Ireland demonstrates, the declaration of a ceasefire was followed by divisive tactics, methods that had already manifested themselves in the Basque case.

In May 2006, the Spanish prime minister said that in one month he would announce the opening of a dialogue with ETA despite the minister of interior's acknowledgment only days before that "the government still lacks the conviction that ETA wants to put an end to violence" (see "El gobierno admite que sigue sin la convicción de que ETA quiere poner fin a la violencia," *El Correo*, May 17, 2006). As later confirmed, the prime minister's announcement was rushed out because Batasuna had threatened to "collapse" the process if certain party members were prosecuted by the National Court.

The prime minister's announcement was followed by another announcement. Contradicting previous positions, the leader of the Basque Socialist Party announced a meeting with the political wing of ETA, although Batasuna was a banned organization. The meeting was an attempt to damage the efficacy of the proscription through a propaganda stunt. The opposition and a widely respected nonpartisan civic movement, ¡Basta Ya!, criticized the move. This influential civic movement argued that "the recognition of Batasuna as a necessary participant inevitably implies the legitimization of violence as a valid political instrument since such a participant doesn't represent anything else but the interests of a terrorist organization which refuses to disappear while imposing conditions before definitely stop[ping] the killing." Furthermore, "such a meeting already represents a political price which is being paid to ETA since it recognizes the group's political wing as a party as legitimate as the ones that they have so cruelly hunted down for all these years." This led ¡Basta Ya! to conclude: "To accept a political negotiation with ETA may lead to throwing away a historic opportunity to defeat the terrorist group for ever."[34]

The government's approach to ETA in this period tended to sideline the negative indications of its activities in order to change the public's widespread rejection of concessions to ETA, vis-à-vis the group's prisoners (*El País*, December 5, 2005). It was common to resort to rhetoric that promised peace and hope. In effect, this became an effective coercive instrument that exploited society's collective longing for a speedy demise of ETA. This rhetoric pressured the public to accept the need to make certain "sacrifices and risks for peace." ETA's ceasefire was followed by a propaganda campaign aimed at presenting previously rejected concessions as reasonable and necessary. The argument that concessions were essential to maintaining the ceasefire stressed the fact that society was worn out by so many decades of terrorism and that a historic opportunity to obtain peace must be grasped in order to avoid further victims.[35]

The government's behavior had real costs. It opened up the possibility of turning a blind eye to violations of the rule of law in the belief that certain aims require dubious means, all of which seriously affect the credibility of the state's institutions. Suspicion increased as the government's policy toward ETA during this period tolerated the group's activities.[36] As has been pointed out, this is what had already happened in Northern Ireland. The resulting political, legal, and moral impunity enjoyed by the IRA allowed it to make a partial recovery politically of the ground it had lost militarily, a situation that could have been repeated in the Basque Country if the same mistakes had been made.

Thus, advocating negotiations with ETA on the grounds that previous governments did the same was actually the best reason for not entering into negotiations, considering how ineffective and even counterproductive they had proved in the past (Domínguez 1998). Over the last three decades, negotiations with ETA failed to contribute to the end of terrorism. On the contrary, ETA's support and legitimacy gradually decreased as a result of governmental policies that included, among other positions, the refusal to contemplate any dialogue with the terrorist group and the banning of Batasuna.

Although the Spanish government altered significantly its policy against ETA in 2007, following the breakdown of the truce, the group was able to make the most of the negotiation process. ETA used the fact that the government had once again agreed to negotiate to strengthen internal cohesion by arguing that in the future the government would also repeat what it had previously said it would never do again. This recurrent mistake by successive Spanish governments allowed ETA to assume that meaningful political negotiations would finally be offered no matter what. As

ETA's documents following the end of the "peace process" demonstrate, such expectations encouraged the continuation of violence by reducing its negative cost for the group.

Conclusions

When assessing the consequences of counterterrorist policies in democratic systems, the rights of those who suffer the terrorist threat are sometimes underestimated. Certain fundamental rights are paramount, the right to life being one of them. Therefore, restrictions imposed on those who are prepared to infringe those rights are not necessarily antidemocratic in intention or outcome. As the experiences of Northern Ireland and the Basque Country reveal, these measures can contribute significantly to the defense of democratic values and the marginalization of terrorist organizations if they are applied by democratic regimes that respect the law.

Of course, states may also go too far in restricting liberties in the name of increased security for their citizens. This need not be the case, however, if democratic regimes comply with the rule of law. The measures described in this chapter increased the liberty of those citizens whose security was threatened. It is true that the liberty of the perpetrators of violence was restricted, but the justified and legitimate purpose was to limit their capacity to deprive citizens in a liberal democracy of their political and civil rights. A democratic system should accept all kinds of beliefs except those that promote violence against the majority that a democracy must protect. A presumed democratic tolerance that allows intolerant ideas to prosper is consenting to the destruction of the values that democracy is supposed to defend. In other words, the failure to respond to challenges such as the ones posed by terrorist groups has highly detrimental consequences for democracy.

The decline of ETA and the IRA opened up the possibility of a definitive eradication of terrorism and a process of political normalization in Northern Ireland and the Basque Country. Nevertheless, their decline and the progressive reduction of violence did not lead to their disbandment; instead, violence was replaced by a new strategy, whereby a reduced level of terrorist activity complemented by other criminal activities was used to exert pressure on legitimate democratic parties. In this way, the experience of Northern Ireland after the IRA ceasefire offers some salient lessons concerning the counterproductive effects of certain policies and attitudes during the transitional phase that a political party associated with a terrorist group must go through in order to become a fully integrated member of the democratic system after the definitive and real cessation of criminal activities.

In light of developments since the IRA ceasefire, the following conclusions apply to the Basque Country. The disarmament and disbandment of ETA are requirements that should be satisfied and rigorously monitored before any dialogue takes place on the question of prisoners, a point on which a significant section of Basque society believes some form of negotiation is necessary.[37] This would prevent ETA from putting pressure on other political and social actors in a scenario where a ceasefire is in effect but an atmosphere of peace cannot be said to exist, given the continued intimidating presence of ETA.

As time has demonstrated in Northern Ireland, the early release of prisoners could have been made contingent on effective and verifiable disbandment and disarmament. The pressure to have activists freed would have encouraged ETA to comply, just as the denial of expectations of success led the IRA to declare a ceasefire in the absence of any major political gains. Thus, if ETA gains concessions on prisoners in exchange for a mere ceasefire declaration, the state is giving up a valuable means of exerting pressure. ETA's ability to use coercion in the subsequent transition process would thus be enhanced. It should not be forgotten that Spanish democracy already provides for the reintegration into society of those who are prepared to renounce violence and to compensate their victims through expressly asking for forgiveness as well as settling the civil claims resulting from the criminal acts in question.

In fact, it is reasonable to argue that if ETA decided to put an end to its campaign, the group's prisoners should still complete their sentences. In Northern Ireland, the demands for justice made by the victims of terrorism were often ignored in the name of political expediency (Alonso 2008a). It is arguable, however, that a democratic society cannot properly advance when such impunity is allowed and injustice is not redressed.

The ending of ETA's campaign seems possible if impunity is not permitted and ETA is required to show that it is unequivocal in its desire to stop using violence and intimidation. In the words of the Pact in Favor of Freedom and Against Terrorism signed by the major Spanish political parties, terrorism must not be allowed to obtain "any political advantage or gain whatsoever." Democracy demands equality, a basic principle that is betrayed when a political party associated with a terrorist group benefits from gestures and concessions that emanate from its association with an illegal actor. Democracy requires governments to uphold the rule of law with fairness and justice. In the Spanish case, this would prevent the democratic deficit that would result if the government were to heed Batasuna's demand that the party's proscription be lifted despite the continuous existence of ETA. The political wing of ETA has also proposed a dual negotiation process, which would take place outside the parliament and without the dissolution of ETA. Some democrats mistakenly see such a circumvention of democratic institutions as necessary for the integration of radicals, despite lack of evidence of ETA's willingness to stand down.

The example of Northern Ireland shows that the existence of a terrorist group in the background tarnishes the political processes in which the party representing it participates because the group's influence leads to coercion and does nothing to bring about the definitive disbandment of the terrorist group. In addition, in circumstances where terrorism has become less murderous, it may come to be accepted. Low-level violence as well as threats, intimidations, extortions, and human rights abuses may become tolerated.

In fact, the Basque Country is probably the only region in western Europe where citizens are regularly deprived of their civil rights and liberties by the coercion of a terrorist group. Despite elections, a significant section of the population is unable to exercise their democratic rights freely, since a fundamental right, the right to life, is still under threat. The seriousness of the situation was demonstrated by events in June 2007 when some elected representatives refused to take office as a result of ETA's pressure and threats. Thousands of Basque citizens live with the permanent protection of bodyguards because their lives are at risk (Llera 2003).

The campaigns of violence perpetrated by nationalist groups like ETA and the IRA aim to undermine the legitimacy of the democratic states in which they take place. Therefore, a solid basis for the resolution of these conflicts can hardly be laid if that legitimacy is undermined once violence has declined. If the integration into the system of those who have threatened democracy is not consistent with democratic principles, as is the case when a political party remains associated with a terrorist organization, the state's legitimacy is weakened. The efficiency of counterterrorism should be measured not only by the decrease of violence but also by the diminished capacity of terrorists to illegally control and affect the governance of the regions where they operate.

The research underlying this chapter was made possible by grants provided by the Spanish Ministerio de Ciencia y Tecnología and Comunidad de Madrid (ref. 06/HSE/0250/2004).

NOTES

1. This experience has also informed the counterterrorist response to violence perpetrated by Muslim extremists in the name of Islam, as demonstrated in Alonso (2007b, 2008b).
2. For an analysis of the motivations of activists in both terrorist groups, see Reinares (2001), Alonso (2003), and Alonso (2006a).
3. See *Northern Ireland Constitution Act 1973* (London: Her Majesty's Stationery Office, July 18, 1973); *Northern Ireland Constitutional Proposals* (London: Her Majesty's Stationery Office, March 1973), cmnd. 5259; and *The Future of Northern Ireland: A Paper for Discussion* (Belfast: Her Majesty's Stationery Office, Northern Ireland Office, October 30, 1972). See also the parliamentary debate on this last document in *Hansard* 846(November 13, 1972): 43 seriatim.
4. Some authors have argued that the use of the military in Northern Ireland had negative consequences for democracy. This interpretation underestimates the degree of the terrorist threat and the inability of the security forces to contain very intense violence, particularly in the early days of the conflict, when the police force was completely inadequate to respond to such a challenge. The support of the army was therefore necessary for policing given the severity of the terrorist campaign. To this extent, it is often overlooked that military units were of key relevance in carrying out undercover operations and very complex surveillance and intelligence-gathering activities and thus complemented the work of the police in this area. The use of the military did not necessarily imply negative consequences for democracy, since counterproductive effects were a result of disproportionate actions and the unprofessional conduct of some members of the army when these happened. The death of civilians in 1972 on Bloody Sunday, when soldiers fired against demonstrators in Derry, and the collusion of some officials with Loyalist terrorist groups are clear examples of this very damaging use of the military.
5. See the relevant data in Euskobarómetro, 2003 to 2008, a regular annual survey conducted by the Department of Political Science and Public Administration at the University of the Basque Country, available at: http://www.ehu.es/euskobarometro.
6. ETA's political wing called for abstention in the 2000 election. In 2002 Batasuna was banned, preventing it from contesting further elections (see Barbería and Unzueta 2003).
7. This negative pattern reversed slightly after the IRA's ceasefire was consolidated and the Good Friday Agreement was signed in 1998. A negative electoral record was also a common pattern for Sinn Féin in the Republic of Ireland, where the party won its first Parliament seat in 1997.
8. For a thorough analysis of the complex system of organizations linked to ETA, their actions, and the nature of such a relationship, see Mata (1993).
9. The judicial report containing these allegations was fully reproduced in the main Basque newspaper, *El Correo*, in October 2002, and was found at:

http://servicios.elcorreodigital.com/vizcaya/pg021018/actualidad/politica/200210/17/RC_auto_garzon.html (accessed October 30, 2002).

10. Euskal Herria, the ethno-linguistic unit claimed by Basque separatists as their homeland, is made up of the three Spanish provinces that form the Basque Country (Guipúzcoa, Álava, and Vizcaya), as well as another Spanish province outside the Basque Autonomous Community, Navarra, and the French departments of Labourd, Soul, and the Lower Navarra portions of Pyrénées.
11. See *Zutabe* (March 2002). *Zutabe* is ETA's internal document published by members of the terrorist group.
12. See, for example, *Zutabe 91* (June 2001), *Zutabe 105* (June 2004), and *Zutabe 104* (April 2004). The internal debate held between 2007 and 2008 within ETA confirmed that the banning of the terrorist group's political wing was very detrimental to ETA. This measure, together with the strengthening of prison sentences, was highlighted by ETA members as two very damaging tools that had been used against the terrorist group.
13. The main nationalist newspapers in the Basque Country provided constant proof of this consensus on their criticism of the banning of Batasuna and questioning of the legality of this measure. See, for example, Joaquín Navarro Estevan, "Gas mostaza," *Deia*, February 23, 2002; Colectivo Ilarra, "La ilegalización de Batasuna," *Gara*, June 6, 2002; Manuel Díaz de Rábado, "La ilegalización de Batasuna," *Deia*, April 19, 2002; "Contra la opinión de la mayoría de los vascos" (editorial), *Deia*, May 18, 2002; and an interview with Arnaldo Otegui in *Gara*, February 24, 2002. See also the view expressed by Joseba Azkárraga, minister for justice of the Basque government, in "Una propuesta inquietante," *El Correo*, February 24, 2002.
14. See, for example, "Rechazo institucional y social a la ilegalización de Batasuna" (editorial), *Gara*, May 18, 2002.
15. Some examples can be found in pieces published by *Gara*, a newspaper that remains supportive of ETA: Joxemari Olarra Agiriano, "Los frutos póstumos del Pacto de Ajuria-Enea," *Gara*, March 5, 2004; "Negación de la voluntad popular" (editorial), *Gara*, June 15, 2003; and "Marcha atrás en el tiempo" (editorial), *Gara*, February 24, 2002.
16. This prohibition was suspended in the Republic of Ireland at the beginning of 1994, when the IRA was making final preparations prior to calling its ceasefire, and months later in the United Kingdom, after the truce had actually been announced.
17. See "Parliamentary Debates," *Hansard* 879 (June 27, 1985): col. 449.
18. For a critical view of this political initiative, see *The Political Vetting of Community Work in Northern Ireland*, The Political Vetting of Community Work Working Group. Belfast: Northern Ireland Council for Voluntary Action, October 1990.
19. As far back as 1976, Gerry Fitt, a prominent figure in the nationalist SDLP, had already warned that certain tenants' associations were controlled by terrorist groups; see Bew and Gillespie (1993, 109).

20. See "Furore at 'Provo Fronts' Charge," *Irish News*, February 5, 1986; Ciaran De Baroid, Frank Liddy, Rowan Davison, and Deirdre McManus, "Put Up or Shut Up Dr. Feeney" (letter to the editor), *Irish News*, February 24, 1986.
21. See, for example, the reports issued by the Independent Monitoring Commission and the security statistics periodically collected by the PSNI (Police Service of Northern Ireland).
22. See Prime Minister's Office, "Prime Minister's Press Conference—15 January," January 16, 2004, available at: http://www.number-10.gov.uk/output/Page5157.asp.
23. See Prime Minister's Office, "Prime Minister's Speech on Northern Ireland—18 November, 2002," February 10, 2003, available at: http://www.number-10.gov.uk/output/Page1732.asp.
24. On the importance of the time factor in the analysis of the conditions of democratization, see Linz (1998).
25. See Fred Halliday, "La ambiciosa estrategia del Sinn Féin," *El País Domingo*, July 17, 2005.
26. On the relationship between terrorist groups and political parties, see Weinberg (1991).
27. See note 22.
28. Although this chapter has focused on the IRA in order to draw a comparison with an ethno-nationalist group like ETA, there are other terrorist groups in Northern Ireland that have also been involved in violence despite the official declarations of ceasefire. The Loyalist UFF (Ulster Freedom Fighters) and UVF (Ulster Volunteer Force) have repeatedly and clearly breached their cessations of violence in the last years. In spite of their constant denunciation and condemnation of these breaches, politicians have very often failed to act by imposing the sanctions that democracy observes for such circumstances.
29. See "Lucha contra el terrorismo" (Fight Against Terrorism), resolution 32, approved by the chamber in plenary session, Congress of Members of Parliament, VIII Legislature, in *Boletín Oficial de las Cortes Generales* (*Official Parliamentary Journal*) 206(May 20, 2005).
30. On the extent of the important political concessions by the Spanish government, see "2005–2007: Proceso de negociación: En busca de un acuerdo político resolutivo: Suplemento documentos," *Gara*, September 23, 2007; *Deia*, July 29, 2007; and *Tiempo*, March 19–27, 2008.
31. See José Luis Barbería, "Los recelos en Francia subsisten pese al fin del proceso de paz" and "ETA dispone de 30 activistas dispuestas a atentar en España," *El País*, April 29, 2007; see also John Ward Anderson, "Spain's Peace Process in Tatters After Basque Separatist Bombing," *Washington Post*, February 18, 2007.
32 For a thorough analysis of ETA's terrorist activities throughout the period of the so-called truce, see Mikel Buesa, "ETA en 'alto el fuego': Nueve meses de actividad terrorista: Quinto informe de verificación de la violencia terrorista:

Documentos foro de Ermua," December 31, 2006, available at: http://www.foroermua.com/html/descargas/5Informe_verificacion061231.pdf.

33. See, for example, *Gara,* May 14, 2006. Furthermore, in August 2006 the terrorist group accused the Spanish government of seriously jeopardizing "the process" and threatened to "respond" to the "state's aggressions" if these did not stop. ETA was referring to the detention of some of its members involved in activities of financing and extortion and to the continuation of the judicial processes against activists already prosecuted (*El País,* August 19, 2006).
34. In fact, ETA had been trying to kill since May 2003 but had failed to do so on many occasions as a result of police successes; see Rogelio Alonso, "Falseando la voluntad asesina de ETA," *ABC,* March 31, 2007.
35. See "Iniciativa ciudadana ¡Basta Ya! pide al PSE que no se reúna con Batasuna," available at the ¡Basta Ya! website: http://www.bastaya.org/uploads/noticias/index.php?id=3598.
36. This attitude is epitomized, for example, in the declarations of the bishop of San Sebastian, Juan María Uriarte, that "the higher good of peace requires all of us to reduce our legitimate aspirations" and, accordingly, "no party interest, no past or present grievances, no act of violence, must obstruct the path towards peace" (quoted in *El Correo,* May 30, 2005).
37. As a result of this attitude, the Spanish government allowed one of ETA's political fronts, a party called ANV (Acción Nacionalista Vasca), to take part in the local elections held in May 2007. The indulgence of the government provided ETA with a relevant success: while obtaining again very significant economic and political resources, the terrorist group could argue that the banning of its political party had been circumvented. In September 2008, the Spanish government decided to ban ANV, clearly exposing the inconsistency of its previous position on the party; see "Contradicciones frente a ETA," *ABC,* May 4, 2007, and Rogelio Alonso, "Los elevados costes de una ineficaz política," *ABC,* June 12, 2007. It is very revealing that a newspaper that was fully supportive of the Spanish government's negotiations and lenient attitude toward ANV later admitted that the government had made a "political" rather than a "judicial" decision when it had not banned the party. Therefore, such interference in judicial power was clearly at odds with fair democratic principles. The contradictory attitude of the Spanish government and those who supported its antiterrorist policy during this period is clearly seen in an editorial in *El País,* "Ilegalizar, deslegitimar," published September 19, 2008.
38. Euskobarómetro, the survey carried out by the University of the Basque Country Department of Political Science and Public Administration and published in July 2005, showed that around 77 percent of the Basque population was in favor of the idea of negotiations between ETA and the Spanish government; see http://www.ehu.es/euskobarometro. Nonetheless, surveys indi-

cate that the majority of Spaniards would support a form of dialogue between the Spanish government and ETA only if the terrorist group gives up violence and without any concessions. See, for example, the survey carried out by Instituto Opina, quoted in *El País*, September 26, 2005.

REFERENCES

Alonso, Rogelio. 2001a. *Irlanda del Norte: Una historia de guerra y la búsqueda de la paz*. Madrid: Editorial Complutense.

———. 2001b. "The Modernization in Irish Republican Thinking Toward the Utility of Violence." *Studies in Conflict and Terrorism* 24: 131–44.

———. 2003. *Matar por Irlanda: El IRA y la lucha armada*. Madrid: Alianza Editorial.

———. 2004. "Pathways Out of Terrorism in Northern Ireland and the Basque Country: The Misrepresentation of the Irish Model." *Terrorism and Political Violence* 16: 695–713.

———. 2005. "El nuevo terrorismo: Factores de cambio y permanencia." In *Un análisis del mal y sus consecuencias*, edited by Amalio Blanco, Rafael del Águila, and José Manuel Sabucedo. Madrid: Editorial Trotta.

———. 2006a. "Individual Motivations for Joining Terrorist Organizations: A Comparative Qualitative Study on Members of ETA and the IRA." In *Social and Psychological Factors in the Genesis of Terrorism*, edited by Jeff Victoroff. Amsterdam: IOS Press.

———. 2006b. "El fenómeno terrorista en España: Principales amenazas y respuestas gubernamentales. *Revista iberoamericana de análisis político* 4–5(November): 14–33.

———. 2007a. *The IRA and Armed Struggle*. London: Routledge.

———. 2007b. "The Madrid Attacks on March 11: An Analysis of the Jihadist Threat in Spain and Main Counterterrorist Measures." In *Combating Terrorism and Insurgency in the Twenty-first Century: International Perspectives*, edited by James Forest. Westport, Conn.: Praeger.

———. 2007c. "La política antiterrorista frente a ETA entre 2004 y 2006: Del consenso al proceso de paz." In *Fuerzas armadas y seguridad pública: Consideraciones en torno al terrorismo y la inmigración*, edited by José González Cusac. Castellón de la Plana: Publicaciones de la Universitat Jaume I.

———. 2008a. "Leaving Terrorism Behind in Northern Ireland and the Basque Country: Reassessing Anti-terrorist Policies and the Peace Processes." In *Leaving Terrorism Behind: Individual and Collective Disengagement*, edited by Tore Bjorgo and John Horgan. London: Routledge.

———. 2008b. "The Evolution of the Terrorist Threat in Spain and the United Kingdom: From Ethno-nationalist Terrorism to Jihadist Terrorism." In *Terror: From Tyrannicide to Terrorism in Europe, 1605–Future*, edited by Bret Bowden. Queensland: University of Queensland Press.

Alonso, Rogelio, and Reinares, Fernando. 2005. "Terrorism, Human Rights, and Law Enforcement in Spain." *Terrorism and Political Violence* 17(1–2): 265–78.

Article 19. 1989. *No Comment: Censorship, Secrecy, and the Irish Troubles.* London: Article 19 and the International Centre on Censorship.

Aughey, Arthur. 2005. *The Politics of Northern Ireland: Beyond the Belfast Agreement.* Abingdon: Routledge.

Barbería, José Luis, and Patxo Unzueta. 2003. *Cómo hemos llegado a esto: La crisis vasca.* Madrid: Taurus.

Bew, Paul, Martyn Frampton, and Iñigo Gurruchaga. 2009. *Talking to Terrorists: Making Peace in Northern Ireland and the Basque Country.* London: Hurst & Company.

Bew, Paul, and Gordon Gillespie. 1993. *Northern Ireland: A Chronology of the Troubles 1969–1993.* Dublin: Gill & Macmillan.

Bloomfield, Kenneth. 2007. *A Tragedy of Errors: The Government and Misgovernment of Northern Ireland.* Liverpool: Liverpool University Press.

Buesa, Mikel. 2006. "Consecuencias económicas del terrorismo nacionalista en el País Vasco." Working paper 5. Madrid: Universidad Complutense, Instituto de Análisis Industrial y Financiero. Available at: www.ucm.es/bucm/cee/iaif.

Burton, Frank. 1978. *The Politics of Legitimacy: Struggles in a Belfast Community.* London: Routledge.

Casadevante, Carlos. 2006. *La nación sin ciudadanos: El dilema del País Vasco.* Madrid: Dilex.

Clarke, Liam, and Kathryn Johnston. 2001. *Martin McGuinness: From Guns to Government.* Edinburgh: Mainstream Publishing Co.

Conversi, Danielle. 1993. "Domino Effect or Internal Developments? The Influences of International Events and Political Ideologies on Catalan and Basque Nationalism." *West European Politics* 16(3): 245–70.

Crenshaw, Martha. 1981. "The Causes of Terrorism." *Comparative Politics* 13: 379–99.

———. 1983. *Terrorism, Legitimacy, and Power: The Consequences of Political Violence.* Middletown, Conn.: Wesleyan University Press.

———. 1991. "How Terrorism Declines." *Terrorism and Political Violence* (3): 69–87.

———. 2003. "The Causes of Terrorism." In *The New Global Terrorism: Characteristics, Causes, Controls,* edited by Charles Kegley. Englewood Cliffs, N.J.: Prentice-Hall.

Domínguez, Florencio. 1998. *De la negociación a la tregua: ¿El final de ETA?* Madrid: Taurus.

———. 2003. *Las raíces del miedo: Euskadi, una sociedad atemorizada.* Madrid: El País Aguilar.

Donohue, Laura. 2008. *The Cost of Counterterrorism: Power, Politics, and Liberty.* Cambridge: Cambridge University Press.

Elorza, Antonio, ed. 2000. *La Historia de ETA.* Madrid: Temas de Hoy.

Europol. 2007. *TE-SAT 2007: EU Terrorism Situation and Trend Report 2007.* The Hague: Corporate Communications.

Ewing, Keith D., and C. A. Gearty. 1990. *Freedom Under Thatcher: Civil Liberties in Modern Britain.* Oxford: Clarendon Press.

Fay, Marie-Therese, Mike Morrissey, and Marie Smyth. 1997. *Mapping Troubles-Related Deaths in Northern Ireland 1969–1994.* Derry: International Conflict Research (INCORE).

———. 1999. *Northern Ireland's Troubles: The Human Costs.* London: Pluto Press.

Funes, María Jesús. 1998. "Social Responses to Political Violence in the Basque Country: Peace Movements and Their Audience." *Journal of Conflict Resolution* 42: 493–510.

Hayes, Bernadette C., and Ian McAllister. 1996. "Public Support for Democratic Values in Northern Ireland." In *Social Attitudes in Northern Ireland: The Fifth Report, 1995–1996,* edited by Richard Breen, Paula Divine, and Lizanne Dowds. Belfast: Appletree Press.

———. 2001. "Sowing Dragon's Teeth: Public Support for Political Violence and Paramilitarism in Northern Ireland." *Political Studies* (49)5: 901–22.

Hogan, Gerard, and Clive Walker. 1989. *Political Violence and the Law in Ireland.* Manchester: Manchester University Press.

Horowitz, Donald. 2002. "Explaining the Northern Ireland Agreement: The Sources of an Unlikely Constitutional Consensus." *British Journal of Political Science* 32: 193–220.

Independent Monitoring Commission (IMC). 2004. *First Report of the Independent Monitoring Commission.* London: Her Majesty's Stationery Office (HMSO) (April 20).

———. 2006a. *Eighth Report of the Independent Monitoring Commission.* London: HMSO (February 1).

———. 2006b. *Twelfth Report of the Independent Monitoring Commission.* London: HMSO (October).

Jaime, Oscar. 2002. *Policía, terrorismo, y cambio político en España, 1976–1996.* Valencia: Tirant lo Blanch.

Jenkins, Brian. 1975. *International Terrorism.* Santa Monica, Calif.: RAND Corporation.

Linz, Juan. 1986. *Conflicto en Euskadi.* Madrid: Espasa Calpe.

———. 1998. "Democracy's Time Constraints." *International Political Science Review* 19: 19–37.

Llera, Francisco. 1993. "Conflicto en Euskadi Revisited." In *Politics, Society, and Democracy: The Case of Spain,* edited by Richard Gunther. Boulder, Colo.: Westview Press.

———. 2003. "La red terrorista: Subcultura de la violencia y nacionalismo en Euskadi." In *La sangre de las naciones: Identidades nacionales y violencia política,* edited by Antonio Robles Egea. Granada: Universidad de Granada.

Lomasky, Loren E. 1991. "The Political Significance of Terrorism." In *Violence, Terrorism, and Justice,* edited by R. G. Frey and Christopher W. Morris. Cambridge: Cambridge University Press.

Mallie, Eamonn, and Patrick Bishop. 1987. *The Provisional IRA.* London: Heinemann.

Mata, José Manuel. 1993. *El nacionalismo vasco radical.* Bilbao: Universidad del País Vasco.

McKittrick, David, Seamus Kelters, Brian Feeney, and Chris Thornton. 1999. *Lost Lives.* Edinburgh: Mainstream Publishing Co.

Mees, Ludger. 2001. "Between Votes and Bullets: Conflicting Ethnic Identities in the Basque Country." *Ethnic and Racial Studies* 24(5): 798–827.

Moloney, Ed. 1991. "Closing Down the Airwaves: The Story of the Broadcasting Ban." In *The Media and Northern Ireland,* edited by Bill Rolston. London: Macmillan.

———. 2002. *A Secret History of the IRA.* London: Penguin.

Morrison, Danny. 1999. *Then the Walls Came Down: A Prison Journal.* Dublin: Mercier Press.

Murdock, Graham. 1991. "Patrolling the Border: British Broadcasting and the Irish Question in the 1980s." *Journal of Communication* (41)4: 104–15.

Neumann, Peter. 2003. *Britain's Long War: British Strategy in the Northern Ireland Conflict, 1969–1998.* Houndmills, Basingstoke: Palgrave Macmillan.

Patterson, Henry. 1997. *The Politics of Illusion: A Political History of the IRA.* London: Serif.

Political Vetting of Community Work Working Group. 1990. *The Political Vetting of Community Work in Northern Ireland.* Belfast: Northern Ireland Council for Voluntary Action (October).

Pollak, Andy. 1993. *A Citizen's Inquiry: The Opsahl Report on Northern Ireland.* Dublin: Lilliput Press.

Rapoport, David. 2004. "The Four Waves of Modern Terrorism." In *Attacking Terrorism: Elements of a Grand Strategy,* edited by Audrey Kurth Cronin and James M. Ludes. Washington, D.C.: Georgetown University Press.

Reinares, Fernando. 2001. *Patriotas de la muerte: Quiénes han militado en ETA y por qué.* Madrid: Taurus.

Reinares, Fernando, and Rogelio Alonso. 2007. "Confronting Ethno-nationalist Terrorism in Spain: Political and Coercive Measures Against ETA." In *Democracy and Counterterrorism: Lessons from the Past,* edited by Louise Richardson and Robert Art. Washington, D.C: United States Institute of Peace Press.

Richards, Anthony. 2007. "The Domestic Threat: The Cases of Northern Ireland and Animal Rights Extremism." In *Homeland Security in the U.K.: Future Preparedness for Terrorist Attack Since 9/11,* edited by Paul Wilkinson. Abingdon: Routledge.

Sawyer, Katherine A. 2003. "Rejection of Weimarian Politics or Betrayal of Democracy? Spain's Proscription of Batasuna Under the European Convention on Human Rights." *American University Law Review* 52: 1532–81.

Schmid, Alex. 1993. "Terrorism and Democracy." In *Western Responses to Terrorism,* edited by Alex P. Schmid and Ronald D. Crelinsten. London: Frank Cass.

———. 2000. "Towards Joint Political Strategies for De-legitimizing the Use of Terrorism." Paper presented to the international conference on "Countering

Terrorism Through Enhanced International Cooperation." Mont Blanc, Italy (September 22–24).

Smith, Michael. 1995. *Fighting for Ireland? The Military Strategy of the Irish Republican Movement*. London: Routledge.

Tejerina, Benjamín. 2001. "Protest Cycle, Political Violence, and Social Movements in the Basque Country." *Nations and Nationalism* 7(1): 39–57.

Tonge, Jonathan. 2006. *Northern Ireland*. Cambridge: Polity.

Uriarte, Edurne. 2003. *Cobardes y rebeldes: Por qué pervive el terrorismo*. Madrid: Temas de Hoy.

Weinberg, Leonard. 1991. "Turning to Terror: The Conditions Under Which Political Parties Turn to Terrorist Activities." *Comparative Politics* 23(4): 423–38.

Wilkinson, Paul. 1990. "Terrorism and Propaganda." In *Terrorism and the Media: Dilemmas for Government, Journalists, and the Public*, edited by Yonah Alexander and Richard Latter. Washington, D.C.: Brassey's.

Woodworth, Paddy. 2001. *Dirty Wars, Clean Hands: ETA, the GAL, and Spanish Democracy*. Cork: University Press.

Whyte, John. 1994. *Interpreting Northern Ireland*. Oxford: Oxford University Press.

CHAPTER 7

FRENCH RESPONSES TO TERRORISM FROM THE ALGERIAN WAR TO THE PRESENT

JEREMY SHAPIRO

France has long been on the "bleeding edge" of terrorism, confronting terrorism in all its guises from bomb-throwing anarchists to transnational networks. This chapter briefly surveys the French experience with counterterrorism over the last fifty years, chronicling the actions that the French government has taken to improve its capacity to fight terrorism and describing the institutional system that has evolved in France to prevent and respond to terrorist attacks. After a long and often painful evolution, that system has become quite adept at preventing terrorist attacks in France while respecting French democratic traditions. But the system is not without its flaws, both in terms of its capacity to deal with terrorism and its effects on civil liberties in general and on the Muslim community in France in particular. The chapter concludes with an assessment and lessons that the French experience holds for other democracies.

The most salient fact about the postwar French experience is the broad range of terrorist threats that France has faced. In the 1950s and 1960s, the French government faced anticolonial terrorism emanating from the war in Algeria as well as right-wing terrorism aimed at preventing France from giving up its Algerian colony. In the 1970s and 1980s, France was

TABLE 7.1 Dominant French Counterterrorism Strategies

Period	Strategy
1950s to 1960s	Emergency
1970s to early 1980s	Sanctuary
Late 1980s	Accommodation
Early 1990s	Suppression
Late 1990s to present	Prevention

Source: Authors' compilation.

often attacked by groups that espoused a radical leftist, anticapitalist philosophy, similar to the Red Brigades (Brigate Rosse) in Italy or the Red Army Faction (Rote Armee Fraktion) in West Germany. As in other European countries, these groups were homegrown and ideologically committed to the overthrow of the capitalist system and to the downfall of American-led imperialism.

In the 1970s and 1980s, France confronted foreign terrorists, both spillovers from conflicts elsewhere in Palestine, Lebanon, and Armenia and state-sponsored terrorism aimed at changing French policy toward Iran, Syria, and Libya. In the 1990s, France struggled with the overflow of the Algerian Civil War into France. In the last decade, France has been a target of transnational Islamist networks emanating from various internationalized wars in the Islamic world, including Afghanistan, Bosnia, Chechnya, and most recently Iraq. Throughout these periods, the most persistent—although probably the least violent—terrorist groups in France have been the regional separatist groups that advocate independence for the Basque Country, Brittany, and especially Corsica.

After fifty years of confronting this terrorism "à tous azimuts," France views the struggle against terrorism as a permanent feature of modern life. Accordingly, French counterterrorism strategy has evolved along with the threats, passing through five basic periods, labeled here as emergency, sanctuary, accommodation, repression, and prevention. Such a periodization is rough and necessarily does some violence to the facts. In each of the periods, most of these strategies were employed to some degree, but the labels are intended to convey the dominant strategy in each period (see table 7.1).

EMERGENCY

In November 1954, the Algerian War of Independence began with attacks against French army positions in various parts of Algeria. The attacks were quickly labeled terrorism, and French prime minister Pierre Mendès-France vowed that "the criminal designs of a few men will be broken by a repression without weakness," declaring that France would never leave Algeria (Bocca 1968, xiii). In the course of the war from 1954 to 1962, approximately 250,000 people were killed in a struggle that involved terrorism in Algeria and metropolitan (European) France, as well as guerrilla attacks throughout Algeria and even conventional military encounters (for casualty figures, see Rich 1999, 97).

Although the Algerian War was fought on many fronts, using many techniques, terrorism was from almost the beginning an integral part of the struggle. The main Algerian resistance group, the Front de Libération Nationale (FLN), adhered to a Maoist insurgency strategy that foresaw moving in slow phases up the ladder of conflict from the creation of a movement to hit-and-run guerrilla attacks, to an eventual conventional military victory. Throughout the conflict, however, the FLN was never able to achieve Mao's third phase of overwhelming the military forces. Even at the moment of their withdrawal from Algeria in 1962, the French maintained complete conventional military superiority and indeed were even very successful at suppressing the insurgency, effectively wiping it out in the major urban areas and keeping guerrillas on the run through an early application of airmobile tactics in the countryside. Also, with effective French border control, exiled FLN leaders and the resources offered by foreign governments were rarely able to play a significant role in the war in Algeria.

In this context, terror attacks against civilians became a critical weapon in the FLN arsenal. Their purpose was to radicalize the conflict by targeting pro-French Muslims and to create a climate of instability that would increase suspicion and divisions between the European and Muslim populations and provoke the French to retaliate indiscriminately against the Muslim population. With few organizational resources and little command and control, terrorist attacks enabled the FLN to inflict a continuing stream of casualties, to erode the will of the French population to continue the struggle, and to keep its struggle high on the international agenda (Porch 1995, 363). At its peak, in March 1956, the FLN was able to mount over twenty-five hundred attacks a month in Algeria. A broadening of the terrorist campaign into metropolitan France in May 1957 magnified these effects by targeting moderate Muslims in France for assassination, blowing up oil storage tanks, gunning down policemen, and even planting explosives in the Eiffel Tower (Connelly 2002, 99, 194–97).

In the event, the combination of terror attacks, moral repugnance at the government's response—especially the resort to torture—and pressure from abroad did indeed have a corrosive effect on the French will to retain

Algeria. In 1958, the politically weak French Fourth Republic collapsed in large part because it could neither pacify Algeria nor muster the necessary domestic consensus to withdraw. The Fourth Republic was replaced by a new governmental structure intended to end partisan squabbling and place control of national security in the hands of a single office, the President of the Republic, and of a single man, the Fifth Republic's first president, World War II hero General Charles de Gaulle.

When de Gaulle, to the surprise of many, indicated his intention to quit Algeria, he inspired an attempted military putsch against his regime in April 1961. That attempt quickly fizzled out, but it inspired a motley amalgam of pied-noirs (European settlers in Algeria) and hard-line military officers to form a terrorist group, the Organization de l'Armée Secrète (OAS), which was intent on using terror tactics gleaned from the FLN to prevent a French withdrawal. The fierce OAS campaign of assassinations and bombings in both Algeria and France amounted to over five thousand attacks between May 1961 and January 1962, including several attempts to assassinate de Gaulle himself (Crenshaw 1995, 503). This further round of violence did little to inspire the French to retain Algeria, but it did represent a critical challenge to the new Fifth Republic's ability to maintain control.

Responses

The response of the French government to both the FLN and the OAS was swift and by many accounts brutal, including summary execution, torture, and various other "extralegal" methods.[1] In both instances, the government viewed these groups as serious threats—in the first instance to France's territorial integrity, and in the second to the survival of the French political regime. Of course, particularly in the case of the FLN, these responses were not primarily understood as counterterrorism.[2] The Algerian War was in essence a classic counterinsurgency effort, informed by the French army's experience in Vietnam. It focused on close territorial control, search-and-destroy operations, and resettlement of the rural population—about 3.5 million people were moved, or 50 percent of the rural population (Rich 1999, 106). Similarly, the struggle against the OAS was viewed less through the prism of counterterrorism than as a prolonged effort to avoid a coup by the military and security services.

In both cases, the government declared various forms of emergency in both metropolitan France and Algeria that allowed it to avail itself of extraordinary powers and to use ad hoc bodies to confront the problem of terrorism. By the end of the war, Algeria had become a fully militarized state where the rule of law was largely suspended. General Jacques Massu, the head of the French paratroopers assigned to pacify Algiers in 1956, estimated that some 40 percent of the male residents of the Casbah were detained at one time or another; torture and collective punishment were common. The government also engaged in various efforts at "direct action" that included bombings against civilian villages that were helping the FLN, assassinations of arms dealers supplying the FLN, and even an attempt to kill the Egyptian leader Gamal Abdel Nasser, whom the French believed was the power behind the Algerian insurgency (Porch 1995, 370–84).

Because the OAS emanated from mainstream French society, government tactics against it were less indiscriminate, just as Dirk Haubrich (this volume) notes in the case of Britain and the IRA. But the close links of the OAS to the French security services and military also compelled the government to resort to extraordinary measures. One such measure was the so-called barbouzes, essentially an unofficial parallel police force of undercover agents, recruited largely from various thuggish elements of French society. Working outside of normal police channels, the barbouzes were tasked with infiltrating the OAS, disrupting its operations, and sometimes assassinating its leaders, although for the most part they succeeded only in generating resentment among the regular police (Harrison 2005, 96–99).

In France, de Gaulle instituted limits on the freedom of the press and allowed special administrative internments for people determined to have been involved in subversion. He activated two special military tribunals primarily in order to try, convict, and punish OAS members outside of the normal judicial system. When one of the tribunals failed to deliver a death sentence for one of the leaders of the April 1961 putsch, de Gaulle replaced it with a new permanent body, the State Security Court (La Cour de Sûreté de l'État), which was intended to deal with crimes that attempted "to substitute an illegal authority for the authority of the state." The cases in front of the court were judged by military officers, its proceedings were secret, and it had extraordinary powers of detention and search, as well as limited rights of appeal. In short, it stood completely outside the normal system of French justice (Stoller 2002, 107). Opposition politicians such as then-Senator François Mitterrand specifically criticized it as an unconstitutional appropriation of judicial power by the executive (see Furniss 1964, 160).

Few lessons about counterterrorism were learned from these responses. Indeed, many of the methods that had proven least productive, such as the use of ad hoc units, were repeated in future episodes. But this period nonetheless established the foundation on which future French counterterrorism policy would be based, principally by bequeathing two general principles on the nature of terrorism. First, the FLN and OAS experiences established just how intractable a problem terrorism could be for modern, democratic societies—particularly when such groups had extensive support abroad. They created a correspondingly strong impulse to avoid conflicts with terrorist organizations.

Second, the Algerian experience demonstrated the essentially political nature of terrorism and consequently the need for a response that was at least partly political. In the French narrative, the FLN succeeded in Algeria not because of military victory on the battlefield or even because its terrorist attacks damaged French society or weakened the French will. Rather, the FLN profited from the fact that effective countermeasures appeared to require a degree of government repression that polarized Algeria, creating the prospect of yet further terrorism while also horrifying French society and damaging France's international standing. In contrast, the OAS failed mostly because it had little support abroad, but also in part because de Gaulle was able to isolate it politically within France and even within the military and security services. For France, the idea that any serious terrorism problem could have a purely repressive solution devoid of political content died a painful death in Algeria.

Sanctuary

Because the experience of the Algerian War and its aftermath made terrorism seem to be such an intractable problem, it created a certain bias within the French political class against applying the label of terrorism, particularly to problems with international dimensions. Various terrorist groups remained active in France, including international terrorists. In June 1975, two French intelligence agents were gunned down in Paris by the well-known international terrorist Carlos the Jackal. The event stunned the public and served as a wake-up call for many in the security services, but the government still resisted labeling the problem as terrorism or formulating an institutional response.[3]

By 1981, there was so little interest in the problem of terrorism in the French intelligence services that the introductory briefings for the new head of the French foreign intelligence agency, the Service de Documentation Extérieur et de Contre-Espionnage (SDECE), contained hardly a mention of the problem (Marion 1991, 22).[4] Similarly, the Direction du Surveillance du Territoire (DST), the French internal intelligence agency, had in 1981, according to one agent, "only the most derisory means" for combating international terrorism (Burdan 1990, 97; de Weck 1991, 25).

In part, this lack of attention to international terrorism within the French intelligence services was part and parcel of the French government's policy on the issue. Since the Algerian War, successive French governments had applied what can best be described as the "sanctuary doctrine" to the problem. The sanctuary doctrine attempted to isolate the country from international terrorism by creating within France a sanctuary both for and from international terrorists, including ETA in neighboring Spain as well as Palestinian groups. This policy required making French policy and soil as neutral as possible with respect to the issues that motivated international terrorism. As a result, international terrorist groups would have nothing to fear and nothing to achieve in France, where their members could operate with impunity as long as they did not perpetrate acts of terrorism within France or against French interests (Porch 1995, 431).

Whatever the moral implications of such a policy, and the Carlos incident notwithstanding, it was a fairly successful tactic for preventing terrorist violence in France. It was applied particularly to achieve the quiescence of the Palestine Liberation Organization (PLO) within France (Wieviorka 1990, 68). The sanctuary doctrine was based on the belief that international terrorism was ultimately a political and a foreign policy problem distinct from law enforcement, and as such required that the government take into account both the interests and the capacities of the French state abroad. The doctrine allowed France to maintain good relations with important states that might have taken exception to French crackdowns on groups they supported, while simultaneously acknowledging that the French ability to prevent foreign-inspired attacks and to punish states and groups outside of French borders was limited. Such attacks were therefore better avoided.

At the same time, the sanctuary doctrine had serious drawbacks that became evident in the early 1980s. First, the doctrine tended to create political problems with the opponents of the terrorists sheltered by France, particularly Spain (in the case of the Basque terrorist group ETA), Israel (in the case of the PLO), and later the United States (in the case of the Fractions Armées Revolutionnaires Libanaise, which assassinated an American diplomat), somewhat offsetting any foreign policy gains. Second, the sanctuary doctrine required the political authorities to maintain secret contact with terrorist groups, who therefore had to be identifiable and reachable. Moreover, this contact did not play well in the domestic political arena and was often politically damaging to current government parties during French political campaigns. Perhaps more fundamentally, the sanctuary doctrine could only effectively protect France when terrorist groups did not directly challenge French interests or seek to change French policy. At the same time, however, the sanctuary doctrine was an expression of weakness and a lack of confidence in the ability of the French state apparatus to prevent or respond to foreign terrorist attacks.

The sanctuary policy clearly ceased to be effective over the course of the early 1980s as France became the European country most affected by international terrorism (Jongman 1992, 44). Nonetheless, French authorities were slow to abandon it, particularly in the case of certain favored groups. For the most part, the increasing inefficacy of the sanctuary doctrine resulted from international political circumstances that brought France into direct conflict with groups and states that used terrorism as a political tool. In retrospect, however, it is also clear that the sanctuary doctrine contained the seeds of its own destruction. The expression of weakness that the sanctuary doctrine represented was not lost on terrorist groups and their state sponsors, and therefore, paradoxically, it encouraged them to use terrorist methods when they decided that their goals demanded a direct challenge to French interests. Moreover, in giving sanctuary and therefore effective support to one terrorist group, France inevitably angered the often equally violent rivals of that group. Finally, the freedom that terrorists had to operate within France, even for the purposes of conducting operations outside of French borders, allowed them to accumulate logistical and operational networks that could easily be turned on their host when the moment was ripe.

This failure of the sanctuary doctrine first manifested itself in attacks that reflected the anger of splinter Palestinian movements at French support for Yasir Arafat's control of the PLO. Thus, for example, an October 1980 attack on a synagogue on the Rue Copernic in Paris appears to have been motivated in part by the struggle between Abu Nidal and Yasir Arafat for leadership of the Palestinian cause. Similarly, an attack at the Rue Marbeuf in the middle of Paris in 1982 was part of a Syrian-Iraqi dispute. The Syrians took advantage of existing Palestinian networks within France to plant a car bomb outside of the offices of a pro-Iraqi newspaper in Paris; one person was killed and sixty-three wounded (Burdan 1990, 162).

These types of attacks were part of rather subtle signaling campaigns whose targets were often other groups or other states. As such, the purpose of these attacks was often not clear to the French authorities, who had little success in tracing the attacks back to their original instigators or in achieving any capacity to prevent future attacks. Such attacks continued fitfully throughout the early 1980s, exhibiting little pattern or apparent purpose, at least from the French perspective. Because of the extremely nebulous nature of the attacks, terrorism began to become a major source of public anxiety and an issue of considerable political controversy within France.

Nonetheless, the sanctuary doctrine was only definitively abandoned in the wake of a series of terror attacks that nearly paralyzed Paris in 1986. Three waves of attacks in February, March, and September targeted large department stores, trains, subways, and public buildings (see table 7.2). In all, at least 14 attacks caused 11 deaths and over 220 injuries. Most of these attacks were claimed by a previously unheard-of group called the CSPPA (Committee for Solidarity with Near Eastern Political Prisoners), whose announced aims were to secure the release of three apparently unrelated terrorist leaders then in French custody.[5] As these attacks progressed, a variety of security measures were introduced, including the offer of a $150,000 reward and the requirement that all non-EU citizens, except the Swiss, acquire a visa to visit France. The government began to allow random identity checks by police and to extend from twenty-four hours to four days the time a suspected terrorist could be held for questioning before being charged. In addition, police instituted bag searches at major stores and government offices, and the government began to reorganize the police administration to get more uniformed officers on the street, especially in sensitive areas.

As a result of these measures and increased public vigilance, French police were able to thwart some attacks and to make some arrests after specific bombings, but the attacks continued, often claimed by the shadowy CSPPA and at other times by other equally unknown groups, such as the Partisans for Right and Freedom. Overall, the French authorities appeared powerless to stop the attacks, perhaps because the terrorists were so well implanted within France, perhaps because they had powerful state sponsors. As the attacks progressed, a defector informed French officials that the demand for the release of prisoners was actually a cover for an overall coordinated terrorist offensive explicitly linked to French interests in the Middle East. The campaign involved not just the bombings on French soil but also attacks against French interests abroad, particularly the taking of French hostages in Beirut (Burdan 1990, 310; Porch 1995, 452).

In the early 1980s, French policy in the Middle East had begun to conflict directly with the policies of Syria, Iran, and Libya, the principal state sponsors of terrorism in the Middle East. Syria saw French participation in the multinational intervention and the civil war in Lebanon as direct

TABLE 7.2 Attacks in France Claimed by the Committee for Solidarity with Near Eastern Political Prisoners, 1986

February 3	A bomb explodes in a shopping gallery on the Champs-Élysées, injuring eight people. An hour later a second bomb is discovered and defused atop the Eiffel Tower.
February 4	A bomb explodes in a Left Bank bookshop, injuring four persons.
February 5	A bomb explodes in an underground sporting goods store in Paris, wounding nine people.
March 17	An explosion and fire in the Paris-Lyons Train à Grande Vitesse (TGV; a high-speed train) injures ten people.
March 20	A bomb explodes in a shopping arcade on the Champs-Élysées. Two people die, and twenty-eight are injured. A few minutes later a second explosive device is found and defused at the Châtelet subway station.
September 4	A bomb is found in a subway train at the Gare de Lyon. The detonator explodes but does not ignite the bomb.
September 8	A bomb explodes in the post office in Paris City Hall, killing one employee and injuring eighteen.
September 12	A lunchtime bomb in a crowded Paris cafeteria injures forty people.
September 14	A bomb is found in a pub on the Champs-Élysées. It explodes when a staff member and two policemen take it to the basement. One policeman dies.
September 15	A bomb explodes at police headquarters in Paris, killing one person and injuring fifty-one others.
September 16	One person is wounded in an explosion in a restaurant in northern Paris.
September 17	A bomb thrown from a passing car explodes in front of a crowded department store on the Left Bank, Rue de Rennes, killing five people and wounding fifty-two. One of the injured later dies of his wounds.

Source: Authors' compilation.

threats to Syrian interests. French opposition to the Libyan invasion of Chad had occasioned friction with the Libyan government. Finally, the most serious frictions were with the government of Iran: in the midst of a devastating war with Iraq, Iran resented France's role as the principal supplier of high-tech weaponry to Saddam Hussein's regime. Iran also claimed that it was owed over $1 billion from contracts broken by France in the wake of the Iranian revolution (Porch 1995, 432). According to the defector, all three regimes worked in concert with existing Palestinian and Lebanese networks in France to perpetrate attacks aimed at forcing the French government to alter its policies in the Middle East.[6]

ACCOMMODATION

With such a direct clash of interests, there was little chance of reviving the sanctuary doctrine as a method of preventing terrorist attacks in France. Indeed, the very fact of the attacks had created enough fear and anger among the French population as to make the idea of negotiating with or harboring terrorists of any sort far too politically risky. More fundamentally, it had become clear that the constant interactions between terrorist groups of all types and potential state sponsors, as well as the constantly changing nature of terrorist political goals, only invited future attack if a country allowed such networks to establish themselves on its soil.. Unfortunately, the inability of the French counterterrorist services to suppress the attacks, either through protective measures at home or through direct action abroad, left the French government with few options for ending the attacks at home or for freeing the French hostages in Lebanon.[7]

The speculation at the time and since has been that this series of attacks ended because the French government decided that the solution to terrorism was accommodation rather than sanctuary or suppression. According to *Le Monde*, a visit to Damascus by French government officials in September 1986 resulted in a deal whereby the Syrians would cease support for terrorism in France, secure the release of French hostages in Lebanon, and provide intelligence on Lebanese terrorists in return for arms, economic aid, and French diplomatic support. Three hostages in Lebanon were released in November 1986, and all were released by the time of the next French presidential election in May 1988. Terrorist attacks in France also ceased, although that no doubt was partly the outcome of the information provided by the defector. A similar deal was apparently struck with the Iranians the next summer when Wahid Gordji, a translator attached to the Iranian embassy in Paris who had been found to have masterminded many of the 1986 attacks and who had taken refuge in the

Iranian embassy, was allowed to leave France.[8] After years of sporadic waves of attacks, France remained largely free of international terrorist attacks on its home soil from 1987 until 1994.

The French government has always denied that such deals took place, and the existence of any arrangement with state sponsors of terror attacks in France remains highly controversial to this day.[9] Nonetheless, it is clear, as Michel Wieviorka (1991, 165) points out, that "faced with international terrorism, France, we might say, followed a policy of diplomatic activities that was guided by the will of terrorist states." The French government withdrew from Lebanese affairs, scaled back dramatically its support to Iraq in the Iran-Iraq War, and settled its debts with Iran in the context of reestablishing diplomatic relations.

Suppression

The French policy of accommodation may have been successful in ending the spate of attacks in France during the 1980s, but accommodation—essentially coerced changes in French foreign policy—could hardly have been the preferred outcome of French policymakers. The failure of the sanctuary doctrine, the lack of capacity to attack terrorist targets abroad, and the inability to prevent attacks at home had revealed a variety of shortcomings in the French system for fighting terrorism at home. Not wanting to return to the days of the emergency measures of the 1960s, French policymakers decided to vastly increase the French institutional capacity to suppress attacks on French soil by strengthening the French police and judicial apparatus in the field of counterterrorism. The French efforts addressed two interrelated problems that had made suppression particularly difficult in France: a lack of coordination and centralization of antiterrorist policies internally, and politicization of the struggle against terrorism.

Lack of Coordination

The fight against terrorism at home was not in any sense institutionalized within the French governmental structures in the early 1980s and therefore was very badly coordinated. At least seven different police services in four different cabinet ministries had a variety of overlapping responsibilities in matters relating to terrorism.[10] These agencies rarely met and often actively distrusted and misled each other, to such an extent that the interior minister in 1981 refused, in the presence of the prime minister, to share intelligence about terrorism with the Direction Générale de la Sécurité Extérieure (DGSE), the foreign intelligence agency, because he claimed it was "a nest of Soviet spies" (Marion 1991, 54). In another example, Direction du Surveillance du Territoire (DST), the domestic intelligence agency, actively cooperated with the New Zealand police in their efforts to prove the complicity of the DGSE in the 1985 bombing of the Greenpeace ship *Rainbow Warrior* in Auckland Harbor (Porch 1995). In the judicial sphere, the local prosecutors and investigators who worked in the location of the attacks handled terrorism cases. Unfortunately, terrorist attacks were rarely isolated incidents, and the specific location of the attack was of little relevance to its investigation or prosecution. With little contact between prosecutors of different jurisdictions who were working on related cases, there was little capacity to integrate information and to discover patterns.

Politicization

Things were little better on the political level. After the election of François Mitterrand and the Socialists in 1981, there was a deep level of distrust between the political authorities in the president's and the prime minister's offices and the police and intelligence services. After twenty-three years of right-wing rule, the Socialists viewed the security services as bastions of right-wing sympathizers. In the 1950s, Mitterrand's political career had been nearly destroyed by false accusations emanating from the security services.[11] Similarly, the security services distrusted the new government and resented the Socialists' decision after their election in 1981 to issue amnesty for many imprisoned terrorists. They even suspected the Socialists of harboring sympathies for some of the extreme leftist terrorist groups, including Action Directe—a prejudice that was reinforced by the fact that one of Mitterrand's advisers, Régis Debray, had fought with Che Guevara in Latin America (Marsaud 2002, 14–16; Guisnel and Violet 1988, 41).

At the same time, the ability to protect the French population from terrorist attacks and to secure the freedom of the French hostages abroad became highly fraught political issues in France during the 1980s (see, for example, Chauvin 1990). The intense political saliency of these issues, in combination with the Socialists' distrust of the existing intelligence services, convinced Mitterrand, harking back to the Algerian experience, to create an ad hoc cell within the presidential palace devoted to the problem of terrorism and staffed with operatives he felt he could trust. The presence of this cell, greatly resented by the established police and intelligence agencies, did little to promote coordination and trust between the numerous agencies necessary to combat the complex phenomenon that terrorism had become by the 1980s. In the end, this cell did little to further the struggle against terrorism and caused a public relations disaster when it was revealed to have planted evidence in order to arrest some suspected Irish terrorists.[12]

Responses

The French response to what had become an overwhelming public outcry for increased security was best embodied in the legislation of September 1986.[13] That legislation created a variety of new organs within the French government that specialized in dealing with terrorist issues and coordinated or centralized the problem of terrorism within the French government. In general, the legislation signaled the move away from accommodation by empowering the justice and interior ministries and sidelining the foreign affairs ministry, which had tended, in retrospect, to place too high a value on maintaining amicable relations with states that sponsored terrorism.

New specialized organizations were created within the interior ministry (Unité de Coordination de la Lutte Anti-Terroriste, UCLAT) and the justice ministry (Service pour Coordination de la Lutte Anti-Terroriste, SCLAT) and were specifically charged with maintaining relationships and information flows.[14] The purpose of these organizations is to make connections between all of the various intelligence and police services within the French government bearing on the question of terrorism. Previously, no single service had specialized in terrorism, and thus no one was responsible for assembling a complete picture from the various institutional sources, for ensuring the smooth flow of information between the various agencies, or for providing coordinated direction to the intelligence and police services for the prevention of terrorism.[15] According to one of the authors of the legislation, this system was explicitly modeled in part on the U.S. National Security Council (NSC) and the interagency process it oversees.[16]

The 1986 legislation also centralized all judicial proceedings relating to terrorism. The State Security Court of the Algerian period was often seen as an instrument of political oppression, particularly by the political opposition on the left. On assuming power in 1981, before the new round of terrorist attacks had gained much force, Mitterrand acted almost immediately on early opposition to the court and eliminated it. But he did not replace it with any specific judicial system for dealing with terrorism.

The 1986 legislation filled this void but did not repeat the mistake of creating a new specialized court outside of the normal judicial system. Although the legislation did take note of the special nature of the terrorist crimes by providing for longer jail terms for acts committed for the purpose of terrorism and for longer periods of detention and investigation in such cases, it nonetheless left the prosecution of terrorist cases within the normal procedures of French justice. Rather than creating an entirely new court, the legislation centralized proceedings relating to terrorism in the existing Trial Court of Paris and left to normal judges the ultimate decision as to the outcome of the cases.

Under this system, a local prosecutor decides whether a crime committed within his or her geographic area of responsibility is related to terrorism, based on a definition of terrorism as "acts committed by individuals or groups that have as a goal to gravely trouble public order by intimidation or terror." If an incident meets that definition, the judge refers the case to specialized prosecutors or magistrates within the Paris court. This system gets around the problem of the small size of local prosecutors' offices and minimizes the danger of reprisals against local officials (particularly a problem with separatist terrorist groups in Corsica). More important perhaps, the system has created within the Trial Court of Paris a small cadre of prosecutors and investigating magistrates who deal only with terrorism cases and who have become established as the lead actors in the French struggle against terrorism.

The investigating magistrate—who is somewhat of a cross between a prosecutor and a judge—has no precise counterpart in the Anglo-Saxon system of justice. An investigating magistrate (an inexact translation of "juge d'instruction") is not an advocate for the prosecution or the defense, but rather is charged with conducting an impartial investigation to determine whether a crime worthy of a prosecution has been committed. Once that determination is made, the investigating magistrate hands the case over to a prosecutor and a defense attorney who, on the basis of the magistrate's investigation, act as advocates in front of a judge (juge de siege). Because these magistrates are intended to be impartial arbiters, they are, at least in theory, not answerable to any political authority and are granted fairly wide powers to open judicial inquiries, authorize search warrants and wiretaps, and issue subpoenas—powers that in the United States would require specific judicial authorization. Within the French judicial system, such magistrates are not unique to terrorism cases. Nevertheless, this institution, which in many circumstances serves merely as an unwieldy extra step in the judicial process, has proven uniquely adaptive to the complex investigations necessary to use judicial procedures to punish and even prevent terrorist actions.[17]

This adaptation occurred because the creation of a small, specialized corps of antiterrorism magistrates created, over time, a competency that almost amounted to an intelligence service in and of itself. The individual magistrates, after years of conducting connected investigations—many of which specifically resulted from evidence gleaned in prior investigations—acquired the type of expertise on the subject of terrorism that is difficult to create within normal judicial institutions. These magistrates even tended to specialize in cases related to specific classes of terrorism, such as separatist or Islamic terrorism.

Finally, the system of specialized investigating magistrates also helped to depoliticize the issue of counterterrorism, although this may not have been an intention of the legislation. As these magistrates became more publicly visible, they achieved a greater capacity to assert their statutory independence from political authorities—if necessary, through resort to the media. Indeed, over time, the investigating magistrates gained a public reputation for implacable opposition to terrorism that stood in stark contrast to the craven image of politicians in the 1980s. With the magistrates taking the role of informed, independent, and pitiless adversaries of terrorism in all its forms, any notion of the French government to return to a policy of sanctuary or accommodation was unlikely to achieve the necessary level of secrecy or public support. Although French politicians were thus denied a degree of control over an important aspect of state policy, they were also relieved of public responsibility, and therefore blame, for failing to solve what they saw as an intractable problem.

Prevention

The new French counterterrorism system was first put to the test in response to the spillover of the Algerian civil war in France. In 1989, the government of Algeria had authorized multiparty elections. However, in 1992, when it appeared that an Islamist party, the Islamic Salvation Front (FIS), was going to win those elections, the army suspended the entire process and declared martial law. The FIS, outlawed by the military government, retreated into a clandestine existence and began to organize an armed struggle. By 1994, a more radical grouping, the Islamic Armed Group (GIA), had succeeded in rallying all of the Algerian Islamist movements under its banner and in gathering external support from Islamists in Tunisia, Libya, and Morocco. This support gave them access to a variety of militants already residing in Europe (Chaliand 2002).

The ascendance of the GIA in Algeria caused the French authorities to reevaluate the threat posed to France by the Algerian civil war. Unlike the FLN and the FIS before it, the GIA did not merely aim at seizing political power in Algeria. Rather, the GIA adhered to the political doctrine of jahiliyya, developed by the Egyptian Islamist thinker Sayyid Qutb (1906 to 1966), which held that the Algerian people and their government existed in a pre-Islamic state. All Algerians were therefore considered takfir (impious ones). Algerians therefore had to submit themselves to the restoration of Islam or die. Through holy war, or jihad, the GIA wanted not just to take power in Algeria but also to reestablish the Caliphate, the only form of government recognized by Islamic tradition. After Algeria, the Caliphate would be extended to the entire world.

To this end, the GIA considered it the right and indeed the duty of Muslims throughout the world to refuse Western laws and to be prepared to make war against the West at any moment. Thus, for the GIA, Algeria was only one theater in a wider war against the West. If the hatred of the GIA Islamists toward the West was virulent, their hatred of France was absolute. France represented "the mother of all sinners" (Laïdi 2002, 193) because France had destroyed Algeria with its colonialism, despoiled its riches for more than a century, and continued, through its support for the junta ruling Algeria, to reduce Algerian Muslims to slavery and to move Algeria away from religion. For the French authorities, this ideological position left little doubt that French territory would from now on be a target.

The extension of the Algerian crisis into France began with the kidnapping of three French consular agents on October 24, 1993, in Algiers. The message carried back by one of the hostages was explicit: the security of French citizens in Algeria was under threat from that moment forward.[18] In response, on November 9, 1993, French authorities launched Operation Chrysanthemum within France. In two days, 110 people in France had been questioned and 87 taken into custody. This wave of arrests was certainly motivated by the hostage-taking, but the arrests were also a response to the general disquiet of the French authorities, who, since 1992, had noticed the arrival in France of numerous members of the FIS as well as other Algerian Islamist groups. For the interior minister, Charles Pasqua, these interrogations also served the purpose of sending the message that the French government intended to suppress Islamist activity within the borders of France. On November 8, 1994, the Chalabi network, the most important support group for Algerian fighters struggling against the Algerian government, was dismantled. Ninety-three people were arrested, fifteen were soon released, and seventy-eight were held over for trial.

In response, on Christmas Day 1994, an Air France flight from Algiers to Paris was hijacked. With this hijacking, the GIA announced its willingness and even desire to strike directly on French soil. As the conditions for releasing the plane, the GIA demanded the abandonment of French aid to Algeria and financial reparations for the damages inflicted on Algerians by France between 1945 and 1962. It also demanded the liberation of FIS leaders as well as the freeing of a former emir of the GIA (Laïdi 2002). On December 26, French commandos assaulted the plane on the tarmac in Marseille and killed the hijackers. Documents found in London demonstrated that the terrorists had intended to crash the plane in Paris, possibly into the Eiffel Tower.

Expecting further attacks, French authorities decided to increase the pressure on the Islamist networks in France and throughout Europe. On June 2, 1995, 400 police officers dismantled a vast European network of support for the GIA and other Algerian groups by arresting 131 people in Paris, Marseille, Perpignan, Tourcoing, and Orléans. Unfortunately, the French intelligence services did not know of the existence of parallel networks in Lyon and in Lille; those groups launched a series of attacks in reprisal.[19] The authorities were thus taken by surprise by the wave of attacks that began on July 25, 1995, killing 10 and wounding over 150 between July and October (see table 7.3). In contrast to the wave of attacks in the 1980s, however, the French authorities were able to track down those responsible and dissolve the networks that supported them within four months.[20]

Responses

Throughout the 1990s, the French magistrates in charge of counterterrorism were concerned with the problem of using their judicial powers to prevent as well as to respond to terrorist attacks. The investigations led by the magistrates throughout this period had permitted them to understand the Islamist movement in a holistic fashion. After many years of such investigations, the magistrates had acquired what amounted to almost a cultural understanding of the Islamist movement. That knowledge turned out to be critical: because it permitted them to reduce the length of the investigations, they could arrest the members of a network more quickly and thus increase the French ability to prevent attacks.

Given the threats that faced France at the beginning of the 1990s, the magistrates decided to give priority to attacking the logistics networks, which they saw as the weak link in terrorist organization. To support themselves financially, the logistics networks of the diverse armed Algerian

TABLE 7.3 Attacks in France by the Islamic Armed Group, July to October 1995

July 11	Assassination of the imam of the mosque on the Rue Myrrha. Moderate and close to the FIS, he had protested against the use of violence on French territory.
July 25	A bomb explodes in the regional transit system at Saint-Michel station in Paris. Eight people die, and eighty-six are wounded.
August 17	A bomb laden with nuts and bolts explodes in a trash can near the Arc de Triomphe, wounding seventeen. Police increase security at public places and interview witnesses to the attack, which is believed to be related to the earlier attack at the Saint-Michel station.
August 26	Authorities discover a bomb planted on a TGV high-speed train track north of Lyons. It fails to detonate.
September 3	A pressure cooker bomb partially explodes in an open market near Place de la Bastille in Paris. Four people are wounded.
September 4	A potentially powerful bomb fails to explode and is found inside a public toilet near an outdoor market in the 15th District in Paris.
September 7	A car bomb explodes outside a Jewish school in a Lyons suburb ten minutes before school lets out. Fourteen people are wounded.
October 6	A gas canister containing nuts and bolts hidden in a trash can explodes near the Maison Blanche subway station in Paris, wounding sixteen people.
October 17	In the eighth terrorist attack or attempted attack in the last three months, a bomb explodes in an underground commuter train at the RER Orsay, wounding thirty people.

Source: Authors' compilation.

groups committed armed robberies and trafficked in credit cards and false documents such as passports. New legislative initiatives in 1995 and 1996 helped the magistrates target the logistics networks by codifying the notion that conspiracy to commit terrorism was itself terrorism.[21] This refinement in the law allowed the investigating magistrates to open investigations and to deploy their expertise and judicial tools before terrorist attacks took place, thereby enhancing their competence not just in punishing terrorist attacks after they took place but also in preventing them in the first place.

Nonetheless, in confronting the Algerian threat, the French authorities still found themselves facing the old problem of a lack of coordination and communication, now particularly between the intelligence agencies and the investigating magistrates at the Ministry of Justice. The investigating magistrates usually availed themselves of the Judicial Police (essentially police detectives) as their investigative arm. At this time, however, the Sixth Section of the Judicial Police (now known as the Division Nationale Anti-Terroriste of the Judicial Police, or DNAT) was facing an increase in Basque and Corsican separatist terrorism, culminating in the unprecedented 1998 assassination of the highest French government official in Corsica, the prefect Claude Érignac. They consequently did not have the internal resources to devote to the Islamist dossiers in the manner the magistrates would have preferred.

The magistrates in charge of Islamist cases thus began to work directly with the Direction du Surveillance du Territoire (DST), the domestic intelligence agency, which previously had communicated with the magistrates primarily through the intermediary of the Judicial Police. The magistrates had decided to make use of the fact that the DST officially had a dual role as an intelligence agency and a judicial police force that could be placed under the authority of a magistrate.[22]

The process of these investigations created a continuing relationship between specific judicial authorities and the DST. These relationships, in turn, inspired a degree of confidence within the DST that it was dealing with people in the judicial arm who understood and shared its concerns about protection of sources and the threat that judicial procedures posed to intelligence operations. The combination of expertise, effective relationships with the intelligence services, and the judicial powers already mentioned eventually created a formidable body for combating terrorism.

As a result, intelligence agents from the DST could now go directly to the magistrate and the prosecutor when they had information that they felt warranted a judicial investigation. If the magistrates decided from the intelligence obtained that there had been or might be a criminal act, they had the power to transform the intelligence investigation into a judicial investigation. Although information acquired before a judicial investigation is not admissible in French court, the opening of an official investigation provides various advantages because the agents in question can from that point onward avail themselves of the magistrates' extensive powers to issue warrants, subpoenas, and wiretaps, the results of which can be used as proof in court.

In effect, the struggle against Islamist terrorists is co-managed by the antiterrorism magistrates and the DST. On the one hand, the magistrates, who decide on the direction of the investigations, remain the masters of the "grand strategy." On the other hand, genuine exchanges are made around a table on the options that present themselves—for example, opening an intelligence investigation, transforming it into a judicial investigation, deciding to follow particular leads. This tight integration of the French intelligence and judicial system allows the latter to act much more quickly and effectively than most judicial authorities.[23]

This system developed in part because of the trust that was forged among specific personalities. Particular magistrates, such as Jean-Louis Bruguière and Jean-François Ricard, accumulated vast experience in understanding Islamist networks, and their personal interactions with the DST counted for a great deal. We can hope that this degree of trust will eventually move beyond personalities and develop into an institutional feature. The magistrates and the DST, however, have each maintained their prerogatives, and the court does not interfere in intelligence missions that have no bearing on judicial cases.[24]

The Globalization of the Struggle

France's struggle with the Islamic Armed Group (GIA) led the French authorities to understand relatively early that the Islamist threat was of a new, complex, and global type. Starting in 1994, the antiterrorism magistrates began to notice the departure of many hard-core GIA militants for Afghan training camps. The interrogations of people belonging to the Lyon cell of the GIA after the 1995 attacks also showed that the GIA had been sending new recruits to Afghanistan since the beginning of the 1990s.

In Afghanistan, they received a military education in small arms and explosives as well as a religious education in radical Islam. French investigations also revealed that the financing for the 1995 attacks came from London. The financier Rachid Ramda was found, in turn, to have financial and other connections with Osama bin Laden and his group of Afghan veterans. Clearly, France's Algerian problem was internationalizing. The subsequent affair of the Roubaix gang supported this conclusion. The Roubaix affair began with several heavily armed robberies in the Roubaix region in January and February 1996 and originally appeared to have no relation to international terrorism. On the eve of the G-7 summit at Lille on March 29, 1996, the gang put a bomb in a car at a police station, though the bomb was discovered and dismantled (Laïdi 2002, 217). Subsequent investigation discovered a link to the Islamist movement, but despite this link, the members of the Roubaix gang were not normal Algerian guerrilla fighters. Rather, they were native-born French citizens and second-generation French North Africans who had converted to radical Islam in France and made their connections with the terrorist movement in Bosnia and Afghanistan. According to French antiterrorism magistrate Jean-Louis Bruguière, "The structure of the organization—and the targets—had changed. The targets were not just in France or Europe."[25] The magistrates were beginning to develop a vision of a global, yet nebulous, Islamist internationale.

Because of this early awareness, the system has evolved only fairly modestly in response to the new wave of attacks since 2001 and the spread of Al Qaeda methods and ideology to other groups. The terrorist attacks in the United States, Spain, and the United Kingdom each spawned new legislation in France and gave incrementally more powers to the police and the magistrates—particularly in the use of video surveillance, the setting of longer penalties for terrorist offenses, gaining greater access to databases on telephone calls and Internet use for counterterrorism purposes, and having increased powers of search and detention. There has also been a greater ability and willingness to enforce laws against hate speech and to deport imams from abroad who espouse a radical Islamist philosophy—thirty-five were deported between the fall of 2003 and the fall of 2005 (Laurence and Vaisse 2006, 245). France has also strengthened its cooperation with foreign governments, particularly with key European partners and the United States. This cooperation includes a top-secret multinational operations cell in Paris that plans counterterrorism operations with various partners, particularly the United States.[26]

French Lessons

In sum, France has developed, largely by costly experiments over nearly fifty years, a fairly effective, although controversial, system for fighting terrorism at home. The French approach is, of course, uniquely French, tailored to France's particular threats and capacities as well as to France's distinct civic culture. It relies on extensive societal surveillance to prevent terrorist cells or logistics networks from forming, a specialized but non-emergency cadre of laws and procedures to take account of the unique nature of the terrorist threat, and preset mobilization plans that can reassure and involve the public in case of an attack. Its effectiveness has been demonstrated by the absence of successful terrorist attacks in France in recent years—despite numerous threats—as well as by the many plots that have been foiled by the authorities in recent years (see table 7.4).

TABLE 7.4 Selected Terrorist Plots Prevented by French Authorities, 1998 to Present

May 1998	In a synchronized operation, police in France, Belgium, Italy, Germany, and Switzerland detained more than eighty Islamic militants suspected of planning terrorist actions during the upcoming World Cup in France.
December 2000	Four men were arrested in Frankfurt, Germany, based on a tip from French authorities. Evidence found in their apartment showed that they intended to blow up the Christmas Market surrounding the cathedral in Strasbourg, France.
October 2001	In France, the Netherlands, Belgium, and Dubai, intelligence and security services arrested fourteen men suspected of planning an attack on the U.S. embassy in Paris.
December 2002	French antiterrorism police arrested nine people planning to blow up the Russian Embassy in Paris. The group's apparent motive was to avenge the deaths of several comrades killed in Chechnya.
January 2003	Based on intelligence provided by French authorities, raids on five homes in North London resulted in the arrests of seven people apparently planning terrorist attacks in Britain. Traces of attempts to manufacture the deadly poison ricin were discovered in one of the apartments.
January 2005	French antiterrorism police arrest three people in Paris involved in smuggling fighters to Iraq. The so-called Buttes-Chaumont network is estimated to have trained some fifty jihadists, six of whom had been arrested or killed in Iraq, including one in a suicide bombing attack in Baghdad.

Source: Authors' compilation.

The system, however, is far from perfect, and French authorities remain aware of an active and dangerous threat. Recent political developments, such as the war in Iraq, the French decision to ban the head scarf in public schools, and the continued activity of various Moroccan and Algerian terrorist groups, keep France both a target and a source of recruits for global jihad. French networks have sent fighters to Iraq, some of whom may have already returned to wage jihad at home, and the Renseignements Généraux (RG) estimates that there are some five thousand Salafists in France, many of whom are potentially dangerous.[27]

One lesson of the French experience is how important it is to deal with terrorism through normal channels, and to include judicial institutions in particular. Terrorism certainly stresses such institutions' capacities, but the persistent nature of terrorism makes it critical to maintain a fair counterterrorism system that commands democratic legitimacy, not only to safeguard liberties but also to wage an effective struggle. The French experience shows that ad hoc or unpopular antiterrorist measures that have little basis in societal values and shallow support may wither away during periods of calm.

Maintaining legitimacy remains a challenge for France, as for any other country. The French system's approach to civil liberties—one that includes detention without charges and pervasive surveillance by the authorities, including of prayer sites—would be unacceptable in many other democracies. The burden of French counterterrorism actions today falls most heavily on France's economically disadvantaged and restive Muslim and Arab population. French counterterrorism policies therefore do pose some risk of adding fuel to the fire of France's already volatile problem of Muslim and Arab integration. In fact, the shooting of a terrorism suspect, Khaled Kelkal, by a special police unit during the 1995 wave of terrorism sparked riots in the Muslim communities of Paris and Lyon.[28] The 2005 riots in Muslim communities throughout France similarly began after the death of suspects fleeing from the police, although they were not terrorist suspects.

As a result, France's counterterrorism apparatus has often been fiercely criticized by the media and human rights groups. Two areas in particular have been the object of acerbic criticisms: the preventive roundups and the associated indiscriminate detention of suspects, as well as the broad powers given to magistrates to conduct these sweeps and detentions with very little oversight. Denunciations of the November 1993 Operation Chrysanthemum as a sweep used the French word "rafle," which specifically evokes the actions taken during the German occupation.[29] Eighty-eight people were interrogated, but only three were incarcerated and put under investigation for "conspiracy in relation to a terrorist enterprise." A variety of media outlets, as well as the Fédération Internationales des Ligues des Droits de l'Homme (FDIH; 1999), declared the arrests "media spectacles" and "destructive of liberty." Such roundups have often swept up people against whom there is no preexisting evidence or people who have nothing to do with the networks but just happen to be present on the day of the sweep. The decision after the 1995 attacks to go after logistics and support networks has only increased the breadth of the sweeps, as demonstrated before the 1998 World Cup in France (discussed later).

Another frequent criticism is that there is no controlling authority over the actions of the antiterrorism magistrates and that the contents of the antiterrorist laws of 1986 and 1996 offer excessive scope for the magistrates to decide what constitutes terrorism or intent to commit terrorism. According to a January 1999 report of the FDIH, a number of jurists and lawyers have expressed reservations about the vagueness of the antiterrorist laws, notably in the Chalabi affair (Fédération Internationales des Ligues des Droits de l'Homme 1999). Not only does the 1986 law heavily concentrate the competences for fighting terrorism in the hands of a limited group of antiterrorism magistrates, but their conclusions are then usually accepted uncritically by the other actors in the judicial system with very little oversight by any outside authority. Thus, of the 138 people the magistrates detained for a trial in the sweeps associated with the dismantlement of the Chalabi network, 51 were ultimately found innocent of complicity in terrorism and released, but not until they had spent more than four years in jail. In 2000 a reform of the judicial system known as the Loi Guigou attempted to respond to the problem by providing for a juge de liberté who needs to approve holding people over beyond the original detention period (now six days for terrorism cases), but this reform has not proved a significant impediment for the investigating magistrates.[30]

In the view of the authorities, arresting a large number of people makes it possible to carry out corroborated interrogations in order to maintain knowledge of networks that are in a perpetual state of evolution. Thus, for example, arrests in early 1998 permitted the authorities to prevent attacks planned on the World Cup, one of which was intended for the Stadium of France. This policy stands in contrast to normal French law, which usually insists that an infraction must have actually taken place before a judicial investigation can begin.

Interestingly, these attacks on the specialized system of antiterrorism enforcement in France have not generally emanated from Muslim civil society groups. Indeed, there has been very little talk about the degree to which this cadre of special antiterrorism legislation contributes to frictions between the Muslim community and the state—a debate that is almost glaring in its absence.[31] The system of investigating magistrates has certainly come under fierce public criticism for abuses and may well be eliminated altogether. But the abuses that have garnered the most attention have come in areas that have nothing to do with counterterrorism—particularly the "Outreau Affair," in which a young investigating magistrate abused his authority to investigate child abuse. On the most mundane level, the explanation is that the Muslim community in France appears to be contending with larger issues: issues of cultural integration and economic opportunity, the plague of "normal" criminal activity in Muslim areas, and the debate over public religious expression dominate the French domestic political agenda. In this highly contentious environment, occasional counterterrorism actions that affect the Muslim population, as well as the associated constant surveillance by the state (usually quite discreet), do not generate much public outcry from within the Muslim community.

In this sense, the outbursts over the killing of Khaled Kelkal, like the November 2005 riots in the Muslim neighborhoods of Paris and other French cities, were more a reflection of the general frustration the French Muslim community feels over its treatment by the police and by society than a specific response to the surveillance and even to the roundups associated with the French counterterrorism apparatus. It seems clear, however, that future dramatic episodes along the lines of the Khelkal shooting could let loose a torrent of social discontent that might find its expression in opposition to the special cadre of antiterrorism laws and methods that, in effect, target the North African community.

Notes

1. For one of numerous such accounts regarding the FLN, see Aussaresses (2001). On the brutality of the response to the OAS, see Bocca (1968).
2. Thus, for example, the post-9/11 English edition of General Paul Aussaresses's (2001) book on his Algerian experience is subtitled "Terrorism and Counterterrorism in Algeria," but the original French subtitle is "Mon témoignage sur la torture" (My Account of the Torture).
3. The French police, however, had a long memory. Carlos was eventually apprehended in 1994 and in 1997 sentenced to life imprisonment.
4. The SDECE was renamed the Direction Générale de la Sécurité Extérieure (DGSE) in 1981.
5. The three leaders were Georges Ibrahim Abdallah, chief of the FARL (Fractions Armées Revolutionnaires Libanaise), the organization that had assassinated Charles Ray, military attaché of the U.S. embassy, and Yaacov Bar-Simen-Tov, second secretary of the Israeli embassy, in Paris in 1982 and had attempted to assassinate Robert Homme, consul general of the U.S. embassy in Strasbourg in 1984; Anis Naccache, a Lebanese Christian who had attempted to assassinate an Iranian dissident on orders from Tehran and in the process killed a neighbor and a French policeman; and Varoujean

Garbidjian, a leader of ASALA (Secret Army for the Liberation of Armenia), which had bombed the Turkish Airlines counter in Orly Airport in Paris in 1983, killing eight.

6. According to Daniel Burdan (1990, 310), the defector, code-named Jabert, claimed that a meeting took place in January 1986 between representatives of Iran, Libya, Syria, and Abu Nidal for the purposes of planning the 1986 campaign of bombing in France.
7. The French foreign intelligence service (DGSE) apparently attempted retaliatory attacks that included a car bombing in Damascus in 1981, an attempted bombing of the Iranian embassy in Beirut in 1983, and a raid on a terrorist training camp in Lebanon in 1986, but these actions either were unsuccessful (both attempts in Lebanon) or had little effect on state behavior (as in Damascus). See Wieviorka (1990, 78–81), Porch (1995, 435), and Wieviorka (1991, 162).
8. See Georges Marion, "Le role des services de renseignement dans les rapports franco-iraniens," *Le Monde*, July 31, 1987.
9. For an example of how this controversy persisted as an issue in French politics into the 2002 presidential election, see "M. Pasqua veut maintenir sa candidature a l'Élysée malgré les affaires: La controverse sur les otages du Liban se poursuit," *Le Monde*, January 10, 2002.
10. At the time, these included, among others, the Police Judiciaire (PJ), the Direction Centrale des Renseignements Généraux (DCRG), the Direction du Surveillance du Territoire (DST), the Police de l'Air and des Frontiers (PAF), the Gendarmerie Nationale, the Direction Générale de la Sécurité Extérieure (DGSE), the Brigade Criminelle, and the Direction de la Protection et de la Sécurité de la Défense (DPSD). For a more complete list, see Guisnel and Violet (1988).
11. In 1954, in what became known as the "Affair of the Leaks" (Affaire des Fuites), the DST had falsely accused then–Interior Minister Mitterrand of leaking information that had brought about the fall of the French garrison at Dien Bien Phu.
12. This affair became known as the "Irlandais de Vincennes Affair." For details, see the memoir of Paul Barril (1984), the Élysée cell member responsible for the affair.
13. At the French government website, see "Loi no. 86-1020 du 9 septembre 1986 relative à la lutte contre le terrorisme et aux atteintes à la sûreté de l'État," http://www.legifrance.gouv.fr.
14. SCLAT was later renamed the Fourteenth Section of the Parquet de Paris.
15. Author interview with a French official, October 2002.
16. See Alain Marsaud, "Pour un 'Conseil de Securité,'" *Le Monde*, December 21, 1985.
17. Author interview with another French official, October 2002. On the advantages and disadvantages of the investigating magistrates in the French legal system, see Soulez Larivière and Dalle (2002) and Leclerc (2002).

18. It should be noted that some people viewed these kidnappings as a manipulation by the Algerian secret services, which wanted to convince French authorities to act against opponents of the Algerian regime in France. See, for example, Samraoui (2003).
19. Author interview with Irène Stoller, October 2002.
20. However, the origin of an apparently linked attack on December 3, 1996, at the Port-Royal RER station remains a mystery.
21. According to article 421-2-1 of the French penal code, inserted on July 22, 1996, "the participation in any group formed or association established with a view to the preparation, marked by one or more material actions, of any of the acts of terrorism provided for under the previous articles shall in addition be an act of terrorism." See the relevant passage from the penal code at the French government website, http://www.legifrance.gouv.fr/html/codes_traduits/code_penal_textan.htm.
22. Author interview with a French official, October 2002.
23. Author interview with Alain Marsaud, October 2002.
24. Author interview with a French official, October 2002.
25. Quoted in Hal Bernton and others, "The Terrorist Within," *Seattle Times*, June 25, 2002. This article is one of an eighteen-part series published in the *Seattle Times* from June 22 to July 8, 2002.
26. For French adaptations since 9/11, see Secrétariat Général de la Défense Nationale (SGDN 2006); on the multinational operations cell, see Dana Priest, "Help from France Key in Covert Operations; Paris's 'Alliance Base' Targets Terrorists," *Washington Post*, July 3, 2005.
27. See Piotr Smolar, "L'antiterrorisme, selon le patron des RG." *Le Monde*, November 25, 2005.
28. See Andrew Jack and Roula Khalaf, "Row over Shooting of French Suspect," *Financial Times*, October 4, 1995.
29. See Erich Inciyan, "Après les coups de filet policiers dans les milieux kurdes et islamistes en France: Le message des operations 'Chrysantheme' et 'Rouge-Rose Monde,'" *Le Monde*, December 2, 1993.
30. Author interview with a French investigating magistrate, October 2005.
31. For an exception that sees French counterterrorism laws as reinforcing social cleavages in French society, see Bigo (2002).

References

Aussaresses, Gen. Paul. 2001. *The Battle of the Casbah: Terrorism and Counterterrorism in Algeria, 1955–1957*. New York: Enigma Books.

Barril, Paul. 1984. *Missions très speciales*. Paris: Presses de la Cité.

Bigo, Didier. 2002. "Reassuring and Protecting: Internal Security Implications of French Participation in the Coalition Against Terrorism." In *Critical Views of September 11*, edited by Eric Hershberg and Kevin W. Moore. New York: New Press.

Bocca, Geoffrey. 1968. *The Secret Army*. Englewood Cliffs, N.J.: Prentice-Hall.

Burdan, Daniel. 1990. *DST: Neuf ans a la division antiterroriste*. Paris: Robert Laffont.

Chaliand, Gerard. 2002. *L'Arme du terrorisme*. Paris: Louis Audibert.

Chauvin, Luc. 1990. "French Diplomacy and the Hostage Crises." In *The Politics of Counterterrorism: The Ordeal of Democratic States*, edited by Barry Rubin. Philadelphia: Foreign Policy Institute.

Connelly, Matthew. 2002. *A Diplomatic Revolution: Algeria's Fight for Independence and the Origin of the Post–Cold War Era*. Oxford: Oxford University Press.

Crenshaw, Martha. 1995. "The Effectiveness of Terrorism in the Algerian War." In *Terrorism in Context*, edited by Martha Crenshaw. University Park: Penn State University Press.

De Weck, Herve. 1991. "Les services de renseignements à coeur ouvert?" *Revue Militaire Suisse* 2: 25.

Fédération Internationale des Ligues des Droits de l'Homme (FDIH). 1999. "France: La porte ouverte a l'arbitraire, no. 271." Rapport d'une mission internationale d'enquête en France sur l'application de la législation antiterroriste (January). Available at: http://www.fidh.org (accessed September 22, 2009).

Furniss, Edgar S., Jr. 1964. *DeGaulle and the French Army*. New York: Twentieth-Century Fund.

Guisnel, Jean, and Bernard Violet. 1988. *Services secrets: Le pouvoir et les services des renseignements sous la présidence de François Mitterrand*. Paris: Éditions La Découverte.

Harrison, Alexander. 2005. *Challenging De Gaulle: The OAS and the Counterrevolution in Algeria 1954–1962*. New York: Hailer Publishing.

Jongman, Albert J. 1992. "Trends in International and Domestic Terrorism in Western Europe, 1968–1988." *Terrorism and Political Violence* 4: 26–76.

Laïdi, Ali, with Ahmed Salam. 2002. *Le jihad en Europe : Les filières du terrorisme en Europe*. Paris: Seuil.

Laurence, Jonathan, and Justin Vaisse. 2006. *Integrating Islam: Political and Religious Challenges in Contemporary France*. Washington, D.C.: Brookings Institution Press.

Leclerc, Henri. 2002. "Pour un nouveau procès penal." In *Notre justice: Le livre vérité de la justice française*, edited by Daniel Soulez Larivière and Hubert Dalle. Paris: Robert Laffont.

Marion, Pierre. 1991. *La mission impossible: À la tête des Services Secrets*. Paris: Calmann-Lévy.

Marsaud, Alain. 2002. *Avant de tout oublier*. Paris: Denoël Impacts.

Porch, Douglas. 1995. *The French Secret Services: A History of French Intelligence from the Dreyfus Affair to the Gulf War*. New York: Farrar, Strauss & Giroux.

Rich, Paul B. 1999. "Insurgency, Revolution, and Crises in Algeria." In *The Counter-insurgent State: Guerrilla Warfare and State-Building in the Twentieth Century*, edited by Paul B. Rich and Richard Stubbs. New York: St. Martin's Press.

Samraoui, Mohammed. 2003. *Chronique des années de sang: Algérie: Comment les services secret ont manipulé les groupes islamistes.* Paris: Denoël Impacts.

Secrétariat Général de la Défense Nationale (SGDN). 2006. *Prevailing Against Terrorism: White Paper on Domestic Security Against Terrorism.* Paris: La Documentation Française.

Soulez Larivière, Daniel, and Hubert Dalle. 2002. *Notre justice: Le livre vérité de la justice française.* Paris: Robert Laffont.

Stoller, Irène. 2002. *Procureur à la 14e Section.* Paris: Michel Lafon.

Wieviorka, Michel. 1990. "French Politics and Strategy on Terrorism." In *The Politics of Counterterrorism: The Ordeal of Democratic States,* edited by Barry Rubin. Philadelphia: Foreign Policy Institute.

———. 1991. "France Faced with Terrorism." *Terrorism* 14(3): 151-70.

Chapter 8

Germany's Response to 9/11: The Importance of Checks and Balances

Giovanni Capoccia

> The Federal Government has devoted itself with the strongest determination to improving protection from terrorism, extremism and religious fundamentalism. We are conscious that these extreme forms of intolerance pose a new threat to the fundamental liberal-democratic order of the Republic. Therefore, we cannot afford any hesitation in implementing the new legal instruments against anti-constitutional and violent organizations with necessary firmness.
>
> Otto Schily, Social Democrat (SPD), Minister of Interior Affairs, January 16, 2003, Plenary Session of the Bundestag[1]

The post-9/11 counterterrorism policies enacted in different countries display important differences. In the United States, the emergence of an international terrorist threat on an unprecedented scale has led to a great increase in the power of the executive (see, for example, Heymann 2003; Ackerman 2004a, 2004b; Scheppele 2004). By contrast, other countries that are potentially exposed to the same threat and are certainly aware of the danger, such as Germany, have retained tighter limits on the power of the executive. What explains these differences? A large literature has emphasized that even in the presence of common external shocks such as 9/11, the foreign and domestic security policies of different countries are the result of the "filtering" of external shocks through the prism of the existing domestic political environment (see, for example, Katzenstein 1996a, 2003). These accounts generally criticize "realist" approaches in international relations, and rightly stress that the "domestic origins of state preferences and their perceptions of the international system . . . cannot be answered by perspectives that focus solely on a state's position in the international system" (Berger 1996, 319). Special emphasis is generally placed on the failure of realist approaches to attribute the appropriate weight to the cultural norms (values, identities, ideologies) that shape the response of countries to security threats (Katzenstein 1996b, 1996c; Jepperson, Wendt, and Katzenstein 1996; Berger 1998). For example, in his interpretation of the changes in German and Japanese counterterrorism policy following 9/11, Peter Katzenstein maintains that a "situational" analysis focused on domestic and international material conditions—such as the number of Muslim immigrants in a country, its geopolitical position, and so on—should be strengthened by an appropriate analysis of the impact of the constitutive and regulatory norms that guide reactions to terrorist threats. According to this view, security policy operates in a normatively "deep" social environment as it ultimately confronts the state with the "enemy within." Thus, in security policymaking, strategic action to pursue certain ends is embedded in thick layers of institutionalized norms (Katzenstein 2003). This position resonates with a large literature in sociological institutionalism: security policymaking is mostly shaped by cultural and social factors that influence the very identity of political actors and decisionmakers and that also define "appropriate" responses to external threats (see, for example, March and Olsen 1989, 2004; Powell and Di Maggio 1991).

This chapter, which analyzes domestic security policymaking in Germany after 9/11, argues that the analysis of cultural norms should be integrated with the analysis of internal institutional dynamics.[2] Domestic institutions—in particular "counter-majoritarian" ones such as federalism and the judiciary—can have an important impact on policy outcomes, in domestic security as well as other areas. In fact, as the literature emphasizes, even the most strongly embedded cultural norms are generally contested (Katzenstein 1996c). Such contestation is not always solved by public deliberation: on the contrary, in some cases it leads to institutional friction between the government and the counter-majoritarian institutions. Post-9/11 Germany offers an example of how a system of checks and balances can limit the expansion of national executive power in matters of internal security and counterterrorism.

Of course, cultural norms inherited from recent history have informed the German public debate on national security. However, counter-majoritarian institutions such as the federal system (and the prerogatives of the Länder in it) and the judicial system (in particular the Federal Constitutional Court) have exerted an important influence on which interpretation of the fundamental cultural norms underlying the 1949 Basic Law has ultimately prevailed in shaping security policy. This has happened even in areas where a different interpretation of inherited norms was accepted by the majority of the political elites and the population. In fact, the range of feasible initiatives in security policy may not be just limited and directed by norms that are diffuse in the population at large (see, for example, Berger 1996). On the contrary, the German case shows that counter-majoritarian institutions may impose interpretations of inherited norms that prevail even over other interpretations that are supported by an overwhelming majority of the political elites and the public. To be sure, the very existence of counter-majoritarian institutions is not exogenous to the fundamental normative concerns characteristic of the Basic Law: the prerogatives of the Länder and the judiciary were designed exactly to enforce those norms in the new Federal Republic. Yet, the limits to government policies provided by such institutions, once they are in place, may be more immediate and constraining for the government than the limits imposed on decision-makers by codes of ideological appropriateness, either directly through cultural scripts (see, for example, March and Olson 2004), or indirectly, through popular pressure (see, for example, Berger 1998).

The analysis shows that, thanks mainly to the actions of counter-majoritarian institutional actors, the pre-2001 normative and institutional framework of the 1949 Basic Law has remained firmly in place, despite the sweeping reforms and policy changes advocated by both political elites and the public in the wake of the 9/11 attacks. Of course, some important policy changes have been introduced, but either they have remained within the rather strict limits imposed by the Basic Law or they represent the continuation of incremental changes that were already under way before 9/11. Most importantly, the powers of the federal executive have not grown significantly. The German security apparatus is still marked by functional fragmentation and federal decentralization, notwithstanding recent calls for centralization to respond more effectively to the new threat of international Islamic terrorism. In those instances in which the central executive has tried, since September 2001, to expand its security powers by supporting an extensive interpretation of the constitutional limits to its action, the judiciary has intervened to stop it, either preventively or ex post facto—that is, by revoking or annulling government decisions and setting clear limits to future governmental action in those spheres. Similarly, the entrenched nature of the federal system has frustrated proposals for the outright centralization of power, making enhanced *coordination* between levels of government the only viable strategy to step up counterterrorism activity.

It is important to note that the literature has given due consideration to the impact of internal political dynamics on the evolution of the normative debate on national security in Germany before 9/11 (see, for example, the excellent analyses in Jepperson, Wendt, and Katzenstein 1996; Katzenstein 1997; Berger 1998). The situation after 9/11 is different for two reasons. First, while it is beyond doubt that security policy has always involved a foreign as well as a domestic dimension (see, for example, Katzenstein 2003), the relative importance of domestic security has grown. The nature of the new international terrorist threat has focused attention on several spheres of domestic policy that earlier had at best a marginal relevance for national security. Post-9/11 security debates involve not only police powers and the regulation of states of emergency but also issues such as asylum, immigration, the rights of minorities, and freedom of religion and religious expression (Chebel d'Appollonia and Reich 2007). Second, as a consequence of this state of affairs, the judiciary is now more likely to intervene on security issues (in the new areas) and to play an important role in enforcing the relevant constitutional norms. By the same token, the federated subunits are likely to resist encroachment on their policy-making powers in these new areas. Thus, given the extended conception of security, the general normative concerns highlighted by several culturalist interpretations of German foreign policy (for example, Banchoff 1999; Markovits and Reich 1997) no longer offer a sufficient basis for understanding security policy as a whole. The friction between the government and the political majority, on the one hand, and counter-majoritarian institutions such as the Länder and the courts, on the other, needs to be taken into account more systematically. Indeed, the German case shows that on important occasions the federal system and the Federal Constitutional Court have gone against the current of the German public and elites, vetoing policies or limiting reforms that enjoyed widespread public support and that were backed by the overwhelming majority of the political class.

In sum, in post-9/11 Germany some changes in the bureaucratic structure of the security institutions have been introduced, new laws have been passed that increase police power against terrorist groups and individuals, and the intensity of investigative activities has been stepped up. The correct way to interpret such innovations, however, is to see them as examples of incremental change in the context of a rather unchanged normative and institutional framework of national security policy.

The first section outlines the key aspects of the normative and institutional context of security policy in Germany. The second section analyzes public opinion on relevant matters in Germany after 2001. The central part of the chapter analyzes continuity and change in different areas of legislation, the institutional structure of the security agencies, and security policy following 9/11. The concluding section draws out the implications of the analysis for the possibility of future reforms in German security policy.

The Normative and Institutional Context of German Security Policy

The question of which norms among the many values and principles that drive political action in a pluralist democracy should be considered fundamental and which should be seen instead as more expendable is obviously debatable (see, for example, Garrett and Weingast 1992). The identification of such "basic principles" is often left to the interpretation of the analyst. In the specific case of national security in the Federal Republic of Germany, however, the risk of subjectivity in this matter can be substantively reduced. In fact, the national security sector underwent a total ideological overhaul in Germany after the defeat in World War II. Indeed, it was clear since its approval in 1949 that some of the principles and norms included in the Grundgesetz (Basic Law), and the institutional arrangements that entrenched and protected them, were more important than others to the ideological foundations of the re-created democratic West German state.

The whole German constitutionalist doctrine is virtually at one in considering the 1949 Basic Law a "double reaction" to the Weimar Republic and its failure, on the one hand, and to the totalitarian Nazi regime, on the other (see, for example, Dürig 1988, 12). These normative bases of the Grundgesetz and the institutional embodiment of such norms were clearly articulated by the founding fathers (and the occupying Allies) during the constitution-making process (see von Doemming, Füsslein, and Matz 1951).[3] To reach this objective, the Basic Law designed a democratic system in which two main normative and institutional principles coexist. The Weimar Republic's foundering against the Nazi challenge led to the immunization and protection of the democratic system from the action of antidemocratic forces. The Basic Law endows the political authorities of the German Federal Republic with the constitutional and legal means to repress the challenges to the constitutional order that emerge from society. And rejection of the Nazi past has led to the establishment of a system in which fundamental rights are universal, constitutionally entrenched, and nonmodifiable—and guaranteed by judicial review exerted by a powerful system of constitutional courts at the federal and state levels. Power is neither actually nor potentially concentrated in a single constitutional organ, and a system of checks and balances is always operational, both within and across territorial levels of government (Dürig 1988; see also, for example, Stern 1977, 416; Karpen 1983, 1988; Weber-Fas 1983; Klein 1983; Starck 1983; Mussgnug 1987; Zieger 1988; Currie 1994; Katzenstein 1996d, 2003).[4]

This "double negative" heritage of the Weimar Republic and the Nazi regime has been visible in most aspects of German postwar constitutional life. Put differently, the historical heritage of the Weimar Republic, on the one hand, and of the Nazi dictatorship, on the other, not only provides the normative "national lenses" through which international crises and their domestic consequences are filtered (Katzenstein 2003, 732; see also Markovits and Reich 1997), but is also at the basis of the institutional framework through which internal threats to the "fundamental liberal-democratic order" (as mentioned in the Basic Law and defined by the Federal Constitutional Court as early as 1952) are viewed and approached in Germany today.[5] In other words, these basic normative principles are made effective by specific institutional arrangements.

The determination to defend the "fundamental liberal-democratic order" of the Federal Republic from its enemies informs the principle of "streitbare Demokratie" (militant democracy), which is one of the defining characteristics of the 1949 Basic Law (see, for example, Jesse 1980; Boventer 1985; Sajò 2004). The prohibition on abusing one's fundamental rights against the constitutional order is not just asserted, however: the Basic Law includes specific rules and attributes powers to limit fundamental rights in case of their abuse. According to article 18, individuals can be stripped of their basic rights if these are used to undermine the "fundamental liberal-democratic order". Articles 9 and 21, respectively, allow for the legal dissolution of political associations and political parties if these are opposed to the fundamental liberal-democratic order. Although the rules on the forfeiture of individual rights have been interpreted narrowly by the Federal Constitutional Court and have not yet been implemented to date (see, for example, Foster and Sule 2002, 202), several political parties and many associations have been banned since 1949 to "defend the Constitution."[6] Apart from the activity of federal and state executives and courts in these respects, the Office for the Protection of the Constitution (Bundesamt für Verfassungsschutz), which has a federal office and sixteen regional branches, is in charge of monitoring extremist groups and individuals and disseminating information on them to the authorities and the public.

The concern about avoiding excessive centralization of power and the risk of authoritarianism is embodied by the constitutionally entrenched, unmodifiable nature of the federal system (article 79[3] of the Basic Law), but also by the particularly powerful position granted to the Länder vis-à-vis the federal level of government and by the strength and independence of the court system at both the state and federal levels (see Currie 1994). In other words, the basic normative principles of reaction against the institutional vulnerability of Weimar and the authoritarianism of the Nazi period have consciously been translated into "institutionalized norms" (Katzenstein 1996c, 20–21), not only "weakly" by simply solemnly asserting them in the text of the Constitution, but also "strongly" by endowing constitutional bodies with powers and prerogatives to enact such principles in German political life.

In the years following 9/11, the determination to defend the fundamental liberal-democratic order of the Federal Republic from its enemies according to the "streitbare Demokratie" principle has constantly been clear in the words and actions of national politicians, and it has also been used to frame the security reforms proposed. In fact, although moments of intense partisan debate on these issues have punctuated German post-war history, the three main German parties, the Social Democrats (SPD), the Christian Democrats (CDU/CSU), and the Liberals (FDP), have for a long time held roughly similar positions on topics of security and law and order.[7] Things have not substantially changed in the post-9/11 period: in its 2002 election manifesto, for example, the SPD talked about security as a citizen's right and a central aim of the Rechtsstaat, a position not essentially different from that of the Liberals and the Christian Democrats. Only the ex-Communist PDS (now the Left Party) has openly criticized the new antiterrorism legislation, stating (in its 2002 manifesto) that it results in discrimination against foreigners and an increase in xenophobia and anti-Muslim sentiments. The party has permanently been in opposition since its creation in 1990, however, and has as yet no serious prospect of being accepted by the moderate left-wing parties as a coalition partner at the federal level.[8] All other parties have supported the new legislation:

even the Greens—who before entering the government in coalition with the Social Democrats in 1998 tended to reject radically any stricter law-and-order measure—played an important part, as members of the governing coalition until 2005, in drafting the new antiterrorism legislation.[9] The Greens stressed that any restrictions of civil liberties should be kept to a minimum (in their 2002 party platform they emphasized the importance of sunset clauses), but did acknowledge that internal security is a legitimate aim of the state and that coercive measures are legitimate to ensure security. In this spirit, for example, they supported the controversial airspace security law (discussed later).[10] Some further disagreements emerged on the occasion of the approval of specific policies, but they were rather limited.

At the same time, however, the limits to such defensive policies against the anticonstitutional forces of terrorism and extremism have proved resilient. Fundamental rights were upheld by the courts, which ruled against the governmental policy on several occasions (discussed later). Moreover, the federal principle still molds the institutional structure of the security apparatuses, despite widespread advocacy for centralization in the public debate. Security institutions present a double kind of fragmentation: the division of responsibility between the federal government (Bund) and the states (Länder) and between different federal agencies. In general terms, internal security and policing are mainly in the hands of the Länder, while areas such as border controls (including security measures at airports and railway stations) and others have been in the remit of the federal government for a few decades now (see, for example, Currie 1994; Glässner 2003).

In fact, the general tendency since the 1950s has been one of slow, incremental centralization in a system that began as almost entirely regionalized, with the federal agencies acquiring some new responsibilities in response to the internal terrorist challenges of the 1970s and 1980s (Busch et al. 1985; Katzenstein 1996d). Yet, despite the renewed pressures for centralization that emerged after 9/11, the territorial and functional fragmentation described earlier still largely exists: on the one hand, federal agencies still have to rely on the Länder police to carry out most of their tasks. On the other hand, the institutional response to the inefficiencies lamented by many in the public debate deriving from the functional fragmentation between federal security bodies has been mainly to improve the coordination mechanisms between agencies rather than to centralize tasks in a single body.

In sum, the fundamental normative principles informing the Basic Law are embodied in specific institutions. The pressure to increase executive powers and to limit rights and guarantees following 9/11, although consistent with the important principle of the "defense of the Constitution" against its enemies, led to overall limited reform. This outcome was mainly due to the counter-majoritarian action of the judiciary and the inertial force of the federal system, both of which have constrained governmental action against terrorism. In fact, the legislative and institutional innovations introduced over the past few years, while enlarging the scope of police action, have largely stayed within the traditional terms of reference set by the Basic Law, despite widespread support among the political elites, the community of policy experts, and the population at large for broader reforms.

The Perception of the Threat: Counterterrorism and Public Opinion in Germany Since 9/11

A great deal of empirical evidence shows that in Germany the threat of international Islamic terrorism was fully perceived by opinion leaders, mainstream politicians, and the public. Later sections describe various moments of the public debate on these issues. Here I present data that show that, in the context of a general deterioration of the attitude toward the Muslim community, the majority of the German public supported the new antiterrorism measures and would have supported even stricter ones.

The Changing Attitude Toward Islam

Although data on the perception of the Muslim community by the German majority before 9/11 are not available, it is an easy guess that the events of 9/11 had a negative effect on that perception. It is interesting to note, however, that this perception has deteriorated even further *since* 9/11. Several surveys show that since the end of 2001 an increasing number of Germans perceive Muslims as a threat and associate them with terrorism. This is particularly worrying given the large number of Muslims residing in Germany (3.5 million, according to the last census). The Office for the Protection of the Constitution reported that fewer than 1 percent of the Muslim resident population are thought to be members of Islamic organizations with extremist ties. Yet the view that some larger Muslim fringe groups harbor extremist views and could constitute a recruiting ground for terrorists is held by an increasingly larger share of the population.

The data show a rather unequivocal picture: Islam is increasingly perceived as a threat and is increasingly associated with terrorism and violence. For example, the "Politbarometer" survey of the renowned German survey agency Forschungsgruppe Wahlen shows that the percentage of

FIGURE 8.1 Association Between Muslims and Terrorism

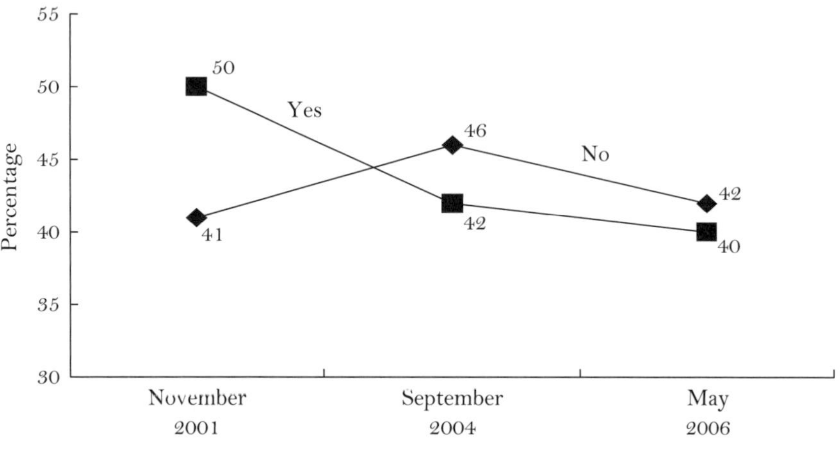

Source: Author's compilation based on Allensbach Survey 265 (November 14, 2001); Survey 215 (September 15, 2004); and Survey 114 (May 17, 2006).
Note: Responses to the Question: "If someone says: 'There are so many Muslims living in Germany. Sometimes I am really afraid that there might be many terrorists among them.' Do you agree?"

respondents perceiving Islam as a threat to Western democracy increased from 36 to 45 percent between 2001 and 2004, while the percentage of those holding the opposite view decreased from 58 to 48 percent in the same period.[11] A similar survey conducted by a different research institute (Allensbach) reveals a similar trend, shown in figure 8.1: while the percentage of those who associate Muslim minorities with terrorist groups has remained stable (and well over 40 percent) since November 2001, the percentage of those who clearly deny such an association has clearly and steadily declined, from 50 percent to 40 percent.

Other public opinion data show a clear decrease over the past five years in the number of those who believe in peaceful coexistence between the Islamic and Western worlds, even if this datum is compared with the same observation *immediately after* 9/11. In May 2006, the percentage of Germans who denied the possibility of peaceful coexistence between the two cultures was observed at 65 percent (it had been 58 percent in December 2001), while a mere 23 percent (29 percent in December 2001; see figure 8.2) believed in the possibility of peaceful coexistence.

FIGURE 8.2 Potential for Peaceful Coexistence Between Islamic and Western Cultures

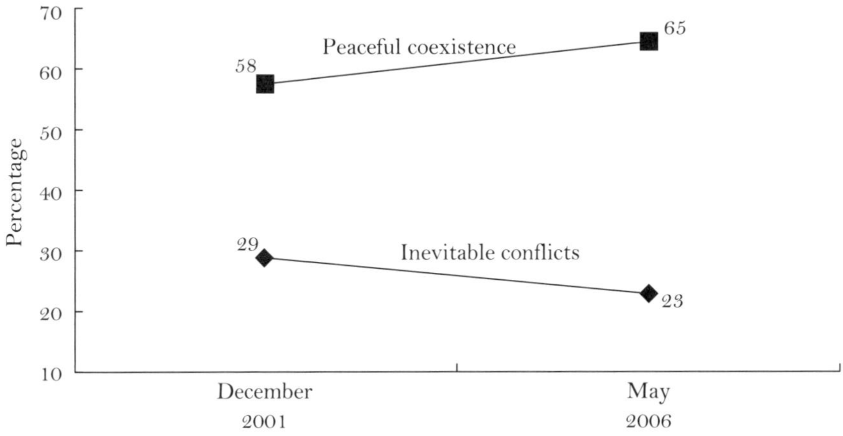

Source: Author's compilation based on: December 2001 question: Allensbacher Jahrbuch der Demoskopie 1998 to 2002, 998; May 2006 question: Allensbach Survey 114 (May 17, 2006).
Notes: Responses to the questions: "Do you think that despite the differences in beliefs and cultural values, a sustained peaceful coexistence between the Western culture and the Arabic-Muslim culture is possible, or that these differences will lead to repeated conflict in the future?" (December 2001) and "What do you think: can the Western and Islamic worlds coexist peacefully, or are these cultures too different, and because of this, severe, repeated conflicts are inevitable?" (May 2006).

These recent trends in German public opinion show an increasingly negative perception of Muslims and of Islamic culture in general. More specific surveys that ask directly about the likelihood of tensions between the larger German population and Muslim minorities show the connection of the deteriorating image of the Muslim community in the eyes of Germans and the possibility that this deteriorating image would lead to actual tensions between the two groups. The trend, shown in figure 8.3, is again very clear: there has been a marked increase (from 49 percent in 2001—after 9/11—to 58 percent in 2006) in the number of those who believe such tension will materialize, and a steady decrease in the number of those who hold the opposite view (from 43 percent in 2001 to 22 percent in May 2006).

Support for Stricter Antiterrorism Measures

In the context of this deterioration of the perception of Muslim minorities, there is clear support in the German public for stricter antiterrorism

FIGURE 8.3 The Likelihood of Tensions Between German Majority and Muslim Minority in Germany

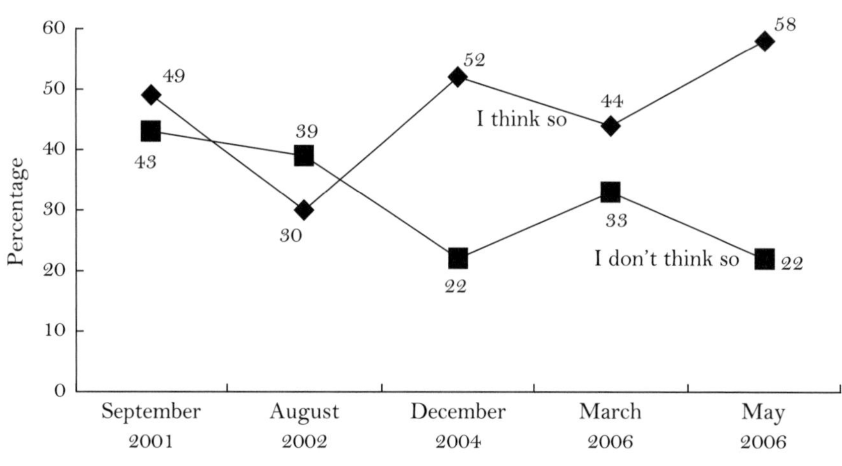

Source: Author's compilation based on Allensbach Survey 114 (May 17, 2006).
Note: Responses to the question: "Do you think that in the near future, tension toward the Muslim population will materialize, or are such developments unlikely in Germany?"

measures. Particularly interesting here are the data for the period between the end of 2001 and the end of 2002, when most of the new antiterrorism legislation was passed. Figure 8.4 shows that there was broad support in the population for stricter counterterrorism policies: an absolute (and growing) majority of respondents considered the new measures adequate, while around 40 percent thought that even more should be done. Many fewer considered the measures excessive, and their number dwindled to a mere 6 percent by November 2002 (data are reported separately for East and West Germany).

No longitudinal survey data are available to detect public opinion trends on the specific question of the equilibrium between security and civil liberties. Several one-off surveys show, however, that the population offered broad support for tightening security even when this was presented as a trade-off with civil liberties. In this respect, the state of German public opinion is broadly comparable to the situation of the 1970s, when the (West) German public was being asked similar questions in the face of terrorist attacks coming from the Rote Armee Fraktion (RAF, or the Red Army Faction). In response to an explicit question asked in 2004 by the survey institute Allensbach, for example, 62 percent of respondents declared themselves ready to accept a restriction of their individual rights in order

FIGURE 8.4 The Adequacy of the Counterterrorism Measures Adopted

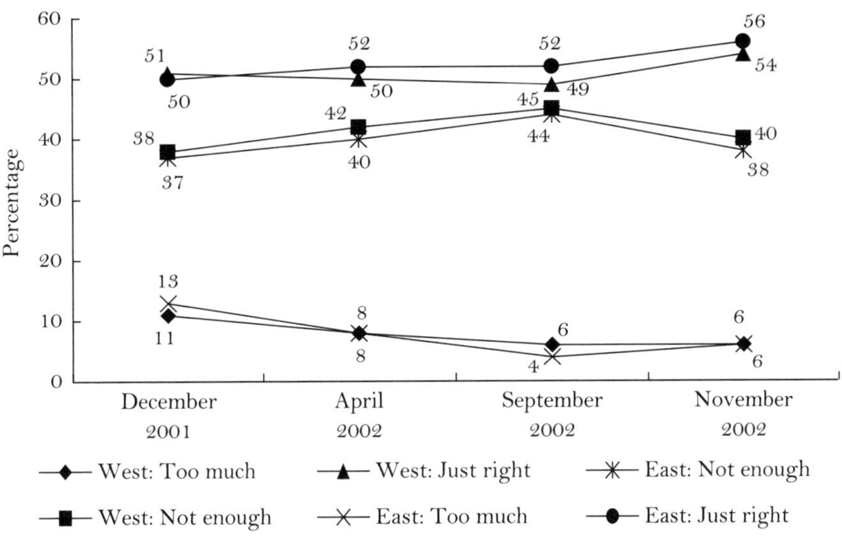

Source: Author's compilation based on Politbarometer West and Politbarometer Ost 2001, "Variable 197: Innere Sicherheit"; Politbarometer West and Politbarometer Ost 2002, "Variable 239: Innere Sicherheit."

Notes: Responses to the question: "After the terror attacks in the United States, stricter security measures were adopted in Germany to guarantee internal security. Do you think that what was done was too much, not enough, or just right?" This picture seems to have remained stable over the years and to not have been an effect of "novelty" brought about by the introduction of the new reforms. In a survey conducted by the Forschungsgruppe Wahlen in March 2004 after the Madrid bombings, 46 percent of people responded that enough was done in Germany to guarantee protection against terrorist attacks, while 44 percent did not think so and 10 percent did not answer. See Politbarometer March II 2004.

to strengthen the fight against terrorism, while only 25 percent said that they would reject any such restriction.[12] The figures for a similar question asked in 1977 were 62 and 26 percent, respectively.[13]

Analyses conducted by the survey institute Emnid in the months immediately following 9/11 also show solid support for tighter security measures, even as a trade-off for freedoms. In November 2001, 61 percent of the respondents answered that they valued "security more than freedom" (against 32 percent who did not), the percentage of those who thought that "security in Germany can only be guaranteed with tighter security measures" was 69 percent (against 29 percent who were of the opposite opinion), and 86 percent (against 13 percent) approved of includ-

TABLE 8.1 Support for Stricter Security Measures

Measure	Respondents Approving
Asylum-seekers should be deported more easily if they are thought to be involved in terrorist activities.	79%
Public places, such as airports, train stations, and shopping malls, should be placed under increasing video surveillance.	78
Organizations that are thought to be supporting terrorist groups should be prohibited from collecting money (donations).	72
The Bundeswehr should be deployed internally, for the protection of people and property.	59
Fingerprints should be recorded in passports.	59
The fingerprints of everyone entering Germany should be collected.	55
Passports should contain biometric data (about the shape of the hands and the face).	51
Those under suspicion of terrorist activity may be taken into custody without proof.	46

Source: Author's compilation based on Allensbach Survey 215 (September 15, 2004).
Note: Responses to the question: "Here is a list of different measures for the fight against terrorism. Please tell me all measures for which you would say: 'Yes, I am happy if something like this should be introduced in Germany.'"

ing fingerprints in passports.[14] Three years later, as the Allensbach survey results reported in table 8.1 show, this situation had not changed substantially.

The most illiberal proposal—taking into custody without proof anyone suspected of terrorism (not a part of the German legal system)—received the lowest rate of approval, but it was still higher than 40 percent. Support for including fingerprints in passports seems to have gone down as well from the high level it reached immediately after 9/11, but it is still close to 60 percent. The overwhelming support for easier deportation of asylum-seekers who are suspected to be terrorists was most likely influenced by the difficulties encountered in expelling the head of the Muslim fundamentalist group Kalifatstaat (Caliphate State; discussed later); that support suggests that the public sees the current system as offering too many hiding places to potential terrorists. Moreover, the datum about donations to suspected supporters of terrorist groups also reveals the worries about the Muslim minorities in Germany and the perception of insufficient controls on existing barriers between legitimate immigrants and terrorist cover-ups. The reform of the asylum and immigration laws passed before 2004 (discussed later) could therefore be seen as still insufficient by large sections of the population. In fact, the data reported in the table are from 2004—that is, *after* most reforms to counterterrorism had been introduced. Finally, the data about the deployment of the Bundeswehr for internal emergencies show great support (59 percent) for this kind of measure, later declared unconstitutional by the Federal Constitutional Court in its official ruling striking down the law on airspace security. Such a measure is unlikely to be revived in the future.[15]

In sum, the analysis of public opinion since 9/11 shows that the German public would largely be in favor of substantially increasing the possibilities for the government to intervene more incisively against terrorism. As emerges from the following analysis, while the federal government has undoubtedly increased its powers to counter international terrorism, it has largely fallen short of acquiring the more incisive powers that would have been supported by the majority of the public and many politicians. This outcome is mainly due to the resilience of the federal arrangement of the security apparatuses and the active interventions of the Federal Constitutional Court. The next section illustrates the legislative, organizational, and policy changes introduced in Germany after September 2001 to counter Islamic terrorism.

Counterterrorism Policies, New Regulations, and Incremental Change

The rules and practices aimed at the "protection of the Constitution" have been fundamental to the institutional architecture of the Federal Republic (probably more so than in any other Western democracy) and were mainly intended to curb the right-wing and left-wing extremism of the fascist/Nazi and Communist traditions, respectively. In the 1970s and 1980s, those principles were invoked against domestic terrorism, which was mainly of leftist origin (see Braunthal 1989).[16] Thus, the new challenge of international Islamic terrorism posed an unprecedented complication to German authorities: the (partial) connection between the "enemies of the Constitution" and the members of ethnic and religious minorities. In fact, German asylum and immigration laws and other institutions affecting religious and ethnic minorities were traditionally relatively generous; moreover, religious associations were exempted by law from the constitutional limits imposed on extreme-right and extreme-left groups.

The post-9/11 reforms of domestic security policy fall into three categories: reforms that expanded and adapted existing rules to the repression of international Islamic terrorism, including the rules on the crime of terrorist associations, police access to social data, and so on, most of which had been introduced in the 1970s and the 1980s to fight domestic terrorism; reforms that addressed relatively new and less-regulated areas, such as money laundering and aviation security; and reforms passed in areas (such as immigration and asylum regulations) that, while bearing an important connection to the new terrorist threat, could have a much greater social impact.

Adapting Existing Rules: The "Antiterror Packages" and the Reform of thc Criminal Code

The German government was very swift in its first reactions to the 9/11 events: only eight days after the attacks the cabinet issued plans for a response to terrorist activities. By December 2001, the parliament had already approved two antiterrorism packages.[17]

The End of "Religions Privilege" The first antiterror measure approved by the German parliament was to withdraw the legal statutory provision, dating back to 1964, that exempted religious groups from the conditions the law imposed on all other associations.[18] The new law extended to religious associations the rules that allow the government to ban all associations that break criminal law or attack the fundamental liberal-democratic order of the Federal Republic.[19] Owing to the excesses of some Muslim associations that openly propagated fundamentalist and radical ideas, this measure had been considered explicitly by the parliamentary Commission of Inquiry in 1998—since it had become increasingly clear that fundamentalist religious groups were pursuing terrorist objectives while hiding under the cloaks of religious organizations—but in the end was not approved. Now the new law was supported by all parties, with the exception of some PDS representatives. In supporting the new measures, the government stressed that they were not intended to restrict religious freedoms but were targeted only at groups that pursued "anti-constitutional goals that are allegedly based on religious beliefs." In other words, the law explicitly aimed to curb the possibility that anticonstitutional organizations could pursue their goals undisturbed by simply defining themselves as "religious" (Glässner 2003, 49).[20] A particular target of this law was the Cologne-based group Kalifatstaat (Caliphate State), led by the cleric Metin Kaplan, who had already repeatedly made national headlines in the previous years for his extremist and fundamentalist statements. The government immediately used the new law to ban the Caliphate State and, after several court trials, to expel Kaplan.[21]

Using the measure against Kaplan found virtually no significant opposition across the political spectrum: the minister of the interior at the time, Otto Schily, a Social Democrat, evoked the principle of "streitbare Demokratie" to justify the new law and its implementation and found a good deal of consensus on this point. The center-right opposition of the time, the FDP and the CDU/CSU, was completely behind the new measure, and even the Greens—at the time the governing partner of the SPD—supported the expulsion despite some internal disagreements.[22] The new law also found widespread support among the population at large: 70 percent of those asked in a survey conducted June 1–3, 2004, agreed that those who, like Kaplan, advocated violence should be expelled even though they risked torture or capital punishment in their home countries.[23] The normative principle of defending the Constitution against its enemies could be applied rigorously against religious fundamentalist organizations after the new law was passed: the government moved immediately against twenty other religious organizations (most of them operating at the regional level) and conducted more than two hundred raids (Katzenstein 2003, 749).[24]

The Law to Fight International Terrorism This law amended more than one hundred regulations in seventeen other laws and five administrative decrees (Katzenstein 2003, 750), with the common objective of strengthening the government's powers of prevention vis-à-vis international terrorism.[25] The law's stated purposes included giving the security services enhanced legal responsibilities; improving the necessary information-sharing between the authorities; preventing the entry of terrorists into Germany and improving border controls; creating the legal basis for the inclusion of biometric data in passports and ID cards to identify extremists; enhancing security checks for workers in security-sensitive installations, including not only governmental agencies but also TV, energy, postal, and telecommunication services; and granting the government access to further social data, including individuals' telephone, banking, employment, and university records, to allow for more-encompassing "profiling" activities—a method of investigation (or rather of preventive identification of potential suspects) that had already been used in the 1970s and 1980s to fight domestic terrorism (see, for example, Katzenstein 1996d). This law also broadened the set of criteria on the basis of which the state could restrict the basic freedoms of individuals and groups for security purposes: reasons for intervention now included not only breaches of criminal law and threats to the fundamental liberal-democratic order but also advocacy of the goal of "undermining the idea of international understanding and world peace."[26]

The bill leading to this law was the subject of internal debate in the two parties supporting the government at the time, the Social Democrats and the Greens (see Glässner 2003, 52), but in the end the law found broad support in the parliament, by the government majority as well as the main opposition party, the Christian Democrats. Only the PDS continued to oppose it on grounds of substance, while the FDP expressed some reservations mainly for the haste with which the law was pushed through parliament, cutting the debate short. Criticisms of the law were voiced in the Bundesrat (the upper chamber of the German parliamentary system composed of representatives of the regional governments) and by the Datenschutzbeauftragten (Federal and Regional Independent Authorities for Data Protection and Freedom of Information). The concerns voiced in the Bundesrat were more about the financial implications of the law for the Länder, whose police forces would be burdened with more tasks as they enforced the substantive limitations of freedom that the law introduced. The Datenschutzbeauftragten had more substantive concerns about some of the new measures being used not to fight terrorism but for other purposes, such as identifying clandestine immigrants, for which a restriction of civil liberties of the kind allowed by the new law was hardly justifiable (Glässner 2003, 52; Gusy 2004, 219).[27] The main outcome of this debate was the inclusion of a five-year sunset clause in the law; the original substance of the bill was not significantly amended. The law was renewed in January 2007.[28]

The Reform of the Criminal Code The new section 129(b) included in the Criminal Code allows prosecution in cases of creation of, participation in, and recruitment and support for foreign criminal and terrorist associations.[29] In particular, it prohibits support for a foreign organization that "contradicts a state order which guarantees the dignity of people, or the peaceful coexistence of the peoples" (Katzenstein 2003, 741). The new section builds on preexisting, connected rules: section 129 of the Criminal Code (on "criminal" associations) had already been supplemented in 1976 with section 129(a), which introduced specific norms aimed at counteracting the activities of "terrorist" associations specifically. Section 129(a) gave exclusive responsibility for prosecuting terrorist organizations to the Federal Prosecution Office (Bundesstaatsanwalt), which was allowed to use data from telecommunications tapping and statistical profiling. These powers have been used to repress Islamic terrorism as well (Wache 2003, 145).

The new section 129(b) simply extends the applicability of sections 129 and 129(a) to criminal and terrorist organizations that are based abroad but whose members carry out their activities in Germany.[30]

Thus, the new section 129(b) hardly represents a radical departure from the pre-9/11 situation:[31] the rationale for its introduction was the inadequacy of the existing section 129(a)—as interpreted by the Federal High Court (Bundesgerichtshof)—which had led to paradoxical situations. The court had clarified that for section 129(a) to apply, a group had to be composed of at least three people who had been associated for a certain time period, who were pursuing common goals, and who perceived themselves as members of an association (Wache 2003, 145).[32] This interpretation had been effective against the domestic terrorist organizations of the 1970s and 1980s but proved insufficient for the prosecution of Islamic terrorist organizations, mainly because it was difficult to prove that an Islamic terrorist cell displayed the requirement of minimum duration deemed necessary for the section to apply (Hirschmann 2003, 395). In fact, an Islamic terrorist cell typically consisted of three or four people who were associated for a very short time in order to prepare one specific attack, after which they would disband and normally leave the country. Section 129(b) eliminated the loophole in the law by making it possible for the courts to apply the law to an "association" based outside of the national territory and to punish individuals' support for such an association even if the prerequisites for a domestic association are lacking.[33]

Countering the New Terrorism: Money Laundering and Aviation Security

Money Laundering To cut off the terrorists' access to financial resources, the parliament amended the law on money laundering in August 2002.[34] The reform introduced a central register of all accounts registered with bank branches or other financial service providers in Germany; the register would store the name, date, and place of birth of the account holder, the type of account, and the date of opening.[35] In addition, the law instituted a central task force within the federal police agency, the Federal Criminal Police Office (Bundeskriminalamt, BKA), called the Financial Intelligence Unit (FIU, Zentrale Analyse- und Informationsstelle für Verdachtsanzeigen), which was specifically responsible for the investigation of money laundering and terrorism financing. The FIU's main task—apart from enhancing awareness of these problems among other institutional actors and the general public—is collecting and examining reports by financial institutions of suspected cases of money laundering and terrorism financing. If the FIU finds evidence of either, the Regional Criminal Offices (Landeskriminalämter, LKÄ) involved can start the actual investigation, under the coordination and supervision of the FIU.

While the new reform does give the FIU (and therefore the BKA) a relatively prominent position, it does not achieve full centralization, as most voices in the debate had advocated. Like the approval of section 129(b), this reform rationalized an underregulated situation that had led to inefficiencies and dysfunction, but without really changing the general institutional framework. In fact, before the reform, absent clear guidelines, these matters had been dealt with rather erratically: financial institutions indiscriminately reported suspected cases of money laundering or terrorism financing to different institutions: the BKA, the LKÄ, the Federal Securities Supervisory Office (Bundesaufsichtsamt für den Wertpapierhandel), the Federal Banking Supervisory Office (Bundesaufsichtsamt für das Kreditwesen), public prosecutors, and others. As a consequence, it was impossible to establish the larger picture of money laundering and terrorism financing and to map the complex networks through which money was transferred, a goal that the new reform is set to achieve.[36]

Aviation Security and the Domestic Role of the Military An important policy area for reacting to the current brand of international terrorism is aviation and border security. The second antiterror package granted the Federal Border Police (Bundesgrenzschutz, BGS) increased responsibility for stopping, interrogating, and identifying people at the national borders. In particular, airport security was stepped up, and the new law introduced the possibility of BGS officers being employed as air marshals (Flugsicherheitsbegleiter). Although these measures were relatively uncontroversial, more wide-ranging reform that would have given the government a freer hand to resort to the military in the event of an internal emergency—in particular the power to decide to shoot down hijacked aircraft threatening to crash into buildings—proved substantially more complicated and ultimately failed. The main obstacle to reform was the opposition of the Federal Constitutional Court.

In the Weimar Republic, the police, though formally separated from the army, had essentially a military character (Katzenstein 1996d, 5–6), and the army played a role in keeping internal security and order (Bisanz and Gerstenberg 2003, 323). Eager to build a different system, the drafters of the 1949 Basic Law differentiated clearly between the functions of the military and those of the police; among other things, they firmly excluded the

Bundeswehr from intervening in internal matters. Only in 1968 did constitutional amendments on states of emergency (Notstandgesetzen) designate a very restricted and controlled role for the Bundeswehr in case of internal emergency. Since then, the Basic Law (article 87[a]) allows the use of the army in domestic security only to support the police and the BGS in the protection of civil objectives when the existence of the Federal Republic, of one of the Länder, or of their fundamental liberal-democratic order is threatened. Article 35 of the Basic Law allows the federal or state governments to ask for the help of the army to respond to a natural catastrophe or a grave accident, but in support of local police forces should these be insufficient to the task. Even in these limited cases, soldiers must behave like police officers and submit to police law, including the general principle of "proportionality" of reaction to disturbers of public peace (Bisanz and Gerstenberg 2003, 324; see also Leggemann 2003).

The new scale of terror attacks demonstrated by the events of 9/11 posed the problem of the intervention of the military in case of internal emergency in rather urgent terms. After, in January 2003, a deranged person flew over the city center of Frankfurt am Main in a small airplane, threatening to crash it into one of the banking district's skyscrapers, the government drafted a bill proposing to authorize military aviation to shoot down any hijacked plane that could be used for a terrorist attack. Although some circles within the government majority and the FDP from the opposition rejected the proposal on the basis of the strict constitutional separation of the police and military (but not the much larger CDU/CSU, which supported the proposal), the government managed to get the new Law on Airspace Security (Luftsicherheitsgesetz) approved in Parliament on January 11, 2005. The law was immediately challenged, however, before the Federal Constitutional Court—a course of action recommended also by the federal president, a bipartisan figure in the German constitutional structure.

In July 2005, while the court's judgment was pending, a man committed suicide by crashing his airplane between the Parliament and Chancellery buildings in Berlin. This incident turned the public debate on the law into a more general debate on the powers of the military in counterterrorism, particularly the possible use of the Bundeswehr to *prevent* a terrorist attack—such as shooting down a hijacked plane.[37] Not even the support for the new regulations from the majority of the government and the opposition, and the public emotion caused by the two incidents involving airplanes crashing or threatening to crash in urban centers, prevented the Federal Constitutional Court from striking down part of the new Law on Airspace Security in February 2006. In particular, the court considered section 14.3 of the law, which allowed shooting down hijacked planes when they were likely to be used as weapons, both procedurally and substantially incompatible with the Basic Law.[38] With respect to the more general issue of the deployment of the Bundeswehr for antiterrorism purposes, the court did remark that the "grave accidents" mentioned in the Basic Law as a possible reason to resort to the military might also include calamities brought about intentionally as well as ongoing actions for which a disastrous outcome can be predicted with certainty. Although this seems to leave some space for the possible deployment of the military against terrorism, the court reiterated that, when acting domestically, the Bundeswehr must not use weaponry that is beyond the equipment of the police.[39]

Given the gravity of the threat, the issue stayed on the nation's political agenda: the "Grand Coalition" (CDU/CSU and SPD) government that took office in 2005 produced a white paper on the topic. While the government committee was working on the white paper, public debate on the issue continued: for example, the CDU/CSU publicly insisted on a change to the Basic Law that would allow greater scope of action for the Bundeswehr in a situation in which, as Chancellor Angela Merkel (Christian Democrat) herself remarked, the distinction between internal and external threat "has become blurred."[40] The new interior minister, Wolfgang Schäuble (Christian Democrat), announced plans to change the Basic Law during the current Parliament (elected in 2005), with the purpose of explicitly including "terrorist attacks" among the situations that would justify the resort to the Bundeswehr for reasons of internal emergency.[41] Although generally more cautious, the SPD nevertheless did not do much to distance itself from this position.

The white paper—which was published in October 2006 and had not yet been turned into a bill at the time of writing—hardly seems to have made significant progress on the thorniest issues.[42] On the possibility of deploying the Bundeswehr for internal emergencies, the white paper states that fighting terrorism is mostly still the task of "federal and Land administrations" and that the Bundeswehr can be employed whenever "such a situation can only be managed with its help." Thus, despite the intentions declared by several leaders of the parties in government (which is now supported by a majority of about three-quarters of the Parliament) and the general approval of the public for a larger use of the military to respond to domestic terrorist attacks, the opposition of the Federal Constitutional Court constituted the real obstacle to reform, thus reasserting the constitutional principle of the limits to executive power even when this is directed against "enemies of the constitution."

Controlling Borders: Asylum, Immigration, and Visa Policy

Several of the 9/11 terrorists were foreign citizens living in the Federal Republic (some of them as students) and one of them, Mohamed Atta, entered the country with three different falsified passports. The connection between asylum, immigration, and visa procedures, on the one hand, and terrorism, on the other, was therefore immediately clear in the eyes of both German legislators and the German public.

Germany has traditionally had a very liberal asylum and immigration policy. Probably more than elsewhere, changes in the German asylum and immigration regulations call into question delicate issues of constitutional and national identity that bear a heavy burden of historical memory. As Britta Walthelm (n.d., 19–20) appropriately puts it, "Against the backdrop of Germany's national-socialist past, the treatment of foreigners and the status of immigrants have always been a sensitive issue in the Federal Republic." The protection of the right of individuals to political asylum is included in article 16(a) of the Basic Law. Traditionally, the courts have interpreted the rights of foreigners and refugees in Germany in an expansive fashion.[43]

This is probably the area of legislation in which prima facie the most radical changes have been introduced post-9/11. A closer look at the data, however, reveals that even in this area the break with the past is less marked than the analysis of formal regulations would indicate. The practical effects of the new reforms, in fact, have been less drastic than the effects of the immigration and asylum reforms introduced in the early 1990s, when constitutional amendments limiting the (until then absolute) right to asylum were introduced.[44] Whereas the 1990s reforms mainly aimed to differentiate between political refugees and economic immigrants in order to prevent the latter from using the "asylum" route to enter Germany, the essence of the 2004 reforms is to allow the government to expel individuals who are suspected terrorists or otherwise represent a threat to the constitutional order and to endow the authorities with new technological instruments to do this.

The main changes introduced in 2004 can be grouped under three headings.[45] First, the new regulations introduced further grounds for the expulsion of immigrants. Section 54, subsections 5 and 5(a), of the new Residence Act (Aufenthaltsgesetz) allows the expulsion of foreigners who are or were members or supporters of an association that supports terrorism, threaten the fundamental liberal-democratic order or the security of the Federal Republic of Germany, participate in violent actions with political aims, publicly call for the use of force, or publicly threaten the use of force. Subsection 6 of the same section allows expulsion if a foreigner makes false or incomplete statements on his or her connections to persons or organizations suspected of supporting international terrorism. Expulsion can also happen (section 55) if an alien resident knowingly gives false information in order to extend their residence permit. Those affected by an expulsion order have the right to an appeal before a court, but while judicial decisions are pending they must register with the police on a weekly basis.

Second, the police now have more power—in cooperation with the German consulates—to conduct background checks on applicants for visas and asylum. This can lead to the refusal of a visa or residence permit to any person considered a possible threat to the fundamental liberal-democratic order or suspected of engaging in or supporting terrorism or acts of violence (Glässner 2003, 50).

Third, the technological profile of identification procedures has also been stepped up, and the data collected during immigration procedures are now integrated with larger police information systems. Fingerprinting is now part of the visa procedure, and identity cards for long-term visas have been made forgery-proof (Walthelm, n.d.). Voice-recording has been introduced as part of the asylum-seeking procedure: this technique allows the identification of an immigrant's country of origin, which in turn helps in establishing his or her identity. After the reforms, the identity-establishing information obtained in connection with the asylum procedure can be stored for ten years. The data collected while implementing these stricter personal identification measures can therefore be cross-checked with other data in the possession of the police for the identification of possible terrorists. For example, the fingerprints of asylum-seekers are automatically matched with those taken by the police at crime scenes, and they are stored by the BKA for further matching. Finally, the Federal Immigration Office (Bundesamt für Migration und Flüchtlinge) is now obliged to give the police access to the Central Alien Register (Ausländerzentralregister).[46] The police are thus able to establish immediately whether a foreigner is lawfully residing in Germany. The register now also includes integrated "visa files" with all of the information related to each person (Glässner 2003, 51).[47]

These legislative changes were explicitly driven by the intention of curbing the "misuse of asylum" and making Germany "a less desirable space for terrorists and 'sleepers.'" Like other post-9/11 reforms, measures similar to those introduced in 2004 had been discussed in previous years, albeit with largely different purposes—for example, to identify illegal residents—but

FIGURE 8.5 Asylum Applications and Refusals, 1991 to 2006

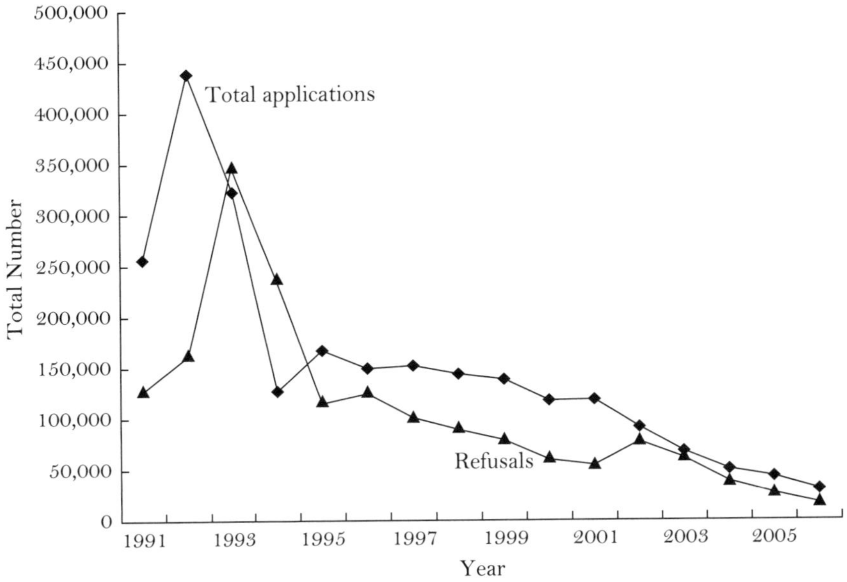

Source: Author's compilation based on official Data from the Bundesamt für Migration und Flüchtlinge (2006, 2007).

in the end they had not been approved because, to many observers, the purposes did not seem to justify the restrictions being advocated. In the new threat environment following 9/11, however, these very same measures have been much less controversial, even though it remains possible that these new police powers could be used for purposes other than the repression and prevention of terrorism (Glässner 2003, 51). In any case, even though after the approval of the new rules the number of applications for asylum went down—in tandem with a stable proportion of rejections—the practical impact of the 2004 legislation has been limited. In fact, if data from the early 1990s are brought into the picture, it becomes clear that the post-2004 changes have simply been the continuation of a trend started more than ten years ago. As illustrated in figure 8.5, the total number of applications for asylum showed a sharp drop in 1993–94 (immediately after the introduction of the reforms of the early 1990s) and has been steadily decreasing since then (Bundesamt für Migration und Flüchtlinge 2006, 2007).[48]

In sum, the data graphed in figure 8.5 show that the 2004 reforms of immigration and asylum regulations simply reinforced a decreasing trend in asylum applications that has been in place since the early 1990s.

Substantially, the new legislation makes it possible for German authorities to refuse asylum to persons who represent a danger from a *political* point of view. Whether the German courts will allow an extensive interpretation of the new norms is still an open question.

The Effect of Federalism: Limited Reform of the Security Agencies

Strictly speaking, the Federal Republic of Germany has never had *one* police organization: what is commonly called "the police" consists in fact of several organizations; operating at different territorial levels, they are connected with each other and coordinate to achieve common goals. The Basic Law gives responsibility for the police to the Länder, and the police force of each Land (all formally independent from each other) is what constitutes the bulk of "the police" in the Federal Republic (Bayley 1985; Busch et al. 1985, 81). Originally, the federal police bodies had only a subordinate and complementary character. Over the postwar era, the federal police bodies have gradually grown in importance and size, without, however, altering the nature of the police system in the Federal Republic as a "decentralized system with multiple, coordinated police forces" (Bayley 1985, 58–59). Seen from this perspective, the last wave of post-9/11 reform of the security agencies—limited in scope overall—is part of a longer trend: again, the reforms introduced do not represent a radical break with the past.

Despite the emphasis that the new laws put on the need for the effectiveness and rapidity of investigative and intelligence actions against terrorists, the reform of the relevant bureaucratic structures was only partial. Five specialized agencies have traditionally dealt with terrorism issues at the federal level: the Office for the Protection of the Constitution (Bundesamt für Verfassungsschutz, BfV), plus the regional LfVs (Landesämter für Verfassungsschutz); the Federal Criminal Police Office (Bundeskriminalamt, BKA), plus the regional LKÄ (Landeskriminalämter); the Federal Intelligence Service (Bundesnachrichtendienst, BND); the Federal Border Police (Bundesgrenzschutz, BGS); and the Military Counterintelligence Service (Militärischer Abschirmdienst, MAD). Centralizing security structures and rethinking the federal division of powers were common concerns in many of the reform proposals aired in the public debate by academics, journalists, and policy experts: many shared the view that a new single federal office to supervise all counterterrorism activities would certainly increase the rapidity and coordination of the actions of the various government agencies (see, for example, Bisanz and Gerstenberg 2003; Hirschmann 2003; Werthebach 2004). It would be impossible to render here the complexity of the public debate on these matters. The general emphasis of most proposals, however, was on the need for better integration and coordination of the different agencies dealing with security in Germany; the "double fragmentation" described earlier seemed to be broadly perceived as the main inadequacy of the German security system (see, for example, Weidenfeld 2004).[49]

Although the power of federal agencies to coordinate their regional branches was increased in some cases (for example, the BKA vis-à-vis the LKÄ in matters of money laundering and terrorism financing), the objective of full centralization was never reached—and is nowhere in sight. Indeed, coordination and information exchange rather than centralization has been the answer to the fragmentation problem: traditionally, the work of the different agencies dealing with internal security was coordinated by a high-ranking official in the Federal Chancellery who convened weekly meetings with representatives of the different intelligence organizations (Katzenstein 1996d, 14). More recently, an "Information Board" was established for the systematic exchange and evaluation of information between the BND, the MAD, the BfV, and the BKA (Wache 2003, 148–49). The rest of this section briefly analyzes the changes introduced or proposed in two important institutions for Germany's internal security policy: the BKA and the Office for the Protection of the Constitution (BfV), as well as their regional counterparts, the LKÄ and the LfV.

The key task of the Office for the Protection of the Constitution, at both the federal and regional levels, is to protect the fundamental liberal-democratic order from groups and individuals that threaten it. This charge translates mainly into collecting information (for which the BfV cooperates with the civilian and military intelligence services) and providing intelligence on extremist groups and their members to the federal and regional governments as well as the courts: the BfV and the LfV have no power of arrest (Glässner 2003, 54). Under the new security legislation, the BfV and the LfV can also target groups and individuals whose activities are directed against the "idea of understanding among peoples and the peaceful coexistence of peoples." Crucially, this new provision allows for the investigation of individuals and groups that prepare terrorist attacks abroad. Moreover, the BfV can also request specific information from banks, financial services, aviation, and telecommunications companies.[50] It can locate cell phones in order to reconstruct terrorist networks and share these data with other security agencies (Glässner 2003, 54–55).[51]

Until the end of the 1960s, direct responsibility for police matters in the Federal Republic (apart from the coordination of the Bereitschaftspolizei) came only through the limited remit of the Federal Criminal Police Office.[52]

When it was established in 1951, the BKA had two main functions: being a loosely coordinating agency of the regional police and, more importantly, acting as a common source of information for the various police agencies. In 1973 the BKA took on a more important role: it was given the power to directly investigate cases of terrorism, international arms traffic, drug-related criminality, and money forgery. During the 1970s, the BKA gained additional prominence because its original mission—storing and elaborating information relevant for police activities—grew significantly in importance: large data sets for preventive identification of possible terrorists were established, and for the same reason, access to existing data sets (of utilities, car registration, and so on) was granted to the police (Busch et al. 1985, 83). The last pre-9/11 reform of the BKA, passed in 1997, slightly extended the agency's brief in collecting information and advising regional police agencies.

The new post-9/11 legislation has continued the trend of incremental extension of the responsibilities of the BKA, some of which have been discussed earlier. In addition to those, section 10 of the Law to Fight International Terrorism gives the BKA the power to collect information on suspected criminal activities *directly*, without first having to go through the regional police agencies. The new law allows the BKA to collect data from public and nonpublic organizations, foreign authorities, and international organizations for the purpose of amending or evaluating essential facts in the execution of its duty to support regional polices in preventing and prosecuting crimes that have a cross-Länder or international nature or are otherwise extremely important. For these crimes, the law simply removed the obligation for the BKA to ask regional police agencies in advance. Additional reforms aimed at further increasing the power of the BKA vis-à-vis regional agencies were discussed in 2007 as part of the general reform plans of the new Grand Coalition government, which aimed to reduce the overall weight of the Länder in various policy areas, but at the time of writing these discussions had not given rise to new legislation.

Police Action and Judicial Control

In response to the domestic terrorist threat of the 1970s and 1980s, the German police decisively abandoned its obsolete, quasi-military approach and mentality and adopted a completely different way of working, one characterized by prevention and massive use of technological methods of investigation (Busch et al. 1985; Katzenstein 1996d). In 1972 the first integrated information database, called INPOL, was created. For each individual investigated by the police, it combined data from different sources—identity data, the investigation folder, convictions, and so on (Dietl 2003). Integrated electronic databases combining social data on large numbers of individuals were a hotly debated police tool in the investigation and repression of domestic terrorism during the 1970s and 1980s: especially in the 1970s, great use was made of statistical "profiling," for the preventive identification of potential terrorists, through resort to the so-called Rasterfahndung (dragnet investigation). In enacting the Rasterfahndung, the police used computer matching of large amounts of statistical data (from utility companies, car registrations, social security agencies, and so on) in the effort to identify clusters of suspicious traits in specific groups. "In brief, preventive or 'intelligent' police work . . . was informed by abstract social categories that the police had defined. It was not informed by any evidence that a targeted individual had engaged in criminal behavior" (Katzenstein 2003, 742). The success of the Rasterfahndung at that time was mixed (Katzenstein 1996).[53] But the same technique was revived after 2001, with even larger and more complex data sets, for use against Islamic terrorists.[54]

The analysis of the resort to profiling-based investigative techniques after 9/11 shows that, despite modern technology's potential to intrude into the personal sphere of citizens, the use of these techniques was never unchecked and the courts did not shy away from ruling against the government counterterrorism policy. In other words, state and federal courts have exerted an effective vigilance toward possible violations of civil rights for reasons of security, preventing the balance between freedom and security from tilting too much in favor of the latter, even in the presence of the new antiterrorism norms introduced after 9/11.

The Resort to Statistical Profiling: The Rasterfahndung

As explained earlier, the introduction in 1976 of section 129(a) of the Criminal Code permitted the state to repress criminal intent as well as criminal behavior. Security legislation approved in the 1970s also gave law enforcement authorities access to social data in general and the data necessary for conducting computer-aided profiling in particular. The post-9/11 antiterrorism legal reforms expanded these possibilities, and so arose the possibility of resorting, as in the 1970s, to the large-scale statistical profiling of entire sectors of the population with the purpose of identifying potential terrorists. The method of the Rasterfahndung was therefore revived in the investigations against Islamic terrorism. Because three of the four pilots involved in the 9/11 attacks had lived legally and inconspicuously in Germany for some time, the technique looked particularly appropriate to identify so-called sleepers—individuals affiliated with Al Qaeda who might be living under the cover of a perfectly legal life.

The federal police authorities cannot, by law, enact a *preventive* dragnet investigation: only the Länder police have this power. Despite the many voices raised in the debate in favor of greater centralization of police activities in matters of counterterrorism, this legal prohibition persisted, and the Länder proved quite jealous of their constitutional prerogatives in police matters. Achieving the necessary coordination between the police forces of the sixteen Länder has been quite arduous at times.[55] The initiative for a coordinated Rasterfahndung came formally from the Standing Committee of the Regional Interior Ministers (Innenministerkonferenz, IMK) in September 2001, when two states, Berlin and Hamburg, had already decided separately to conduct similar dragnet investigations in their territory. The IMK decided that each Land would initiate its own investigation, and in order to achieve comparable and reliable results, it impaneled the Coordination Group on International Terrorism (Koordinierungsgruppe Internationaler Terrorismus, KIT), which brings together two IMK subcommittees with representatives from the Federal Intelligence Service, the Office for the Protection of the Constitution, the Federal Border Police, the army, and the Federal Prosecution Authority. The KIT is headed by a representative of the Federal Criminal Police Office.

The KIT suggested a standard profile for the Rasterfahndung that would be implemented in all the Länder and was largely based on the social characteristics of the known perpetrators of 9/11: male, eighteen to forty years old, current or former student, Islamic, legal resident of Germany, and originating from one of a list of twenty-six Muslim countries (see Kant 2005, 14). These recommendations were followed in fifteen of the sixteen Länder. (North Rhine–Westphalia deviated from them.)[56] The technical difficulties of integrating different regional databases did not take long to emerge: data coming from Länder authorities was occasionally incomplete (birth dates, for example, were not collected in all states), and different Länder used different software and formatted the data differently.

The Landeskriminalämter screened the records of residents' registration offices and universities and the Central Foreigners' Register (Ausländerzentralregister) to identify individuals who matched the defined profile. The results were then passed on to the BKA, whose "sleepers database" subsequently had thirty-two thousand entries (Kant 2005, 15).[57] The BKA then determined how many of these individuals belonged to certain categories of people (ninety-six categories in total, for a total of more than 4 million individuals) who could possess the relevant knowledge to carry out a terrorist attack or who were familiar with places that could constitute possible terrorist targets. These categories included, for example, individuals who had a piloting license or were attending a course to obtain it, members of sporting aviation associations, employees of airports, nuclear power plants, chemical plants, the rail service, laboratories, and other research institutes, and also students of the German language at the Goethe Institutes. The comparison of these two databases, in March 2002, yielded 1,689 potential sleepers.[58] Those individuals were then investigated by the police of their Land, but after one year not one sleeper had been identified. Seven individuals suspected of being members of a terrorist cell in Hamburg were arrested, but they did not fit the statistical profile (Katzenstein 2003, 751). The databases were deleted in June and July 2003. In the whole process, data were collected and analyzed on about 8.3 million individuals (Kant 2005). Hence, the large effort put into the Rasterfahndung did not, in the end, lead to any substantial results (Glässner 2003; Kant 2005).

The Intervention of the Courts

The resort to the Rasterfahndung enjoyed broad support in all parties, even that of the Datenschutzbeauftragten (Authorities for Data Protection), which, in an official conference held in 2002, supported the effort provided the data was deleted once the procedure had been completed. In the political debate, only the PDS and some circles within the Greens emphasized the twofold risk of violating the principle of the presumption of innocence and the right to "informational self-determination" (individuals about whom data are collected in the Rasterfahndung are not notified), as well as the danger of alienating Muslim minorities. Again, the main opposition to the Rasterfahndung came from the judiciary, at both the regional and the federal level.

Some state courts got in the way of the new investigation, either delaying it or forcing the authorities to change the legal framework under which the Rasterfahndung could be implemented. At the beginning of 2002, regional courts in Berlin and Hesse declared the Rasterfahndung illegal, since no "imminent threat" of a terrorist attack (as prescribed by the regional police laws of those Länder) was present, and the "mere possibility" of a terrorist attack was not sufficient to justify the encroachment on individual rights that this kind of investigation would entail. Following these rulings, the police authorities of each Land had to suspend the investigation. In Berlin, the LKÄ appealed the decision, and in April 2002 the regional Court of Appeal sustained its case, hence giving the green light to resume the investigation. In Hesse, the regional parliament had to quickly change the regional police law (in March 2002) to justify a more flexible resort to the Rasterfahndung, which could then be resumed in that Land too. The tribulations of the Rasterfahndung in Hesse did not end there, however, as further complaints were brought to the administrative courts of that Land: in November 2002, the lower Administrative Court in Giessen ruled against the Rasterfahndung. Again, the case went to appeal, and only in February 2003 did the Regional High Administrative Court confirm the legality of the Rasterfahndung in Hesse.

After the Rasterfahndung was completed, the final opposition to it came from the Federal Constitutional Court, which in its ruling of April 4, 2006, declared it unconstitutional.[59] While reasserting the constitutionality of the regional laws on which the Rasterfahndung was based, the court considered that the actual decision to carry out the investigation had unduly misinterpreted the law, which required the existence of a "concrete danger."[60] The court maintained that a Rasterfahndung constitutes a significant interference with the right to privacy and data protection. A violation of that right could be justified only in the presence of concrete leads to a planned attack or information about the presence of suspected terrorists in Germany. A simple general perception of a threat of a terrorist attack is not enough, the court argued, since there will always be international crises in whose context terrorist attacks can occur, and therefore such a threat can never be entirely eliminated.[61] This decision of the Federal Constitutional Court is likely to have consequences for the future, especially for the behavior of regional courts. In the ruling, the Federal Constitutional Court urged them to assess more carefully each time whether the conditions for a Rasterfahndung are present.

The reactions to the decision of the Federal Constitutional Court show the different views held by most of the political forces and by the highest representative of the judiciary on this matter—thus indirectly confirming the independent influence of courts in dictating the interpretation of the constitutional principles that should guide security policy. In fact, the court's decision was heavily criticized by many CDU/CSU national politicians for tying the hands of the police in the face of national danger. The SPD was not as vocal, but it should be kept in mind that the party dominated the federal government at the time of the implementation of the Rasterfahndung and that the Rasterfahndung was first started in SPD-ruled Länder. Indeed, regional SPD politicians criticized the ruling, even suggesting publicly that the government should try to find ways to revive the Rasterfahndung, while formally respecting the court's decision. FDP representatives such as the former justice minister Sabine Leutheusser-Schnarrenberger approved the court's decision as upholding the rule of law. Their position, however, seems to reveal a partisan intent rather than a principled disagreement. In fact, no substantial opposition came from the FDP *while* the Rasterfahndung was being carried out by regional governments, some of which were supported by the FDP.[62]

Conclusion

The German case shows that institutions—and in particular counter-majoritarian institutions—matter in domestic security policy. To be sure, inherited norms are important too.[63] For example, the notion of "streitbare Demokratie," a normative order that requires the defense of democracy against its enemies, was explicitly articulated in the political debate in Germany as the normative justification for the special antiterrorism legislation approved after 9/11. The extent to which this principle has penetrated German political culture is also shown by the broad support in opinion polls for strong governmental action against extremists and terrorists. However, this popular support did not influence the judiciary, which intervened to veto several important security policies, nor was it sufficient to generate wide-ranging reform of the territorially and functionally fragmented security apparatus. The complex division of responsibilities in domestic security policy was criticized by many as the possible cause of inefficiencies and delays in the face of crises. Centralizing police responsibilities was widely debated, and there were attempts to enhance the central government's power to intervene in various matters of internal security. Whenever the political authorities tried to overstep the constitutional mark, however, the courts—and in particular the Federal Constitutional Court—acted as very effective watchdogs over the existing division of responsibilities between the federal government and the Länder in matters of national security. The institutional safeguards incorporated into the Basic Law to avoid "excessive" centralization of power—such as federalism, the separation between police and security services, and the many restrictions on the use of the Bundeswehr in internal emergencies—are still firmly in place, mainly thanks to the action of the courts. Thus, institutional vetoes ensured the prevalence of the fundamental constitutional principle of the safeguards against excesses in the exercise of executive power, even when executive action is justified with the principle—also enshrined in the Basic Law—of defending the constitution against its "enemies".

The discussion here should not conceal the fact that some changes have indeed been introduced: for example, the powers of the police have been increased, more data are now available for investigations, and immigration and asylum have been restricted. As shown in the analysis, however, these trends were mostly already under way before 9/11. They were intended to adapt institutions and policies to the needs of a country that was turning into a country of immigration to an extent unprecedented in its history. The political shock of 9/11 simply removed some of the political obstacles to their approval. Finally, some reforms—such as the regulatory reforms related to money laundering—were induced by the country's international commitments and could generally be carried out within the existing constitutional framework.

Whether the new norms and actions have been successful is still an open question. A natural yardstick of comparison for the post-9/11 situation is the antiterrorism legislative reforms and police activities of the 1970s and the 1980s: then as now, new ad hoc laws, tailored to the characteristics of the terrorist threat, were passed and new police methods were introduced (see, for example, Horbatiuk 1979–80; Katzenstein 1996d). The post-9/11 reaction to Islamic terrorism has been built on those rules and experiences, innovating where it was appropriate, given the new threat environment, and where it was politically and constitutionally possible. Katzenstein (2003, 757), among others, has highlighted the relative lack of success of the police actions undertaken since 9/11. Although this is true insofar as visible effects are concerned, perhaps more credit should go to the ability of the recent reforms and police initiatives to prevent public pro-terrorist activity. In other words, police activity targeting the Islamic associations and communities that breached the new laws, as well as individual suspects, has probably restricted the field of action of potential terrorists, who would normally find refuge in these circles and use them as cover for their activities. It is obviously difficult to substantiate this counterfactual argument with hard evidence, but the argument in question has been made by some commentators. For example, Hirschmann (2003, 396) writes, "Many police actions against suspects have sent extremists the message that they can no longer carry out their activities undisturbed."[64]

This leads to another question: how likely is it that further reforms will be introduced, and how far-reaching will they be? The majority of security experts hold the view that the current system is far from ideal. In the current situation, inefficiencies in the distribution of information and duplication of work are still frequent problems, despite all the reforms devoted to increasing coordination and encouraging a smoother flow of information between security agencies. A reform to give the BKA further proactive responsibilities in counterterrorism activities is being discussed at the time of writing, but even the reformed BKA would still be far from this ideal. Similarly, proposals for the reform of the Office for the Protection of the Constitution have been put forward (see, for example, Hirschmann 2003; Werthebach 2004), but they have not been turned into formal proposals for institutional rearrangement by the federal government.

Be that as it may, this chapter has shown that the decisive element in the success of these proposals will be their capacity to overcome the likely opposition of the courts and the resistance of some aspects of the federal system. The record after 9/11 is quite clear: change has been possible only within the existing allocation of responsibilities in the context of the existing federal system, and the courts have managed to impose their own interpretation (less favorable to extending executive powers, even those used against enemies of the constitution) of the Basic Law's fundamental principles. At this stage, for example, overcoming the likely opposition of the Federal Constitutional Court on key issues such as the deployment of the military for internal terrorism emergencies would take amending the Basic Law; such a proposal is not on the agenda at the time of writing, and it is unlikely to be in the near future.

In sum, security policy certainly represents a "norm-intense" social environment, since in principle it deals with the "enemy within" (Katzenstein 2003, 736–37). And norms have undoubtedly shown their importance in the case of Germany. Even the most resilient norms, however, are always at least partially contested, and the resolution of this contestation is often the outcome of clashes between different institutions. In Germany, counter-majoritarian institutions such as the federal system and the judiciary have proved their vitality even in the atmosphere of political urgency following 9/11.

I thank Martha Crenshaw, Phil Heymann, Robert Pape, Louise Richardson, and the participants in the Radcliffe "Advanced Seminar on Terrorism," at the Radcliffe Institute for Advanced Study, Harvard University, December 4–6, 2006, for their comments on earlier versions of this chapter. The usual disclaimer applies. I also thank Anne-Marie Grandke and Bettina Hahn for excellent research assistance.

Notes

1. Reported in Hirschmann and Leggemann (2003, 10); translation by the author.
2. For a more general analysis of both foreign and domestic security policies in post-9/11 Germany, see Katzenstein (2003).
3. The German constitutional doctrine has emphasized the importance of other institutional arrangements intended to realize the same constitutional principles: the important responsibilities given to the Länder in the implementation of federal policies, or in the legislative process at the federal level (see, for example, Weber-Fas 1983); and the rejection of the direct election of the head of state (see, for example, Mussgnug 1987), as well as of any institution of direct democracy (see, for example, Greifeld 1983; Böckenförde 1985), to avoid any plebiscitarian temptation, which doomed the Weimar Republic. Others mention the constitutional provision of the constructive vote of no confidence (by which the executive cannot be replaced if another coalition is not ready to take its place) and the corrections to proportionality in the federal and state electoral systems, both of which are supposed to increase government stability (see, for example, Hübner 1984; Nohlen 1986; Zieger 1988).
4. As a German constitutional lawyer put it, "The democratic principle, which can be translated in very many different ways, found in the *Grundgesetz* a characteristically liberal and representative normative connotation. This is particularly clear in the existing parliamentary system as well as in the constitutional principle of the 'fundamental liberal-democratic order' . . . this system is also characterized by the specificities of a democracy which is federal, 'social' and 'protected'" (quoted in Weber-Fas 1983, 51–52). Virtually the same description can be found in the whole German postwar constitutional doctrine.
5. The court has defined the fundamental liberal-democratic order as including "the rule of law (responsible government, legality of administration, and judicial independence); separation of powers; popular sovereignty and democratic decision-making based on the majority principle; guaranteed human rights; and a multi-party system granting equal opportunities to all parties, including the right to form a parliamentary opposition"; see BVerfGE 2, 1–79, translated in Braunthal (1989, 310).
6. Only the Federal Constitutional Court can ban a political party, while political associations, which unlike parties do not participate in elections, can be disbanded by a decree of the executive.
7. Most of the repressive antiterrorism laws and reforms of the 1970s, for example, were passed by a center-left Social Democrat–Liberal majority, with the agreement of the Christian Democratic opposition of the time (Braunthal 1989).

8. In an official statement, the party accused the SPD/Green coalition of exacerbating fear and mistrust in society with its domestic security policies. See Die Linke im Bundestag—Service Newsletter, available at: http://www.linksfraktion.de/newsletter_view.php?newsletter=1980535644 (accessed October 2006).
9. Although they have backed the rest of the antiterrorism measures, the Greens initially opposed the creation of biometric passports, which were introduced in 2005. The Liberals (FDP) were in a similar position (although the FDP did not oppose the collection of DNA data for criminals). It should be noted, however, that the FDP has been in opposition as of 1998, and its position could change should it again become part of the government.
10. See, for example, Matthias Geis, "Die Staat lieben lernen," *Die Zeit*, February 3, 2005.
11. Question: "What do you think about Islam? Do you think that Islam represents a threat to Western democracy, or don't you think so?" See Politbarometer 2001, "Variable 200: Islam als Bedrohung" (April 1, 2004), summary available at: http://www.forschungsgruppe.de/Umfragen_und_Publikationen/Politbarometer/Archiv/Politbarometer_2004/PB_April_I_2004/(accessed June 2008). Disclaimer: The Politbarometer Surveys quoted in this chapter were conducted by the Forschungsgruppe Wahlen Mannheim and made available by the Zentralarchiv für empirische Sozialforschung, University of Köln, Germany. Responsibility for the analysis and interpretation of these data is entirely the author's.
12. Allensbach Survey 215, September 15, 2004. The exact wording of the question was: "If in the fight against terrorism, the influence of the state and the police must be strengthened, would you accept a curbing of your personal rights through measures such as surveillance and searches, or would you reject this?"
13. See ibid., which compares data from 1977 and 2004 for the following question: "If in the fight against terrorism, the influence of the state and the police must be strengthened, would you accept a curbing of your personal rights through measures such as surveillance and searches, or would you reject this?" Data available from Allensbach.
14. See "Wahlen in Deutschland—Sicherheit 2001" available at: http://www.aillyacum.de/Dt/Wahlen-Deutschland/2001/Sicherheit11.html (accessed March 2007). The exact wordings of the questions were: "As a citizen, do you value security more than freedom?"; "Can security in Germany only be guaranteed with tighter security measures?"; and "In the future, should passports contain the fingerprints of their holders?" Data from Emnid (November 2, 2001).
15. This datum seems to be quite robust. A separate survey conducted by Allensbach at about the same time ("Some have suggested that to fight terrorism, the mandate of the Bundeswehr should be extended, so that it is

able to act internally and fulfil police tasks or border security. Do you think this is right or not right?") shows a figure of 61 percent in support of the engagement of the Bundeswehr in internal emergency situations, versus a mere 23 percent against the idea. Allensbacher Berichte Survey 7, "Mehr als jeder zweite befürchtet einen Terroranschlag in Deutschland" (2004), available at: http://www.ifd-allensbach.de/news/prd_0407.html (accessed November 2006).

16. The literature (especially in German) on the terrorist threat in Germany during the 1970s and 1980s is vast. Examples of English-language analyses of the terrorist movements are Della Porta (1995), Kolinsky (1988), and Corves (1978); for state responses, see Horbatiuk (1979–80), Thomaneck (1985), Finn (1991), and Katzenstein (1996d). The most encompassing study on the organization of the German police forces, including the reforms passed to counter domestic terrorism, is Busch et al. (1985).

17. It should be noted that important existing repressive provisions could be invoked *unchanged* against Islamic terrorists. This was the case, for example, with the Radikalenerlass ("radicals' decree"), famously introduced in 1972 to screen left- and right-wing extremists from the civil service. The decree was applied quite extensively (and controversially) in those years: about 3.5 million people were investigated as potential political extremists after 1972; about 10,000 were unable to enter or remain in the civil service; and 130 were fired—see, for example, Histor (1992). After 9/11, the decree was used only once—against a Muslim teacher who wore a head scarf in the classroom. See Jochen Leffers, "Lehrerin darf vorerst mit Kopftuch unterrichten," Spiegel Online (September 24, 2003), available at: http://www.spiegel.de/jahreschronik/0,1518,275907,00.html (accessed October 2006); Thomas Darnstädt and Caroline Schmidt, "Stuttgarter Leitkultur," *Der Spiegel*, November 3, 2003, 50; Dietmar Hipp, "Nonnen retten den Islam," Spiegel Online (July 8, 2006), available at: http://www.spiegel.de/schulspiegel/0,1518,425678,00.html (accessed October 2006). Another example, as the federal justice minister made publicly clear in May 2004, is that of the controversial restrictions to the rights of defense counsel: introduced in criminal procedure law during the 1970s, these restrictions in certain cases allow detainees to be excluded from the trial room or barred from any contact with their lawyers (see Finn 1991; Grönewold 1993). See Federal Minister of Justice Brigitte Zypries, "Freedom, Democracy, and the Rule of Law Against the Background of International Terrorism," speech given May 10, 2004, Washington, D.C., available at: http://www.fesdc.org/Speeches%20+%20Papers/zypries051004.html (accessed June 2006).

18. The law (Erstes Änderungsgesetz zum Vereinsgesetz, December 4, 2001), approved by both chambers in November 2001, has been called the "first security package," or the "first antiterror package," in public debate. It came into force on December 8, 2001.

19. Another counterterrorism law extended the possible reasons for an association ban to include the existence of a "threat to the idea of international understanding and world peace" as one of the association's goals.
20. The federal government identified three groups that might be affected: "fundamentalist Islamic groups" that did not disavow the possibility of violence; groups that used the "religion privilege" to circumvent the provisions of the law; and groups (as yet unknown in Germany) that prophesied the end of the world and encouraged mass suicide. See Bundestag, *Blickpunkt Bundestag* (September 2001), available at: http://www.bundestag.de/bp/2001/bp0109/0109033a.html (accessed August 2006).
21. Although the ban of the Caliphate State was finally upheld by both the Federal Administrative Court and the Federal Constitutional Court, lower courts substantially delayed Kaplan's expulsion by opposing the government's act on the basis of potential violation of human rights. For a reconstruction of the facts, see "Im Labyrhint des Kalifen," *Der Spiegel*, June 7, 2004.
22. Ibid.; see also "Kaplan erwartet Hochverrat-Prozess," *Der Spiegel*, October 13, 2004.
23. The exact wording of the question was "Should persons such as Metin Kaplan, who advocate violence in Germany, be expelled even when they face persecution, torture or death in their home country?" (translated by the author). The result across the sample of about one thousand interviewees was 70 percent "yes," 20 percent "no," and 5 percent "don't know." Broken down by party preference (without reporting the "don't know" data), the split was 66 percent "yes" to 27 percent "no" among SPD voters, 75 percent "yes" to 22 percent "no" among CDU/CSU voters, and 82 percent "yes" to 14 percent "no" among FDP voters. The Greens' electors showed more division, with 49 percent in favor and 43 percent against, but the party expressed no official disagreement with Kaplan's expulsion. See "TNS Infratest," *Der Spiegel*, June 7, 2004.
24. The Servant of Islam, an important Muslim association, was banned along with the Caliphate State. In August 2002, the interior minister used the new legislation to ban Al-Aqsa, an Islamic organization accused of collecting donations for Hamas in order to support the families of suicide bombers in Israel. (Three years later, the successor organization, Yatim Children's Aid, was also banned.) In September 2002, the police searched about one hundred mosques, apartments, and public venues. Many arrests were made, and the minister of the interior banned sixteen Islamic associations that had been active mainly at the local or regional level. In January 2003, the Hizb ut-Tahrir al-Islami (HuT) was also banned throughout the Federal Republic. December 2003 saw one of the largest police operations in the history of the Germany: 5,500 officers searched 1,170 properties in 13 states. See *Süddeutsche Zeitung*, December 12, 2003; *Frankfurter Rundschau*, October 18, 2003,

and December 12, 2003; and the list of forbidden Islamist organizations at Bundesamt für Verfassungsschutz: http://www.verfassungsschutz.de/de/arbeitsfelder/af_islamismus/zahlen_und_fakten_islamismus/zafais_3_verbotene_islam_org.html (accessed October 2006).

25. Gesetz zur Bekämpfung des internationalen Terrorismus (Terrorismusbekämpfungsgesetz; January 9, 2002), called the "second security package," or the "second antiterror package," in public parlance. The second antiterror package, approved by both chambers in December 2001, came into force in January 2002.
26. The law specifies this concept as follows: "1. Limiting or endangering the political process, the peaceful living together of Germans and foreigners or of different groups of foreigners in the Federal Republic, public security or order, or other significant interests of the Federal Republic of Germany. 2. Running counter to the obligations of the Federal Republic of Germany under international law. 3. Supporting tendencies outside the Federal Republic, the aims or means of which are incompatible with a state order that respects the dignity of humanity. 4. Supporting, encouraging or calling for the use of violence as a means of achieving political, religious or other aims. 5. Supporting associations inside or outside the Federal Republic which carry out, support or threaten attacks on people or goods." See Terrorismusbekämpfungsgesetz, sect. 9.
27. *Süddeutsche Zeitung*, October 27–28, 2001, 5, quoted in Glässner (2003, 52). In 1983 the Federal Constitutional Court had established that public institutions could collect and share individuals' personal data for purposes established by the law (BVerfGE 65, 1, 44).
28. Gesetz zur Ergänzung des Terrorismusbekämpfungsgesetz (Terrorismusbekämpfungsergänzungsgesetz), Bundesgesetzblatt, 2007, part 1, no. 1, published in Bonn (January 10, 2007), available at: www.cilip.de (accessed November 2007).
29. Thirty-fourth Strafrechtsänderungsgesetz (August 22, 2002).
30. Prosecution has no limits if the group is based in another EU member state. For nonmember states, the section applies if the activities of the group are carried out in Germany, if the perpetrator or the victim is German, or if either of them is in Germany at the time of the crime. Furthermore, to safeguard diplomatic relations, prosecution in these cases is submitted to the federal government for approval (Wache 2003, 151).
31. The extension of the applicability of sections 129 and 129(a) was accompanied by a tightening of their wording: a newly punishable offense was not just "advertising" (Sympathiewerbung) terrorist organizations but, more specifically, advertising "with the end of recruiting members and supporters" (um Mitglieder oder Unterstützer werben). A later proposal of the CDU/CSU to reinsert "Sympathiewerbung" was not accepted. See Tröndle and Fischer (2004, §129a, no. 20).

32. The "integrative" interpretation of the court was necessary because section 129(a) describes what in German legalese is called a Vorfelddelikt ("run-up crime"), which allows the prosecution of individuals if they belong to an organization whose goals include committing crimes of a certain gravity (such as murder) even *before* those crimes are committed or even planned (Katzenstein 2003).
33. The urgency of this problem became clear when the Oberlandesgericht (Regional High Court) in Frankfurt am Main was called upon to judge the four members of an Islamic terrorist cell who (while in Germany) organized a bomb attack on the Christmas Market in Strasbourg in 2000. The police arrested them in December 2000, just before they could carry out their plans, and the prosecutor charged them with, among other things, forming a terrorist association on the basis of section 129(a) of the Criminal Code. The court in 2003 finally condemned the defendants to prison sentences of between ten and twelve years; it also ruled, however, that section 129(a) could not be applied to the case (even though the new legislation had been passed in the intervening time, the principle of favor rei was applied) and that therefore the individuals could not be considered as having formed a terrorist organization, since there was evidence that they had not planned further attacks and some of them had already bought airline tickets to leave the country (Wache 2003, 146).
34. Geldwäschebekämpfungsgesetz (August 8, 2002).
35. The law does not allow the collection of data on an account's balance, transactions, or returns on interest. The Datenschutzbeauftragten and financial institutions opposed these changes during the debate before the law was passed; in fact, one of the most controversial issues considered was whether data could also be used to identify tax evaders.
36. This reform could also be framed in terms of multilateralism in foreign policy, another principle derived from the Basic Law (Katzenstein 2003). Until this reform, in fact, Germany had been a laggard in this respect vis-à-vis other countries. Despite being one of the founding members of the Financial Action Task Force (FATF), an intergovernmental body founded by the G-7 in 1989 in response to the increased threat posed by international money laundering (since 2001, the FATF has also dealt with international terrorism financing), Germany had not yet fully implemented the relevant recommendations that accompanied its creation. One of these recommendations was to establish a central register of suspected cases of money laundering and terrorism financing. The main obstacle to the establishment of such a central body was the resistance of the Länder to giving up their responsibilities in this area. Now fourteen officials work in the central FIU, while about three hundred officials work on money laundering and terrorism financing across all Länder. The FIU is staffed by federal police officers, like the rest of the BKA, and it uses external consultants for more technical matters. See *Welt am Sonntag*, September 30, 2001.

37. Several experts proposed an enhanced role for the Bundeswehr in both external and internal tasks (see, for example, Weisser 2004; Naumann 2004). For very detailed proposals on how the Bundeswehr could support the actions of other security agencies beyond military intervention (for example, by providing know-how, technology, reserved information, or logistical support), see, for example, Gusy (2004).
38. In the ruling, the court first made clear that the Basic Law does not allow the federal government to pass such a law: article 35 of the Basic Law allows the armed forces to help the Länder in case of natural disasters and severe casualties, but it prohibits the use of specific military armament for these purposes, and it allows the employment of the armed forces only as "police-like" forces. Since section 14.3 of the Luftsicherheitsgesetz provided for a military deployment of the armed forces, the court judged that the federal government had overstepped its powers as established by the Basic Law. From a substantial point of view, the court held that section 14.3 of the new law clashed with articles 1.1 and 2.2 of the Basic Law, which protect the basic rights to human dignity and life. The new law would have been in compliance with the Basic Law if it had allowed shooting down only pilot-less aircraft or aircraft carrying persons planning to use the plane as a weapon against other individuals. The new law, however, allowed shooting down airplanes carrying innocent crew or passengers. BVerfG, 1 BvR 357/05, February 15, 2006, available at: http://www.bverfg.de/entscheidungen/rs20060215_1bvr035705.html (accessed November 2006).
39. BVerfGE, 1 BvR 357/05, February 15, 2006, para. 105–9. The court also explicitly stated that its ruling did not aim to evaluate criminal liability in the case of an actual shooting; that ruling dealt exclusively with the constitutionality of the Luftsicherheitsgesetz. This may hint at the possibility that a military commander could make an illegal decision in an emergency situation and be tried for it in a criminal court afterward.
40. *Süddeutsche Zeitung*, February 18, 2006.
41. *Süddeutsche Zeitung*, April 5, 2006.
42. See Bundesministerium der Verteidigung, *Weissbuch 2006 zur Sicherheitspolitik Deutschlands und zur Zukunft der Bundeswehr*, available at: http://merln.ndu.edu/whitepapers/Germany_Weissbuch_2006_mB_sig.pdf (accessed September 2009). Throughout its text, the white paper is consistent with the normative framework of the Basic Law (such as multilateralism; see Katzenstein 2003) and with reforms introduced well before 9/11, such as the possibility of deploying the army in international missions under very strict conditions. See Severin Weiland, "Weissbuch zwischen Wehrpflicht und Weltpolitik," Spiegel Online (October 25, 2006), available at: http://www.spiegel.de/politik/deutschland/0,1518,444354,00.html (accessed November 2007).
43. For example, the consolidation of the rights of the Gastarbeiter (the guest workers who entered Germany mainly between the 1950s and the 1970s)

with those of permanent residents was greatly helped by judicial interpretation of the laws rather than by new legislation. The courts also kept their expansive interpretation of the rights of foreigners in the later phase, when most economic immigrants went the "asylum" route rather than the old route of "imported labor" (Walthelm, n.d.).

44. The Gesetz zur Änderung des Grundgesetzes (Law Amending the Basic Law) of June 28, 1993, added article 16(a) to the Basic Law, which subjected the concession of political asylum to a series of conditions, mainly having to do with the effective violation of human rights in the applicant's country of origin.
45. More specifically, a new Zuwanderungsgesetz (Immigration Act) was passed on July 30, 2004, to go into force on January 1, 2005. Among other things, section 1 of the new law replaced the old Ausländergesetz (Foreigners Act) with the Aufenthaltsgesetz (Residence Act). Section 2 of the same law introduced the Gesetz über die allgemeine Freizügigkeit von Unionsbürgern (Act on the General Freedom of Movement of EU Citizens), newly regulating migration within the EU and replacing the 1980 Aufenthaltsgesetz/EWG (Residence Act/EEC). Section 3 changed the Asylverfahrensgesetz (Act on Asylum Procedures).
46. The Ausländerzentralregister is an official database that stores personal information on all foreigners who have or have had a residence permit, who are seeking or have sought asylum, or who are admitted asylum-seekers.
47. The new Aufenthaltsgesetz also introduced new integration measures such as integration courses and programs (sects. 43–45).
48. Data for 2007, available only for the period of January to September at the time of writing, show that even the decreasing trend in asylum applications may now have reached the bottom: 23,206 applications were filed in the first nine months of the year. Assuming that the trend remained stable for the remaining quarter, this would yield about 29,000 applications, against the 30,100 filed in 2006. Furthermore, based on the same data and assumptions, the percentage of refusals may have been slightly declining between 2006 and 2007: 13,864 applications were rejected in the first nine months of 2007. This might yield a total of about 17,000 refusals at the end of the year against the 21,029 in 2006 (Bundesamt für Migration und Flüchtlinge 2007).
49. For example, the authoritative Bertelsmann Foundation proposed, among other things, to increase the centralization of power for the BfV and the BKA against their respective regional branches (Weidenfeld 2004, 17). More cooperation in various forms—from the swap of functionaries to the integration of different agencies into a "network" scheme between the BKA, BND, BGS, and BfV—was also advocated, especially in the access and evaluation of information through the establishment of a general database on

"international terror" and agreements on evaluation procedures (Gusy 2004). Security reforms were sometimes seen as part of more-encompassing schemes to reform the German federal system. For example, Kai Hirschmann proposed to turn the sixteen LfVs into nine regional branches of the national BfV. This reform would have to be carried out in the context of a prospective general reduction of the number of Länder from sixteen to nine and would follow the example of the reform of the Bundesbank (the Federal Central Bank) and the Landesbanken (reduced to nine and turned into regional branches of the Bundesbank) introduced after the European Monetary Union (Hirschmann 2003, 398).

50. The same right has been granted to the civilian Federal Intelligence Service (BND), which can now request information on account-holders and monetary transactions and investments. The Military Counterespionage Service (MAD) has also benefited from the extension of the protected constitutional objects to "understanding between peoples and peaceful coexistence of peoples," being now entitled to gather information on any member of the armed forces or any civilian working in the Ministry of Defense whose activities may be directed against such understanding and coexistence. The MAD cannot, however, request financial information on the same people (Glässner 2003, 55).
51. The problem of data sharing and the common evolution of information between different agencies was a long-standing one in German security policy and goes back at least thirty years, but it has been made substantially more urgent by the increased amount of data now available owing to the enhanced technological possibilities in telecommunications (the Internet, satellites, and so on) and consequently in data collection (Wache 2003, 147).
52. Established in 1950 and coordinated by the Federal Interior Ministry, the Bereitschaftspolizei is an integral part of the Länderpolizeien. Its primary functions are crowd control and assisting the Länderpolizeien in cases of riots, civil disturbances, or catastrophes.
53. The 1970s use of the Rasterfahndung led to the arrest of only one terrorist, RAF member Rolf Heissler, in 1979 (Katzenstein 1996d).
54. For this purpose, new data storage systems had to be created from scratch: attempts to update the INPOL system to adapt it to post-9/11 requirements have encountered the technical and political difficulties associated with the integration of the different standards and procedures of each Land and thus have been unsuccessful. Dietl (2003, 195) reports, for example, that for the crime of car theft, each of the Länder insisted that its own form be integrated into the system, making for sixteen different standards.
55. A Rasterfahndung at the federal level, on the basis of section 98(a) of the Code of Criminal Procedure, is possible only for the purpose of tracking an offender; thus, it would have a repressive rather than preventive purpose. Having decided to carry out a Rasterfahndung with preventive purposes, the

Conference of the Regional Ministers of Interior Affairs chose to ground the initiative in regional police laws, which allow a preventive Rasterfahndung. Regional police laws vary, however, between Länder. For example, in some Länder, carrying out a Rasterfahndung requires prior judicial approval, while in others there is no such need. Moreover, the laws define the circumstances justifying a resort to this kind of investigation differently, variously prescribing the "imminence" of a threat or the presence of "concrete leads" to a future threat or allowing a Rasterfahndung on the mere basis of the "perception" of such a threat by the authorities. Finally, in three Länder (Bremen, Schleswig-Holstein, and Lower Saxony), a Rasterfahndung was not possible at all, and police laws had to be quickly amended.

56. In North Rhine–Westphalia, the authorities collected information on *all* men (German as well as non-German) age eighteen to forty and justified this procedure by pointing to the possibility of sleepers who held German citizenship. Moreover, universities in that Land did not have information on the religious affiliation and national origin of their students. As a result, the authorities in North Rhine–Westphalia collected information on 5 million individuals. This was later challenged before the Regional High Court, which ruled that while the use of the Rasterfahndung itself was justified given the threat coming from Islamic terrorism, collecting data on all ("non-profiled") citizens of a certain age group was not legal.
57. The legal basis for this procedure was provided by BKA-Gesetz, sects. 7 and 28 (BT-Drucksache 14/7249, p. 3).
58. The process of data cleaning was long and complicated. The first comparison of the databases resulted in more than 101,000 relevant matches. This result, however, contained false identities (different individuals with the same name) and double matches (individuals in the sleepers database who were featured more than once in the comparison database). To clear the result of these false matches, the BKA returned all matches to the respective LKÄ, which cleared up the data manually. The number of potential suspects was thus reduced to 3,450. Further screening reduced the number of potential suspects to 1,689 (Kant 2005).
59. BVerfGE, 1 BvR 518/02, April 4, 2006; see http://www.bverfg.de/entscheidungen/rs20060404_1bvr051802.html (accessed August 2006). The case was brought to the court by a student of Moroccan origin who complained about the inappropriate use of his personal data by his university.
60. BVerfGE, 1 BvR 518/02, April 4, 2006, para. 154.
61. BVerfGE, 1 BvR 518/02, April 4, 2006, para. 147.
62. On the political debate on the court's ruling, see "Sicherheitspolitik: Kippt Karlsruhe die Rasterfahndung?" Spiegel Online (May 22, 2006); "Grundsatzurteil: Verfassungsrichter schränken Rasterfahndung ein," Spiegel Online (May 23, 2006); "Analyse: Karlsruhe dezimiert das Arsenal der Terror-Fahnder," Spiegel Online (May 23, 2006); "Reaktionen: 'Besorgnis

erregende Entscheidung,'" Spiegel Online (May 23, 2006); and "Angriff auf Karlsruhe," *Der Spiegel*, August 28, 2006.

63. The pattern of continuity and limited change in counterterrorism policies after 9/11 is not exclusive to Germany but can be observed in other European countries as well. See, for example, Martin Schain's (2007) analysis of France and the United Kingdom; see also Haubrich (2003) and Foley (2007).
64. These considerations echo parts of the debate in the 1970s and early 1980s. For example, Geoffrey Pridham (1981, 50–51), evaluating the police preventive and repressive action against the RAF in 1981, wrote that the German security system "clearly has had an impact in helping to reduce terrorist activities in the Federal Republic despite the well-publicized cases of inefficiency and in some respects rigidity."

References

Ackerman, Bruce. 2004a. "The Emergency Constitution." *Yale Law Journal* 113(5): 1029–91.

———. 2004b. "This Is Not a War." *Yale Law Journal* 113(8): 1871–1907.

Allensbach Survey. Various years. Allensbach, Germany: Institut fuer Demoskopie Allensbach. Available at: http://www.ifd-allensbach.de (accessed September 20, 2009).

Banchoff, Thomas. 1999. *The German Problem Transformed: Institutions, Politics, and Foreign Policy, 1945–1995.* Ann Arbor: University of Michigan Press.

Bayley, David. 1985. *Patterns of Policing: An International Comparative Perspective.* New Brunswick, N.J.: Rutgers University Press.

Berger, Thomas 1996. "Norms, Identity, and National Security in Germany and Japan." In *The Culture of National Security: Norms and Identity in World Politics,* edited by Peter J. Katzenstein. New York: Columbia University Press.

———. 1998. *Cultures of Antimilitarism: National Security in Germany and Japan.* Baltimore: Johns Hopkins University Press.

Bisanz, Stefan, and Uwe Gerstenberg. 2003. "Neue Sicherheitsstrukturen als Antwort auf terroristische Anschläge." In *Der Kampf gegen den Terrorismus,* edited by Kai Hirschmann and Christian Leggemann. Berlin: Strategies und Handlungserfordernisse in Deutschland.

Böckenförde, Ernst-Wolfgang. 1985. "Democrazia e rappresentanza." *Quaderni Costituzionali* 2(August): 227–63.

Boventer, Gregor Paul. 1985. *Grenzen politischer Freiheit im demokratischen Staat: Das Konzept der streitbaren Demokratie im internationaler Vergleich.* Berlin: Duncker & Humblot.

Braunthal, Gerhard. 1989. "Public Order and Civil Liberties." In *Developments in West German Politics,* edited by Gordon Smith, William E. Paterson, and Peter H. Merkl. Durham, N.C.: Duke University Press.

Bundesamt für Migration und Flüchtlinge. 2006. *Aktuelle Zahlen zu Asyl.* Nürnberg: Bundesamt für Migration und Flüchtlinge. Available at: http://www.bamf.de/cln_006/nn_442496/SharedDocs/Anlagen/DE/DasBAMF/Downloads/Statistik/statistik-auflage15-4-aktuell-asyl,templateId=raw,property=publicationFile.pdf/statistik-auflage15-4-aktuell-asyl.pdf (accessed November 2006).

———. 2007. *Asyl in Zahlen 2006.* Nürnberg: Bundesamt für Migration und Flüchtlinge. Available at: http://www.bamf.de/cln_006/nn_442496/SharedDocs/Anlagen/DE/DasBAMF/Publikationen/broschuere-asyl-in-zahlen-2006.html Accessed March 2007.

Busch, Heiner, A. Funk, V. Karuss, W.-D. Narr, and F. Werkentin. 1985. *Die Polizei in der Bundesrepublik.* Frankfurt: Campus.

Chebel d'Appollonia, Ariana, and Simon Reich, eds. 2007. *Immigration, Integration, and Security: America and Europe in Comparative Perspective.* Pittsburgh: Pittsburgh University Press.

Corves, Erich. 1978. "Terrorism and Criminal Police Operations in the Federal Republic of Germany." In *Terrorism and Criminal Justice,* edited by Ronald D. Crelisten, Danielle Laberge-Altmejd, and Denis Szabo. Toronto: Lexington Books.

Currie, David. 1994. *The Constitution of the Federal Republic of Germany.* Chicago: University of Chicago Press.

Della Porta, Donatella. 1995. *Social Movements, Political Violence, and the State.* Cambridge: Cambridge University Press.

Dietl, Wilhelm. 2003. "Das Informationssystem der Deutschen Polizei." In *Der Kampf gegen den Terrorismus,* edited by Kai Hirschmann and Christian Leggemann. Berlin: Strategies und Handlungserfordernisse in Deutschland.

Dürig, Günther. 1988. "An Introduction to the Basic Law of the Federal Republic of Germany." In *The Constitution of the Federal Republic of Germany,* edited by Ulrich Karpen. Baden-Baden: Nomos.

Finn, John E. 1991. *Constitutions in Crisis: Political Violence and the Rule of Law.* Oxford: Oxford University Press.

Foley, Frank. 2007. "Reforming Counterterrorism: Institutions and Organizational Routines in France and the United Kingdom." Paper presented to the annual meeting of the American Political Science Association. Chicago (August 30–September 2).

Forschungsgruppe Wahlen. Various years. Politbarometer Surveys [dataset]. Mannheim, Germany: Forschungsgruppe Wahlen Manheim. Available at http://www.gesis.org/dienstleistungen/daten/umfragedaten/politbarometer/?0= (accessed September 20, 2009).

Foster, Nigel, and Satish Sule. 2002. *German Legal System and Laws,* 3rd ed. Oxford: Oxford University Press.

Garrett, Geoffrey, and Barry Weingast. 1992. "Ideas, Interests, and Institutions." In *Ideas and Foreign Policy,* edited by Judith Goldstein and Robert Keohane. Ithaca, N.Y.: Cornell University Press.

Glässner, Gert Joachim. 2003. "Internal Security and the New Anti-Terrorism Act." *German Politics* 12(1): 43–58.

Greifeld, Andreas. 1983. *Volksentscheid durch Parlamente: Wahlen und Abstimmungen vor dem Grundgesetz der Demokratie.* Berlin: Duncker & Humblot.

Grönewold, Kurt. 1993. "The German Federal Republic's Response and Civil Liberties." In *Western Responses to Terrorism,* edited by Alex P. Schmid and Ronald D. Crelinsten. London: Cass.

Gusy, Christoph. 2004. "Die Vernetzung innerer und äusserer Sicherheitsinstitutionen in der Bundesrepublik Deutschland." In *Herausforderung Terrorismus: Die Zukunft der Sicherheit,* edited by Werner Weidenfeld. Wiesbaden: Verlag für Sozialwissenschaften.

Haubrich, Dirk. 2003. "September 11, Anti-Terror Laws, and Civil Liberties: Britain, France, and Germany Compared." *Government and Opposition* 38(1): 3–28.

Heymann, Philip. 2003. *Freedom, Terrorism, and Security.* Cambridge, Mass.: MIT Press.

Hirschmann, Kai. 2003. "Die Agenda der Zukunft: Die Folgen des Irak-Krieges, neue Konfliktkonstellationen und islamistische Strukturen in Deutschland." In *Der Kampf gegen den Terrorismus,* edited by Kai Hirschmann and Christian Leggemann. Berlin: Strategies und Handlungserfordernisse in Deutschland.

Hirschmann, Kai, and Christian Leggemann, eds. 2003. *Der Kampf gegen den Terrorismus.* Berlin: Strategies und Handlungserfordernisse in Deutschland.

Histor, Manfred. 1992. *Willy Brandts vergessene Opfer,* 2nd ed. Freiburg: Ahriman Verlag.

Horbatiuk, Kevin G. 1979–80. "Anti-Terrorism: The West German Approach." *Fordham International Law Review* 167(3): 167–91.

Hübner, Emil. 1984. *Wahlsysteme und ihre mögliche Wirkungen unter speziellen Berücksichtigung der Bundesrepublik Deutschland.* Munich: Bayerische Landeszentrale für politische Bildung.

Jepperson, Ronald, Alexander Wendt, and Peter J. Katzenstein. 1996. "Norms, Identity, and Culture in National Security." In *The Culture of National Security: Norms and Identity in World Politics,* edited by Peter J. Katzenstein. New York: Columbia University Press.

Jesse, Eckard. 1980. *Streitbare Demokratie: Theorie, Praxis, und Herausforderungen in der Bundesrepublik Deutschland.* Berlin: Colloquium.

Kant, Martina. 2005. "Bilanz der Rasterfahndung nach dem 11. September 2001." *Buergerechte & Polizei/CILIP* 80(1): 13–21.

Karpen, Ulrich. 1983. "Application of the Basic Law." In *Main Principles of the German Basic Law,* edited by Christian Starck. Baden-Baden: Nomos.

———. 1988. "The Constitution of the Federal Republic of Germany." In *Essays on the Basic Rights and Principles of the Basic Law, with a Translation of the Basic Law.* Baden-Baden: Nomos.

Katzenstein, Peter J. 1996a. *The Culture of National Security.* New York: Columbia University Press.

———. 1996b. "Introduction." In *The Culture of National Security*, edited by Peter J. Katzenstein. New York: Columbia University Press.

———. 1996c. *Cultural Norms and National Security: Police and Military in Postwar Japan*. Ithaca, N.Y.: Cornell University Press.

———. 1996d. "West Germany's Internal Security Policy: State and Violence in the 1970s and 1980s." Occasional paper 28. Ithaca, N.Y.: Cornell University, Center for International Studies, Western Societies Program.

———. 1997. "United Germany in an Integrating Europe." In *Tamed Power: Germany in Europe*, edited by Peter J. Katzenstein. Ithaca, N.Y.: Cornell University Press.

———. 2003. "Same War—Different Views: Germany, Japan, and Counterterrorism." *International Organization* 57(4): 731–60.

Klein, Eckart. 1983. "The Concept of the Basic Law." In *Main Principles of the German Basic Law*, edited by Christian Starck. Baden-Baden: Nomos.

Kolinsky, Eva. 1988. "Terrorism in West Germany." In *The Threat of Terrorism*, edited by Juliet Lodge. London: Wheatsheaf.

Leggemann, Christian. 2003. "Der Einsatz von Streitkräften zur Terrorismusbekämfung: Die aktuelle Debatte in Deutschland." In *Der Kampf gegen den Terrorismus*, edited by Kai Hirschmann and Christian Leggemann. Berlin: Strategies und Handlungserfordernisse in Deutschland.

March, James G., and Johan P. Olsen. 1989. *Rediscovering Institutions*. New York: Free Press.

———. 2004. "The Logic of Appropriateness." Working paper 04/09. Oslo: Advanced Research on the Europeanisation of the Nation State (ARENA).

Markovits, Andrei S., and Simon Reich. 1997. *The German Predicament: Memory and Power in the New Europe*. Ithaca, N.Y.: Cornell University Press.

Mussgnug, Reinhard. 1987. "Zustandekommen des Grundgesetzes und Entstehen der Bundesrepublik Deutschland." In *Handbuch des Staatrechts der Bundesrepublik Deutschland*, vol. 1, edited by Josef Isensee and Paul Kirchhof. Heidelberg: Müller.

Naumann, Klaus. 2004. "Die Organization der Sicherheit unter neuen Herausforderungen und die Zukunft der Bundeswehr." In *Herausforderung Terrorismus: Die Zukunft der Sicherheit*, edited by Werner Weidenfeld. Wiesbaden: Verlag für Sozialwissenschaften.

Nohlen, Dieter. 1986. *Wahlrecht und Parteiensystem*. Opladen: Leske & Budrich.

Powell, Walter W., and Paul J. Di Maggio, eds. 1991. *The New Institutionalism in Organizational Analysis*. Chicago: University of Chicago Press.

Pridham, Geoffrey. 1981. "Terrorism and the State in West Germany During the 1970s: A Threat to Stability or a Case of Political Overreaction?" In *Terrorism: A Challenge to the State*, edited by Juliet Lodge. New York: St. Martin's Press.

Sajò, Andras, ed. 2004. *Militant Democracy*. Utrecht, The Netherlands: Eleven International Publishing.

Schain, Martin. 2007. "Immigration Policy and Reactions to Terrorism After September 11." In *Immigration, Integration, and Security: America and Europe in Com-*

parative Perspective, edited by Ariana Chebel d'Appollonia and Simon Reich. Pittsburgh: Pittsburgh University Press.

Scheppele, Kim Lane. 2004. "Law in a Time of Emergency: States of Exception and the Temptations of 9/11." *University of Pennsylvania Law Review* 6(5): 1001–83.

Starck, Christian. 1983. "Introduction." In *Main Principles of the German Basic Law,* edited by Christian Starck. Baden-Baden: Nomos.

Stern, Klaus. 1977. *Das Staatsrecht der Bundesrepublik Deutschland: Band I—Grundbegriffe und Grundlagen des Staatsrechts. Stukturprinzipien der Verfassung.* Munich: Beck.

Thomaneck, Jurgen. 1985. "Police and Public Order in the Federal Republic of Germany." In *Police and Public Order in Europe,* edited by John Roach and Jurgen Thomaneck. London: Croom Helm.

Tröndle, Herbert, and Thomas Fischer. 2004. *Strafgesetzbuch und Nebengesetze,* 52nd ed. Munich: Beck.

Von Doemming, Klaus-Berto, Rudolf Werner Füsslein, and Werner Matz. 1951. "Entstehungsgeschichte der Artikel des Grundgesetzes." *Jahrbuch des öffentlichen Rechts* (Neue Folge) 1.

Wache, Volkhard. 2003. "Die Strafverfolgung islamisticher Terrorismus." In *Der Kampf gegen den Terrorismus,* edited by Kai Hirschmann and Christian Leggemann. Berlin: Strategies und Handlungserfordernisse in Deutschland.

Walthelm, Britta. N.d. "Immigration and Asylum Policies in Great Britain and Germany After September 11." European Union policy papers. Manchester: University of Manchester. Available at: http://www.socialsciences.manchester.ac.uk/politics/research/research_groups/epru/publishing.htm (accessed June 2006).

Weber-Fas, Rudolf. 1983. *Das Grundgesetz: Einführung in das Verfassungsrecht der Bundesrepublik Deutschland.* Berlin: Duncker & Humblot.

Weidenfeld, Werner. 2004. "Für ein System kooperativer Sicherheit." In *Herausforderung Terrorismus: Die Zukunft der Sicherheit,* edited by Werner Weidenfeld. Wiesbaden: Verlag für Sozialwissenschaften.

Weisser, Ulrich. 2004. "Die veränderte Sicherheitslage: NATO und EU vor neuen Herausforderungen -Konsequenzen für deutschen Sicherheitspolitik und Streitkräfte." In *Herausforderung Terrorismus: Die Zukunft der Sicherheit,* edited by Werner Weidenfeld. Wiesbaden: Verlag für Sozialwissenschaften.

Werthebach, Eckart. 2004. "Deutsche Sicherheitsstrukturen im 21. jahrhundert." *Aus Politik und Zeitgeschichte* 44: 5–13.

Zieger, Gottfried. 1988. "Staats- und Verfassungsordnung der Bundesrepublik Deutschland." In *Das deutsche Volk und seine staatliche Gestalt,* edited by Dieter Blumewitz and Gottfried Zieger. Köln: Wissenschaft und Politik.

CHAPTER 9

THE CONSEQUENCES OF COUNTERTERRORIST POLICIES IN ISRAEL

AMI PEDAHZUR AND ARIE PERLIGER

Violent attacks against civilians for the purpose of terror constituted an integral part of the strategies carried out by both Jewish and Arab factions in Palestine during the years of the British Mandate, especially after 1936 (Kimmerling and Migdal 2002; Lachman 1982; Lustick 1995). The founding of the Israeli state on May 14, 1948, led to a war between Israel and its neighboring Arab countries that lasted for more than a year. By the end of the war, the new State of Israel controlled much more land than was initially allocated in accordance with the United Nations partition plan.[1] A Palestinian state in fact was never established. Israel, Jordan, and Egypt annexed sections of land that had initially been offered to the Palestinians by the United Nations, and approximately 900,000 Palestinians became refugees.[2]

The first decade after the war was marked by a relative decline in the levels of violence on both sides. The terrorist attacks perpetrated against Israeli civilians were carried out by the fedayeen—groups of Palestinian refugees most of whom were armed by the Egyptian regime and served its interests (Yaari 1975). These attacks were the precipitating factor in the formation of the official Israeli counterterrorism policy (Goren, August 16,

2006; Shavit, August 16, 2006). This policy, which at the time was called a "retaliatory policy," consisted of military raids against Arab military and civilian centers as an immediate response to attacks against Israelis. The reasoning behind these reprisals was to prove to the Arabs that Israel would not tolerate acts of violence in its territory and that those who perpetrated these acts would have to pay a high price (Ganor 2003, 75). By engaging in this policy, the Israeli elite was hoping to deter Arab leaders from sponsoring terrorism. Questions of democratic acceptability and human rights violations related to the implementation of this policy were not even discussed at the time (Morris 1996, 228–30). At any rate, the goal was not attained. All in all, the "retaliatory policy" ended in a severe escalation between Israel and Arab countries—most prominently Egypt—and in the killing of dozens of innocent civilians (Morris 1996, 446–54). What is more, the policy did not bring an end to terrorism.

On October 10, 1959, the Movement for the Liberation of Palestine (Fatah) was established, and on January 1, 1965, three members of the new group attempted to execute its first terrorist attack on Israeli soil (Shavit, August 16, 2006). Two years later, following the Israeli occupation of the West Bank, East Jerusalem, and the Gaza Strip in the Six-Day War, the conflict between Israel and the Palestinians intensified. Not only were 950,000 Palestinian refugees now under direct Israeli military occupation, but by 1968 the Israeli settler movement had started to expand to the West Bank.[3] Jewish settlements were established first in the Hebron area and then all over the occupied territories.[4] By that time, the popularity of the Fatah had skyrocketed, and its leader, Yasir Arafat, had taken over the leadership of the Palestine Liberation Organization (PLO), which served as an umbrella organization for the different Palestinian ideological factions.

The following years were marked by an unprecedented wave of attacks against Israeli and Jewish targets, both in Israel and abroad. Terrorism had turned from a relatively marginal item on the agenda of the Israeli security establishment to a major one (Zohar, August 17, 2006). This was reflected in the expansion of counterterrorism intelligence branches and the formation of new special counterterrorism units. The attacks did not alter, however, the major premise of Israeli counterterrorism policy—deterrence and containment (Ganor 2003, 75–78). The question was: how could these goals be attained? The emerging policy involved intensive intelligence gathering and strikes against PLO activists, camps, and in some cases even sponsoring states (Byman 2005, 145). While this policy was aimed at coping with the symptoms of the problem, Israel actually intensified its root causes by annexing East Jerusalem and, most prominently, by rapidly expanding

Jewish settlements in the West Bank (Zertal and Eldar 2004, 132–37; Schiff and Yaari 1990, 54; Shalev 1990, 36–40).

The 1980s were marked by two important developments. First, the PLO forces were driven out of Lebanon by the Israel Defense Forces (IDF) in the summer of 1982. Arafat and his supporters had to relocate their headquarters to Tunis. Second, local Palestinian factions in the West Bank and the Gaza Strip gained more prominence. Among those factions, two were particularly significant: the Palestinian Islamic Jihad (PIJ), which was established in 1981, and Hamas, which was formed six years later. The first group is a relatively small and elitist organization, and the latter is a mass social and political movement, but they share similar ideologies that are a mixture of religious and nationalist ideas. The two groups refused to join the PLO and subsequently became the major opposition front to the Oslo Accords signed between Israel and the PLO on September 13, 1993. These agreements were supposed to be the first step in the reconciliation process between Israelis and Palestinians; however, they turned out to be the starting point of an unprecedented era of violence in the region.

Exactly five months prior to the signing of the Oslo Accords, on April 13, 1993, Hamas launched its first suicide bomber. In the following years, suicide attacks would prove to be an extremely effective weapon.[5] Such operations are not costly to carry out and have proven to be highly effective in terms of their lethality and the panic they induce. Furthermore, the Israeli security establishment had no prepared routines for countering these attacks and hence had to start experimenting with different response procedures. Only ten years after the first suicide attack, Israel found a mechanism that enabled it to cope with this tactic effectively. As with similar procedures in the past, however, Israel's various responses were aimed at the symptoms rather than the root causes, and in fact those responses intensified the hostility of the Palestinians toward Israel and the support for the use of violence.[6] The Palestinian factions then turned to the use of high-trajectory weapons. These rockets have proven to be less lethal than human bombs; however, they have had a profound psychological impact.

Two criteria should serve as the basis for evaluating Israeli counterterrorism policy: effectiveness and democratic acceptability. On both measures, Israel does not score very high. Despite Israel's continuous efforts to find effective counterterrorism policies, Palestinian terrorism has never ceased. In fact, it has only intensified over the years. One of the prevailing myths in Israeli popular discourse is that "Arabs understand only the language of force." This myth has been reflected in the counterterrorism measures employed by the state. Harsh measures have always been preferred over more moderate ones. When those measures have proven futile, even harsher tools have been adopted. At the same time, the root causes of Palestinian terrorism have not been addressed. Israeli officials have never considered the seizing of Palestinian lands and the proliferation of Jewish settlements in the West Bank as terrorism-motivating factors. The outcome has been devastating for both societies. In the following sections, we offer and then test a framework aimed at explaining what led Israel to a situation in which its democratic foundations have been compromised and at the same time terrorism has not disappeared.

Israel's Counterterrorism Policies and the Quality of Democracy: A Framework for Analysis

The paradox of democratic countries being confronted with the challenges of terrorism has preoccupied scholars for years. The essence of this paradox is that an effective struggle against terrorism exacts a high toll in terms of the basic civil rights that a democratic regime should offer its citizens and residents (Chalk 1995; Crenshaw 2001; Schmid 1992; Wilkinson 2000). Two models have been proposed to describe the two extremes of this paradox. The "war" model assumes that terrorism is an act of war that challenges the legitimate foundations of the state or political system and therefore amounts to a serious threat that must be fought aggressively with military force and civilian intelligence agencies. Hence, this model mostly rejects the conventional constraints of democratic acceptability (Crelinsten and Schmid 1992; Chalk 1995; Sederberg 1995). The "criminal justice" model, on the other hand, approaches terrorism as a violent criminal action in the civilian sphere; hence, the struggle against the elements of terrorism should be undertaken by the police force and the legal system (Crelinsten and Schmid 1992; Clutterbuck 2004; Pedahzur and Ranstorp 2001; Wilkinson 1986, 125). Generally lacking in the studies that have examined the implementation of these models are answers to these questions: Why do certain countries adhere to a specific model? And under which conditions might they shift to the other?

Most counterterrorism practices employed by Israel correspond with the war model in its most extreme version (Ganor 2003, 48; Catignani 2005a, 2005b). The results of Israeli policy have been in total contrast to the country's initial goals: Israeli practices have generated poor outcomes, and Palestinian animosity toward Israel has only increased. These effects have played into the hands of the different insurgent groups and led to an escalation in terrorist campaigns. At the same time, the quality of Israeli democracy has declined, and Israel's standing as the only democracy in the Middle East has been compromised. For example, the ongoing adoption of war model–type measures over the years has reduced the ability of a growing proportion of Israeli residents to exercise basic civil and political rights. The Palestinian population from the West Bank and Gaza, Israeli Arabs, and, in the last decade, left-wing activists have all suffered from a diminished ability to organize politically, to engage in effective political protest, and to sustain their civil rights.[7] Other signs of the decline in the democratic foundations of the Israeli state have been the dramatic upsurge in administrative detentions, from several hundred during the early 1970s to more than ten thousand during the 1990s,[8] the growing use of military force in security assignments in the interstate civilian arena, and a sharp drop in public trust in political and legal institutions. At the same time, levels of trust in the military establishment have remained very high, partly owing to the dominant role of the military sector in the implementation of the war model, as well as the minor role of the civilian leadership, which in many cases has been perceived as trying to diminish the military efforts to combat terrorism effectively.

In this chapter, we offer a framework for explaining Israel's paradoxical decision to adhere to the war model. The aim of terrorism is to create fear. As a result, terrorized populations in democratic countries are expected to apply pressure on elites to make concessions (Pape 2003, 2005). On the other hand, humans who face such threats tend to react with force (Hobfoll, Canetti-Nisim, and Johnson 2006). Politically, this means that in times of security crises individuals "rally around the flag" and automatically support their leaders (Bennett 1990; Mueller 1970; Scheufele, Nisbet, and Ostman 2005). Israelis are no different. In times of intense terrorist threats, they show high levels of support for militant policies as well as an almost absolute trust in the armed forces (Ben-Dor, Pedahzur, and Hasisi 2003). Contrary to the argument presented by those who advocate an "elitist theory of tolerance," according to which the political elite is less inclined to choose the militant path (Sullivan et al. 1993), the Israeli parliamentary elite tends to reflect the attitudes of its constituents (Pedahzur 2003, 132–33). As a parliamentary democracy, Israel has an executive branch that is elected by the legislature, and hence policymakers themselves tend to exhibit ideas similar to those of Parliament members. However, the consistent adherence to the militant route cannot be attributed only to the desire of politicians to satisfy the demands of their constituents or even their own primordial fears. Israel reflects a "nation in arms" culture (Ben-Eliezer 2001).[9] The elite units of the armed forces and the intelligence community have become equivalent to the old boy network of Ivy League universities in the United States. Israeli political leadership is recruited from the armed forces. Leaders who have spent most of their lives in uniform find it hard to look beyond military solutions (Peri 2006, 21–22; Kober 2001; Wald 1987) and often tend to favor the recommendations made by their buddies in the security establishment to which they formerly belonged (Peri 2006, 21–22; Inbar 1998). The major role of the security establishment in Israel has also had a significant impact on leaders with little military experience. Many of them are inclined to regard the military and intelligence communities as the most significant authority when security affairs and foreign relations are at stake (Peri 2003). Since the Ministry of Defense, the intelligence community, and especially the army have their own interests and preferences, they often formulate and present alternative modes of operation to policymakers in ways that lead to decisions that conform with their preferences (Shelah and Limor 2007, 55). Despite the fact that the power of the army in Israel is far more "silent" in comparison to the role of the military in other democracies—most prominently Turkey—some scholars argue that the immense influence of the military elite on Israeli political systems, as well as the wide support it enjoys from the Israeli public, enables it to usurp the policymaking process (Peri 2006, 81; Inbar 1998; Wald 1987; Lissak 1998; Ben-Eliezer 1995b).

The tendency of both the legislative and executive branches to give preference to offensive measures leaves the burden of defending the foundations of the Israeli democracy on the Supreme Court. Most scholars agree that the court, especially under the leadership of former chief justice Aharon Barak, who advocated "judicial activism," has been the most prominent force standing up for the protection of the democratic foundations of the state. Justices are not recruited from the "security elite," have no commitment to a specific constituency, and most often benefit from a broad educational background with emphasis on constitutional law and the legal foundations of democracies.[10] Yet, not everyone agrees with this argument. According to Baruch Kimmerling (2002) and Yoram Peri (2006, 171–72), the Supreme Court is not so different from the other branches of government and tends to marginalize democratic principles when they do not correspond with security needs. According to Peri (2006), this tendency is reflected in the many decisions made in relation to Israel's counterterrorism policies over the last two decades, especially during the Al-Aqsa Intifada.

To sum up our argument, Israel has been led to implement the war model of counterterrorism by the tendency of its political leadership to try to satisfy its constituency, which leads to a demand for extreme counterterrorism measures; by a "nation in arms" culture that is manifested in the military establishment's extensive influence on the political leadership; and by the Supreme Court's tendency to avoid confrontations with military establishment policies. In the following analysis of five recent Israeli counterterrorism policies, we confirm our contention that the outcome of Israel's adoption of the war model has in fact been an escalation of violence and a negative influence on the quality of the Israeli democracy.

The Demolition of Houses

The idea of demolishing the houses of families of terrorists was introduced by Israel in the late 1960s. However, this policy was applied as a measure of deterrence only in the late 1980s, following the outbreak of the first Intifada. Initially, the Israeli Ministry of Defense, headed by the late Yitzhak Rabin and with the backing of the Israeli Supreme Court and a bloc of central and right parties in the Israeli Parliament (which held the majority of seats in the Knesset at the time), enforced this measure against the families of youngsters who were involved in street riots.[11] Most of the legislators as well as the Supreme Court justices accepted the security establishment's underlying assumption that the importance of the "house" and "land" concepts to the Palestinians would make parents put pressure on their teenage sons to refrain from joining the ranks of the protesters. By the time the Oslo Accords were signed, 432 houses had been demolished. No proof has been provided demonstrating that this policy had any effect on the cessation of the Intifada (Shalev 1990, 127–29).

Nevertheless, the ascendance of suicide terrorism led Israel to reenact this policy in the anticipation that the pain inflicted on their families would deter suicide bombers and their dispatchers. Seventeen houses were demolished between 1996 and 1997. Increasing doubts among Israeli policymakers regarding the effectiveness of this measure, however, led to a complete halt of its enforcement. But then the unprecedented number of suicide attacks perpetrated during the first two years of the Al-Aqsa Intifada led the Sharon cabinet to reconsider its policies. On July 31, 2002, the Israeli government decided to reintroduce this measure. From the summer of 2002 until January 2005, 668 houses were torn down.[12]

Interestingly enough, the decision to abandon this policy was not the outcome of increasing international pressure or concern about the serious human rights issues it provoked; rather, it was based on the conclusion of a military investigation committee that the policy was futile.[13] An analysis of the inconsistent statements made by Israeli policymakers and military officials regarding the effectiveness of house demolitions over the years essentially reflects their helplessness and confusion. As early as 1988, former chief of staff Dan Shomron explained to the Foreign Relations and Security Parliamentary Committee that the house demolition policy could provoke a backlash in the long run.[14] Seventeen years later, his assessment was proven correct. No correlation has ever been found between the house demolition policy and a reduction in the number of suicide attacks.[15] In point of fact, over the years it became evident that the parents of suicide bombers rarely knew that their children intended to perpetrate such attacks, and so they never had an opportunity to stop them.[16] The organizations and networks to which the suicide bombers belonged reassured them that their families would not be harmed. Many families were in fact compensated financially, either by the organizations or the states that supported them.[17] Moreover, during the years of the Al-Aqsa Intifada, it became quite obvious that the bombers themselves had a relatively small role in perpetrating the attacks (Pedahzur and Perliger 2006). Some of them were highly indoctrinated, while others were motivated by vengeance. Deterrence seems to have been irrelevant under the circumstances.

From a different aspect, Israel's argument that the demolition of houses was one component in a legitimate war against terrorism was received with a significant degree of distrust by the international media, by civil right movements throughout the world and in Israel, and by several Knesset members from left-wing parties.[18] The latter two groups led a continuous campaign to coerce the Israeli government into altering its policy, which they claimed was actually aimed at innocent civilians and which harmed the Palestinians' right to shelter. Furthermore, it was often being implemented out of military operational considerations other than deterrence.[19] Naturally, this campaign undermined the attempts of the Israeli Ministry of Foreign Affairs to portray Israel as the real victim of terrorism.

A review of the Supreme Court's verdicts on the subject of the demolition of houses reinforces our earlier suggestion that the Supreme Court tends to close ranks with the policies presented by the political elite and the security establishment. The policy of house demolitions is not part of the Israeli Penal Code. It is an administrative procedure adopted by Israel from the British Mandate Defense Regulations (1945).[20] The mandate to apply this regulation was grounded in the fact that, since the day it was established, Israel has been under a constant "state of emergency" made legislatively possible every year by a repeated—almost automatic—vote in the Knesset. The relatively liberal stance of the Supreme Court on domestic political issues is not reflected in its decisions regarding Palestinian issues

(Kimmerling 2002). Palestinians who received a notice from the military authorities that their house was about to be demolished filed over 150 appeals to the Supreme Court. Only in a smattering of these cases did the justices veto the execution of the decision (Kretzmer 2002, 145–70).[21] A review of the court's decisions confirms that in the majority of cases the justices declared that they were highly concerned about the fact that the act of demolition was injurious to basic civil rights and that they also demanded from the security authorities substantial proof that the specified demolition would in fact improve security.[22] Nonetheless, in the absolute majority of cases, and although the material presented by the state was not always fully convincing, they accepted unanimously the security establishment's argument that the demolition policy had proven to be a highly effective tool of deterrence against future terrorists as well as a legitimate policy for solving immediate security issues, such as using the policy to destroy buildings that had been used as cover for terrorists ambushing IDF convoys.[23] The courts approved the demolition by claiming that it was crucial in order to save the lives of Israeli citizens and that the policy's harm to civil rights was proportional to its benefits.

As noted earlier, despite the fact that the state made a very compelling argument in court regarding the expediency of this policy, the Ministry of Defense abandoned it altogether because it proved ineffective.

It can be concluded that the policy of house demolitions did not deter terrorists, but rather increased the animosity of Palestinians toward Israel. Moreover, it severely undermined some of the basic foundations of a democratic regime, such as the dictates to avoid collective punishments and to adhere to the laws that enforce domestic and international civil liberties (Shnayderman 2004, 44).

Targeted Killings

Another tactic that draws attention to the dilemma of finding a balance between counterterrorism courses of action and democratic values is the policy of "targeted killings." These days, "targeted killings" have become almost synonymous with air strikes aimed at insurgents and their leaders. This measure has been utilized extensively by Israel since the outbreak of the Al-Aqsa Intifada. The initial aim of this method was to stop "ticking bombs." In other words, when all other measures had been exhausted, targeted killings were supposed to strike at terrorists who were dispatched on a deadly mission (Byman and Dicter 2006). However, as indicated by Yuval Diskin, head of the General Security Service (GSS) and the person responsible for developing this tactic, its use quickly expanded from "ticking bombs" to "ticking infrastructures." This vague term refers to dispatchers and local leaders of terrorist cells.[24] By 2004 it had become obvious that the targets of this policy had expanded once more and now included political leaders of different Palestinian factions, such as Ahmed Yassin and Abdel Aziz al-Rantissi.

Assassinations of Palestinian militants are not new to the Israeli-Palestinian conflict. Following the massacre of eleven athletes in the Munich Olympic Games, the Israeli cabinet led by Golda Meir launched operations Wrath of God and Spring of Youth during which Mossad agents and special military forces—most prominently Sayeret Matkal—were deployed to assassinate members of the Fatah and the Popular Front for the Liberation of Palestine (PFLP) in Europe and Lebanon (Goren, August 16, 2006).[25] Both of these operations enjoyed consensual support in the Knesset as well as with the Israeli public (Klein 2006, 94–101). A decade after the end of this campaign, on April 16, 1988, the Israeli elite units Sayeret Matkal and Shayetet 13, aided by Mossad operatives, landed on a Tunisian beach and raided the house of one of the five founders of the Fatah, Khalil Al-Wazir, also known as Abu Jihad.[26] He was killed in his living room while his wife and children looked on (Zonder 2000, 244–45). More than seven years later, two men riding a motorcycle shot Fathi Shaqaqi, the leader of the Palestinian Islamic Jihad, at close range, in the town of Sliema in Malta. Despite the fact that Israel never acknowledged its involvement in the killing, it is widely accepted that members of Kidon—the Mossad's operational unit—pulled off this attack.[27] At any rate, in this case as well, most of the Israeli public and the political echelons did not dispute the legitimacy of the method of operation (Druker and Shelah 2005, 158–59, 162).

The basic procedure leading to such killings has not changed much over the years. The Israeli prime minister, heads of the intelligence community and the IDF, and sometimes the government legal counsel serve as an unofficial tribunal—formerly known as the X Committee (Ganor 2003, 148). They review the case of each target, look for moral justification to launch the operation, and discuss its potential legal and political outcomes (Navot, August 14, 2006). During the Al-Aqsa Intifada, the process gradually became much more expeditious and centralized owing to the frequency of its use as well as the close relationship that evolved between the head of the GSS, Avi Dichter, and Prime Minister Ariel Sharon. When an opportunity for such an action was indicated by intelligence, Dichter and Sharon got together and decided by themselves whether or not to carry out the assassination. Also, significant tactical changes were made. In the past, Israel relied heavily on Mossad operatives and special units. In some cases, such as the January 5, 1996, assassination of Yahya Ayyash ("The Engineer"), one of the masterminds of the Hamas suicide bombing tactic, a more sophisticated method was chosen. GSS operatives planted an explosive device in his cell phone and remote-activated the device when he tried to answer the call they had placed.[28] A year and a half later, an attempt to kill Hamas political leader Khaled Mashal by poison injection in Amman failed and led to a major diplomatic scandal (Ganor 2003, 75–78). As mentioned earlier, during the years of the Al-Aqsa Intifada, this policy became almost routine. Air force Apache helicopter pilots executed most of the killings while receiving real-time tactical intelligence from the General Security Service (Harhel and Issacharoff 2004).

As with the house demolition policy, neither the Israeli security establishment nor the academic community agreed on the moral justifications (Gross 2003; Kretzmer 2005) or effectiveness of the assassination policy; nevertheless, they assumed that its aim was to diminish the capabilities of different terrorist groups in perpetrating attacks against Israel (Byman 2006; Hafez and Hatfield 2006).

While some argue that this policy forces terrorist leaders to focus all their efforts on ensuring their own survival and hence impairs their ability to perpetrate further attacks (Byman 2006), others note that the loose network structure of the Palestinian groups diminishes the effect of the killing of a specific person (Pedahzur and Perliger 2006). Moreover, the extensive use of targeted killings by air strikes often kills innocent noncombatants—otherwise known as "collateral damage." The most blatant example was the incident of the targeted killing of Salah Shahada, an influential Hamas leader in the Gaza Strip. The bomb that was dropped on his house, which weighed more than 2,200 pounds, killed him and fifteen others, including innocent children and women. Events such as these increase the level of animosity toward Israel not only among the groups whose activists were killed but also in the victimized community (Bloom 2004). The outcome is revenge operations that enjoy the support of the community (Hafez and Hatfield 2006).

As with the house demolition policy, public debate regarding this policy was almost completely absent from the Israeli public arena as well as from the legislative branch.[29] Several reasons can be provided in explanation. First, the unprecedented waves of suicide attacks on the Israeli streets had led the Israeli public and its leaders to adopt any "medicine" introduced by the security establishment for especially violent acts and made it easier to disregard the problematic moral issues—that is, the fact that the state was in effect imposing death sentences, sometimes en masse, without going through standard legal procedures. The feeling among the public was that terrorism had become a strategic threat; hence, moral issues should be set aside until the survival of the collective was ensured (Arian 2003). Second, the security establishment, at least in the first years of the Intifada, strongly supported this tactic and considered it part of the Israeli security forces' long-running offensive legacy of bringing the war to the enemy's territory. The great influence of the security leadership in the decisionmaking process regarding security issues, as well as the high levels of trust it enjoyed among the Israeli public, silenced almost every voice that doubted the effectiveness of the targeted killings.[30] The fact that most of the central political figures in the government at the time of the Intifada were veterans of the security establishment who highly supported the offensive approach of targeted killings and acts of retaliation (Ariel Sharon, Benjamin Ben-Eliezer, Shaul Mofaz, and Ehud Barak) only facilitated the security establishment's ability to make a case for the adoption of these methods and to silence the objectors. Finally, in many cases it was even argued that targeted killings served domestic political purposes rather than real counterterrorism needs (Harhel and Issacharoff 2004, 195). By availing themselves of the high profile of assassination operations, political leaders aspired to show the public that they were in effect winning the battle against terrorism. Accordingly, these same political leaders were motivated to use their power to reduce any moral controversy regarding this policy in the public or political arena.

The fact that even the Israeli judicial system found its own ways to refrain from condemning this policy also contributed to the absence of any genuine public debate on the subject. The attorney general and military legal advisers drafted guidelines for the implementation of targeted killings that were ambiguous enough to include different scenarios (Harhel and Issacharoff 2004, 200). In general, justification for assassinations was provided when there was reasonable indication that the actions of some figures could lead to the harm of Israeli civilians. As for the Supreme Court, it dragged its feet for almost five years and refrained from addressing appeals filed by Palestinians regarding the legality of this policy, some of which dated back to the year 2001.[31] Without providing any type of rationale for its evasive conduct, the Supreme Court thus approved de facto the implementation of the policy. Finally, in December 2005, the court announced its decision. The panel of justices, which included retiring president Aaron Barak, the newly appointed president Dorit Bienisch, and the vice president Mishael Cheshin, unanimously decided that the use of targeted killings could be continued. They acknowledged the security establishment's contention that this method was crucial for defending the citizens' safety and right to security. At the same time, however, they introduced several conditions for carrying out this method in an attempt to ensure that it would do as little harm as possible to the state's democratic foundations. More specifically, the Supreme Court concluded in its decision that Palestinian terrorist suspects should not enjoy the rights provided to soldiers by law of war, since they were not "legal warriors" as defined by international law. The justices also noted that terrorists were actually illegal warriors—civilians who participated in hostile actions and engaged in war against the state—and thus should not enjoy any immunity from state forces and operations. The justices emphasized, however, that these civilians should be targeted only under several conditions. The targeted figures should be *directly* and *continually* involved in hostile counterstate violent operations, which could include the transportation and financing of terrorists as well as involvement in intelligence operations. Moreover, they should be targeted only when there was no other means of restraining them or preventing their activities. As for collateral damage, here the court used the term "proportionality": the authorities should verify whether the benefits of the targeted killings justified the potential harm to innocent civilians.

To conclude, as many critics of the decision pointed out, the Supreme Court in fact "decided not to decide" and in this way legitimized the execution of civilians en masse without adequate regulation from the legal system or due process.

The Question of Citizenship

According to the Israeli "Law of Return," the state's major immigration law, an individual who can provide evidence of his or her ascription to the Jewish nation by offering proof that one of his or her grandparents was a Jew is automatically granted citizenship. The ability of individuals who cannot provide evidence of such a relationship to gain citizenship is much more limited.

Apart from the relatively large community of foreign workers, Israeli immigration policy mostly affects Palestinians. Since the establishment of the State of Israel, the close ties between the Palestinian citizens of Israel and the Palestinians who reside in Jordan and Egypt (and later the Palestinians of the Palestinian National Authority) have not weakened. Many of them belong to the same extended families—families that have been torn apart by wars and changing borders (Kadman 1999, 19). These ties have naturally led to a relatively high rate of marriage among Palestinians on both sides of the border. One of the major benefits for Palestinians who marry citizens of Israel is the chance to live in a more prosperous environment and sometimes to even secure citizenship (Kadman 1999, 18). Moreover, over the years the Israeli and Palestinian economies have become interdependent. Palestinian workers from the West Bank and Gaza became the dominant workforce in the Israeli economy in the construction business, in most of the services, and in unskilled jobs. On the other hand, the majority of the Palestinian population became dependent on the jobs provided by the Israeli economy for their livelihood.[32]

In 1993, six years after the outbreak of the first Intifada, and as a result of the upsurge of terrorist knifing attacks, Israel closed its gates to the majority of the Palestinian workers. The minister of defense, Yitzhak Rabin, explained the decision in his own words: "We are in a major dilemma; closing the gates will harm thousands of Palestinian workers, but terrorism must be stopped" (quoted in Soffer 1993). Many of those Palestinian workers had married into the families of Palestinian citizens of Israel. The previously open borders between Israel and Palestinian lands had allowed them to move freely, and thus many of them never went to the trouble of trying to obtain Israeli citizenship. The new "closure policy" led to an increase in the number of citizenship applications filed by Palestinians. Most of them just wanted to be able to live with their spouses and children in Israel.[33] For the Israeli ministries of defense and interior, this was an unexpected and undesired outcome. First, they feared that Palestinians who were granted a citizen or permanent resident status would help facilitate terrorist attacks (Stein 2006). Second, there were rising concerns that Israel would be flooded by Palestinians who would then become citizens and pose a "demographic threat" to the Jewish character of the state (Amnesty International 2004).[34]

In 1999, following a petition to the Supreme Court by Palestinians who alleged that they had been subjected to discrimination, the State of Israel promised to modify its policy and allow Palestinians who married Israeli citizens temporary resident status in Israel, which then might be convertible into permanent status after five years (Kohn 2006).[35] By 2002, however, two years into the Al-Aqsa Intifada, the state had backed off its promise and decided to freeze the process. The official reason offered by the General Security Service was that terrorist cells from the West Bank were exploiting this security breach and had recruited at least twenty Palestinian men who had temporary resident status to help carry out suicide attacks in Israel (Internal Affairs Committee of the Knesset Protocol, July 14, 2003).[36]

A year later, in the summer of 2003, by a majority of fifty-three to twenty-five, the Israeli Parliament amended its Citizenship Law in a way that enabled the state to decline permanent residence and citizenship applications on the basis of security reasons (Davidov et al. 2004). The Arab parties as well as the left-wing parties of Meretz and Labor opposed the law, declaring it a black stain on Israeli democracy that harmed Israel's democratic foundations by discriminating against a large number of its citizens on ethnic grounds and showing the Israeli regime to be greatly insensitive to the humanitarian problem caused by the law. However, the other central, right, and religious parties placed security concerns above democratic acceptability and supported the law, and many of them also did not hesitate to declare that the law was an effective mechanism in preventing changes in the demographic balance between Jews and Arabs.

Two years later, in the wake of the decline in the number of suicide attacks, the ongoing pressure of civil rights organizations, and the fear that the law would not stand up to the scrutiny of the Supreme Court, several of the Citizenship Law restrictions were waived. The fact that Prime Minister Sharon needed the support of the left-wing parties for the approval of his disengagement plan also helped. According to the new amendment, Palestinian men above the age of thirty-five and women above the age of twenty-five were eligible for resident status upon marrying a citizen of Israel. The revision of the law was approved only following an authorization of the head of the General Security Service, who assured the legislature that older Palestinians in these age groups were less likely to become suicide bombers.[37] This amendment was criticized by Israeli civil rights organizations, the European Union, and the United Nations for violating human rights based on ethnic or nationalist prejudice.[38]

The Israeli Supreme Court was asked to address this issue, and its ruling was one of the most dramatic resolutions ever passed by this court. In May 2006, following months of deliberations, a decision was finally made. Six justices accepted the state's reasoning, while five others contested it. The justices who approved the law contended that they were convinced that the law was crucial in order to defend the citizens of Israel from terrorism and that violations of human rights by the law were proportional given the security threats posed by Palestinians. The justices who rejected the state's position argued that other available alternatives would cause less offense to civil liberties than the current problematic law (such as individual scrutiny of those applying for Israeli citizenship) and that its harm to the democratic foundations of the state, and especially the right to equality and family life, was much greater than its benefits. These justices reinforced their claims by stating that absolute security was not reachable, hence the state should take reasonable risks in order to preserve its democratic foundations.

At any rate, the Supreme Court again issued a stamp of legitimacy to the highly repressive Israeli response to terrorism. In June 2006, backed by this verdict, the government formed a new committee whose aim was to draft new legislation that would make the process of becoming an Israeli citizen even more difficult.

The "Security Fence" or the "Apartheid Wall"?

The barrier that Israel has been erecting between its territory and Palestinian land has led to various semantic debates, as illustrated in the title to this section; more importantly, the barrier has also provoked political and legal debates.[39] Two main questions have been discussed in public and legal forums since late 2001: Is Israel allowed to pursue a unilateral decision regarding the creation of a border? And is it legal to annex Palestinian lands while pursuing this policy?

The decision to establish the barrier was reached only in 2002, in the midst of a continuous campaign of suicide attacks in the Israeli heartland. However, the fact that the overwhelming majority of suicide bombers entered Israeli territory from the West Bank with no difficulty (Israel Ministry of Defense 2004), as well as the fact that a security fence built around the Gaza Strip had almost completely prevented the infiltration of Palestinians from this region to Israel, led the military and the Ministry of Defense to promote the idea of a "barrier" as a temporary security measure long before it was adopted. Yet for a long time it was rejected by both Palestinians and Israeli right-wing political parties.[40] While the Palestinians were hoping to reach an agreement that would serve as a basis for the erection of an international border between two viable states, the Israeli settler movement feared that such a barrier would eventually become a permanent border and lead to the isolation and even dismantling of settlements on the eastern side of the wall.

Yet the overwhelming number of civilian casualties in the Israeli heartland forced the cabinet led by Ariel Sharon to pursue the "seam zone" plan.[41] This idea was to create a barrier between Israeli and Palestinian territories that would consist of two layers of a "smart electronic fence" and a buffer zone between them as well as on both outer sides. The width of the barrier was designed to be between fifty and seventy meters.[42] Only 4 percent of the total barrier length, mostly in Jerusalem, has been built as a concrete wall (Israel Ministry of Defense 2006).

It was extremely important for the Sharon cabinet to emphasize that the barrier was a temporary security measure taken against suicide bombers. However, neither the Palestinians nor the settlers accepted this argument, both sides contending that Israel was actually trying to create a fait accompli on the ground and unilaterally establish the future border between the two states.[43]

In the short run, the barrier seemed to be a success story, at least from the Israeli point of view. The dramatic decrease in the number of successful suicide attacks was presented by Israel as the major reason for its continuous efforts to complete the project. Yet it is important to note that there were other views. For example, Avi Dichter, former head of the General Security Service and minister for internal security, gave more credit to Israeli HUMINT (intelligence information obtained from human sources) in the West Bank, which made it feasible to stop the perpetration of suicide attacks in the planning stages.[44]

Doubts about the short-term effectiveness of the barrier are minor, however, in comparison to the skepticism over its long-term implications. As mentioned earlier, the legitimacy of the barrier is debated with regard to different issues. Although both the majority of Palestinians and the international community may have accepted the idea of a partition erected on the "Green Line" (the pre-1967 border),[45] the route of the fence proposed by Israel has been severely criticized by the International Court in The Hague, among many others.[46] According to the Israeli executive branch, security needs call for the inclusion of Palestinian lands in the areas surrounded by the fence. As a result, Palestinian farmers are cut off from their fields, which now serve as part of the "buffer zone." In Jerusalem, where the route of the fence is particularly complicated, neighborhoods have been split in two by the wall—a situation that is tearing families apart and that prevents individuals from getting to their workplaces as well as from receiving medical and other services.[47] Another major issue is the security of the Jewish settlers in the West Bank. Checkpoints and fences surround other population centers in the West Bank and are aimed at protecting settlers residing on the eastern side of the West Bank; the barrier is not meant to replace this security system.[48] Consequently, not only are Palestinians unable to move freely into Israeli territory, but in many cases it is almost impossible to move from one Palestinian town to another.[49]

The barrier was marketed to the Israeli public as an immediate remedy for the suicide bombings phenomenon, and hence, unsurprisingly, approval rates for completing the barrier are consistently very high.[50] Most Israelis do not know about the problems created by the course-plotting of the fence, and even those who do have an idea show very little understanding of Palestinian needs.[51] For them, the most important issue is to halt terrorism in the short run. This is a myopic perspective that does not take into consideration the fact that the unilateral erection of a barrier that annexes Palestinian lands and imposes more restrictions on civilians only intensifies the animosity and fuels the motivation among Palestinians to retaliate.[52]

While policymakers express widespread support for the barrier plan in their statements and actions, the Supreme Court—which, as mentioned, backed the security establishment on issues such as house demolitions, the Citizenship Law, and to a certain extent the targeted killings policy—has adopted a more active approach. The comparatively more active role of the court in this case is a result of several factors. To begin with, the harm to civil liberties caused by the fence was much more salient and included large sections of the Palestinian population—indeed, entire villages—whereas previous measures injured a smaller portion of the population. Moreover, while the counterterrorism measures of targeted killings and house demolitions were directed against the offenders and their families, the victims in the case of the fence were a vast civilian population whose connection to terrorism was negligible. Finally, while it is hard to find effective alternatives to targeted killings and the Citizenship Law, creating new routes for the fence that would lessen the harm to innocent Palestinians was a relatively simpler action.

Although justices generally have given a lot of weight to the state's position and thus authorized the confiscation of Palestinian lands for security purposes, they again emphasize the concept of "proportionality" forcing the state to strike a balance between its security needs and the basic human rights of Palestinians.[53] Moreover, the state was severely criticized by Chief Justice Aharon Barak when it appeared that in some places the barrier route was dictated by political rather than security considerations.[54] All in all, decisions made by the Israeli Supreme Court in regard to the route of the barrier were much more convenient for the Israeli security establishment than the rulings handed down by the International Court of Justice. However, the International Court's pronouncement was never enforced, owing to a lack of jurisdiction,[55] but decisions made by the Israeli Supreme Court have forced the Ministry of Defense more than once to tear down parts of the barrier and rebuild it closer to the Green Line.[56] The last Supreme Court decision in this vein was given on September 4, 2007, when the court ordered the state to again reroute the fence near the village of Belien. In the original route, Israel had annexed more than two thousand square miles of village lands. With the new route, most of the village lands were returned to village residents.

Tolerance in Parliament

The only question on which the Supreme Court has forcefully confronted the legislature has been in regard to party disqualification. The first decision to ban political parties from taking part in parliamentary elections was issued by the Supreme Court in 1965. The court disqualified the Arab Nationalist party Al-Ard (the Socialist List), arguing that its platform undermined the right of Israel to exist as a Jewish state. In the beginning of the 1980s, with the increase in public support for Kach, Rabbi Kahane's racist political party, party prohibition became central on the public agenda. The concern that extreme parties such as Kach would take advantage of the Israeli elections system's relatively lenient conditions of competition raised the need to institutionalize regulating mechanisms that would keep in check such possibly excessive attitudes.[57] In 1985 an amendment to the Basic Law, Knesset 7(a), declared that those parties whose platform rejected the Jewish character of the state or its democratic foundations would not be allowed to compete in the political arena.

In countries such as France, India, Germany, and Spain, for every appeal of the disqualification of a political party, a dialogue is conducted between the executive and legislative authorities, on the one hand, and the judicial authority, on the other (Nolte and Fox 1995). In Israel, however, the status of the legislative authority is especially significant because the Central Elections Committee (CEC) is the first legal instance in which an appeal for the disqualification of a political party is deliberated. It is also important to note that this committee is composed of delegates from different political parties and led by the head of the Supreme Court and that its original function consisted mainly of supervision over the electoral procedure. The Supreme Court plays a role only as a second instance.

Toward the end of the year 2000, a short while after the eruption of the Al-Aqsa Intifada, the Knesset plenary session became the scene of a struggle between Arab members of the Knesset who intensified their objections to the Israeli occupation and expressed support for the Palestinian uprising and Jewish members who regarded the uprising as insupportable behavior (Schueftan 2002). Justice Mishael Cheshin, who was already in the position of chairman of the Central Elections Committee for the elections to the Sixteenth Knesset and who was aware of the increasing tensions, signaled that despite these tensions in the Knesset he had no intention of readily endorsing decisions that would lead to the disqualification of lists, including those that rejected the Jewish character of the state. As far as certain Knesset members were concerned, this state of affairs could not be tolerated. At the end of the year 2001, the Knesset passed the initiative proposed by member of parliament (MP) Yisrael Katz from the Likud relating to section 7(a). Apart from the fact that it was now possible to disqualify individual candidates as well as lists, the significant alteration in the revised version of the section was that in addition to the clause that enabled the disqualification of an Arab party by reason of its rejection of the Jewish character of the State of Israel, it was now possible to ban a list or a candidate also on the basis of their support for the armed struggle of a hostile country or terrorist organization against the State of Israel (Pedahzur 2003).

However, this was only the tip-off to the events that then took place at the Central Elections Committee (CEC). The CEC had to decide on three weighty issues closely linked to the delicate balance between the protection of the governing system and basic democratic liberties. Specifically, these were the debates on the matter of one racist Jewish list—Herut—and the issue of MPs Ahmad Tibi and Azmi Bishara and the Balad list. In these three cases, representatives from the political elite acted in polarized dissent against the position of the CEC chairman so that ultimately Baruch Marzel, the head of Herut and a well-known Jewish militant candidate, was approved, while MPs Tibi and Bishara, both of whom were never accused of involvement in terrorism, were disqualified. Eleven justices of the Supreme Court who presided over these three cases unanimously elected to overturn the CEC decision and authorized Ahmad Tibi's candidature. Furthermore, a majority of seven judges against four ruled in approval of the candidacy of Azmi Bishara. Only in the case of Baruch Marzel, once again with a majority of seven-to-four, did the original CEC decision remain unaffected.

As might have been anticipated, activists from the political elites did not remain indifferent to the Supreme Court's decision. A few hours after the announcement of the Supreme Court's ruling, the chairman of the right-wing "National Unity" list, MP Avigdor Lieberman, stated that once again he was witness to a patronizing body that was both disparaging of the Israeli parliament and oblivious to the public's inner feelings. He promised to take immediate action and establish an institutional court. The position of the chairman of the National Religious Party, Efi Eitam, was not much different and reflected the stance of the rest of the right-wing faction on the CEC. In his opinion, the Supreme Court had passed a resolution that was unreceptive to the disposition of a public who was compelled to hear, at the height of a war with scores of casualties, words in praise of terrorism (Shmueli and Sumphalbi 2003).

Conclusion

The analyzed case studies show that time and again Israel has chosen to adopt counterterrorism measures that are unsuccessful in deterring the perpetrators of terrorism and that also fail to reduce the level of the violence and its intensity. Also, the fact that most of these measures are grave violations of basic civil rights and basic democratic principles, thus intensifying the decline in the quality of the Israeli democracy, has not led Israeli policymakers to seek alternative measures.

In addition to confirmation of these conclusions, we find that the paradoxical decision of Israeli policymakers to implement the measures discussed in this chapter resulted from the fact that they enjoyed the backing of the judicial system, from the influence on them of the security establishment's militant point of view, and especially from the influence of their constituents' demands for an extreme response. However, several more insights may be drawn from the Israeli case.

First, the intensity of violence has a direct influence on the type of measures the state tends to adopt and on how willing it is to sacrifice its democratic acceptability. In all the counterterrorism measures discussed here, the willingness of the political leadership to use them grew as Palestinian violence became more and more extensive, until its peak in 2002, when more than 1,400 Israelis were injured and around 391 were killed.

Second, this analysis supports the claim that "while public opinion does not govern, it may set limits on what governments do" (Qualter 1991). The relative dearth of public debate among the majority of the Israeli public on the moral dimensions of the enforced counterterrorism measures gave policymakers both the legitimization and the latitude to use measures that are a far cry from what is acceptable in a regime that adheres to the notion of being a liberal democracy. Moreover, in many cases the opposition (mostly from left-wing parties and movements) was depicted as holding treacherous views, a fact that intensified the legitimacy of the counterterrorism measures.

Finally, it seems that Israel's extreme response was also fostered by the fact that most of the Palestinian violence until mid-2002, when most of the measures discussed were implemented in the most extensive manner, resulted from the activities of fundamentalist and revolutionary groups that rejected any conciliatory process with Israel. This proposition—that democracies tend to act more forcefully against revolutionary groups—should of course be examined more meticulously, but at least in the Israeli case it seems to find some support.

To conclude, based on the failure to contain terrorism and on the deterioration of its democratic principles, it appears that Israel has no other choice but to "think outside the box" and revise its counterterrorism policies. Any such revision will involve rethinking the "war model" that has prevailed for decades and adopting a more flexible and "conciliatory" approach that will leave civilians outside the cycle of violence.

Notes

1. United Nations Resolution 181 was a solution designed to end the Jewish-Arab conflict in Palestine by partitioning Mandatory Palestine into two independent states, one Jewish and the other Arab. The resolution was based on the recommendations of the United Nations Special Committee on Palestine (UNSCOP) committee and set up by the United Nations in May 1947 following Great Britain's return of the mandate over Palestine. Resolution 181 was adopted by the General Assembly of the United Nations on November 29, 1947, with the support of thirty-three countries, the opposition of thirteen, and ten abstentions. See Avalon Project at Yale Law School, http://www.yale.edu/lawweb/avalon/un/res181.htm (accessed August 22, 2006).
2. The number of Palestinian refugees has long been a matter of dispute. Since 1949, Arab spokespeople have claimed that the number is between 900,000 and 1 million, while spokespeople for the Israeli government have usually set the number at about 520,000. The Economic Delegation of the United Nations and the United Nations Relief and Works Agency for Palestinian Refugees in the Near East (UNRWA) set the number at 726,000 people. Other estimates fall in between the numbers claimed by Israeli and Arab spokespeople. For example, in February 1949, the British set the number of refugees at 810,000—530,000 of them in the territory of Palestine and 280,000 in the other Arab countries. Palestinian refugees have also settled in various countries: in Jordan, there are 315,000; in Egypt, 177,000, in the Gaza Strip, 165,000; in Syria, 70,000; and in Lebanon, 70,000. The rest of the refugees settled in the Persian Gulf states. The civil status of these refugees also varies from country to country. In Lebanon only about one-quarter of the refugees have received Lebanese citizenship, either by marriage or by pressure from the various ethnic groups that succeeded in gaining citizenship for some of those who share their ethnicity. In Jordan all official rights were granted to refugees, but there is still concealed discrimination. In Syria refugees lack citizenship and political rights but are granted all social rights, and in Egypt refugees possess all civil rights, which were accorded to them in 1952. See Morris (1996, 19 [Hebrew]) and Ashbel and Soffer (2001, 16–17 [Hebrew]).
3. Following the Six-Day War (also known as the 1967 War), there were 950,000 Palestinians in the occupied territories (West Bank and Gaza) left over from the population of 1.4 million Palestinians prior to the war.

According to UNRWA data on the state of Palestinian refugees in 1972, during that year 278,255 registered refugees lived in the West Bank and another 567,324 registered refugees lived in the Gaza Strip. See Abu-Lughod (1971).

4. The first official settlement, Gush Etzion, was founded in September 1967; over the years 1967 to 2004, 118 additional settlements were founded and received official recognition from the Israeli government. Additionally, there are more than 100 unrecognized settlements in the West Bank. For a detailed discussion of the Israeli settlements in the West Bank, see Zertal and Eldar (2004).
5. The average number of casualties (both dead and wounded) in a suicide attack carried out by using an explosives-packed belt during the period 1993 to 2003 was 58.35, and the average number in a suicide car bomb was 43.59. By contrast, the number of casualties at this time from a bomb attack was 8.37 victims, from shooting 3.7, and from stabbing 1.6. Data available at: http://www.laits.utexas.edu/tiger (accessed August 17, 2006).
6. For example, in July 2001, 58 percent of the Palestinians in the Palestinian National Authority (PNA) supported armed attacks against Israeli civilians inside Israel, but by October 2003, 75 percent supported suicide attacks against Israeli civilian targets; see Palestinian Center for Policy and Survey Research (PSR) at: http://www.pcpsr.org/survey/index.html.
7. See "Incitement and Silencing Criticism," *Haaretz*, December 24, 2002; Efrat Wies and Roi Nahmias, "Jerusalem: The Islamic Movement Rally Was Dispersed," *Ynet News*, August 23, 2007, available at: http://www.ynet.co.il/articles/0,7340,L-3440909,00.html (accessed August 17, 2006).
8. Abraham Pachter, "Administrative Detention: Overview," *NFS*, February 26, 2004, available at: http://www.nfc.co.il/Archive/0018-D-5186-00.html?tag=00-10-03 (accessed August 17, 2006).
9. The notion refers to a model in which the boundaries between the military sector and the civilian sector are inconsistent, and thus the two sectors interact in a wide range of situations. While some scholars see the Israeli case of a "nation in arms" as a response to survival and nation construction needs (see Luckham 1971), others perceive it as a political means of legitimizing solutions to political problems with military means (see Ben-Eliezer 1995a).
10. Moshe Hanegbi, "Yes, Beheading Heads," *Haaretz*, October 8, 2006 (Hebrew); Shlomo Cohen, "The Public Trust the Supreme Court," *Israel Attorneys Journal* (February 2003), available at: http://www.israelbar.org.il/article_inner.asp?catID=193&pgID=26718 (Hebrew).
11. Gerta G. LaBelle, "Troops Raze Houses, Settlers to Make Own Arrests," Associated Press, January 26, 1989; see also Israeli High Court of Justice, plea 4112/90 (September 24 and 24, 1990; October 31, 1990); Knesset Protocol, August 22, 1988; February 21, 1989; February 7, 1990.
12. For statistics on house demolitions carried out by Israel, see B'tselem, "House Demolitions as Punishment: Statistics on Punitive House Demolitions," avail-

able at: http://www.btselem.org/english/Punitive_Demolitions/Statistics.asp (accessed August 19, 2006).

13. Amos Harhel, "Commission Appointed by IDF Chief of Staff: Stop Demolitions [of] Houses of Terrorists—Produces More Damage Than Benefit," *Haaretz*, February 17, 2005 (Hebrew).
14. Avi Bnayahu, "IDF Was Not Affected by the Uprising," *Al Hamishmar*, November 9, 1988 (Hebrew).
15. Amos Harhel, "IDF Will Stop Demolishing Terrorists' Houses on Territories," *Haaretz*, February 18, 2005 (Hebrew).
16. Zvi Barhel, "Houses Demolition—Verified and Tested," *Haaretz*, August 16, 2002 (Hebrew).
17. "Salaries for Suicide Bombers," *CBS News*, April 3, 2002, available at: http://www.cbsnews.com/stories/2002/04/03/world/main505316.shtml (accessed August 19, 2006); see also Ken Layne, "Saddam Pays 25K for Palestinian Bombers," *Fox News*, March 26, 2002, available at: http://www.foxnews.com/story/0,2933,48822,00.html (accessed August 19, 2006).
18. For example, see the relationship between the media and Human Rights Watch during IDF's Operation Rainbow, conducted May 18–24, 2004, in Human Rights Watch, "Razing Rafah: Mass Home Demolitions in the Gaza Strip" (October 2004), available at: http://hrw.org/reports/2004/rafah1004/rafah1004text.pdf (accessed August 20, 2006).
19. "Q&A: Israel's House Demolition Policy," *BBC News*, May 16, 2004, available at: http://news.bbc.co.uk/2/hi/middle_east/3718981.stm.
20. The Defense Regulations (1945) were promulgated by the British Mandatory Government to ensure public security, impose public order, prevent uprisings, and maintain the provision of necessary services to the public. The regulations enable the authorities to take various steps for security reasons: administrative detentions, restrictions on movement, property confiscations, classifications of organizations as illegal, newspaper shutdowns, curfews, expulsions, and bans on assembly. In 1948 the State of Israel incorporated the Defense Regulations into its legal system, by the power of section 11 of the Law and Administration Ordinance. When the occupied territories were captured in 1967, these regulations were imposed on the territories, and through the years Israel has made wide use of them for punishment and deterrence. See Ben-Zvi (2005).
21. See, for example, *Salah A-Din et al. v. IDF Commander Officer in Judea and Samaria*, HC 6868/02; *Nimer v. IDF Commander Officer in Judea and Samaria*, HC 299/90; and *Nesman et al. v. IDF Commander Officer in Gaza Strip*, HC 802/89.
22. See, for example, Israeli High Court of Justice, plea 893/04; Israeli High Court of Justice, plea 4694/04 (March 4, 2009).
23. See B'tselem, "House Demolitions as Punishment in the Eyes of International Law" (2006, Hebrew), available at: http://www.btselem.org/Hebrew/Punitive_Demolitions/Legal_basis.asp (accessed August 19, 2006).

24. Zeev Schiff, "Targeted Assassinations: From Ticking Bomb to Ticking Infrastructure," *Haaretz*, September 10, 2003 (Hebrew).
25. Sayeret Matkal (General Staff Reconnaissance Unit—Unit 269) is a military commando unit that is part of the Intelligence Branch and directly subordinate to the General Staff of the IDF. Set up in 1957 on the basis of the model of the Special Air Service (SAS) Regiment of Britain, the unit's original mission was to collect military intelligence information in enemy territory, but it has also been used in various military operations. Over the years the Sayeret Matkal has become famous for its operations, which include gaining control of the hijacked Sabena Airlines plane at the Ben-Gurion Airport on May 9, 1972, and its participation in the Entebbe Operation on July 3, 1976. See Eshel (2002, 21); for additional information, see Zonder (2000).
26. Shayetet 13 (Naval Commando) is the elite navy unit whose mission is to carry out naval operations across enemy borders—such as attacks on naval vessels in enemy ports and on important facilities during wartime—and to collect intelligence information on enemy operations. Shayetet 13 operations have included taking part in the attack on Green Island (July 20, 1969) and the Spring of Youth operation (April 9–10, 1973). Since the beginning of the Al-Aqsa Intifada, the unit has also carried out activities in Judaa and Samaria that include detaining terror activists. See Blanche (1998); Katz (1998). See also Israeli Special Forces database, "Shayetet 13," available at: http://www.isayeret.com/content/units/sea/shayetet/article.htm (accessed August 21, 2006).
27. "Israel Unleashes Its Death Squads," *Sunday Herald Sun*, January 19, 2003.
28. Eitan Rabin, "The Cell Phone Rang, Yahya Ayyash Answered, and the Cell Phone Exploded," *Haaretz*, January 7, 1996 (Hebrew).
29. This is attested to by the fact that the only public discussion initiated in Israeli society regarding the legitimacy of the policy of targeted killings came after the July 22, 2002, assassination of Salah Shahada, when fifteen innocent civilians were also killed. The protest was ignited when the chief of the air force, Dan Halutz (who later became IDF chief of staff between 2005 and 2006), asserted that he felt no pangs of conscience about the killing of the innocent. One of the reactions in this particular case was the "pilots' letter" in which a number of reserve pilots expressed their opposition to participating in the targeted killings policy.
30. Atila Shumfalby and Anat Bershkovski, "The Labor Party: The General Secretary Against Deals in the Primaries," *Ynet News*, January 2, 2006, available at: http://www.ynet.co.il/articles/0,7340,L-3193451,00.html; Amos Harhel, "The IDF Show Moral Justification for Targeted Killings," *Haaretz*, September 5, 2003 (Hebrew).
31. See *Seeham Thabet v. Prime Minister of Israel*, HC 192/01; *MK Mohammed Barakeh v. Prime Minister of Israel and Minister of Defense*, HC 5872/01; *Public Committee Against Torture and Palestinian Society for the Protection of Human Rights and the Environment v. Government of Israel et al.*, HC 769/02.

32. For example, during the 1980s, 40 percent of the construction workforce was Palestinian; see Romanov and Zusman (2003).
33. Amnesty International, "Israel and the Occupied Territories: Torn Apart: Families Split by Discriminatory Policies" (July 12, 2004), Available at: http://web.amnesty.org/library/pdf/MDE150632004ENGLISH/$File/MDE1506304.pdf (accessed August 19, 2006).
34. See also note 33. The demographic threat is an argument that has arisen in the last decade in Israeli society: it asserts that the Jewish majority in the State of Israel may be reduced and may even disappear and that this development would lead to the abolition of the idea of the Jewish state, a state in which Jews are a majority. According to this argument, the threat derives from the high natural rate of population increase among Palestinians in contrast to Jews. Among Jews, the natural increase in population is 1 percent, while among Arabs it is 3.5 percent. At this rate, in 2020 the Jewish population will be reduced and will represent 65 percent of the population, compared to 70 percent in 2004. If this situation were to continue to the point where the Jewish population amounted to only 50 to 60 percent of the population within the borders of 1967, the numerical parity might lead the Arab population to demand a change in the Jewish character of the state and thus bring an end to the definition of the state as "the state of the Jewish nation." See Soffer and Evgeniya (2004).
35. See also Israel High Court ruling in *Stamka et al. v. The Minister of the Interior et al.*, HC 3648/97, and the state's response of September 7, 1999, in *Issa et al. v. The Minister of the Interior*, HC 338/98.
36. See Internal Affairs Committee of the Knesset, protocol of July 14, 2003 (Hebrew), available at: http://knesset.gov.il/protocols/data/rtf/pnim/2003-07-14-01.rtf (accessed August 17, 2006).
37. See "Sharon Approved Recommendations to Limit Married Israeli-Arabs's Eligibility for Citizenship—There Is a Need to Preserve the Jewish Nature of the State," *Bambili News*, April 5, 2005 (Hebrew).
38. See Ambassador Giancarlo Chevallard, head of the European Commission Delegation, "Statement Regarding the Nationality and Entry into Israel Law (Temporary Order) 2003," August 4, 2003; see also UN Committee on the Elimination of Racial Discrimination, "Decision 2(63)," August 14, 2003, available at: http://www.unhchr.ch/tbs/doc.nsf/(Symbol)/CCPR.CO.78.ISR.En?Opendocument (accessed August 18, 2006).
39. One of the salient aspects of the disagreement regarding the "security barrier" is the struggle over what to call it. The Israeli government uses terms with positive connotations, such as the "security fence," the "separation obstacle," and the "border obstacle." By contrast, the Palestinians use names that not only have negative connotations—such as the "separation wall" and the "apartheid wall"—but also emphasize the type of construction, that is, a wall within cities. The compromise between the two types of terms is the concept of a "barrier," which is perceived as having neutral content.

40. Diana Bahur, "Love, Don't Love, Love . . . ," *Ynet News*, August 4, 2003 (Hebrew), available at: http://www.ynet.co.il/articles/0,7340,L-2713493,00.html (accessed August 15, 2006).
41. See Gideon Alon, "Government Approved Separation Fence; Peres Threatened to Resign," *Haaretz*, June 24, 2002 (Hebrew).
42. *Council of Beit Sourik v. Government of Israel*, HC 2056/04.
43. See Haggai Hoberman, "And Thanks to Sharon and the Security Fence," *Hazofe*, April 4, 2004 (Hebrew), available at: http://hazofe.co.il/web/newsnew/katava6.asp?Modul=24&id=22729&Word=&gilayon=1954&mador (accessed August 19, 2006).
44. Ari Shavit, "Has Disengagement Succeeded?" *Haaretz*, July 7, 2006 (Hebrew). According to NATO, HUMINT is defined as "a category of intelligence derived from information which has been accumulated and supplied by human sources." HUMINT includes information gleaned from both confidential sources, such as secret agents, and public sources, such as interviews with individuals who may be hostile, neutral, or friendly.
45. The most prominent confirmation of this position was the Geneva Accord, which was signed by representatives of the Palestinian leadership and which firmly stated that the border between the two countries would be based on the Green Line. See Palestinian Peace Coalition, "The Geneva Accord: A Model Israeli-Palestinian Peace Agreement," available at: http://www.geneva-accord.org (accessed August 19, 2006).
46. The International Court in The Hague also stated that the fence was being built to assist the ongoing settlement of Israeli citizens in the West Bank, which is in contradiction to the Fourth Geneva Accord. Hence, the court called for an immediate halt to fence construction.
47. Ibrahim Habib, "In the Heart of Wall: Separation Wall and Its Damage to the Right to Health and to the Palestinian Hospitals in the East Jerusalem" (2005, Hebrew), available at Physicians for Human Rights: http://www.phr.org.il/phr/files/articlefile_1134503727497.pdf (accessed August 17, 2006).
48. September 9, 2006; see also Layne (2003).
49. Center for the Defense of the Individual, "Report: Freedom of Movement" (2006, Hebrew), available at: http://www.hamoked.org.il/items/12901.pdf (accessed August 17, 2006); International Commission of Jurists, "Israel's Separation Barrier: Challenges to the Rule of Law and Human Rights," Geneva: International Commission of Jurists (2006), available at: http://www.icj.org/IMG/pdf/Israel_s_Separation_Barrier-2.pdf (accessed August 17, 2006).
50. For the data, see Tami Steinmetz Center for Peace Research, "Peace Index for June 2003, July 2003, October 2003, February 2004, June 2004, and April 2006," available at: http://www.tau.ac.il/peace/ (accessed August 18, 2006).
51. See B'tselem, "Third of Public Doesn't Know the Path of the Fence" (press release, 2006, Hebrew), available at: http://www.btselem.org/hebrew/Press_Releases/20060131.asp (accessed August 18, 2006).

52. See Barak Ravid and Itamar Inbari, "Continuing to Build the Security Fence Will Lead to Violence," *Maariv*, September 15, 2005 (Hebrew).
53. *Council of Beit Sourik v. Government of Israel*, HC 2056/04.
54. *Hasin et al. v. Government of Israel and IDF Commander in the West Bank*, HC 2732/05.
55. Efrat Forsher, "High Court: Dismantle Fence in Alfi Menashe," *Maariv*, September 15, 2005 (Hebrew) (Forsher 2006).
56. See *Council of Beit Sourik v. Government of Israel*, HC 2056/04; *Mraabe et al. v. Prime Minister of Israel et al.*, HC 7957/04; *Hasin et al. v. Government of Israel and IDF Commander in the West Bank*, HC 2732/05; *Municipality of Bethlehem v. State of Israel et al.*, HC 1890/03.
57. The threshold of the Israeli electoral system was for many years just 1 percent; in 1996 it was raised to 1.5 percent, and in the early 2000s to 2 percent.

References

Abu-Lughod, Janet L. 1971. "The Demographic Transformation of Palestine." In *The Transformation of Palestine: Essays on the Origin and Development of the Arab-Israeli Conflict*, edited by Ibrahim Abu-Lughod. Evanston, Ill.: Northwestern University Press.

Amnesty International Report. 2004. "Israel and the Occupied Territories, Torn Apart: Families Split by Discriminatory Policies." Amnesty International, July 2004. Available at: http://web.amnesty.org/library/pdf/MDE150632004 ENGLISH/$File/MDE1506304.pdf (accessed August 19, 2006).

Arian, Asher. 2003. "Israel Public Opinion on National Security." JCSS Publications. Tel Aviv: Tel Aviv University (Hebrew).

Ashbel, Dan, and Arnon Soffer. 2001. "Palestinian Refugees from 1948: Background, Sides, Positions, and Recommendations for Solution." *National Security* 1: 16–17 (Hebrew).

Ben-Dor, Gabriel, Ami Pedahzur, and Badi Hasisi. 2003. "Anti-Liberalism and the Use of Force in Israeli Democracy." *Journal of Political and Military Sociology* 31(1): 119–42.

Ben-Eliezer, Uri. 1995a. "A Nation in Arms: State, Nation, and Militarism in Israel's First Years." *Comparative Studies in Society and History* 37(2): 264–85.

———. 1995b. *Through the Gun Sight: The Emergence of Israeli Militarism 1936–1956.* Tel-Aviv: Dvir (Hebrew).

———. 2001. "From a Nation-in-Arms to a Postmodern Army: Military Politics in 'New Times' Israel." *Democratic Culture* 4–5: 55–98 (Hebrew).

Bennett, W. Lance. 1990. "Toward a Theory of Press-State Relations in United States." *Journal of Communication* 40(2): 103–25.

Ben-Zvi, Abraham. 2005. "The Limits of Israel's Democracy in the Shadow of Security." *Taiwan Journal of Democracy* 1(2): 4–6.

Blanche, Ed. 1998. "Israel Intelligence Agencies Under Fire." *Janes Intelligence Review* 10(1): 20.

Bloom, Mia M. 2004. "Palestinian Suicide Bombing: Public Support, Market Share, and Outbidding." *Political Science Quarterly* 119(1): 84–105.

Byman, Daniel L. 2005. *Deadly Connections: States That Sponsor Terrorism.* Cambridge: Cambridge University Press.

———. 2006. "Do Targeted Killings Work?" *Foreign Affairs* 85(2): 95–113.

Byman, Daniel L., and Avi Dicter. 2006. "Israel's Lessons for Fighting Terrorists and Their Implications for the United States." Analysis paper 8. Washington, D.C.: Brookings Institution, Saban Center for Middle East Policy.

Catignani, Sergio. 2005a. "The Strategic Impasse in Low-Intensity Conflicts: The Gap Between Israeli Counter-Insurgency Strategy and Tactics During the Al-Aqsa Intifada." *Journal of Strategic Studies* 28(1): 57–75.

———. 2005b. "The Security Imperative in Counterterror Operations: The Israeli Fight Against Suicidal Terror." *Terrorism and Political Violence* 17(1–2): 245–64.

Chalk, Peter. 1995. "The Liberal Response to Terrorism." *Terrorism and Political Violence* 7(4): 10–44.

Clutterbuck, Lindsay. 2004. "Law Enforcement." In *Attacking Terrorism*, edited by Luds James and Cronin Audrey. Washington, D.C.: Georgetown University Press.

Crelinsten, Ronald D., and Alex Schmid. 1992. "Western Response to Terrorism: A Twenty-Five-Year Balance Sheet." *Terrorism and Political Violence* 4(4): 307–40.

Crenshaw, Martha. 2001. "Counterterrorism Policy and the Political Process." *Studies in Conflict and Terrorism* 24(5): 329–37.

Davidov, Guy, Yonatan Yuval, Ilan Saban, and Amnon Reichman. 2004. "State or Family? Citizenship Law and the Entrance to Israel (Temporary Provision)—2003." *Lawatch* 1(2): 63–64 (Hebrew).

Druker, Raviv, and Ofer Shelah. 2005. *Boomerang.* Jerusalem: Keter (Hebrew).

Eshel, David. 2002. "Israel Refines Its Preemptive Approach to Counterterrorism." *Janes Intelligence Review* 14(9): 21.

Forsher, Efrat. 2006. "Forbidden by the High Court, Built by Construction Companies, Approved by State Prosecutor." *NRG News*, November 11, 2006. Available in English at: http://www.awalls.org/ma_ariv_forbidden_by_the_high_court_built_by_contruction_companies_approved_by_state_prosecutor.

Ganor, Boaz. 2003. *The Counter-Terrorism Puzzle: A Guide for Decision Makers.* Herzliya: Interdisciplinary Center Publications (Hebrew).

Goren, Samuel (former commander in the Mossad and Israel Defense Forces Intelligence). Interview with the author. August 16, 2006, Ramat-Gan, Israel.

Gross, Michael J. 2003. "Fighting by Other Means in the Mideast: A Critical Analysis of Israel's Assassination Policy." *Political Studies* 51: 350–68.

Hafez, Mohammed M., and Joseph M. Hatfield. 2006. "Do Targeted Assassinations Work? A Multivariate Analysis of Israel's Controversial Tactic During the Al-Aqsa Uprising." *Studies in Conflict and Terrorism* 29(4): 359–82.

Harhel, Amos, and Avi Issacharoff. 2004. *The Seventh War.* Tel Aviv: Mishkal (Hebrew).

Hobfoll, Stevan E., Daphna Canetti-Nisim, and Robert J. Johnson. 2006. "Exposure to Terrorism, Stress-Related Mental Health Symptoms, and Defensive Coping Among Jews and Arabs in Israel." *Journal of Consulting and Clinical Psychology* 74(2): 207–18.

Inbar, Efraim. 1998. "Israeli National Security 1973–1996." *Annals of the American Academy of Political and Social Science* 555: 62–81.

Internal Affairs Committee of the Knesset. 2003. Protocal, July 14, 2003 (Hebrew). Available at: http://knesset.gov.il/protocols/data/rft/pnim/2003-07-14-01.rtf (accessed August 17, 2006).

Israel Ministry of Defense. 2004. *Security Fence: Background, Data, and Security Plan* (February, Hebrew). Available at: http://www.securityfence.mod.gov.il/Pages/Heb/default.htm (accessed December 2, 2009).

———. 2006. *Security Fence: Obstacle Structure* (April 30, Hebrew). Available at: http://www.securityfence.mod.gov.il/Pages/Heb/mivne.htm (accessed August 17, 2006).

Kadman, Noga. 1999. *Families Torn Apart: Separation of Palestinian Families in the Occupied Territories.* Jerusalem: B'tselem (Hebrew).

Katz, Samuel M. 1998. "Incident at Ansariya." *Janes Intelligence Review* 10(1): 26–28.

Kimmerling, Baruch. 2002. "Jurisdiction in an Immigrant-Settler Society: The 'Jewish and Democratic State.'" *Comparative Political Studies* 35(10): 1119–44.

Kimmerling, Baruch, and Joel S. Migdal. 2002. *Palestinians: The Making of a People.* Jerusalem: Keter Publishers (Hebrew).

Klein, J. Aaron. 2006. *Striking Back: The 1972 Munich Olympics Massacre and Israel's Deadly Response.* Tel Aviv: Lamiskal (Hebrew).

Kober, Avi. 2001. "Israeli War Objectives into an Era of Negativism." In *Israel's National Security Towards the Twenty-first Century*, edited by Uri Bar-Joseph. London: Frank Cass.

Kohn, Orna. 2006. "Initial Comments on the Supreme Court's Ruling on the Nationality and Entry into Israel Law." *Adalah's Newsletter* 25: 1–2.

Kretzmer, David. 2002. *The Occupation of Justice: The Supreme Court of Israel and the Occupied Territories.* Albany: State University of New York Press.

———. 2005. "Targeted Killing of Suspected Terrorists: Extra-Judicial Executions or Legitimate Means of Defense?" *European Journal of International Law* 16(2): 205–12.

Lachman, Shai. 1982. "Arab Rebellion and Terrorism in Palestine 1929–1939: The Case of Sheikh Izz al-Din al-Qassam and His Movement." In *Zionism and Arabism in Palestine and Israel*, edited by Elie Kedourie and Sylvia G. Haim. London: Frank Cass.

Layne, Yehezkel. 2003. *Bad Wall: Human Rights Violations as a Result of Security Barrier.* Jerusalem: B'tselem (Hebrew).

Lissak, Moshe. 1998. "A Militaristic Society, or a Nation in Uniform." In *Security Concerns: Insight from the Israeli Experience*, edited by Daniel Bartal, Dan Jacobson, and Aharon Klieman. London: JAI Press.

Luckham, A. R. 1971. "A Comparative Typology of Civil-Military Relations." *Government and Opposition* 6: 17–20.

Lustick, Ian S. 1995. "Terrorism in Israeli-Arab Conflict: Targets and Audiences." In *Terrorism in Context*, edited by Martha Crenshaw. University Park: Pennsylvania State University Press.

Morris, Benny. 1996. *Israel's Border Wars, 1949–1956: Arab Infiltration, Israel Retaliation, and the Countdown to the Suez War.* Tel-Aviv: Am Oved Publishers (Hebrew).

Mueller, John E. 1970. "Presidential Popularity from Truman to Johnson." *American Political Science Review* 64: 18–34.

Navot, Nahik (former commander in the Mossad). Interview with the author. August 14, 2006, Ramat Hasharon.

Nolte, George, and Gregory Fox. 1995. "Intolerant Democracies." *Harvard International Law Journal* 3(6): 1–7.

Pape, A. Robert. 2003. "The Strategic Logic of Suicide Terrorism." *American Political Science Review* 97(3): 344–61.

———. 2005. *Dying to Win: The Strategic Logic of Suicide Terrorism.* New York: Random House.

Pedahzur, Ami. 2003. "Who's Guarding Democracy? Struggle Between the Elites Toward the Elections to the Knesset Sixteen." In *The Elections in Israel 2003*, edited by Asher Arian and Michal Shamir. Jerusalem: Israel Democracy Institute.

Pedahzur, Ami, and Arie Perliger. 2006. "The Changing Nature of Suicide Attacks: A Social Network Perspective." *Social Forces* 84(4): 1983–2004.

Pedahzur, Ami, and Magnus Ranstorp. 2001. "A Tertiary Model Countering Terrorism in Liberal Democracies: The Case of Israel." *Terrorism and Political Violence* 13(2): 1–26.

Peri, Yoram. 2003. "'The Democratic Putsch' in the Elections of 1999." In *In the Name of Security: The Sociology of Peace and War in Israel in Changing Times*, edited by Majid Al-Haj and Uri Ben-Eliezer. Haifa: University of Haifa Publishers (Hebrew).

———. 2006. *Generals in the Cabinet Room: How the Military Shapes Israeli Policy.* Washington, D.C.: United States Institute of Peace Press.

Qualter, Terence. 1991. "The Role of the Mass Media in Limiting the Public Agenda." In *Manipulating Public Opinion*, edited by Michael Margolis and Gary Mauser. Pacific Grove, Cal.: Brooks/Cole Publishing.

Romanov, Dmitry, and Noam Zusman. 2003. "Foreign Workers in the Construction Business: Current Situation and Policy Implications." Jerusalem: Bank of Israel (July, Hebrew). Available at: http://www.bankisrael.gov.il/deptdata/mehkar/papers/dp0306h.pdf (accessed August 20, 2006).

Schiff, Zeev, and Ehud Yaari. 1990. *Intifada.* Jerusalem: Shoken (Hebrew).

Scheufele, Dietram A., Matthew C. Nisbet, and Ronald E. Ostman. 2005. "September 11 News Coverage, Public Opinion, and Support for Civil Liberties." *Mass Communication and Society* 8(3): 197–218.

Schmid, Alex P. 1992. "Terrorism and Democracy." *Terrorism and Political Violence* (4)4: 14–15.

Schueftan, Dan. 2002. *Korah Hahafrada.* Tel Aviv: Zmora Bitan.

Sederberg, Peter. 1995. "Conciliation as Counter-Terrorist Strategy." *Journal of Peace Research* 32(1): 295–312.

Shalev, Aryeh. 1990. *The Intifada: Causes and Effects.* Tel Aviv: Jaffe Center for Strategic Studies (Hebrew).

Shavit, Shabtai (former head of the Mossad). Interview with the author. August 16, 2006, Herzlia, Israel.

Shelah, Ofer, and Yoav Limor. 2007. *Captives of Lebanon.* Tel Aviv: Miskal (Hebrew).

Shnayderman, Ronen. 2004. *Through No Fault of Their Own: Punitive House Demolitions During the Al-Aqsa Intifada.* Jerusalem: B'tselem (Hebrew).

Smadar, Shmueli, and Attila Sumphalbi. 2003. "Rage on the Right: The Supreme Court is a Branch of the Meretz Party.a" *Ynet news*, September 1, 2003. Available at: http://www.ynet.co.il/articles/0,7340,L-2364113,00.html.

Soffer, Arnon. 1993. "Full Equal Rights for Arabs—Is it Possible?" *Nativ* 2(31): 50–54.

Soffer, Arnon, and Bistrov Evgeniya. 2004. "Israel Demography 2004–2020 in Light of the Disengagement Plan." Haifa: University of Haifa, Cathedra of Geostrategy (Hebrew). Available at: http://geo.haifa.ac.il/~chstrategy/publications/books/demography04/demography2004-2020.pdf (accessed August 20, 2006).

Stein, Yael. 2006. *Quiet Transfer Continues: Revoking Citizenship Status and Social Rights from the Eastern Jerusalem Residents.* Jerusalem: B'tselem (Hebrew).

Sullivan, John L., Pat Walsh, Michal Shamir, David J. Barnum, and James L. Gibson. 1993. "Why Politicians Are More Tolerant: Selective Recruitment and Socialization Among Political Elites in Britain, Israel, New Zealand, and the United States." *British Journal of Political Science* 23: 51–76.

Wald, Emanuel. 1987. *The Curse of the Broken Vessels.* Tel Aviv: Shoken (Hebrew).

Wilkinson, Paul. 1986. *Terrorism and the Liberal State*, 2d ed. London: Macmillan.

———. 2000. *Terrorism and the Liberal State.* Hong Kong: Macmillan.

Yaari, Ehud. 1975. *Egypt and the Fedayeen, 1953–1956.* Giv'at Haviva: Center for Arab and Afro-Asian Studies (Hebrew).

Zertal, Idith, and Akiva Eldar. 2004. *Lords of the Land.* Tel Aviv: Kisseret.

Zohar, Gabi (former head of the Terrorism Arena in the IDF Intelligence). Interview with the author. August 17, 2006, Kfar Saba, Israel.

Zonder, Moshe. 2000. *The Elite Unit of Israel.* Jerusalem: Keter (Hebrew).

CHAPTER 10

TERRORISM AS CONVENTIONAL SECURITY FOR DEMOCRACIES: AMERICA, JAPAN, AND MILITARY ACTION IN THE ASIA-PACIFIC

DAVID LEHENY

Because of their vulnerability both to attack and to political exploitation, democracies face in terrorism a particularly double-edged threat. As other chapters in this volume note, open and liberal societies present a wide array of targets to organizations that would use the space afforded by civil liberties to recruit and plan attacks, and these groups can also count on a relatively free press to publicize and even sensationalize attacks. Terrorist groups are not the only beneficiaries of the expansion of fear. Even one attack—the possible detonation of a "dirty bomb," the release of anthrax in a crowded mall, the deliberate crashing of a passenger plane into a national landmark—might be ruinous. As a result, it might make sense to remove, overcome, or simply ignore the legal and constitutional burdens, no matter how constitutive of democracy itself, that would allow a terrorist to escape detection and capture or allow a captured terrorist to "lawyer up," thumbing his or her nose at desperate investigators as the clock ticks. In this view, the growth of the state's coercive capacity—the amassment of unprecedented government databases with information on virtually all private telephone calls, the suspension of habeas corpus rights and the routinization of violence against terrorist suspects, the increasing abrogation of search-and-seizure restrictions—is simply something to be expected in a time of emergency. But if the health of a democracy is measured at least in part in the robust defense of civil liberties against the powers of the state, even a decline in the risk of an attack may reflect a Pyrrhic victory for citizens and a decisive loss for liberal institutions.

In part for this reason, debates over the relationship between democracy and terrorism often build from the liberty-versus-security tension that epitomizes state efforts to combat terrorism. And yet the very reference to security in this equation displays how curious the exclusive focus on law enforcement and intelligence abuses actually is. After all, when scholars discuss "security politics," terrorism represents only a small part of the larger literature; indeed, this was a major source of embarrassment to international relations scholars in the wake of the September 11 attacks. Even as security specialists have argued that we need to address terrorism as a national security concern, they have been slow to develop theoretical frameworks and arguments that incorporate terrorist organizations and state responses into broader debates about how governments pursue national security. And if we consider terrorism more broadly in security debates, the implications for democracies grow even wider and more troubling.

Indeed, the character of a democracy is more than the sum of its formal institutions. For example, whatever else is implied by its separation of powers, single-member districts, and federalism, American democracy is incomprehensible in its operation and preoccupations without attention to racial politics, the role of Christianity, and regional economic inequality. French democracy, aside from its mixed presidential/parliamentary system and institutional links to the European Union, is characterized by the nature of its welfare and employment bargains and by postcolonial immigration; together these forces have shaped the nature of inequality and stakeholding in France. And Japanese democracy has long been marked, more than anything else, by a bitter division over the role of the military.

In this chapter, I consider the types of challenges that terrorism poses to democratic states in terms of their military activities and efforts, focusing especially on post-9/11 Japan. I describe initially the tensions in Japanese security and counterterrorism policies before 2001, a long postwar period during which Japanese pacifism emanated largely from a political impasse over the state's right to use violence. I then turn to the example of the Iraq War, for which the September 11 attacks helped to break a potential logjam in the aspirations of some Bush administration officials to attack and depose

Saddam Hussein's regime; indeed, terrorism in this case seems intimately linked to the political logic underlying a democracy's decision to wage war. In the next section, I argue that this policy was a crucial step outside of the prevailing international framing of international terrorism as a law enforcement issue, a framing that has constrained debate despite the absence of clear evidence that law enforcement is more successful than other approaches, such as the employment of military force or political negotiations. I then turn to debates over the relationships between democracy and the military, arguing that the primary theoretical paradigm used—the "democratic peace" theory—offers, for whatever its problems, at least intellectually coherent if empirically suspicious monadic claims about how democratic institutions might theoretically constrain the use of force. Finally, I return to the discussion of Japan, arguing that the speed and structure of Japan's dramatic military steps since 9/11 can only be understood by examining how those attacks permitted a fundamental reframing of Japan's primary security nightmares as "terrorist" and thus as requiring the same kinds of military tools that the Bush administration had chosen in its "war on terror."

Pacifism and Democracy in Japan

Both historically and politically, Japan's postwar democracy and tight limits on the role of the military are inextricably linked. The military coup that eliminated Japan's proto-democratic government in 1931 was itself the culmination of fierce battles between military authorities, civilian advisers to the emperor, and the political party leaders who had been gaining ground since the end of the First World War. In the immediate aftermath of the Second World War, which had been ruinous for Japan, U.S. occupation authorities found that their initial goal, that of pacifying Japan, would be a relatively simple matter: its armed forces had largely been obliterated by imperial overstretch, and its war potential had been utterly destroyed by the relentless American bombing of military and manufacturing sites. Of greater urgency and attention was the rebuilding of Japan, particularly under the looming shadow of the Cold War, as a democratic and prosperous nation. Occupation authorities, many of them young men raised under the ideals of the New Deal, sought to achieve this by grafting progressive notions of rights and equality onto the more palatable remnants of Japan's Meiji Constitution. Foremost among the American contributions to the 1947 Constitution was article IX, a renunciation of the right to war as well as the maintenance of armed forces.

For the Japanese left, the American occupation initially seemed like a godsend. Persecuted viciously by the militarist government, leftists saw American-written freedoms as crucial guarantors of their own political viability. Leftists in Japan would soon be disillusioned, however, by American-supported red purges as U.S. occupation authorities grew wary of an activist labor movement that might simultaneously upset the prospects for economic growth and weaken Japan's pro-American, anti-Soviet position. But the left's distrust of the military remained a constant force, and defense of the constitution—even if co-authored by Americans—became the most important rallying cry of postwar progressives. Indeed, American officials quickly found that their own ardor for a pacifist Japan dimmed as they sought military allies against Communist movements in Korea and elsewhere. But Japanese progressives, along with wary conservatives like Prime Minister Shigeru Yoshida (who felt Japan's economic reconstruction would be derailed by military activity), held the line in the early postwar years.[1]

Yoshida's rival, Nobusuke Kishi, would cross that line, with crucial and determining consequences for Japan's postwar democracy. Kishi, an economic policymaker jailed (though not convicted) by U.S. occupation authorities for his activities in Manchuria during World War II, survived the tumult of the early postwar years to rejoin right-wing colleagues in the bewildering transition to a formerly despised political system. Immediately after his 1948 release from Sugamo Prison, he drove to the residence of the prime minister to meet his brother (and the future prime minister), Eisaku Satô, reportedly saying to him, "Strange, isn't it? We're all democrats now" (Samuels 2001, online). For Kishi, the transition to democracy was certainly the lesser of the potential evils in the budding U.S.-Soviet rivalry; a fervent anticommunist, he hoped to revise the Constitution, gut article IX, rearm Japan, and ally as a nearly equal partner with the United States, providing some of the autonomy lost with Japan's 1945 defeat. Kishi's subsequent foray into party politics would help to establish the Japan Democratic Party, which joined forces with Yoshida's Liberal Party in 1955 to prevent a victory by a reenergized Japan Socialist Party. The new Liberal Democratic Party (LDP) would become the dominant party in postwar Japanese politics, solely or in coalition with smaller parties, and would control the government for roughly fifty of the next fifty-two years.

Even aside from his three years (1957 to 1960) as prime minister, Kishi left indelible marks on Japan's postwar politics, but none were broader or more momentous than his efforts in 1959 and 1960 to extend and strengthen the U.S.-Japan military alliance, simultaneously increasing

Japan's responsibilities for its self-defense and connecting it tightly to U.S. foreign policy decisions. In a drama pitting Kishi against Socialists (who deplored Japan's militarist path and its connection to a U.S. government seen as imperialistic), his own party's moderates (who worried that the treaty would overcommit Japan's resources to military funding rather than economic development), and even his rightist allies (who feared loss of autonomy to the United States), Kishi aimed to make good on a promise to President Dwight Eisenhower to ratify the treaty. After a particularly bruising fight with Socialist Diet members who had blockaded the Diet building to prevent action on the treaty, Kishi managed to secure an affirmative vote only by holding a midnight Diet session without informing the Socialists. The questionable legality of the maneuver only exacerbated in the eyes of many the loss of democratic decorum. Indeed, hundreds of thousands of protesters streamed into the streets of Tokyo, surrounding the Diet; the ensuing riot culminated in hundreds of arrests and injuries. Having lost any ability to maintain cabinet or legislative cohesion, Kishi resigned.

The consequences for Japan were profound. His successor, Hayato Ikeda, immediately moved military and constitutional issues off the government's agenda and pledged to focus on the country's economic growth with his vaunted "Income Doubling Plan." Quite aside from any evaluation of whether Ikeda's program made economic sense (by most accounts, Japan's industrial development had already primed it for rapid growth in the 1960s with or without any special action from the prime minister), the political ramifications would dominate Japan's next three decades. Advocates of a stronger military role or a revised constitution were largely silenced within the LDP itself, while successful leaders focused on bread-and-butter issues for a middle-class and then affluent society. Legislative battles with Socialists continued over taxes, subsidies, and routine foreign policy issues, but compromise and incremental changes in Japan's security posture became the norm. While the left-right divide over the proper role for Japan's military continued to dominate ideological debates for the next decades, Japan's postwar democracy was decisively shaped by a stalemate on major changes in foreign policy and security policy. Indeed, Japan's commitment to peace diplomacy was not the result of any inherent pacifism in the Japanese national character; nor was it attributable to unanimity on the lessons of Hiroshima and Nagasaki. It was instead the product of a political maelstrom that had claimed the career of a powerful and shrewd prime minister and threatened to do the same to any others who might try to make something less popular than national economic growth the cornerstone of their political values.

Although Japan's security role has grown and expanded over time, including participation in UN peacekeeping operations and extension of Japan's responsibilities under the security treaty with the United States, all of this was achieved without revision of the 1947 Constitution. Article IX had, through reinterpretation, become one of the most alarmingly elastic constitutional provisions in any advanced industrial democracy, but it stood formally unchallenged for decades, largely because it was seen as an untouchable feature of the democratic landscape. Some scholars have explained Japan's security behavior with reference to neorealist theory, such as Jennifer Lind's (2004) claim that Japan engaged in "buck-passing" by free-riding on U.S. security commitments. But whatever strategic efficacy there may have been in Japan's security stance, there is little doubt that strong antimilitarist pressures played a crucial role in Japan's postwar democracy. Where some have written of a broad "culture of antimilitarism" (see, for example, Berger 1998), Peter J. Katzenstein (1996) has argued that tight political restrictions on the use of force reflected decisionmaking norms particular to Japan's postwar democracy. For Katzenstein, Japan is a nonmajoritarian democracy in that the strongly held views of minority parties must be respected to preserve legislative peace. After the 1960 riots, the LDP remained remarkably sensitive to many of the Socialists' primary concerns, particularly with regard to the reestablishment of Japanese military power. And while Socialists could fulminate against LDP economic policies, the privatization of national infrastructure, and policies on women, it could expect restraint in the LDP's handling of security issues. This did not prevent changes in Japanese security policy, but such restraint certainly slowed and circumscribed them.

In other words, however else we conceptualize Japan's postwar era—as a period of high-speed economic growth, of battles over nationalism and political stature, of an awakening civil society—its democracy was marked primarily by a deep split over the state's use of force. For many of Japan's most important postwar intellectuals and activists, the health of Japan's democracy was contingent on the government's fidelity to principles of pacifism and restraint. Where other countries might have debated decisions about going to war or about using the military to solve specific problems, Japanese activists debated whether the military should exist at all. And although conservatives have achieved major victories through euphemism (creating "self-defense forces" rather than an army) and reinterpretation (the U.S.-Japan treaty and various Peacekeeping Operations [PKOs] were not themselves considered aspects of "collective security"),

Japan's security policies since World War II have been distinguished by extraordinary restraint, just as Japan's parliamentary politics has been marked by extraordinary sensitivity to antimilitarist concerns.

Limits on Japanese Counterterrorism

Japanese counterterrorism policy has long reflected similar restrictions on the state's use of force, and the political impasse on security policy also limited the government's willingness to engage international terrorism except in truly extraordinary circumstances. Although the U.S. occupation authorities would famously leave economic ministries largely untouched in the aftermath of World War II, they abolished the wartime Home Ministry, which had administered, among other things, internal security, police, and propaganda functions. Japan's police would be organized primarily on a prefectural level, with national guidance in the hands of a largely defanged National Police Agency (NPA). Indeed, one of Kishi's unaccomplished goals as prime minister had been a rapid expansion of the NPA's capabilities, including more attention to "political" crimes and fewer American-instituted restrictions on searches and seizures (Samuels 2001). To this day, the NPA's powers are largely informal, and its authority has come largely through clever leveraging of prefectural police departments and through strict attention to "community policing," based largely on the kôban (police box) system. Police officers serving in kôban become neighborhood guides and sources of neighborhood security; they also build connections to residents in order to get advance word of suspicious persons or activity in the area (Bayley 1991; Friman et al. 2006).

The energized student movements of Kishi's era, combined with some of the more militant labor organizers in the 1950s and 1960s, became the primary targets of relentless NPA and PSA (Public Security Agency) investigation, especially under the auspices of the Anti-Surveillance Law—one of the first pieces of legislation passed after the end of the U.S. occupation. For the police, the primary political threats in postwar Japan have been leftists opposed to traditional sources of authority, such as the emperor, LDP members (like Kishi) with direct connections to the wartime past, and key pillars of the business community. And so the splintering and militarization of the student movement, particularly after the 1968 riots, led to a generation of intense police activity, with infiltration of student groups, harassment (often through intrusive surveillance) of progressive and labor organizations, and sometimes outright physical intimidation of leftists.[2]

For the more militant students, going underground with the various factions of the Japanese Red Army (JRA) became a clear option. Seen at the time as a Japanese counterpart to the European terrorist groups of the day (such as Germany's Red Army Faction or the Italian Red Brigades), the JRA was a distinctively menacing and splintered group. Its notorious early strikes in Japan (including a 1970 hijacking that ended with most of the culprits—somewhat unhappily for them, it now seems [Steinhoff 2004]—fleeing to North Korea) were superseded in infamy and cruelty by subsequent attacks overseas. In the brutal 1972 Lod Airport massacre in Israel, for instance, a small number of JRA members hoping to demonstrate common cause with Palestinian groups opened fire with automatic weapons, killing twenty-four people. The JRA's history is certainly tortured and frenetic enough to deserve significant attention, and among its most striking results was its effect on Japanese counterterrorism policy.

In one sense, the effect was limited. Because of long-standing mistrust—even among some in the ruling LDP—of overly extensive police authority, the NPA continued to operate against the JRA within extraordinary constraints. A 1972 siege in Nagano prefecture put these in sharp relief. Local police evidently stumbled on a group of JRA members in the midst of an internal purge (which would claim the lives of twelve), forcing the group's members to flee. Several JRA members entered a couple's mountain cottage, taking the wife hostage and starting one of the most heavily covered media dramas in postwar Japanese history. During the ten-day standoff, the NPA dispatched an official along with elite officers of Tokyo's Metropolitan Police Department to work with the local police to end the crisis. Atsuyuki Sassa, the NPA official on the scene, would later publish a popular but self-serving and often-criticized account of the siege in which he pointed out that he faced an absurd situation. Facing armed JRA gunmen who routinely took shots at the police (who were themselves divided, with the local cops suspicious of the Tokyo visitors), Sassa had been instructed to rescue the hostage; to maintain a good relationship with local officials; to represent the NPA effectively to a national media suspicious of the abuse of police authority; and to do so without the use of guns.

Ultimately knocking a hole in the cottage with a wrecking ball, the police managed to rescue the hostage and arrest most of the JRA members, though some had perished in a final mop-up of the internal purge. Memorialized in several books and also a popular film based on Sassa's (1996) book, the Asama mountain cottage incident illustrated the manner in which police authorities tried to work within existing constraints (and occasionally to push for minor and incremental change) rather than to abrogate them.[3] As with policies on international security, the police behaved in this way not because of an innate allergy to the use of force in the maintenance of social order, but rather because of the omnipresent threat that police misdeeds would tip the political balance to left-wing forces eager to roll back many of the state's powers vis-à-vis citizens. Because the police were tasked with maintaining public safety without themselves becoming a visible threat, their tactics relied heavily on intense and steady pressure—largely through obvious surveillance and through constant efforts to recruit informants—on suspicious organizations.

For decades, such suspicion was focused on the political left. The NPA and PSA made little secret of their targeting of labor unions, the Japan Communist Party, and remnants of the Japanese Red Army. For the security authorities, "terrorism" meant left-leaning activism and militancy and little beyond that. Indeed, this preoccupation with the left (with somewhat greater consideration paid to the civil liberties of religious and other organizations) contributed to the state's near-total blindness to the Aum Shinrikyo cult, which carried out the deadly 1995 sarin gas attack (Friman et al. 2006; see also Hardacre 2003). When arrest was difficult or impossible, the police largely made do with expulsion: JRA members would flee to North Korea or the Middle East, trying (to decreasing effect) to make common cause with Communist and nationalist movements elsewhere. For years the Japanese government would outsource some of its counterterrorist needs, making side deals with Arab governments, like Syria's, to ensure that JRA members would be monitored and harassed by local authorities during, for example, overseas trips by the emperor, which might otherwise offer appealing targets (Katzenstein 2002, 49).

With regard to international terrorism, this was mostly as far as Japanese policy would go. Japan's National Police Agency had displayed little interest in international policing, and indeed the Japanese government had signed on to international conventions on terrorism with some reluctance, fearing a loss of flexibility in handling terrorist crises. First publicly, such as in the Dhaka hijacking of 1977, and then secretively, as in the kidnapping of Japanese geologists by the Islamic Movement of Uzbekistan in Kyrgyzstan in 1999, the Japanese government had gained a reputation for bargaining with terrorist groups to rescue its citizens (Friman et al. 2006; Itabashi, Masamichi, and Leheny 2002; Leheny 2001–2002). Japanese police were primarily concerned with the incremental expansion of investigative authority at home and had little interest in courting controversy by engaging the much thornier world of international conflict, where Japan's hands were tied less by its disquietingly elastic constitutional limits on the military than by political deadlock shaped both by public opinion and by parliamentary norms.

Iraq, Terrorism, and the "One-Percent Doctrine"

It is not difficult to envision how terrorist violence can break political logjams over security politics; indeed, the Iraq War offers a striking case in point. Counterfactuals are a tricky business, and there is no easy way to determine whether the Bush administration would have chosen to attack Iraq had the September 11 attacks not occurred. Left-leaning authors in the United States have long flagged the Project for the New American Century (PNAC), headed by William Kristol and including future Bush administration officials like Paul Wolfowitz, as the intellectual source of the focus on Iraq, a focus that many have associated with PNAC's commitment to Israeli security (see, for example, Austin 2004). Critics have countered that the charge that a PNAC-inspired plan to invade Iraq dictated U.S. foreign policy both oversimplifies the political context and smacks of anti-Semitic conspiracy theories (see, for example, David Brooks, "The Era of Distortion," *New York Times*, January 6, 2004). Wherever one locates the origin of the administration's interest in regime change in Iraq—and it is likely that a variety of concerns shaped policy—there is little doubt that key representatives for George W. Bush, during his 2000 campaign for the presidency, clearly signaled the goal of removing Saddam Hussein from power, labeling his country a "rogue state." Condoleezza Rice, then Bush's foreign policy adviser, wrote a 2000 article for *Foreign Affairs* widely seen as encompassing the candidate's foreign policy platform. In it, she argued:

> As history marches toward markets and democracy, some states have been left by the side of the road. Iraq is the prototype. Saddam Hussein's regime is isolated, his conventional military power has been severely weakened, his people live in poverty and terror, and he has no useful place in international politics. He is therefore determined to develop WMD [weapons of mass destruction]. Nothing will change until Saddam is gone, so the United States must mobilize whatever resources it can, including support from his opposition, to remove him. (Rice 2000, 60)

Although she would go on to criticize Kim Jong Il and the Clinton administration's handling of North Korea, she stopped well short of calling for the removal of the North Korean leader. Whether or not an invasion of Iraq was an idée fixe before 2001, its possibility was hardly a secret.

Yet there is a difference between rogue states and terrorists: a presumption of the rationality of states (even rogue states that may have little regard for international law but have a healthy sense of self-preservation). This presumption is strongly shaped by realpolitik and neorealist conceptions of global politics. In the same article, Rice herself made the point, possibly contradicting her earlier position on Iraq, that the United States would need to pursue missile defense:

> These regimes are living on borrowed time, so there need be no sense of panic about them. Rather, the first line of defense should be a clear and classical statement of deterrence—if they do acquire WMD, their weapons will be unusable because any attempt to use them will bring national obliteration. Second, we should accelerate efforts to defend against these weapons. This is the most important reason to deploy national and theater missile defenses as soon as possible, to focus attention on U.S. homeland defenses against chemical and biological agents, and to expand intelligence capabilities against terrorism of all kinds. (Rice 2000, 61)

This is the statement of a superpower, one confident that it can obliterate any other nation should it choose to do so. Since the end of the Cold War—and particularly as post–Cold War revelations made clear just how rickety Soviet military power had become by the late 1980s—there was simply no conventional military threat capable of challenging the United States. Advocates of improved American defense capabilities had been forced to develop increasingly odd jargon to make their case, including the claim that America's primary threats would be "asymmetric," a clunky euphemism for "weak." Indeed, during the 2000 electoral campaign, the very effort to define American national interest became a crucial issue, given that no state—and possibly no collection of states—could have directly challenged American military power and hoped to survive.

My interest here is not in castigating the Bush administration—as others, like Richard Clarke (2004) have done—for failing to take seriously enough the threat of Al Qaeda, and not for the apparent interest in Iraq in the immediate wake of the September 11 attacks (noted, among others, by Suskind 2004, 187–89; Woodward 2004, 24–26). Rather, I aim only at making the relatively uncontroversial point that while some administration officials probably hoped for an invasion of Iraq even during the early days of the Bush administration, it was anything but a certainty, in part because of the obvious question of how Saddam Hussein's regime, even if armed with nuclear weapons, could threaten the United States given the guarantee of a swift and overpowering American response. The September 11 attacks, however, raised a powerful new specter, the very type idealized in counterterrorism conventions and agreements aimed at reducing arenas of global disorder. Terrorist groups, unlike states, could hide in the aftermath of an attack, and also unlike states, they might ideally be motivated by millenarian ideologies rather than by calculations of self-interest; like states, however, terrorist groups might now be expected to carry out mass-casualty attacks that would be just as deadly and visible as almost anything a rogue regime might attempt. The destructive power formerly presumed to be that of states alone, and always presumed to be amenable to the rational calculations of state leaders, might now be marshaled and used by irrational, secretive, and blindly ideological organizations ostensibly outside of the direct reach of the U.S. government.

Where advisor Condoleezza Rice had emphasized the importance of deterrence, Vice President Richard Cheney could now argue that even a "one percent chance" that weapons of mass destruction might find their way into the hands of a terrorist would have to be treated as a certainty, justifying preemptive military action as well as the myriad other tactics the Bush administration has used in its "war on terror" (Suskind 2006). In the terminology of Barry Buzan, Ole Waever, and Jaap de Wilde (1998, 21–42), counterterrorism policy had been "securitized" in that terrorism had been raised as such a spectral threat that any number of measures that might otherwise have been considered improper could now be accepted as necessary and even normal. Had the September 11 attacks not occurred, it would have been difficult for National Security Advisor Rice to say famously, with reference to Saddam Hussein's purported WMD capabilities, "We don't want the smoking gun to be a mushroom cloud," as she did in a CNN interview in September 2002. But if the delivery system were to be not the Iraqi regime's archaic missiles but rather a suitcase in the hands of Al Qaeda, to whom the Bush administration repeatedly linked Hussein, the threat was far more persuasive to the public, if little more realistic.

Terrorism as Criminality and Disorder

For all the potential that terrorism has for justifying armed conflict, it has not usually been defined primarily as a military phenomenon in diplomatic debates and international institutions. This in itself is curious, in that terrorism's open-endedness as a phenomenon could leave it open to exploitation by elites seeking to circumvent international legal norms in considering military options. The unending and deeply politicized terminological political debates surrounding terrorism (Hoffman 1999, 15–17) reflect its conceptual complexity, both as an object of social scientific analysis and as a target for aggressive policymaking. Although focusing specifically on nonstate violence may draw attention to the special organizational tactics that nonstate movements might pursue (see, for example, Crenshaw 1985) and addressing terrorists' goals in fomenting fear among an enemy population can help analysts to address the role of the mass media in the spread of modern terrorism, it is less clear that terrorism is directly susceptible to uniform remedies or responses. Indeed, the increasing efforts to develop typologies of terrorist organizations—"old" versus "new" terrorism, or millenarian-religious as opposed to ethno-nationalist—suggest a growing awareness among analysts and policymakers that terrorism is not itself a discrete phenomenon, like malaria, for which "draining the swamps" is a self-evidently available countermeasure.

Even the recent history of counterterrorism displays a breathtaking array of tactics and tools that have had varied consequences across national contexts. Beheading a terrorist organization, as the Peruvian government ostensibly did in 1992 by arresting Sendero Luminoso's Abimael Guzmán, may succeed in degrading the group's ability to recruit and operate (though Sendero factions would regroup in a limited manner within a decade). In other cases, however, the consequences are likely to be minimal. Few, for example, were willing to claim that the 2006 death of Abu Musab al-Zarqawi would have any effect on continuing terrorist attacks or the insurgency in Iraq. Similarly, British troops have long been portrayed as part of the problem in Northern Ireland, particularly as a legacy of the brutal shooting of Catholic demonstrators during the Bloody Sunday demonstration of 1972. Yet the skills developed in this period may have possibly helped the British military work more effectively during its probably doomed efforts in Iraq by encouraging soldiers to win the "hearts and minds" of Iraqi civilians while using lethal force against insurgents (Chin 2007). And even though negotiations and the ransoms paid by private firms in Colombia and other areas with major industries in kidnapping have probably encouraged longer-terms cycles of violence, political negotiations in areas like Northern Ireland, Sri Lanka, and Israel have been seen as crucial to reducing terrorist violence. Terrorist conflicts, embedded as they are in highly specific local contexts, seem to be variously susceptible to a wide variety of tactics and tools, ranging from military measures to political negotiations to criminal justice proceedings.

None of this is at all controversial as an analytical matter, but the structure of international agreements on counterterrorism strongly suggests that, as a matter of policy, terrorism is primarily constructed and understood as a criminal justice phenomenon. Using the tools available to international institutions, particularly the G-5/G-7/G-8, states have encouraged the development and elaboration of laws that criminalize certain activities, regulate others, and demand a larger role for the state in monitoring the behavior of citizens, residents, and local organizations. Initially, transnational agreements on terrorism reflected their Cold War origins by essentially banning that small range of activities that the United States and the Soviet Union had a strong interest in proscribing. While the American and Soviet governments continued to provide financial and military support to militants engaged in local conflicts in places like Angola, Nicaragua, and Afghanistan—where combatants used tactics that would easily meet relatively standard definitions of terrorism—international conventions sought to ban the "murder of diplomatic agents," the "hijacking of commercial airliners," and other specific acts. The international counterterrorism regime, marked largely by U.S.-Soviet disagreements over the legitimacy of different kinds of movements, could at least find common ground in prohibiting certain tactics that might imperil the citizens of the superpowers themselves.

Particularly after the end of the Cold War and the inclusion of Russia as the newest G-8 member, however, counterterrorism agreements began to take on a different cast, not simply banning specific activities but also compelling signatories to engage in more rigorous monitoring, surveillance, and control of the potentially lawless elements in their midst. In addition to a G-8 convention mandating greater state control over the diffusion of explosive materials, more recently the major powers—chief among them France and the United States—have pushed aggressively for cooperation to combat the financing of terrorism. Potentially suspect are the financial transfers that drift through largely unmonitored accounts in the Cayman Islands, through the Islamic hawalas (credit associations) that received substantial coverage after the September 11 attacks, or through the sort of charities that, in Northern Ireland, might have been called the "widows' and children's funds" and that are now allegedly central to Islamist networks. By cooperating on intelligence, surveillance, and potential prosecution of the relevant financial actors, states ostensibly can reduce the risk of terrorism. To do so, they reduce the range of activities and transactions considered to be purely private and demand that they be brought instead into a legal and rationalized environment that renders social and economic activity transparent, or at least legible to state authority (on "legibility" and rational order, see Scott 1998).

These steps require the world to become a more orderly place—a place ordered by specific and regulated channels for engaging in a wide variety of social activities. That is, counterterrorism agreements essentially define the threat of terrorism as a subset of the threat of disorder, which can be challenged only through the construction of legal apparatuses that systematize the tools for evaluating and regulating the desired range of action. Indeed, when governments discuss the spread of "counterterrorism" tools, they often do so by referring to governments' "capacity building" to track financial flows, protect "homeland security," and develop the "civil society" institutions that channel discontent and grievances into safe and orderly outlets rather than into paroxysms of rage and uncontrolled violence. Capacity building becomes the spread of a specific set of institutions.[4]

For the most part, military measures fall outside of these agreements and debates, as do the political negotiations that are frequently central to the long-term amelioration of terrorist disputes. Just as Cold War–era conventions clearly demonstrated a sensitivity to the range of options acceptable to adversaries in the long ideological struggle, so too have post-1991 agreements demonstrated a continued reluctance to promote measures on which states might have obviously different interests. For example, even a cursory glance at major terrorist conflicts (such as in Northern Ireland) reveals areas where concessions by states have been crucial to reducing the risk of violence. But encoding the idea of concessions or negotiations in these agreements would in essence legitimize nonstate violent movements, elevating them to the same level as states; as a result, these political negotiations are generally defined as "peace talks" or a "political opening" rather than as components of "counterterrorism."[5] Similarly, an emphasis on military force would legitimize exactly the type of cross-border incursions, premised on the threat of terrorism, that many nations opposed in the U.S.-led invasion of Iraq in 2003. Even the United States, while seeking international support for the attack, has not suggested a global agreement on "preemptive war" in general terms; this right is ostensibly reserved for the United States and is not to be granted to other states, which might wield this authority with less restraint and sobriety than Washington.

Although counterterrorism specialists broadly agree that terrorism is too diverse a phenomenon to be uniformly resolvable through the types of tools dictated in transnational counterterrorism agreements, there is broad multinational support for this understanding of terrorism as a problem primarily to be handled through intelligence and law enforcement. In large part, this derives from the role that advanced industrial democracies have played in drafting the most widely used and cited agreements, first at the G-5/G-7/G-8 level and then as often adopted fitfully at the United Nations and other forums. And so there is a palpable mismatch between the recognition of terrorism as a highly complex issue that can barely be considered a specific or contextless problem and the increasingly rigorous efforts of leading democratic nations to encode counterterrorism solutions as intelligence and criminal justice issues.

Terror, Iraq, and the Democratic Peace

This exclusion of military tools from counterterrorism agreements seems all the more peculiar when one considers the centrality of the military to the modern state. Theorists of state formation have long focused on the decisive role that war and the creation of standing armies had on the development both of nations and of the modern political apparatus that governs them, primarily for two related reasons. First, the larger national armies relied in part on the use of a national consciousness to motivate self-sacrifice, as well as on the development of increasingly sophisticated drill techniques that forced people to cooperate on a much larger and more impersonal scale than ever before (McNeill 1982, 117–43). Second, the construction of the increasingly elaborate tax systems that were necessary for funding these forces, and which entailed more sophisticated monitoring and calculation techniques, helped to produce the system of rationalized and ostensibly nonarbitrary institutions that typify modern states (Tilly 1993; Levi 1989; Elias 1939/1982). Those countries in which the armed forces are legally contested (for example, Japan) or largely absent (for example, Costa Rica) are notable because military force is elsewhere considered de rigueur, a crucial symbol of the state.

Indeed, the military is so central as a legitimating emblem of the modern state that a wide array of terrorist organizations, particularly left-wing or secessionist forces, have adopted military language to describe themselves. The Irish Republican Army, for example, self-consciously modeled itself as a military force, complete with quartermasters and brigades, and a political wing, Sinn Féin. The Japanese Red Army, despite its odd organizational structure, adopted military motifs, as have the FARC (Revolutionary Armed Forces of Colombia) in Colombia, the Red Brigades in Italy, and the Tamil Tigers in Sri Lanka. It is largely for this reason that officials have often preferred to focus on law enforcement approaches: treated as crime rather than as a military matter, terrorism is delegitimized, and terrorist organizations are not elevated to the level of political adversaries, as they would be if treated as armies. And so military motifs are deeply embedded in terrorist conflicts, even as there is consistent pressure among officials to frame the problem as a matter for law enforcement and criminal justice systems.

This framing has penetrated scholarly and popular discourse so decisively that debates over the relationship between democracy and terrorism have tended to focus almost exclusively on the way in which the enhanced circumstances of terrorism may subvert the limits generally placed on the role of the police and prosecutors. But in considering the range of potential state responses—by thinking additionally of military tools, for example—we can identify different types of consequences. A hallmark of democratic governance is the separation of police and military functions: the military is reserved primarily to confront external threats that require the use of force, the police are used as more specific administrators of local criminal law, and both are subject to strict limitations on the state's rights vis-à-vis its citizens. Indeed, proponents of democratization have lamented that terrorism presents a special risk to international efforts to pressure developing nations into separating their criminal justice and military functions (Nolte 2004, 14–15). Particularly in areas where military forces have been responsible for ghastly human rights abuses—ranging from Indonesia to Brazil—their isolation from internal policing seems to be an absolute prerequisite to the development of the state-society split seen as essential to democracy. In the case of newly democratizing nations, the emphasis on law enforcement is almost a bulwark against control by military authorities. For advanced liberal democracies with a history of civilian control over the military and a limited role for the army in domestic politics, the challenges differ.

The relationship between democracy and military engagement has been drawn most explicitly in the "democratic peace" literature. Theorists of democratic peace, building from Immanuel Kant, have argued alternately that democracies are less likely to fight wars than are authoritarian governments and that they are less likely to fight one another than other potential dyads (democratic versus authoritarian states, or authoritarian states against one another). In his classic article series on the subject, Michael W. Doyle (1983a, 208) argues that in Kant's view of liberalism, the most important feature for foreign affairs was the relationship between individual rights and sovereignty: "The state is subject neither to the external authority of other states nor to the internal authority of special prerogatives held, for example, by monarchs or military castes over foreign policy." Doyle carefully points out that there is nothing inherently pacifistic about liberal government and that while democratic states have carved out a sphere of peaceful interaction based in part on perceptions of shared values and economic common interests, the "imprudent vehemence" of liberal states in dealing with nonliberal governments might make them even more prone to violent conflict with their nondemocratic counterparts (Doyle 1983b). The most widely noted outcome of this research agenda, however, has not been the articulation of the specific conditions that would lead a democracy to go to war against a nondemocracy, but rather a vigorous debate over the notion that liberal states do not fight one another.

This was a predictable outcome. By stipulating that common regime types might ameliorate security dilemmas and reduce the risk of conflict, democratic peace theorists posed a direct and empirically defensible challenge to the neorealist school (for example, Waltz 1979), which attributed patterns of conflict and balancing to the distribution of power resources rather than to the internal political dynamics of different states. One set of scholars, including John Oneal and Bruce Russett, have generated data sets that seem to establish a lower rate, or even an absence, of military conflict between democracies (see, for example, Oneal and Russett 2001), and so much of the debate over the viability of the democratic peace theory has focused on the terminological and methodological issues involved in defining democracy, measuring conflict, and disentangling the variables weighing on individual observations (see, for example, Green, Kim, and Yoon 2001).

More recently, the debate has shifted to the apparent mismatch between the most commonly proposed empirical finding by democratic peace theorists—the relative absence of conflict between democratic dyads—and the theoretical claims on which the argument is based. One critic has argued that there is no a priori reason to assume that democratic norms of consultation, negotiation, and legal settlement at home are shared internationally, even among other democracies (Rosato 2003, 588–91). Others have refined the point by suggesting that democratic peace theory is essentially a monadic argument in that its most coherent claims are based primarily on the nature of democracies themselves rather than on something specific to the interactions *between* democracies. Yet this should mean that democracies are less likely to engage in military conflict than other types of government in all cases, not just in fighting against other democracies. That is, the majority of democratic peace studies make essentially monadic claims regarding the nature of democratic restraints on conflict: war is costly for democratically elected leaders because citizens can institutionally hold them accountable for unacceptable losses of life and property in a protracted or failed conflict. John Ferejohn and Frances Rosenbluth (2008) have developed a game-theoretic monadic model to account for the conditions under which democratic leaders will be likely to go to war based in large part on their expectation, particularly against nondemocratic governments that face difficulty in marshaling resources, of the likelihood of rapid success. Even here, however, the purpose is an essentially critical one: to undermine the theoretical basis of the democratic peace literature and to replace it with calculations of competitive global interest and domestic political conflict. With an extraordinary collection of empirical research aimed at determining or disproving the existence of a democratic peace, the issue remains a contested and unsettled academic matter.

It has entered popular discourse, however, as something of a received truth, and it played a crucial role in the Bush administration's rationale for the 2003 invasion of Iraq. Although the principal claim behind the war was Saddam Hussein's purported creation and marshaling of weapons of mass destruction (WMD), President Bush himself frequently drew attention to the threat that nondemocratic states such as Iraq posed to peace, particularly after the WMD rationale proved to be incorrect or even fraudulent.[6] One of the primary figures in the democratic peace debate, Yale's Bruce Russett (2005), even argued shortly after the war had begun that the administration's employment of the theory in establishing a rationale for going to war represented a profound misuse of its central tenets, as most such theorists had never suggested that establishing democracy through force would be an easy or manageable foreign policy prescription. Prompted in part by the Iraq War, two of America's foremost international relations scholars published a book refining democratic peace theory to take account of the pressures encouraging newly democratizing nations to go to war, perhaps at even higher rates than do most autocracies (Mansfield and Snyder 2005). As a component of the war on terror, the Iraq campaign has thus served as an opportunity primarily to debate the wisdom of promoting democratization through force as a tool for preventing future interstate conflict.

As a result, the prevailing security studies literature on democracy and military engagement has largely avoided the issue of terrorism, just as the prevailing policy and political science literature on democracy and terrorism has largely avoided the issue of military engagement. And yet the recent use of terrorism as a crucial justification for the American invasion of Iraq suggests that the increasingly visible potential for mass-casualty terrorism may have important consequences for security politics in democratic nations, consequences largely unaddressed in the recent revisions to democratic peace theory. At least in theory, because citizens can more easily hold their leaders accountable, democratic systems may offer some bulwark against irresponsible or unjustifiable military attacks, particularly when there is no imminent threat from the target. International terrorism—which political leaders can cast as a danger unconstrained by rational self-interest or by moral judgment—can now pose an apparently existential threat. This threat from small groups of people, operating across boundaries, undeterred by the niceties of international diplomacy, has in the American case served as a crucial justification for invading another nation and toppling its regime. The record suggests that if invading Iraq was a strictly American preoccupation, the use of terrorism to justify major security policy changes to a democratic public is not.

International Terrorism and the Reshaping of Japanese Security Politics

It is largely for this reason that the rapid changes in Japanese security policy since 2001 have been breathtaking. Following the September 11 attacks, Prime Minister Junichiro Koizumi pledged extensive and unprecedented levels of Japanese support for American military activities in the war on terror. The dispatch of Japanese Maritime Self-Defense Force units to the Indian Ocean in support of American military activities against the Taliban was the first use of Japanese troops in support of combat operations since the end of the Second World War; their deployment far from the East Asian context—and the political sensitivities of Japan's neighbors, like China and South Korea—might have been especially opportune for Japanese hawks (Midford 2002). The 2004 deployment of Ground Self-Defense Force troops to Iraq was an even more dramatic extension of Japan's security role: celebrated by Japanese hawks as a step toward Japan's emergence as a "normal" military power, it was decried by the left as a betrayal of the Constitution and a symbol of Japan's reemergence as a militarist society. And in the wake of North Korean missile tests in the summer of 2006, Chief Cabinet Secretary Shinzo Abe—already the obvious successor to Koizumi—announced that Japan's right to self-defense might have to be reinterpreted to include the possibility of a preemptive attack.

The shifts have been so striking that analysts of Japanese politics have struggled to find an appropriate explanation, though in some sense the result seems overdetermined. Koizumi is himself the product of the hawkish faction in the Liberal Democratic Party (formerly Kishi's faction), one increasingly seen as having been kept largely out of power by stronger factions that were primarily interested in industrial and trade policy. The collapse of the Japan Socialist Party (JSP) following the privatization of Japan National Railways and the consequent evisceration of the public-sector unions that had been the JSP's base removed the main electoral obstacle to fundamental security policy change. And the end of the Cold War, combined with the rise of Chinese power, dramatically altered the global context in which Japanese leaders and voters considered threats and options. But like the invasion of Iraq, which had been considered desirable by some Bush administration officials even before the September 11 attacks, the Koizumi cabinet's rapid choices reflected policy changes long pushed by Japanese hawks. And their pattern suggests that in Japan, as in the United States, the ambiguously defined threat of terrorism played a crucial political role in helping to justify these shifts in policy.

Even while holding Japanese military expenditures to only 1 percent of the national budget, the Japanese Self-Defense Forces are a highly capable fighting force, competent to defend Japan, by virtually any reckoning, from potential conventional threats in the region. During the Cold War, the possibility of Soviet invasion lingered long enough in the Japanese popular imagination to spur the Japan Defense Agency (JDA) to consider "emergency laws" freeing the military to disobey standard civilian law in the event of military contingencies.[7] An initial plan—which JDA members feared would be politically controversial because it smacked of unchecked military authority in a nation still badly marked by the legacies of a militarist government—was prepared secretly in 1963 as a component of the "Three Arrows" research project that simulated Communist invasions of South Korea. A JSP legislator called attention to the project on the floor of the Diet, badly embarrassing then–prime minister Satô. Satô, who had known nothing of the plan, had no choice but to kill it, rebuking the JDA's plans and the secretive manner in which they were developed (Tatsumi 2002; Murata 1998, 9). Although the JDA would continue to consider emergency legislation in the 1970s, a number of its members recognized that this type of policy shift, while aligning Japan with the security stance of other nations like the United States, was unlikely to be of any use in the event of a real conflict; after all, a conflict between the United States and the Soviet Union was likely to go nuclear quite quickly, rendering meaningless the Self-Defence Force's (SDF) ability to operate freely on Japanese soil. One of the JDA's most respected leaders, Seiki Nishihiro, remarked, "If deterrence fails and there's a war with the Soviets, Japan's going to be scorched earth. You think Japanese are going to support that war? Fine, continue to study the issue, but let's keep the plans locked up in a safe" (Furukawa 2002, 96).

Indeed, whatever romantic images of a "normal" Japanese military might have danced in the minds of hawkish legislators, Japanese security debates have long been marked by shrewd calculations of threat and self-interest. Even with the growing power and apparent ambition of China, Japanese journals and newspapers have long regarded China's potential military threat to Japan as relatively minimal. After all, while the People's Liberation Army is a highly capable fighting force that could do serious damage to the Japanese mainland, it is not entirely clear how China, lacking much in the way of a blue-water navy, could land sufficient numbers of Chinese troops on Japanese shores to pose a significant conventional danger. And the Chinese leadership, even if considered crude and villainous in some of the more right-leaning accounts, displays fairly straightforward calculations of self-interest that have convinced most Japanese policymakers that Beijing would be unlikely to use nuclear or other unconventional weapons against Japan.

And so the threat commonly put forth in recent Japanese public debates emanates from Pyongyang, and is virtually indistinguishable, in the popular imagination, from terrorism; indeed, it is usually labeled as such. Like American views of Al Qaeda, North Korea is generally conceptualized in Japanese debates as irrationally ideological, secretive, and prone to attacks with unconscionable levels of violence. Missile tests over Japanese airspace have been, of course, particularly alarming, but they are far from the only—and perhaps not even the most salient—feature of domestic Japanese debates. The later-confirmed rumors that North Korean operatives had kidnapped over a dozen Japanese in the 1970s and early 1980s, ostensibly to bring them to Pyongyang as language teachers for spies in training, had helped to define North Korea as, in the words of widely read conservative pundit Keitarô Hasegawa (2003, 42), a moji-dôri tero kokka—the "quintessential terrorist state."

Equally disconcerting was the evidence that North Korean undocumented vessels were continuing to arrive in Japan regularly. Although most specialists argue that they are primarily drug smugglers bringing amphetamines into Japan, the public discourse has taken a far darker view, one encouraged by parliamentary hawks. When Iku Asô (1997/2003), a former journalist, published his novel *Sensen fukoku* (Declaration of War) in 1997, he tapped into and shaped prevailing public concerns by writing of a group of North Korean operatives who were smuggled into Japan to attack a nuclear power station. Later made into a film, the novel figured into parliamentary debates when lawmakers commented both on the detailed extent of Asô's knowledge about police capabilities and on the real-ism of the scenario itself (Kawabe 2004, 107). And indeed, many chafed at the constitutional restrictions on the use of force that seemed even to limit the ability of Japan to fire on "suspicious boats" (fushinsen) entering Japanese waters; Maritime Self-Defense Force (MSDF) ships had fired warning shots at one in 2000, though it had gotten away.

The September 11 attacks therefore had two simultaneous implications for Japanese politics. On the one hand, the emphatic demand by the United States—personified by Deputy Secretary of State Richard Armitage during his trip to Tokyo shortly after the attacks—that Japan provide whatever support was requested by its alliance partner placed a hard expectation on the meaning of the U.S.-Japan alliance; mere financial contributions, as Japan had provided in the first Persian Gulf War, would not suffice when the U.S. government determined against whom it would retaliate (McCormack 2004, 38). But the image of a massive attack on a metropolis waged by subversives already inside the country added teeth to the already popular claims that North Korean operatives were entering Japan at will, plotting nuclear and other strikes on Japanese soil. And while October 2001 is primarily remembered in Japan for the passage of the Support for Antiterrorism Special Measures Law, which authorized the use of Japanese forces in support of American antiterror missions, its passage was accompanied simultaneously by a revision of the Coast Guard Law that specifically authorized the Coast Guard to open fire on suspicious boats in Japanese waters. Existing laws already permitted the use of this type of force if necessary, but they had never been put to the test, and the revision provided crucial political cover.

Almost immediately, the revision became politically if not legally relevant. Within two months, on December 22, 2001, Japan Coast Guard ships spotted an unidentified boat that began to escape at a suspiciously high speed, presumably with an engine far more powerful than most small fishing boats would have. After a twenty-hour chase, the Coast Guard patrol boats, acting under the orders of the Coast Guard's commander, who followed the chase in real time, tried to cut off the boat's escape into Chinese waters by trapping it with ropes. Sailors on the vessel, later identified as North Korean, began to shoot at the Japanese boat, provoking a brief firefight that ended only when someone on the vessel evidently used a self-destruct device to scuttle the boat, sinking it just inside of China's Exclusive Economic Zone (Valencia and Ji 2002). Crucially, the legal revision was not actually invoked in the Coast Guard's decision (Yomiuri Shimbun Kyushu Bureau 2002), suggesting that it had been legally unnecessary for justifying the use of force. But it did provide crucial political cover, preparing legislators and the public alike for the idea that Japanese forces would be authorized to kill foreign threats. After Japan received permission to raise and inspect the vessel, the Coast Guard put it on display for nearly a year at Tokyo's Museum of Maritime Science, where it was described not as a "suspicious boat" (fushinsen) but rather as an "operations boat" (kôsakusen). Despite the fact that witnesses aboard the Coast Guard patrol boats described the sailors as dumping white pills (presumably amphetamines) overboard and thereby raising the probability that they were drug smugglers, the boat had essentially been rechristened as a direct threat to Japan, the kind that could be handled, like America's threat from Al Qaeda, only with the creation of a robust military response.

The Japanese Coast Guard serves as a quasi-military bridge between civilian police authority and military power. While the Japanese government has long maintained a policy of keeping military expenditures below 1 percent of the national budget—in keeping with continued claims that Japan's top foreign policy priority is peace—the figure does not include the extensive and rapidly growing funding for the Japan Coast Guard. But the Coast Guard itself has clearly been used as an alternative to naval military force. Indeed, the Coast Guard's forces, measured by tonnage, are roughly 65 percent of the size of the entire Chinese surface fleet, and although they lack missiles, their deck-mounted cannons provide an intimidating deterrent to most potential naval opponents in the region. Japan has maintained a policy of not providing military aid or exporting weapons overseas, but its donation of armed patrol boats to the Indonesian Coast Guard has been described, with an almost visible wink, as nothing more than law enforcement cooperation (see Samuels 2007, 79).

Japan had long stood outside of international agreements on terrorism, signing on to the relatively easy ones to implement at home while foot-dragging on more politically difficult measures, such as the convention against the financing of terror. Moreover, Japanese police forces, primarily concerned with extending authority for law enforcement at home rather than enhancing their global reach, have shown little interest in contributing to international intelligence efforts on transnational movements like Al Qaeda. And until recently, advocates of a more muscular security policy focusing on the military had been uninterested in discussing terrorism, which they viewed as a "crisis management" problem rather than a "national security" issue. But the malleability of the perceived North Korean threat, combined with American efforts to militarize counterterrorism after September 11, provided a crucial opportunity to recast the democratic balance on national security. Left-leaning actors in Japan had long suggested that Japan maintain a pacifist foreign policy under the shadow of U.S. protection, and they had been buttressed by the widespread expectation that China had no interest in major military adventures. But these arguments seemed to crumble in the face of an irrational, treacherous, subversive threat—analytically distinguishable from terrorism, yet described conventionally as "terrorist" within Japan—that could unleash the same kinds of terrors that now inhabited the nightmares of Americans.

Indeed, the revision of the Coast Guard Law and the shooting of the North Korean vessel clearly served as the crucial precedent for the revision of Japan's emergency laws, completed in 2006. One influential Japanese leftist, Hitotsubashi University's Osamu Watanabe (2002), charged that this had been part of a strategic plan by the Koizumi cabinet: to start with that legal revision, to establish emergency laws, and finally to revise Japan's 1947 Constitution, specifically article IX. In a sense, hawks conceded the point, laying out the justification for the changes in roughly the same order: suspicious boats, unconventional threats, limits on the Self-Defense Forces during emergencies, and an outdated constitution preventing Japan from defending itself (see, for example, Nakayama 2002). For advocates of a renegotiation of Japan's position on national defense, arguably the central debate in Japan's postwar democracy, September 11 came as a powerful deus ex machina. Where they had largely avoided discussion of terrorism, which long seemed relevant as a military issue only for special forces units in which the Japan Defense Agency (JDA) had little interest, they now had the opportunity to define small, unidentified boats—primarily drug smugglers, by most accounts—as potential military threats that justified a dramatic enhancement of the state's military authority.

The pattern is remarkable. The Liberal Democratic Party (LDP) hawks and their allies in the JDA have managed to achieve key Cold War–era policy goals, such as the creation of "emergency laws" that are themselves plans for responding to a large-scale invasion of Japan, hardly a likely eventuality at any point in the future. They have also moved quickly toward constitutional revision, which an LDP committee drafted in 2005.[8] None of this would have been considered part of a counterterrorism strategy before the September 11 attacks, and no Japanese counterterrorism specialists emphasized that there were meaningful links between security policy reform and Japanese handling of terrorism. And yet the strange path taken toward these reforms—including the recasting of "suspicious boats" as potential terrorist threats, akin to the 9/11 hijackers in their intent and danger—reflects the deliberate and strategic use of the gray area of terrorism to blur the boundary between policing, such as by the Coast Guard, and the right of the Japanese state to use lethal military force against foreign enemies. The Bush administration's decision to emphasize military action as the appropriate response to terrorism provided a new avenue for considering how major changes in Japanese defense policy might be made less controversial, and the malleability of terrorism as a security concern made it more difficult for political opponents to deny that Japan was at risk. After all, who could deny that small numbers of North Korean operatives could come in and out of Japan with relative ease, or that 9/11 had shown that small numbers could cause grave harm? In this view, leaving Japan's constitution unrevised, leaving its emergency laws unratified, and leaving its national emphasis on pacifism rather than self-preservation collectively represented an invitation to disaster.

Conclusion

These changes may be beneficial for Japan, of course, and a critique of terrorism's use in democratic debate about the role of the military should not be taken as an indictment of Japan's right to self-defense. After all, although China seems to have no territorial designs on Japan, the expansion of its own blue-water fleet suggests an ability to project power that may threaten Japanese economic and security interests in the long run. Although Japanese efforts to develop theater missile defense (TMD) capability to counter North Korean threats have generally developed on a track outside of debates about the government's overall military stance, enhanced Japanese military functions might, if employed judiciously, provide additional options for deterring North Korean aggression. And Japan's postwar democracy has demonstrated itself to be no less responsible in its handling of foreign policy than most other advanced industrial nations, suggesting that it would not pose an unusual danger even if better armed.

But the rise of a hawkish foreign policy has added an element of uncertainty even to American security calculations in the region, and it is now difficult to consider tensions in the Asia-Pacific without taking into account a more muscular and vocal Japanese presence, better armed and more assertive about both Japan's past and its future. And these transformations, while certainly affected by changes in the regional security context and in Japan's own party politics, bear the imprint, in their speed and trajectory, of the use of international terrorism as a justification. When faced with domestic terrorist threats, Japanese leaders have responded with restraint and with concern about public worries about the spread of police authority. Until recently, they have expressed little interest in engaging international terrorism in anything approximating the terms of even America's pre-9/11 counterterrorism policy. But the images of small numbers of conspirators able to wound a superpower allowed the redefinition of problems that had been little more than nuisances as potential existential threats, the kind that justify a major shift in national security policy. Terrorism thus recast the political debate that had, more than any other, defined Japan's postwar democracy; in doing so, it has also changed the contours of security activity in the Asia-Pacific, with still unknown consequences.

International agreements on terrorism have long emphasized its status as a problem primarily for law enforcement, simultaneously delegitimizing terrorists as political actors and ostensibly limiting the use of terrorism as a pretext for armed conflict between states. Although there may be good reasons for this approach, a thorough examination of the relationships between terrorism and democracy requires that we go beyond the tensions involved in the state's police power against its own citizens. As a security threat of increasing scale and plasticity, terrorism provides opportunities for political actors of all stripes to redefine their preferred approaches to national security as effective for combating terrorism as well. The world has already seen one advanced industrial democracy invade another nation, justified to no small degree by the potential terrorist threat posed by that regime and its alleged proxies. We are now witnessing another industrial democracy, located in a highly volatile region, taking its most dramatic military steps of the postwar era, largely with reference to a threat that policymakers, politicians, and pundits all describe as primarily terrorist in nature. This makes them neither right nor wrong, either in their characterization of the threat or the appropriate responses. But it suggests that terrorism's hold on our imaginations gives it a special power in those nations where those with imaginations have the authority to vote.

I thank Martha Crenshaw for her insightful comments on an earlier draft of this chapter. I also thank John Meyer for initially suggesting the connection between terrorism and disorder. Following convention in English-language international relations scholarship, I render Japanese names in Western order (given name, then family name). My discussion of post-9/11 Japanese counterterrorism policy draws largely from *Think Global, Fear Local* (Leheny 2006), especially chapter 6.

NOTES

1. For the best English-language study of the occupation, see Dower (1999).
2. For a fascinating discussion of the police, see Katzenstein and Tsujinaka (2001).

3. The director Masato Harada's terrific 2002 film *Totsunyûseyo: Asama sansô jiken* (released in English as *The Choice of Hercules* but perhaps best understood as *Siege! The Asama Cottage Incident*) largely builds from Sassa's account. Director Wakamatsu Kôji's 2008 film *United Red Army* examines the incident from inside the Red Army's purge, evidently from a perspective more sympathetic to that of the JRA members (Hirasawa 2007). On the history and structure of the Red Army through this period, see Steinhoff 1989.
4. I adapt this claim from Aksartova (2005, 38): "The trope of 'capacity-building' so common in the development discourse is precisely about that: replacing local knowledge and practices (what James C. Scott calls *mêtis*) with Western-style formal organizations."
5. I am indebted to Martha Crenshaw for making this point in correspondence.
6. During a visit to Osan Air Base in the Republic of Korea in November 2005, President Bush defended the Iraq War by saying, "History has proven that free nations are peaceful nations and that democracies do not fight their neighbors. By advancing the hope of freedom and democracy for others, we'll make our own freedom more secure." See the White House website at: http://www.whitehouse.gov/news/releases/2005/11/20051119-5.html (accessed July 8, 2006).
7. In early 2007, the JDA was upgraded in status, becoming the Ministry of Defense (MOD). Because most of the empirical material in this chapter is drawn from 2001 to early 2006, and for the sake of consistency, I refer to it as the JDA.
8. The text (in Japanese) of the LDP's proposal, in various drafts, is available at: http://www.jimin.jp/jimin/shin_kenpou/shiryou/index.html.

References

Aksartova, Saadat. 2005. "Civil Society from Abroad: U.S. Donors in the Former Soviet Union." Ph.D. diss., Princeton University, Department of Sociology.

Asô, Iku. 2003. *Sensen fukoku* (Declaration of War). Tokyo: Kôdansha. (Orig. pub. in 1997.)

Austin, Andrew. 2004. "Bush and Sharon: Securing the Realm." *From the Left* 25(2, Spring–Summer): 5–6.

Bayley, David H. 1991. *Forces of Order: Policing Modern Japan*, rev. ed. Berkeley: University of California Press.

Berger, Thomas U. 1998. *Cultures of Antimilitarism: National Security in Germany and Japan.* Baltimore: Johns Hopkins University Press.

Buzan, Barry, Ole Waever, and Jaap de Wilde. 1998. *Security: A New Framework for Analysis.* Boulder, Colo.: Lynne Rienner.

Chin, Warren. 2007. "Examining the Application of British Counterinsurgency Doctrine by the American Army in Iraq." *Small Wars & Insurgencies* 18(1): 1–26.

Clarke, Richard A. 2004. *Against All Enemies: Inside America's War on Terror.* New York: Free Press.

Crenshaw, Martha. 1985. "An Organizational Approach to the Analysis of Political Terrorism." *Orbis* 29(3, Fall): 465–89.

Dower, John. 1999. *Embracing Defeat: Japan in the Wake of World War II.* New York: W. W. Norton.

Doyle, Michael W. 1983a. "Kant, Liberal Legacies, and Foreign Affairs." *Philosophy and Public Affairs* 12(3, Summer): 205–35.

———. 1983b. "Kant, Liberal Legacies, and Foreign Affairs, Part 2." *Philosophy and Public Affairs* 12(4, Fall): 323–53.

Elias, Norbert. 1982. *The Civilizing Process,* vol. 2, *State Formation and Civilization.* Oxford: Blackwell. (Orig. pub. in 1939.)

Ferejohn, John, and Rosenbluth, Frances. 2008. "Warlike Democracies." *Journal of Conflict Resolution* 52(1): 3–38.

Friman, H. Richard, Peter J. Katzenstein, David Leheny, and Nobuo Okawara. 2006. "Immovable Object? Japan's Security Policy in East Asia." In *Beyond Japan: The Dynamics of East Asian Regionalism,* edited by Peter J. Katzenstein and Takashi Shiraishi. Ithaca, N.Y.: Cornell University Press.

Furukawa, Atsushi. 2002. "Yûji hôsei no rekishiteki hatten: Mitsuya kenkyû kara nichibei gaidorain kanrenhô made" (The Historical Development of Emergency Laws, from the "Three Arrows Research Project" to the U.S.-Japan Guidelines Legislation). In *Yûji hôsei o kentô suru: "9.11 igo" o heiwa kenpô no shiza kara toinaosu* (Considering the Emergency Laws: Using the Peace Constitution to Question the Aftermath of 9/11), edited by Toshihiro Yamauchi. Tokyo: Hôritsu bunkasha.

Green, Donald P., Soo Yeon Kim, and David H. Yoon. 2001. "Dirty Pool." *International Security* 55(2, Spring): 441–68.

Hardacre, Helen. 2003. "After Aum: Religion and Civil Society in Japan." In *The State of Civil Society in Japan,* edited by Frank J. Schwartz and Susan J. Pharr. Cambridge: Cambridge University Press.

Hasegawa, Keitarô. 2003. *Kitachôsen no saishû ketsumatsu: Higashi ajia no reisen wa kaku hôkai suru* (The Final Outcome for North Korea: The Collapse of the East Asian Cold War). Tokyo: PHP.

Hirasawa, Go. 2007. "Cold Mountains, Red Armies." *Vertigo* 3(4, Winter): 15.

Hoffman, Bruce. 1999. *Inside Terrorism.* New York: Columbia University Press.

Itabashi, Isao, Ogawara Masamichi, and David Leheny. 2002. "Japan." In *Combating Terrorism: Strategies of Ten Countries,* edited by Yonah Alexander. Ann Arbor: University of Michigan Press.

Katzenstein, Peter J. 1996. *Cultural Norms and National Security: Police and Military in Postwar Japan.* Ithaca, N.Y.: Cornell University Press.

———. 2002. "September 11 in Comparative Perspective: The Antiterrorism Campaigns of Germany and Japan." *Dialogue-IO* (Spring): 45–56.

Katzenstein, Peter J. and Tsujinaka, Yutaka. 1991. *Defending the Japanese State: Structures, Norms, and the Political Responses to Terrorism and Violent Social Protest in the 1970s and 1980s.* Ithaca, N.Y.: Cornell University East Asian Studies Program. Available at: http://search.barnesandnoble.com/Defending-the-Japanese-State/Peter-J-Katzenstein/e/9780939657537/?itm=2 (accessed September 23, 2009).

Kawabe, Katsurô. 2004. *Rachi wa naze fuseganakatta no ka—Nihon keisatsu no jôhô haisen (Why Couldn't We Prevent the Abductions: How the Japanese Police Lost the Intelligence Battle).* Tokyo: Chikuma Shinshô.

Leheny, David. 2001–2002. "Tokyo Confronts Terror." *Policy Review* 110 (December–January): 37–47.

———. 2006. *Think Global, Fear Local: Sex, Violence, and Anxiety in Contemporary Japan.* Ithaca, N.Y.: Cornell University Press.

Levi, Margaret. 1989. *Of Rule and Revenue.* Berkeley: University of California Press.

Lind, Jennifer M. 2004. "Pacifism or Passing the Buck?: Testing Theories of Japanese Security Policy." *International Security* 29(1): 92–121.

Mansfield, Edward D., and Jack Snyder. 2005. *Electing to Fight: Why Emerging Democracies Go to War.* Cambridge, Mass.: MIT Press.

McCormack, Gavan. 2004. "Remilitarizing Japan." *New Left Review* 29 (October–November): 29–45.

McNeill, William H. 1982. *The Pursuit of Power: Technology, Armed Force, and Society Since AD 1000.* Chicago: University of Chicago Press.

Midford, Paul. 2002. "The Logic of Reassurance and Japan's Grand Strategy." *Security Studies* 11(3): 1–43. Available at: http://www.informaworld.com/smpp/content%7Edb=all%7Econtent=a714005337 (accessed September 23, 2009).

Murata, Koji. 1998. "The Origins and Evolution of the Korean-American Alliance: A Japanese Perspective." Discussion paper. Stanford, Calif.: Stanford University, Asia-Pacific Center, America's Alliances with Japan and Korea in a Changing Northeast Asia Project (August).

Nakayama, Takashi. 2002. *Nihonkai gunji kinchô* (Military Tensions in the Sea of Japan). Tokyo: Chûô Shinsho La Clef.

Nolte, Detlief. 2004. "Problems of Latin American Security and Its Implications for Europe: A German Perspective." Jean Monnet/Robert Schumann Paper Series, vol. 4, no. 11. Miami: University of Miami, Miami European Union Center.

Oneal, John R., and Bruce Russett. 2001. "Clear and Clean: The Fixed Effects of the Liberal Peace." *International Security* 55(2, Spring): 469–85.

Rice, Condoleezza. 2000. "Campaign 2000: Promoting the National Interest." *Foreign Affairs* 79(1, January–February): 45–62.

Rosato, Sebastian. 2003. "The Flawed Logic of Democratic Peace Theory." *American Political Science Review* 97(4, November): 585–602.

Russett, Bruce. 2005. "Bushwhacking the Democratic Peace." *International Studies Perspectives* 6: 395–408.

Samuels, Richard J. 2001. "Kishi and Corruption: An Anatomy of the 1955 System." Working paper 83. San Francisco: University of San Francisco, Center for the

Pacific Rim, Japan Policy Research Institute (JPRI) (December). Available at: http://www.jpri.org/publications/workingpapers/wp83.html (accessed August 19, 2007).

———. 2007. *Securing Japan: Tokyo's Grand Strategy and the Future of East Asia.* Ithaca, N.Y.: Cornell University Press.

Sassa, Atsuyuki. 1996. *Rengô Sekigun "Asama sansô" jiken* (The Japanese Red Army's Asama Cottage Incident). Tokyo: Bungei Shunju.

Scott, James C. 1998. *Seeing Like a State: How Certain Schemes to Improve the Human Condition Have Failed.* New Haven, Conn.: Yale University Press.

Steinhoff, Patricia G. 1989. "Hijackers, Bombers, and Bank Robbers: Managerial Style in the Japanese Red Army." *Journal of Asian Studies* 48(4, November): 724–40.

———. 2004. "Kidnapped Japanese in North Korea: The New Left Connection." *Journal of Japanese Studies* 30(1, Winter): 123–42.

Suskind, Ron. 2004. *The Price of Loyalty: George W. Bush, the White House, and the Education of Paul O'Neill.* New York: Simon & Schuster.

———. 2006. *The One Percent Doctrine.* New York: Simon & Schuster.

Tatsumi, Yuki. 2002. "Yuji Hosei: Japan Should Not Repeat the Mistakes of the Past." *PacNet Newsletter* (Center for Strategic and International Studies) 17(April 26). Available at: http://csis.org/publication/pacnet-17-april-26-yuji-hosei-japan-should-not-repeat-mistake-past (accessed May 11, 2004).

Tilly, Charles. 1993. *Capital, Coercion, and European States, AD 990–1992.* Oxford: Blackwell.

Valencia, Mark J., and Ji Guoxing. 2002. "The 'North Korean' Ship and U.S. Spy Plane Incidents." *Asian Survey* 42(5, October): 723–32.

Waltz, Kenneth. 1979. *Theory of International Politics.* New York: McGraw-Hill.

Watanabe, Osamu. 2002. "9.11 jiken to Nihon no taigai, kokunai seisaku" (9/11 and Japan's Diplomatic and Domestic Policies). In *Yûji hôsei o kentô suru: "9.11 igo" o heiwa kenpô no shiza kara toinaosu* (Considering the Emergency Laws: Using the Peace Constitution to Question the Aftermath of 9/11), edited by Toshihiro Yamauchi. Tokyo: Hôritsu bunkasha.

Woodward, Bob. 2004. *Plan of Attack.* New York: Simon & Schuster.

Yomiuri Shimbun Kyushu Bureau. 2002. "Rensai: 20 jikan no kôjô" (Serial: The Twenty-Hour Tug-of-War). Available at: http://kyushu.yomiuri.co.jp/special/fushinsen/fushinsen-main.htm (Japanese; accessed May 13, 2004).

Index

Boldface numbers refer to figures and tables.